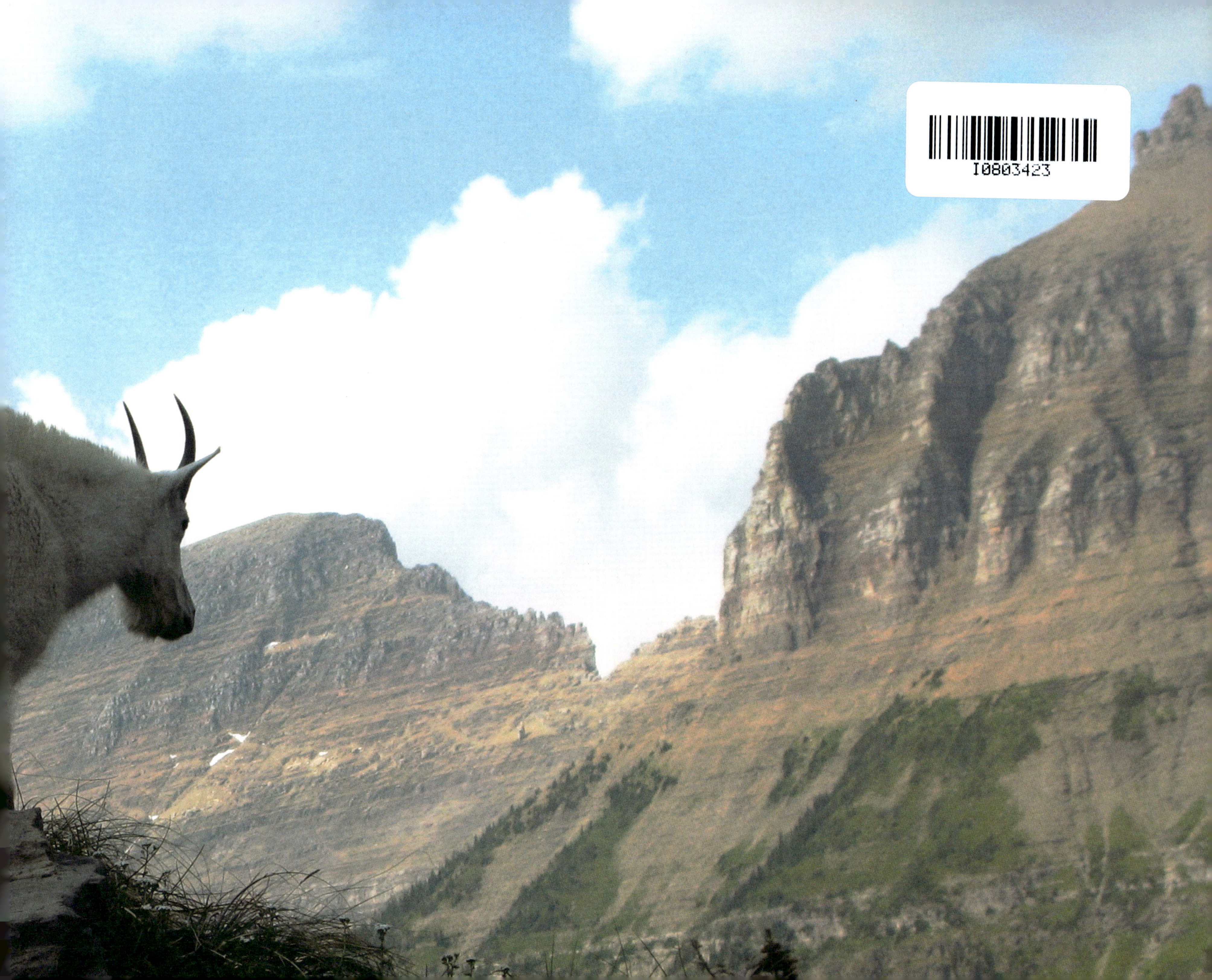

Schiffer Publishing®

Ready to Write a Book?

We're always seeking authors for a wide variety of topics. This is your opportunity to shine! See our website to view an extensive list of our titles. If this idea appeals to you, we'd love to hear from you. Review our book submission guidelines at our website by clicking on the "Submit a Book Proposal" link. Then email your proposal and ideas to **info@schifferbooks.com** or write to the attention of **Acquisitions** at the address below. You can also call 610-593-1777 to make an appointment to speak with an editor.

Schiffer Publishing has books covering a wide variety of interests including:

Antiques, Collectibles, & The Arts
Advertising • Automobilia • Black Collectibles • Breweriana • Ceramics • Clocks • Corkscrews • Decoys • Dolls • Fine Art • Folk Art • Furniture • Graphic Art • Holidays • Hunting • Jewelry • Kitchen • Lighting • Leatherwork • Metalware • Native American Crafts • Nautical • Pinball • Quilts • Rugs • Sports • Teddy Bears • Telephones • Textiles • Toys • Video Games • Vintage Fashion • Watches • Writing Instruments and more.

Design, Lifestyle, & D-I-Y
Architecture • Astrology • Counter Culture • Culinary Arts • Erotica • Interior Design • Kitchens and Baths • Landscaping • Numerology • Paranormal • Pin-Ups • Pop Art • Tarot • Tattooing • Textile Design • UFOs • Witchcraft • Basketry • Beads & Jewelry Making • Carving • Furniture Making • Gourds • Home & Garden • Metalwork • Modeling • Pyrography • Sculpture • Textiles • Weaving • Wood Turning • Tools and more.

Military, Aviation, & Automotive History
WWI & WWII Armor/Aviation: German • U.S. • British • Russian • the Jet Age • Unit Biographies and Autobiographies • Edged Weapons • Firearms • Uniforms and more.

Maritime
Seamanship • Navigation • Ship Management • Towing • Transportation • Boats & Boat Building • Medical • Legal and more.

Regional
History • Children's Books • Architecture • Photography • Landscaping • Paranormal • Souvenir • Guidebooks • Cooking and more.

To learn more, go to **www.schifferbooks.com**
Call 610-593-1777, 8:30a.m.-5:30 p.m. EST
or write to 4880 Lower Valley Road
Atglen, PA 19310 USA
and ask for a free catalog(s).

In the UK and Europe contact
Bushwood Books at 44 (0) 20 8392-8585
info@bushwoodbooks.co.uk

Bookmark printed in China

G-1

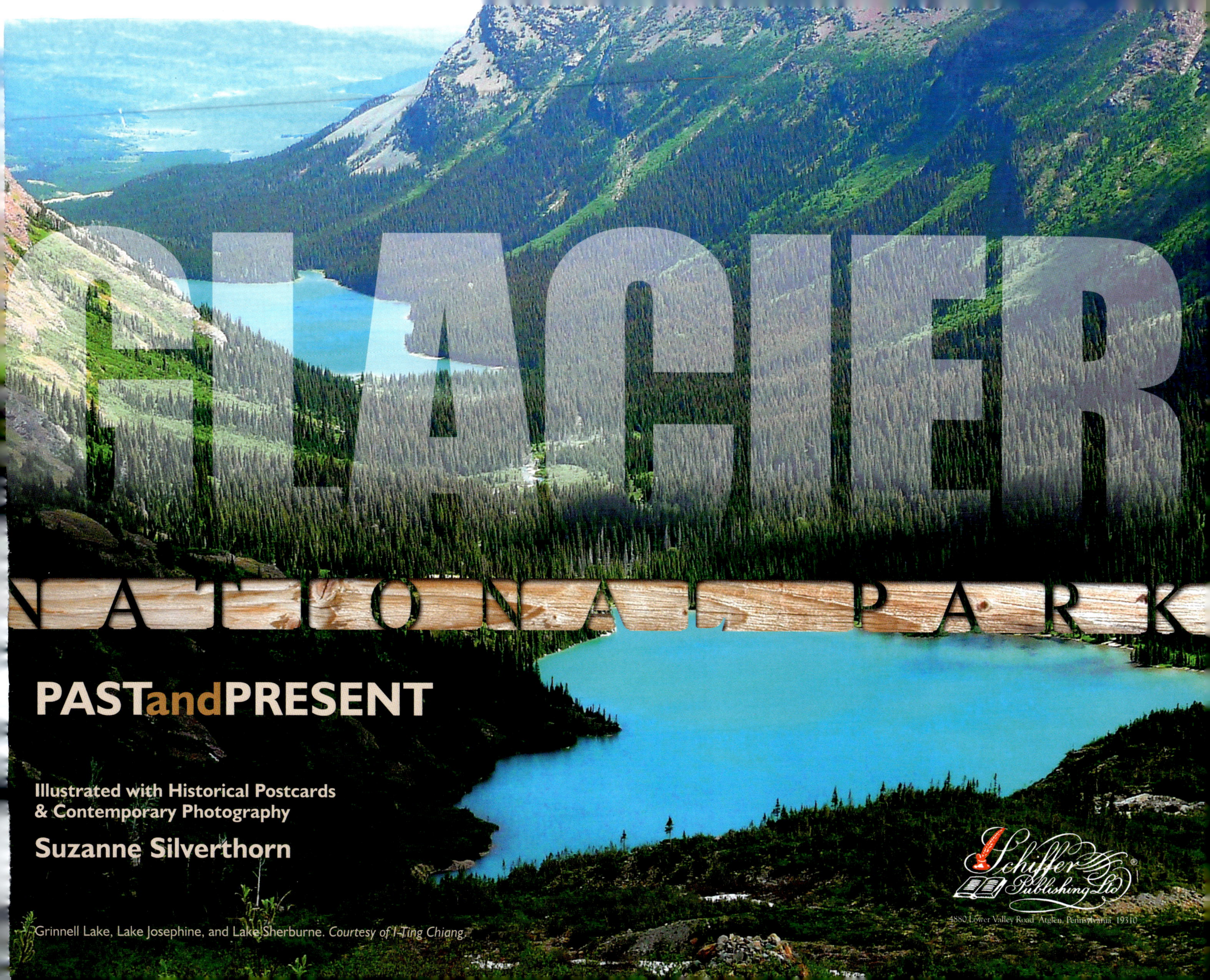

GLACIER NATIONAL PARK

PAST and PRESENT

Illustrated with Historical Postcards
& Contemporary Photography

Suzanne Silverthorn

Schiffer® Publishing Ltd
4880 Lower Valley Road Atglen, Pennsylvania 19310

Grinnell Lake, Lake Josephine, and Lake Sherburne. *Courtesy of I-Ting Chiang.*

Other Schiffer Books By The Author:
Rocky Mountain Tour, 978-0-7643-2848-0, $24.95
Cabin Style: Decorating with Rustic, Adirondack, and Western Collectibles, 0-7643-2019-X, $29.95

Library of Congress Control Number: 2011939056

Designed by Justin Watkinson Cover by Bruce Waters
Type set in Castellar/Humanst521 BT

ISBN: 978-0-7643-3857-1
Printed in China

Schiffer Books are available at special discounts for bulk purchases for sales promotions or premiums. Special editions, including personalized covers, corporate imprints, and excerpts can be created in large quantities for special needs. For more information contact the publisher:

Published by Schiffer Publishing Ltd.
4880 Lower Valley Road
Atglen, PA 19310
Phone: (610) 593-1777; Fax: (610) 593-2002
E-mail: Info@schifferbooks.com

For the largest selection of fine reference books on this and related subjects, please visit our website at:
www.schifferbooks.com
We are always looking for people to write books on new and related subjects.
If you have an idea for a book, please contact us at
proposals@schifferbooks.com

This book may be purchased from the publisher.
Include $5.00 for shipping.
Please try your bookstore first.
You may write for a free catalog.

In Europe, Schiffer books are distributed by
Bushwood Books
6 Marksbury Ave.
Kew Gardens
Surrey TW9 4JF England
Phone: 44 (0) 20 8392 8585; Fax: 44 (0) 20 8392 9876
E-mail: info@bushwoodbooks.co.uk
Website: www.bushwoodbooks.co.uk

Cover photo courtesy Bryan and Nicole Kohrmann; Blackfeet Indian Encampment, St. Mary Lake HTT Co. postcard photographed by Kiser; McDonald Hotel Albertype Co. postcard published by Glacier Park Hotel Co.; Travel decal by Lindgren-Turner Co. Also pictured is the Many Glacier Hotel. Back cover hand-colored postcards of Trick Falls (Running Eagle Falls) and Going-to-the-Sun Mountain, photographed by Hileman and published by Albertype Co. The items in this book are from the author's personal collection unless otherwise noted.

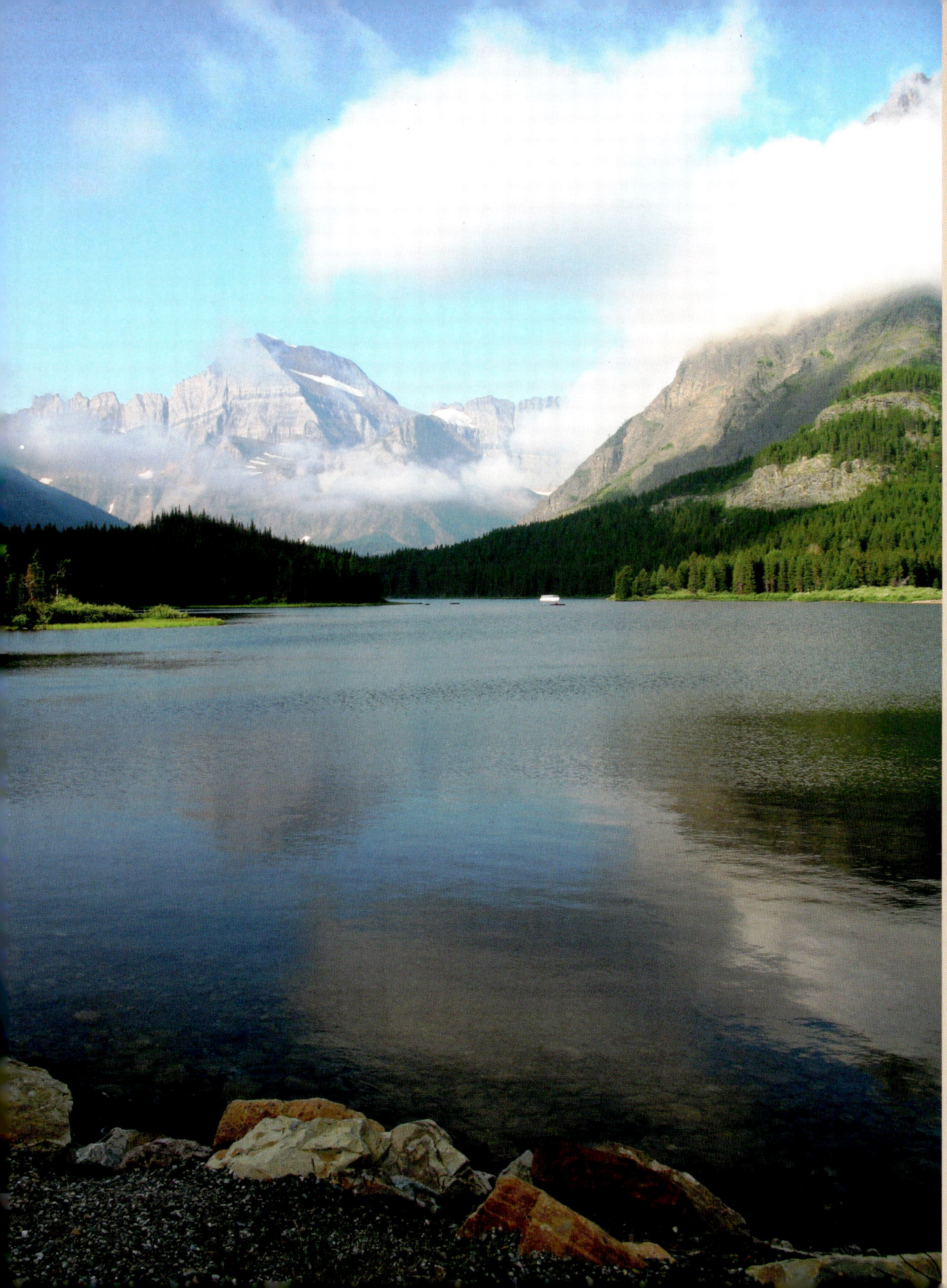

CONTENTS

Swiftcurrent Lake

INTRODUCTION

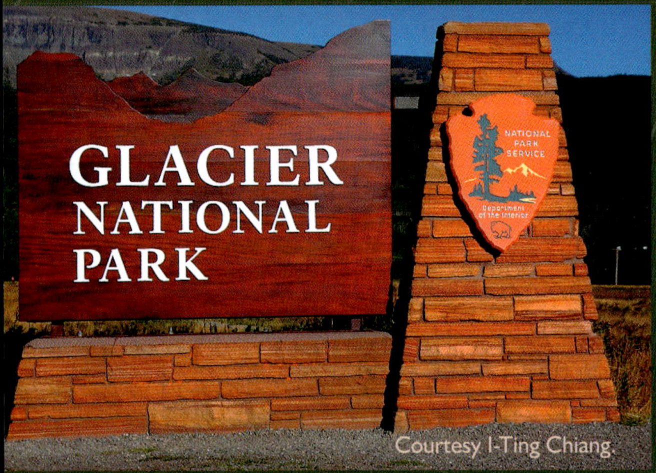

Courtesy I-Ting Chiang.

In the early days of Glacier National Park, as in other newly-established parks, the railroads saw great promise in these picturesque lands. With an eye toward increasing passenger service, the railroads laid out far-reaching plans to showcase these spectacular wonders. Architects were hired to design lodges that would provide a combination of luxury and adventure for the wealthy travelers, while pack horses, stagecoaches, and automobile concessions were established to provide additional sightseeing within the parks. Led by the Great Northern Railway and its "See America First" campaign, the railroads joined in promoting cross-country leisure travel across the Western United States by offering tour packages that included stops at the national parks.

As the years passed and the once rugged roads were improved, rail travel was replaced in popularity by automobile travel and access to the national parks was no longer limited to the wealthy. To accommodate the increase in motoring travel to Glacier National Park, inexpensive auto cabins, motels, and campgrounds were added. This was especially true after the Going-to-the-Sun Road was opened in 1933. Park facilities have continued to evolve to adapt to visitor needs, including renovations of the grand lodges, award-winning visitor centers, and improved roads and campgrounds.

Glacier National Park retains its popularity with nearly two million visitors each year, providing photographic moments at every turn. In this book, today's settings are paired with early day images used to promote the Great Northern Railway's enterprises.

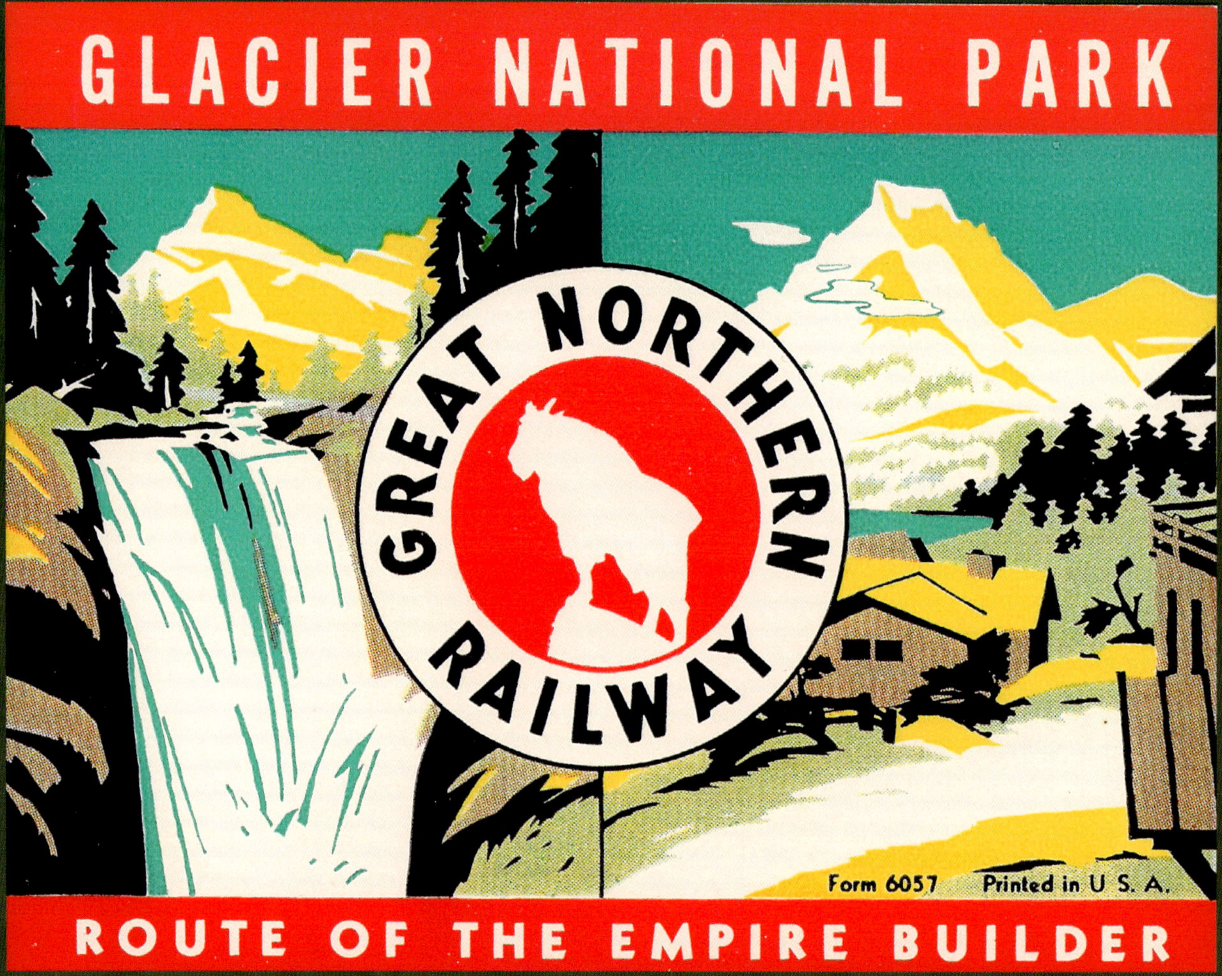

Vintage decal used to promote railway travel to Glacier National Park.

GLACIER NATIONAL PARK: THE HISTORY

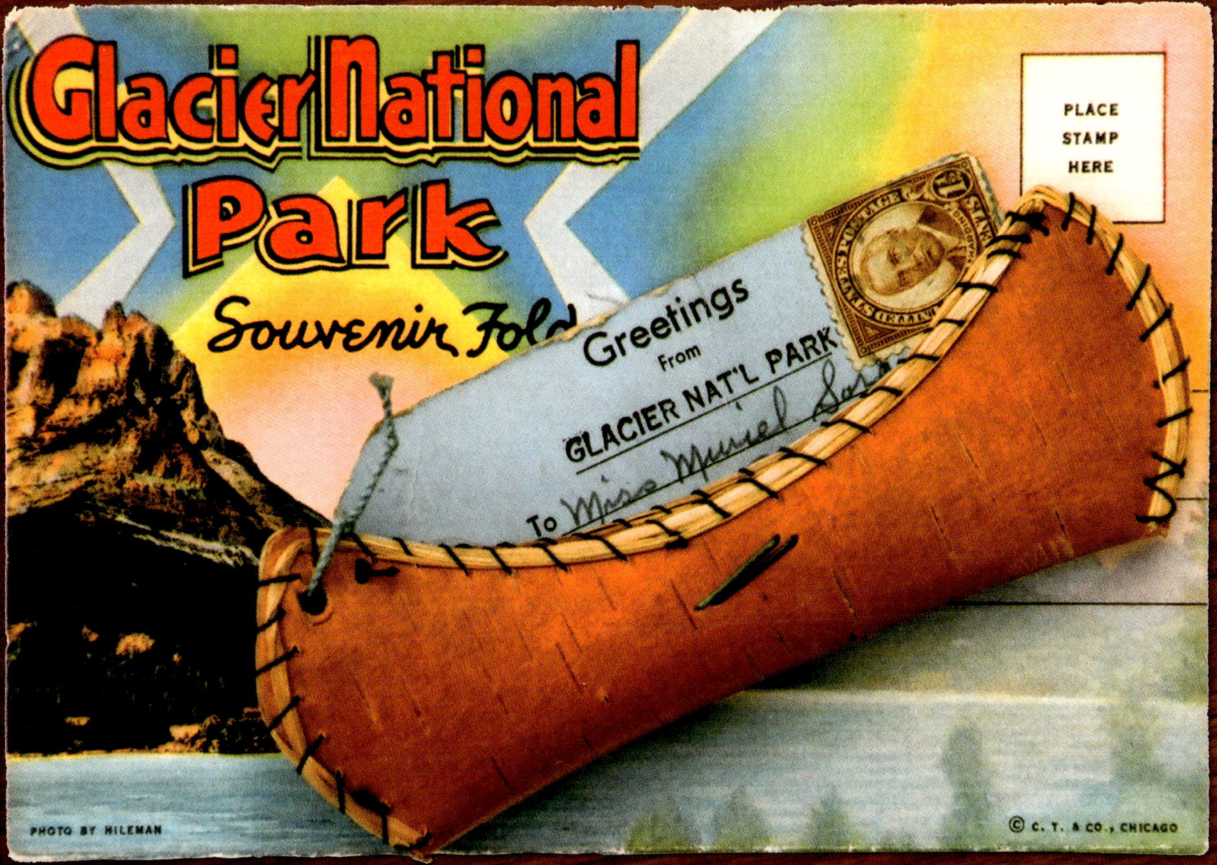

Glacier National Park souvenir folder by Curt Teich. Also pictured is a souvenir canoe.

Thousands of years in the making, Glacier National Park is known as the "Crown of the Continent" and is named for its towering glaciers, which have been grinding and cutting away at the earth's surface since the Ice Age. The result is a landscape of rugged peaks, lush valleys, and glacier-fed lakes, rivers, and streams of magnificent beauty.

The park is vast at more than one million acres. It contains hundreds of lakes, 175 mountains, 750 miles of trails, and is home to a variety of flora and fauna.

HISTORIC DATES

The following information is from the U.S. Department of Interior and Glacier National Park Centennial 2010.

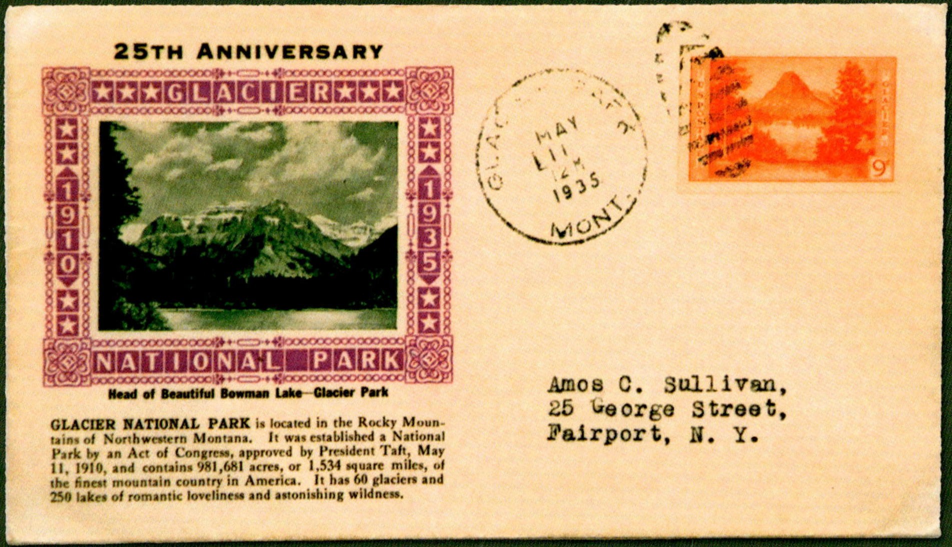

Commemorative cachet and postmark from 1935 celebrating the twenty-fifth anniversary of the establishment of Glacier National Park in 1910 by President Taft.

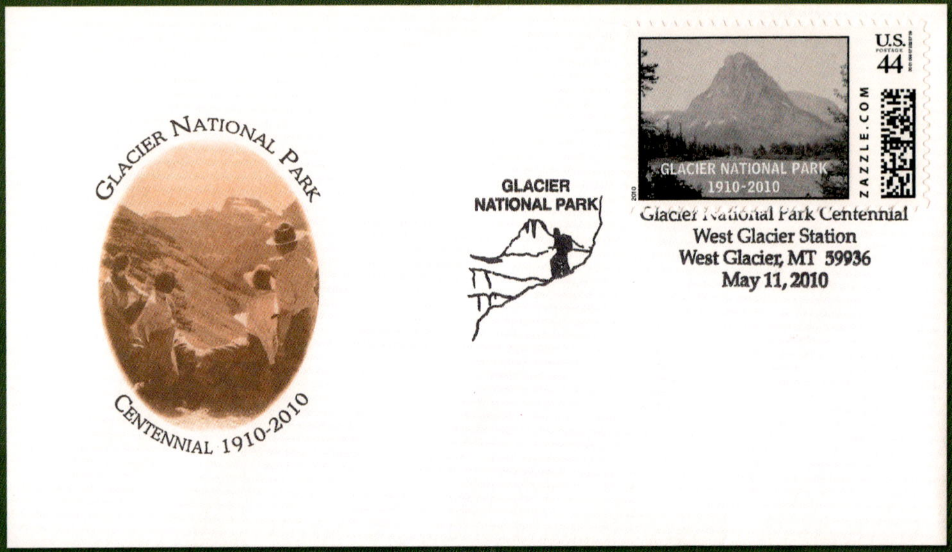

In 2010, the Glacier Association and the U.S. Postal Service joined together on May 11 to mark the 100th anniversary of the park with this pictorial postmark event featuring a specially-created cachet.

1816

The eastern part of the park is said to have been explored by Hugh Monroe of the Hudson's Bay Company.

1853

A. W. Tinkham, engineer of the exploration party with Isaac I. Stevens, Governor of Washington Territory, crossed Cut Bank Pass.

1854

James Doty explored the eastern base of the range and camped on Lower St. Mary Lake.

1861

Northwest Boundary Commission completed a survey of the 49th parallel from the Pacific Ocean to the Continental Divide at the northern boundary of the park.

1872

The international boundary survey that fixed the northern boundary of the park reached the Continental Divide from the east.

1891

The Great Northern Railway line is built through Marias Pass.

1892

Great Northern Railway added passenger service to Belton.

1901

George Bird Grinnell began advocating for the conservation of the park area in *Century* magazine.

1910

Glacier National Park was established with a bill signed on May 11th.

Great Northern Railway opened its first hotel in the new Glacier National Park when Belton Chalet opened in June.

1911

Major W. R. Logan became the first superintendent.

1919

Construction of road begins from Apgar to Logan Creek.

1932

Canada's Waterton and the United States' Glacier parks combined to become the Waterton-Glacier International Peace Park.

1933

Going-to-the-Sun Road was dedicated.

1936

Heaven's Peak fire destroys 14,000 acres, including over half of the Swiftcurrent cabins and most of the Many Glacier Chalet buildings.

1938

Chief Mountain International Road opened to Waterton Lakes National Park.

1944

Businesses in the park closed because of World War II. They reopened in 1946.

1960

Great Northern Railway sold the last of its Glacier Park properties.

1964

Flooding caused damage to roads, buildings, and trails.

1988

The Red Bench fire burned 27,000 acres in the western part of the park.

2003

Wildfires burned 138,000 acres in park.

2004

Plans are announced for the restoration of Going-to-the-Sun Road.

2006

Flooding destroyed trails, roads, highway, and bridges.

2010

Scientists estimate glaciers could disappear by 2020 if climate patterns continue.

100th anniversary celebration.

Anniversary logo courtesy of Glacier Association and Glacier Centennial Coordinator.

THE BLACKFEET NATIVES

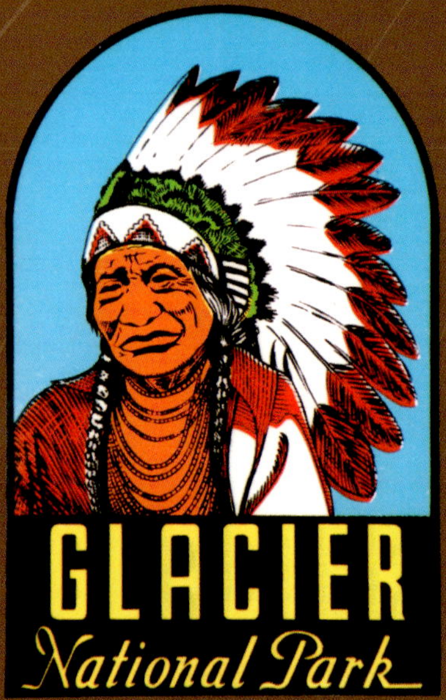

Decal manufactured by Lindgren-Turner Co.

Upon arrival of the frontier explorers in the early 1800s, native peoples had already made claim to the Rocky Mountain region. They may have been the ancestors of an earlier presence dating back thousands of years. The Blackfeet natives lived in the prairies to the east while the Flatheads and others occupied the valleys to the west.

By the mid-1800s the Blackfeet had accepted a treaty and the Blackfeet Indian Reservation was established in 1855. The reservation encompassed portions of the current park from the east to the Continental Divide. Following the discovery of gold and silver in the late 1800s, the government purchased 800,000 acres from the Blackfeet and the area was opened to prospectors and miners. The mining claims were later abandoned and attention returned to exploration, homesteading, and the eventual creation of the park.

The Museum of the Plains Indian is located in nearby Browning and is administered by the Indian Arts and Crafts Board of the U.S. Department of the Interior.

When the Great Northern Railway and Louis W. Hill became involved in developing hotels and other lodging in Glacier National Park, the Blackfeet natives were an integral part of Hill's publicity campaign attracting national attention and intrigue. The railroad's official photographer, Fred Kiser, is thought to have coined the "See America First" motto to entice the country's wealthy travelers to visit the park. This early advertisement promotes the park with the caption, "I saw America First." Matchbook by Diamond Match Co.

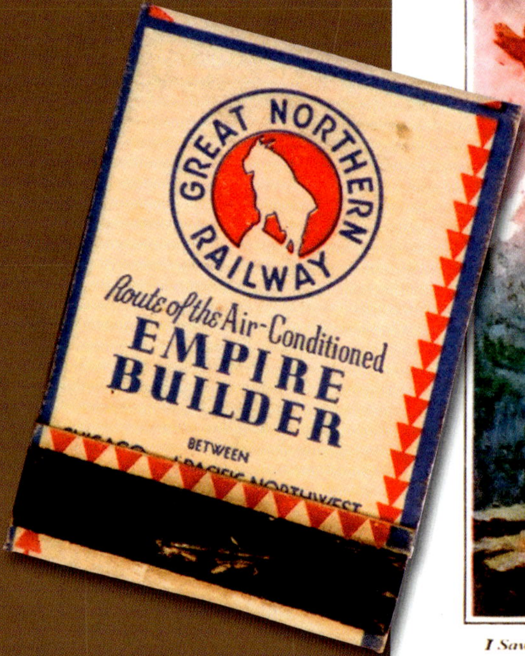

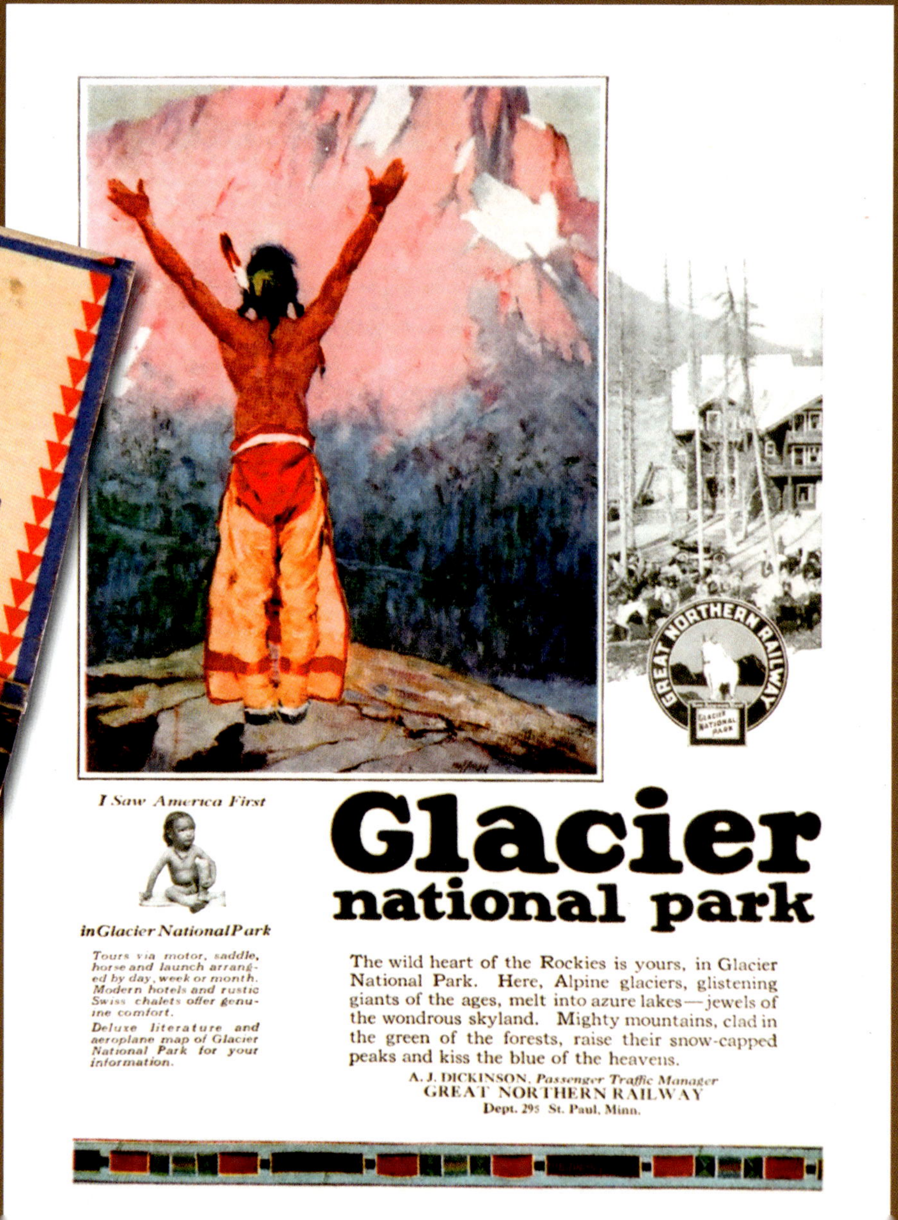

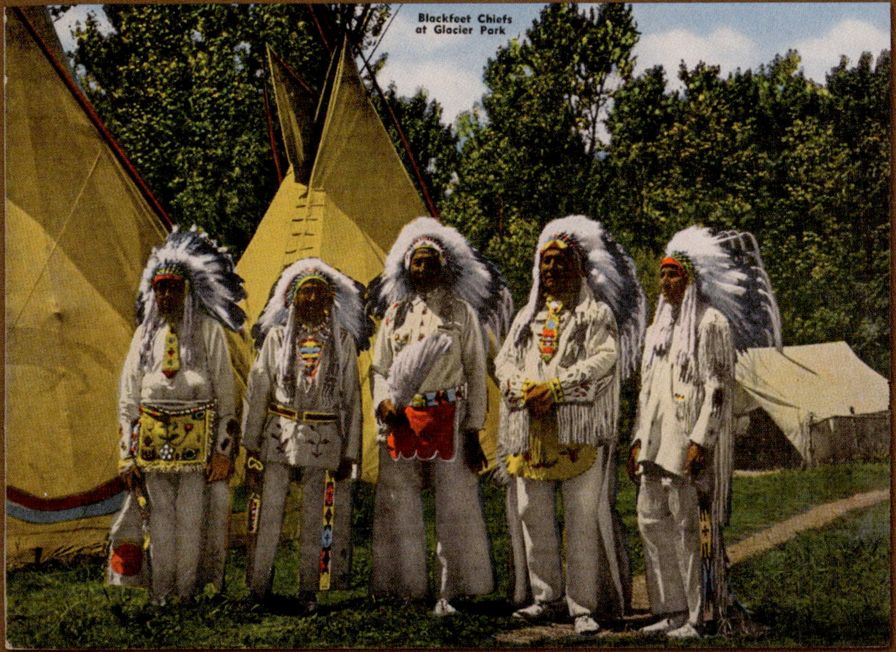

The presence of the Blackfeet natives continued to be prominently featured in the park's promotional materials into the 1950s, as shown in this linen postcard by E. C. Kropp Co. and purchased by vacationers in 1953. The pictured Chiefs are (left to right) Under Mouse, Night Gun, Bull Child, Last Star, and Wades-in-the-Water.

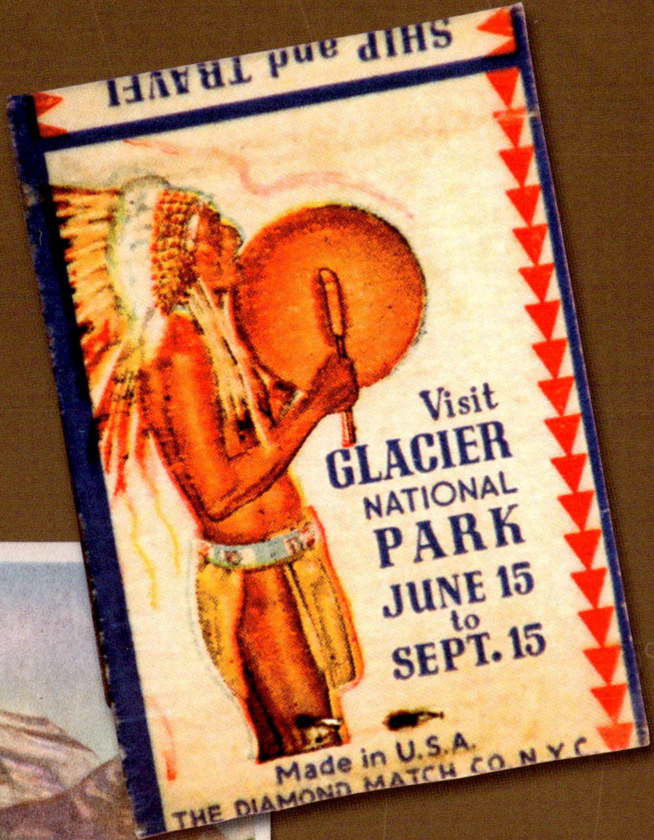

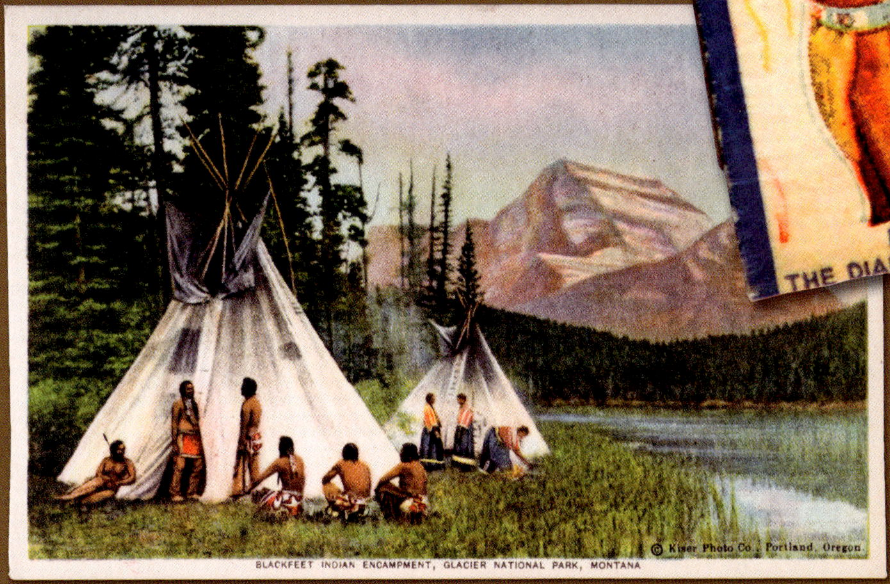

Hill arranged for the Blackfeet natives to set up their camps on the grounds of the Glacier Park Hotel and in other areas to replicate a living history. They were hired to entertain guests by singing, dancing, and providing demonstrations of their native skills. This postcard featuring a Blackfeet encampment at Glacier is one of a series of cards marked "Great Northern Railway. See America First Series." Postcard photo by Fred H. Kiser, the official photographer for the railroad, who spent six summers capturing Glacier's mountain scenery. This early matchbook by Diamond Match Co. also features a Blackfeet native on its cover.

TRANSPORTATION RAILS AND ROADS

The Great Northern Railway began passenger service to Belton in 1892 before the area became a national park. The Oriental Limited was the train operated by Great Northern between St. Paul, Minnesota, and Seattle, Washington, beginning in 1905. Glacier Park visitors could ride the train from the east to eventually reach their Glacier Park destination. Louis Hill, who was in charge of building many of the early Glacier Park facilities, used Oriental touches in decorating many of the establishments to tie-in with his railroad's Oriental Limited trains.

The company added another railroad station near the Glacier Park Hotel circa 1913 when the hotel opened. After introduction of the Empire Builder line in 1929, the Oriental Limited was no longer popular and was discontinued by 1931; it was revived in 1947. Visitors can still enjoy a train trip to the park via the Empire Builder on Amtrak while many others arrive by car.

William and James Brewster provided the first public transportation in Glacier National Park beginning in 1912. When their stage coaches and auto chauffeurs were unable to satisfy the railroad, arrangements were made with a new concessionaire, the Glacier Park Transportation Co., for use of its auto-stages circa 1914. The vehicles evolved into the popular red buses which are still in use.

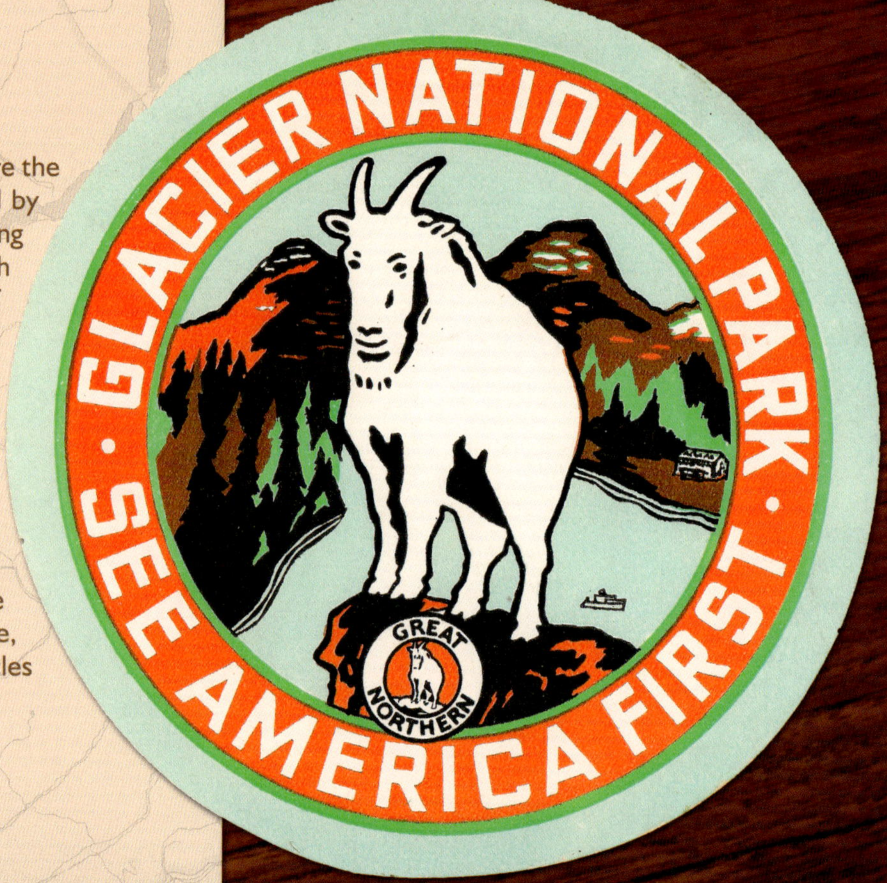

The "See America First" campaign was used by the railroad to showcase adventurous travel in the Western United States as an alternative to the traditional European tours made popular by wealthy Easterners.

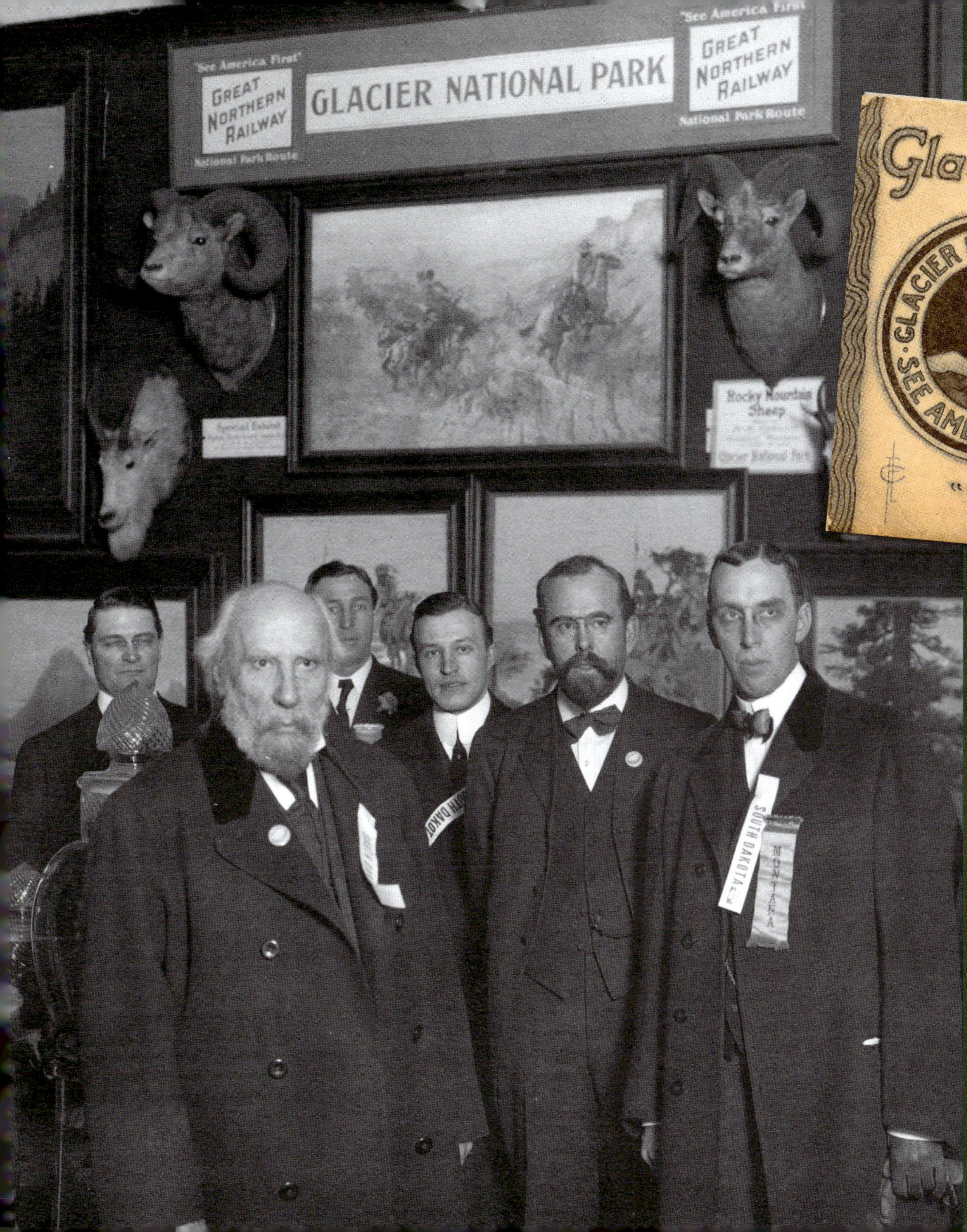

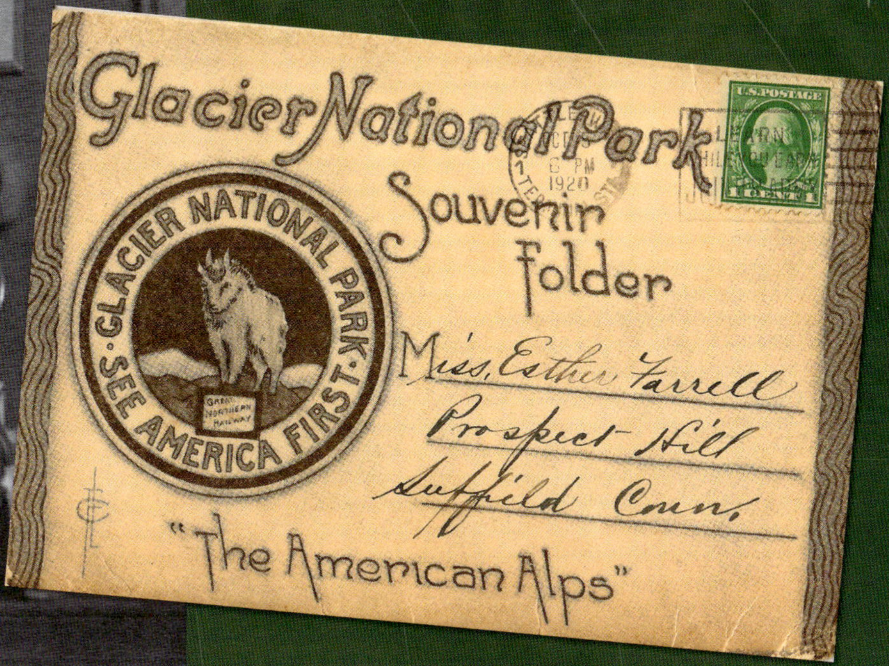

By 1920, when this Great Northern Railway souvenir folder was mailed, the railroad was promoting the park as "The American Alps" to showcase the rugged beauty that could be found in the United States. This folder includes twenty such scenes photographed by Fred Kiser.

The Great Northern Railway Co. was founded in 1889 by railroad tycoon James J. Hill, who used existing rail lines and added new ones to create the country's northernmost transcontinental route stretching from St. Paul, Minnesota, to Seattle, Washington. The line's most pivotal route was through Marias Pass as it crossed the Continental Divide in northwestern Montana near what would become Glacier National Park. The route was charted by John F. Stevens, Hill's engineer, and at 5,213 feet above sea level, it became the easiest and lowest rail line through the northern Rockies. This photograph from 1911 shows James J. Hill (left) and his son Louis W. Hill (with beard) and their associates in the early days of Glacier National Park. *Courtesy of Minnesota Historical Society.*

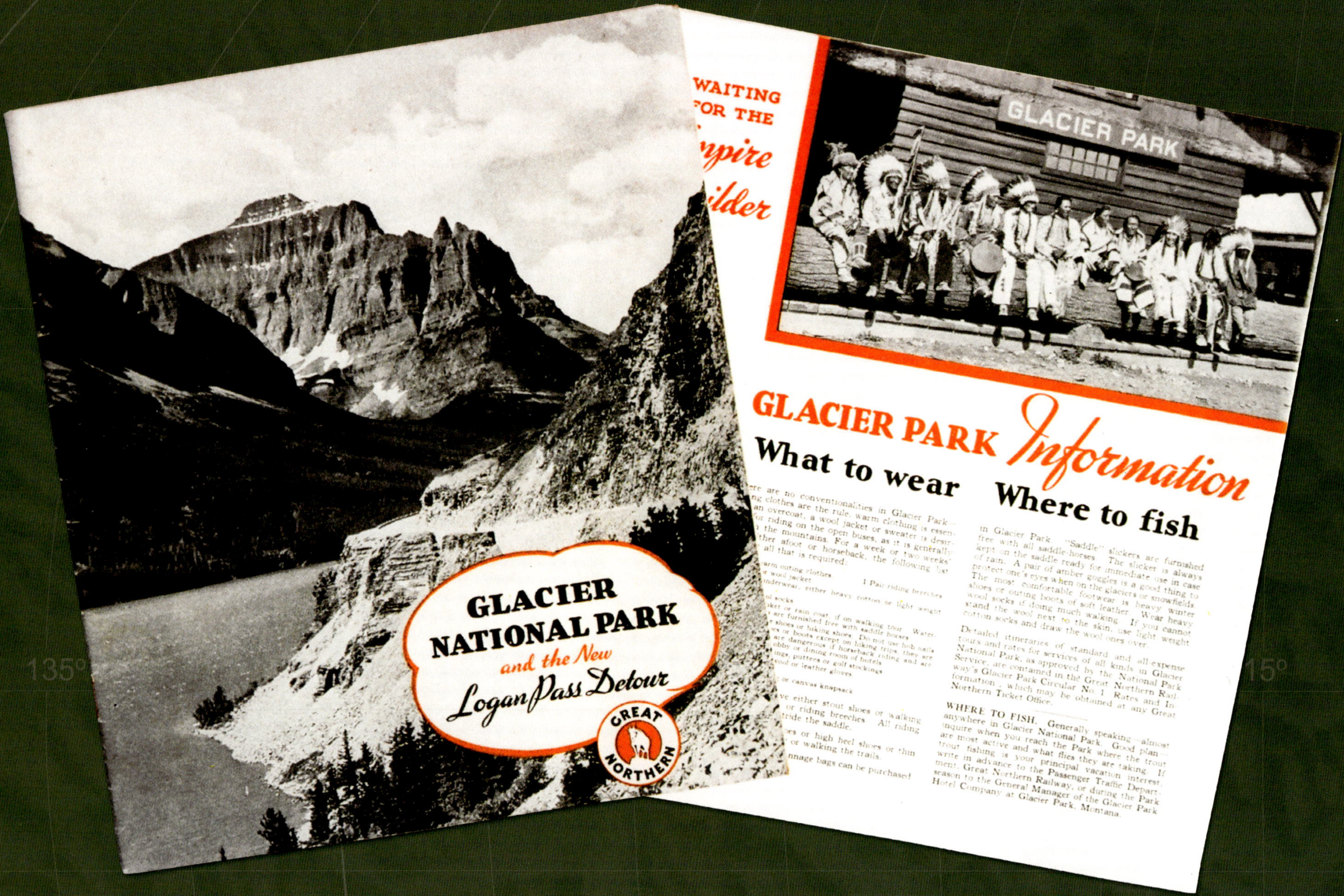

The East Glacier Park Station is still in use. It opened circa 1913. In the early days Blackfeet natives were staged at the station to greet tourists as they arrived. The Blackfeet were available to pose for pictures or visit with the fascinated tourists to make their visits all the more memorable. The Blackfeet welcome picture was included in this Great Northern Railway brochure issued to promote the new Logan Pass completed in 1932.

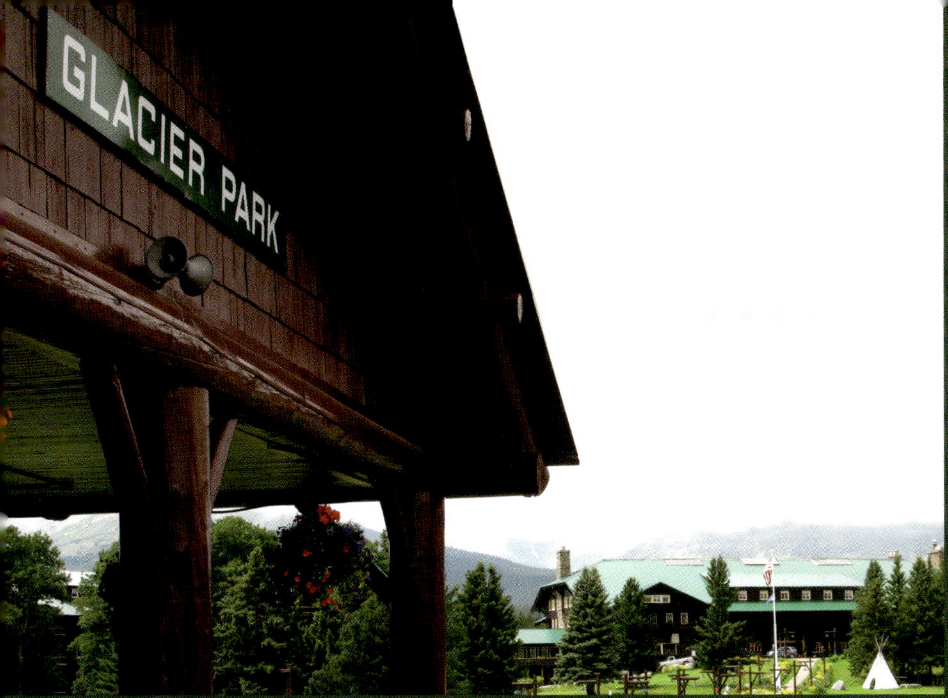

The East Glacier Park Station serves passengers who ride the Empire Builder to the park via Amtrak. The Glacier Park Lodge is conveniently located nearby.

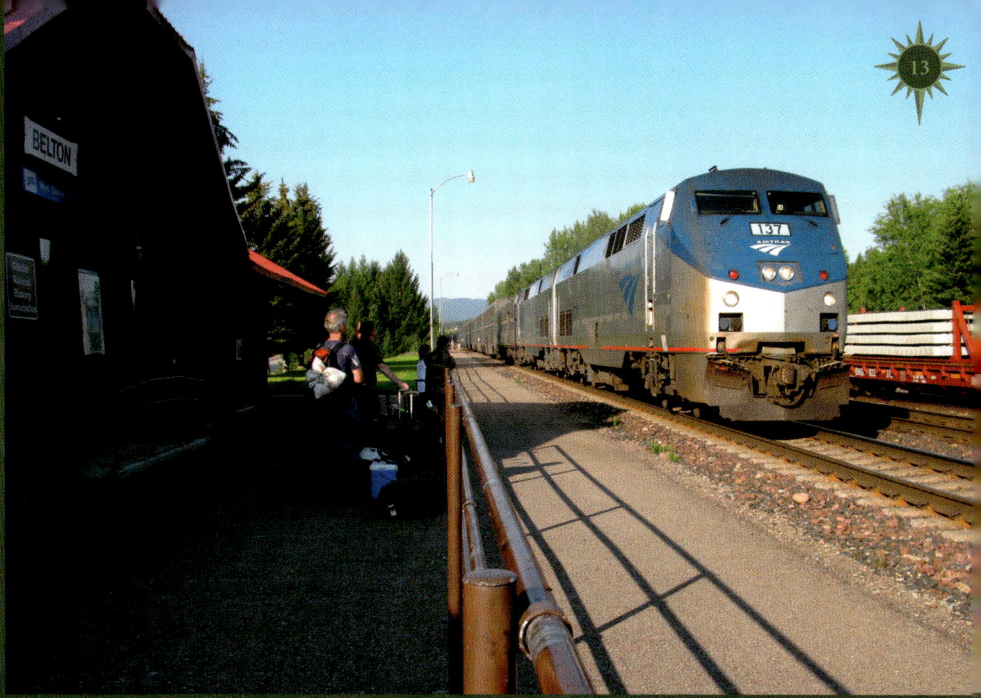

Passengers prepare for the arrival of the Amtrak Empire Builder as it pulls into the West Glacier Station at Belton on a recent summer day.

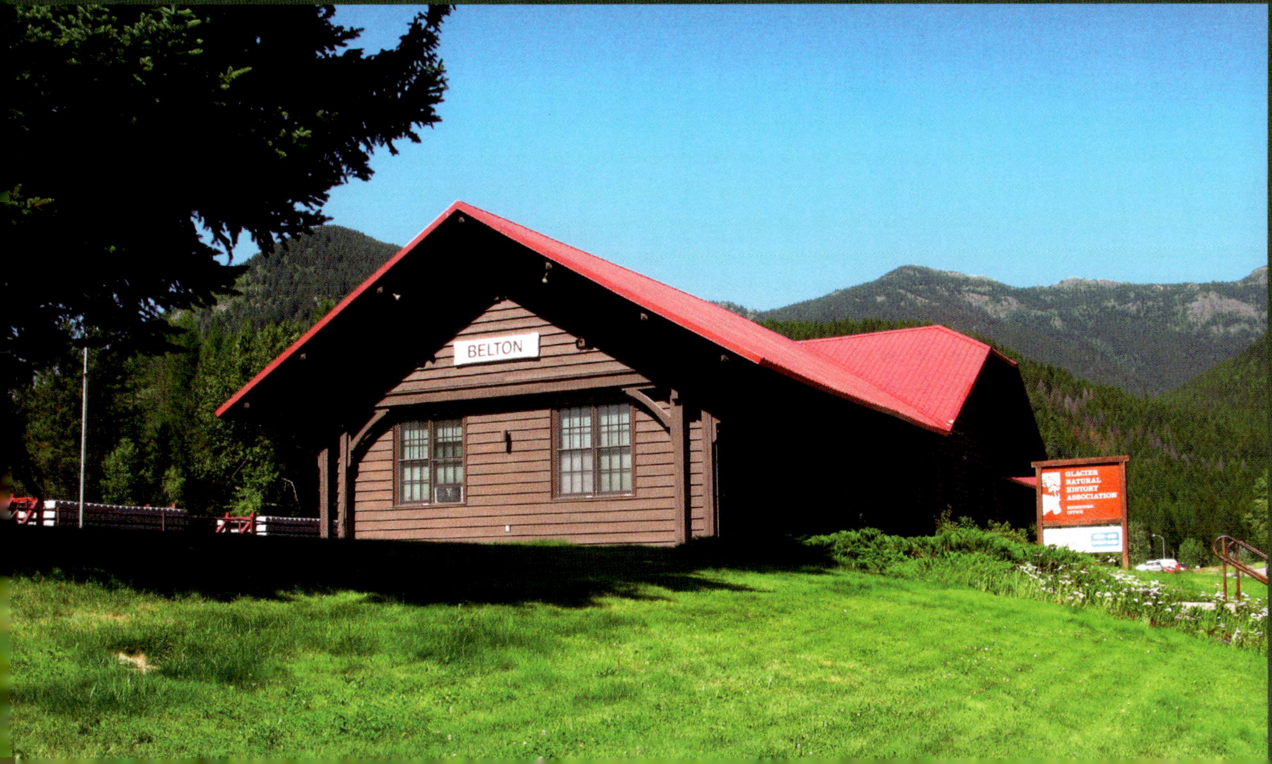

In 1891, two box cars were used to create a primitive train station at Belton for the Great Northern Railway. Passenger service began on August 14, 1892. The makeshift station served the area until a permanent station was built between 1907 and 1910. It is located on the outskirts of the park and its construction began the Great Northern Railway's more than fifty-year involvement with businesses in the park. In 1991, the Glacier Association renovated the depot for use as its headquarters and warehouse. The West Glacier Station is a scheduled stop for Amtrak's Empire Builder with service from Portland and Seattle to Chicago.

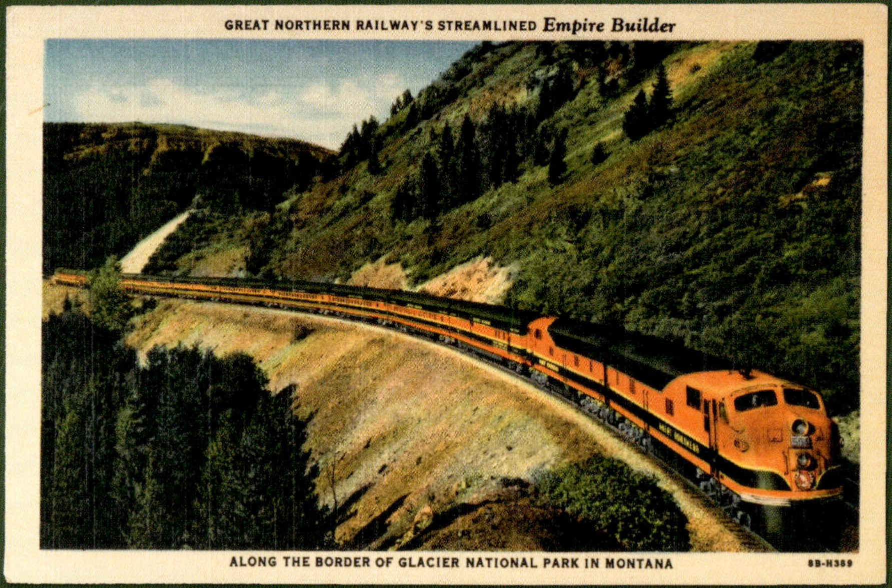

The first Empire Builder passenger train was introduced in 1929 just before the stock market crash. It was named in honor of founder James Hill's success in building a railroad dynasty. Air-conditioning was added to the train in 1935. During World War II, the train suspended stops in Glacier Park because of the increased business of moving troops. In 1947, the Empire Builder became a streamliner train and, in 1951, the Mid-Century Empire Builder was introduced. It offered reclining coach seats, dining car reservations, and drinking fountains. The Great Dome Empire Builder began service in 1955 where passengers could get a birds-eye view of the spectacular sights along the transcontinental route. Postcard of the Streamliner Empire Builder by Curteich. The matchbook was made by the Diamond Match Co.

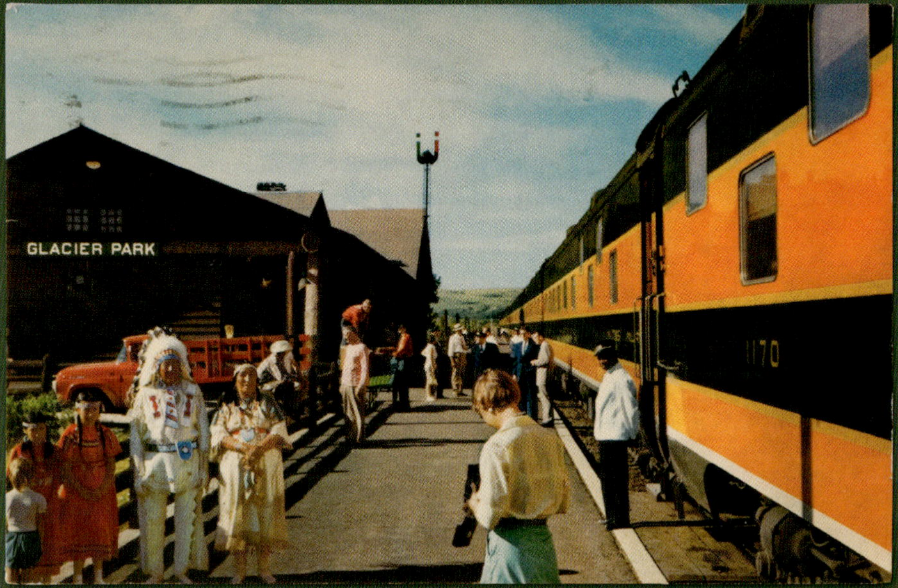

At East Glacier Park Station, the Blackfeet, in their native dress, pose for pictures upon arrival of the Western Star, which was introduced in 1951. Amtrak took over the Empire Builder name in 1971. A year earlier, the Great Northern Railway and three other railroads merged to become the Burlington Northern Railroad. Great Northern Railway Co. postcard made by H. S. Crocker. The matchbook, made by the Ohio Match Co., shows the Empire Builder and the Western Star.

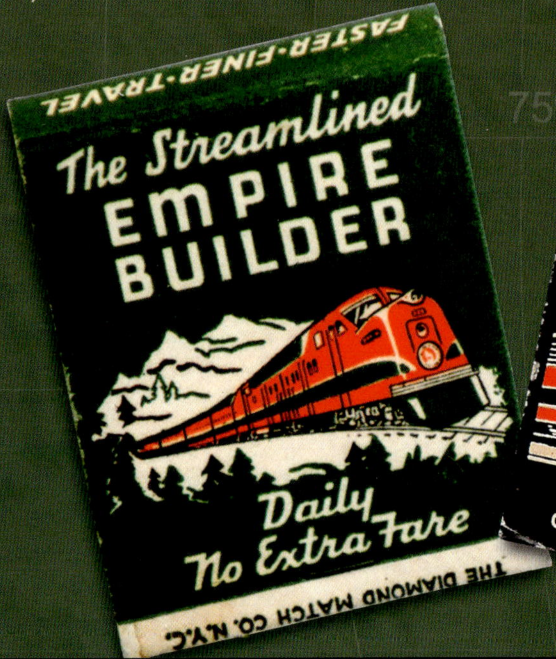

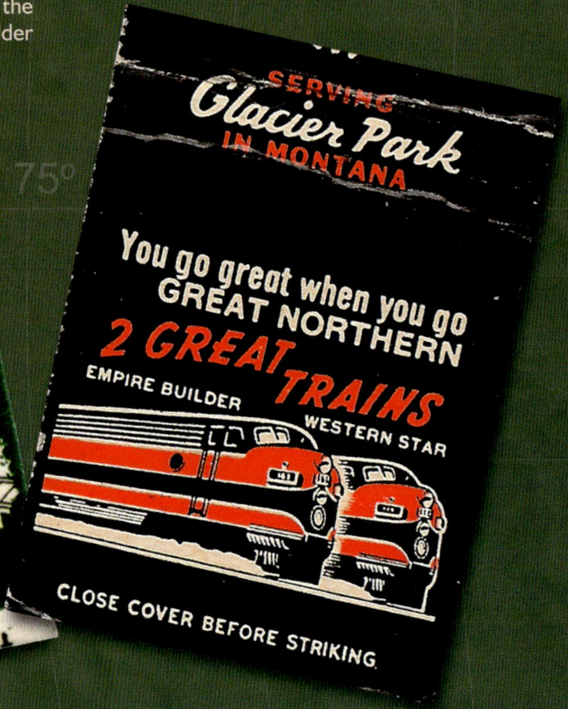

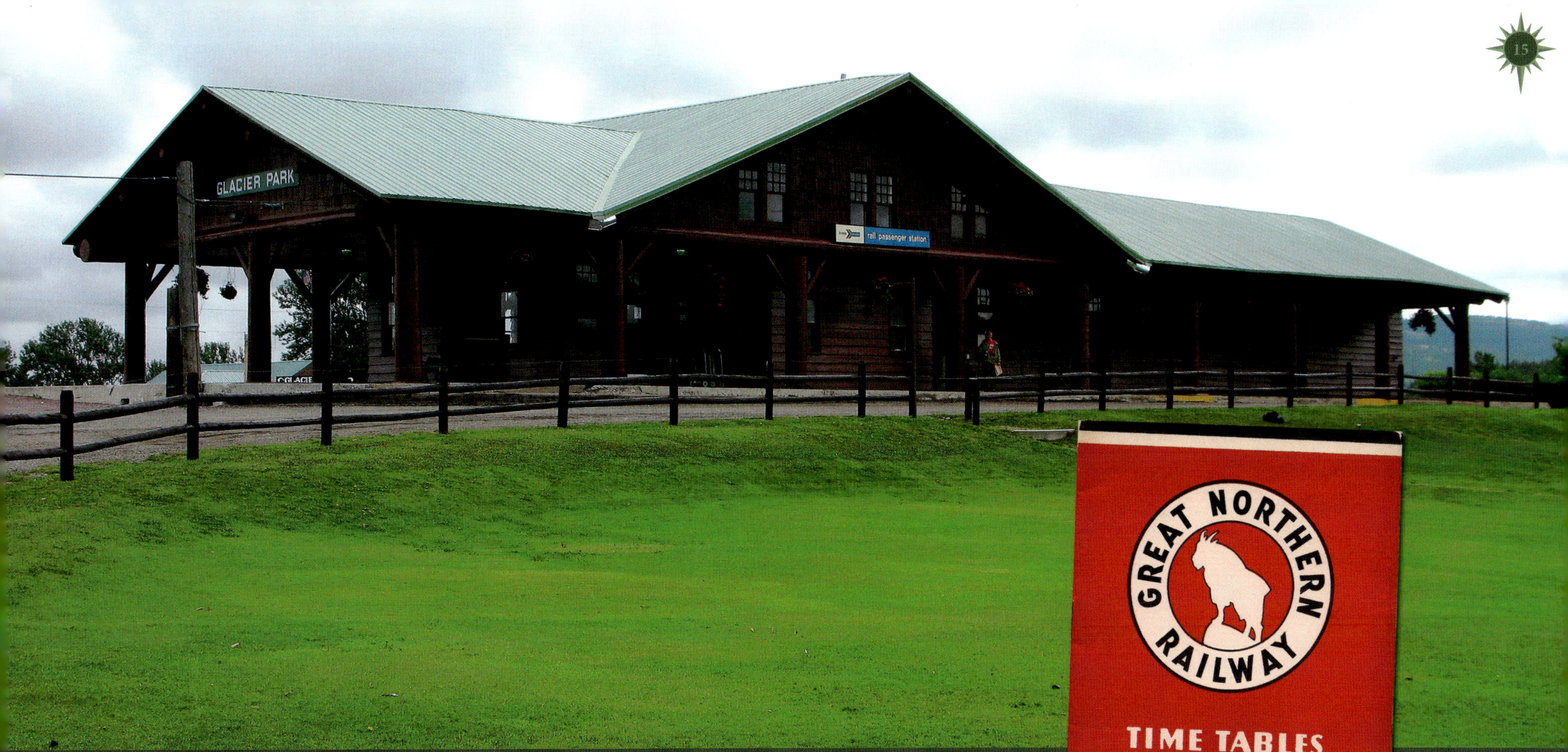

While fewer visitors arrive by train these days, the East Glacier Park Station provides plenty of nostalgia for train travelers. The station looks much as it did when it was built and provides a wonderful setting for a short walk to the Glacier Park Lodge for a modern day stopover.

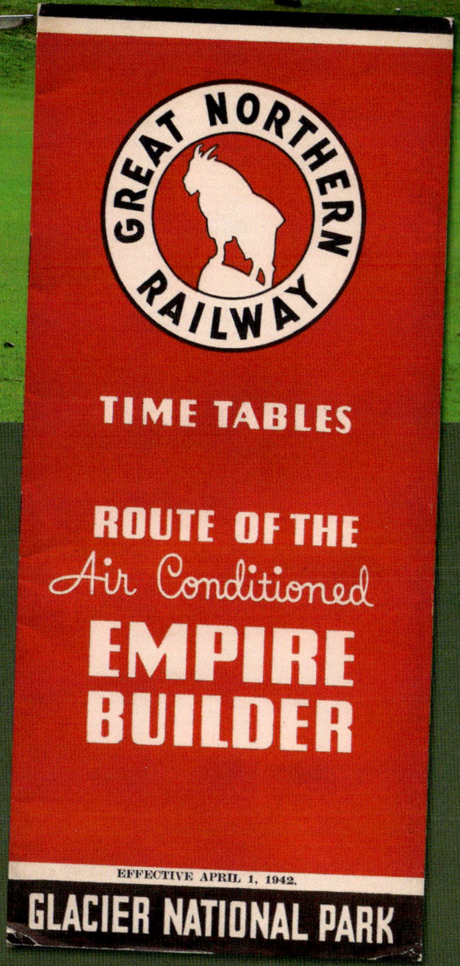

This Great Northern Railway timetable for the Empire Builder dates from 1942 and boasts of the advantages of train travel as "safe, economical, fast and comfortable." Round trip fares from Chicago to Glacier Park were $67.00. Stopovers at Glacier were allowed on all train tickets from June 20th through September 8th that year at either Glacier Park Station or at Belton to permit passengers to make trips through the park.

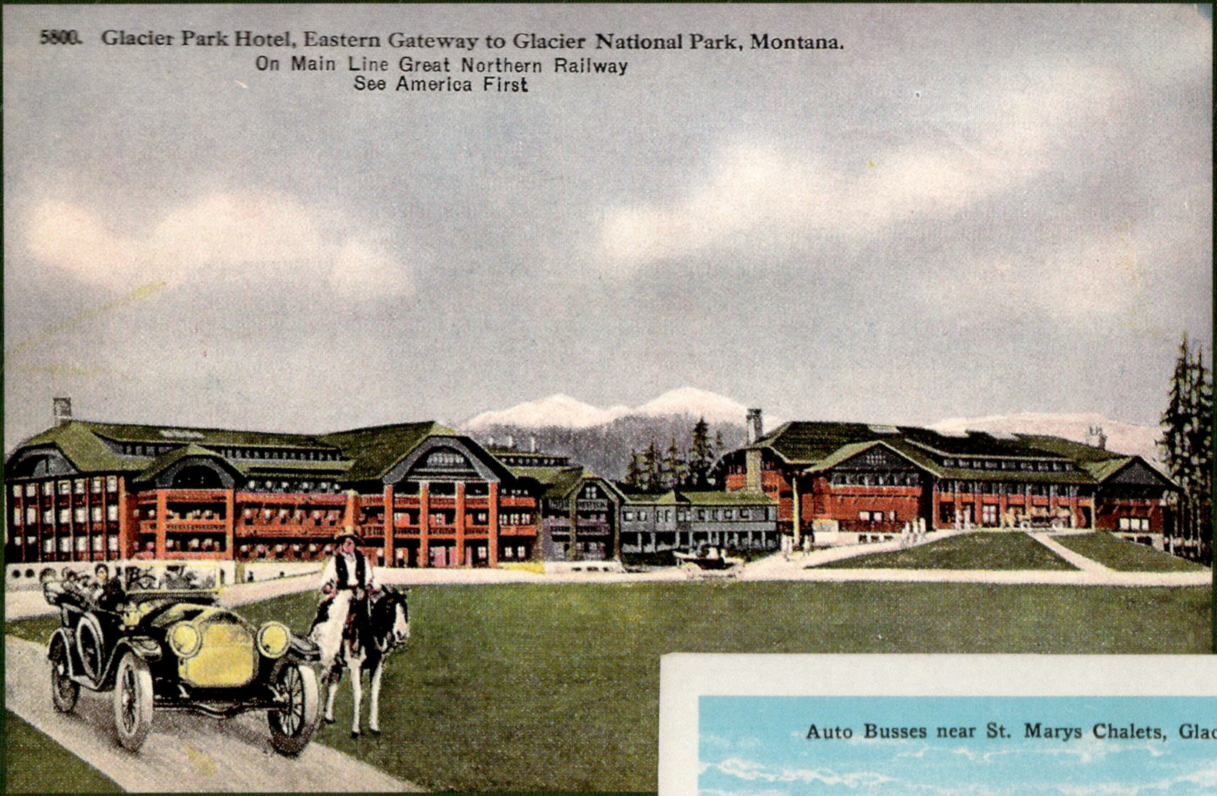

This viewcard from an early "See America First" souvenir folder, published by Great Northern, features motorized and non-motorized transportation options provided within the park. The Glacier Park Hotel is pictured in the background.

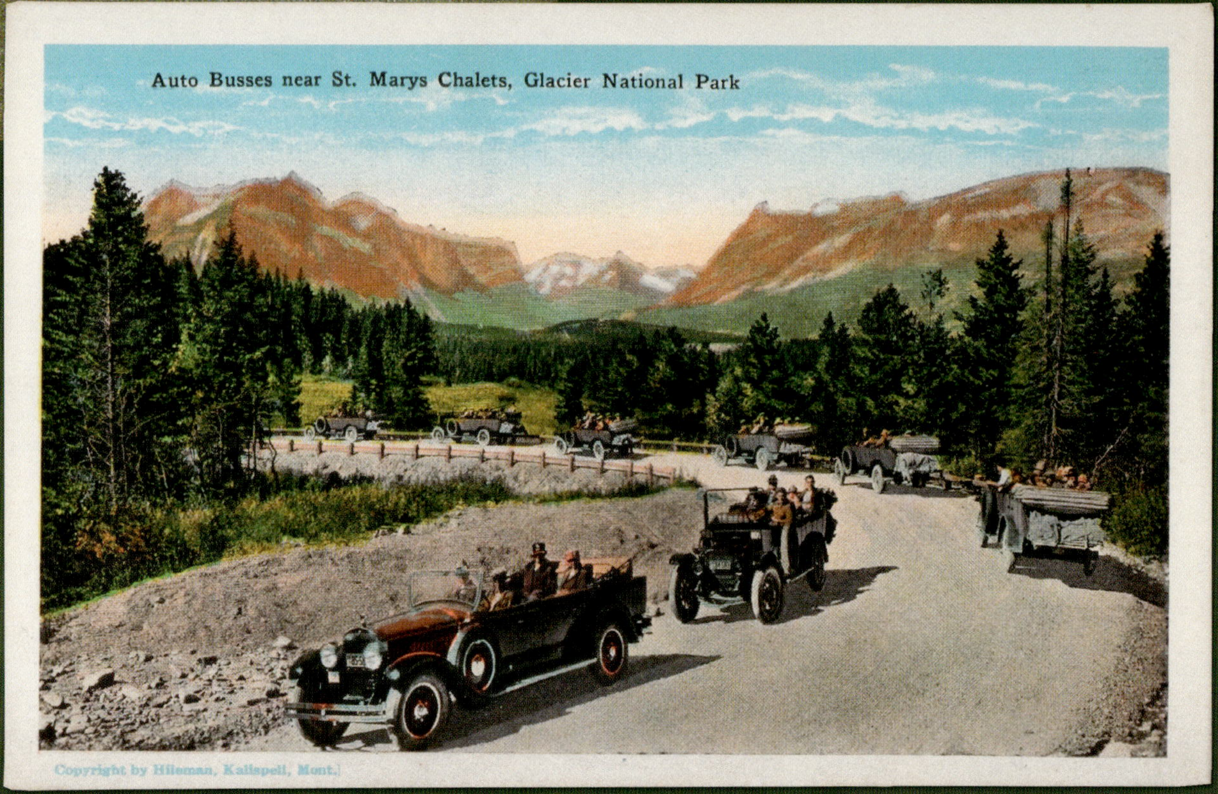

In 1914, the concession for automobile transportation was transferred from the original leasehold, Brewster Brothers, to the Glacier Park Transportation Co. Owned by Roe Emery, the new concession used a fleet of auto-stages manufactured by the White Motor Co. By the mid 1930s, two types of vehicles were in use, as pictured in this postcard published by the Glacier Park Hotel showing a caravan of "auto-busses" near St. Mary Chalets.

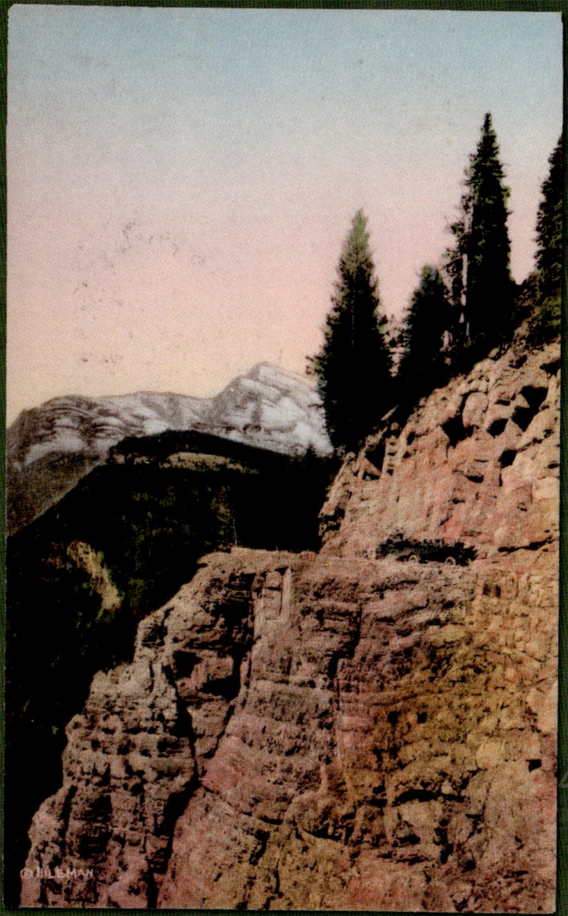

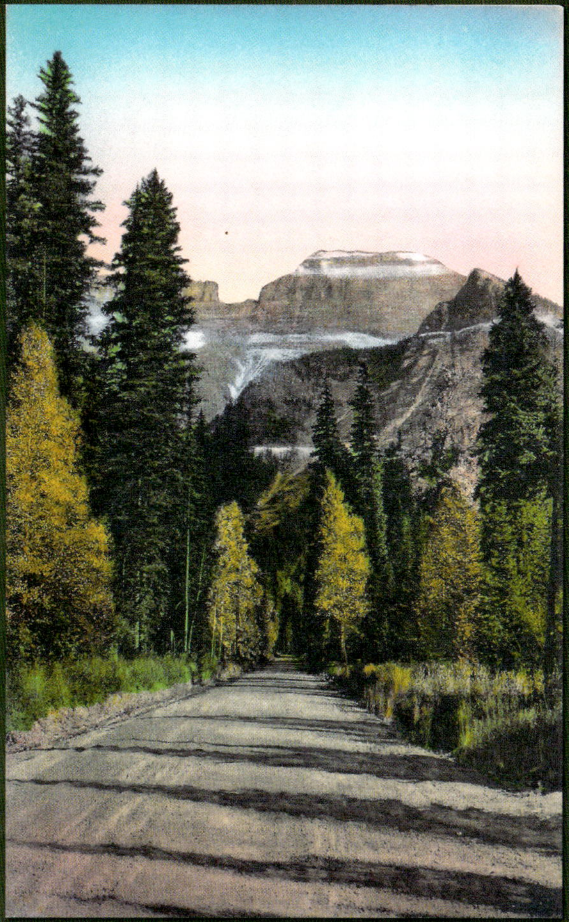

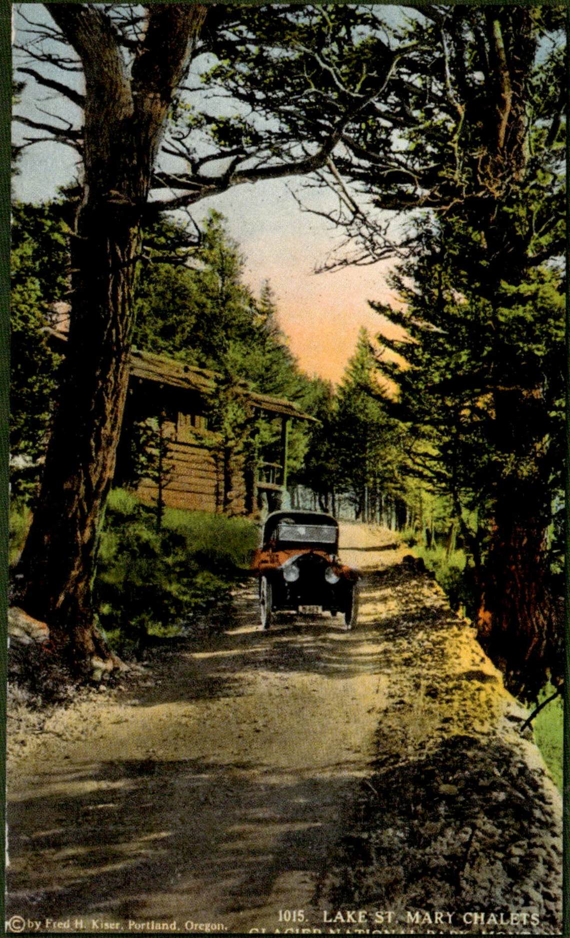

These hand-colored postcards by the Albertype Co. show the Trans-Mountain Road before it was finished and renamed Going-to-the-Sun Road. The road received its first federal construction funds in 1921. Private automobiles were used in the park as early as 1912. An early vehicle traveling near St. Mary Chalets is pictured on another postcard view photographed by Fred Kiser.

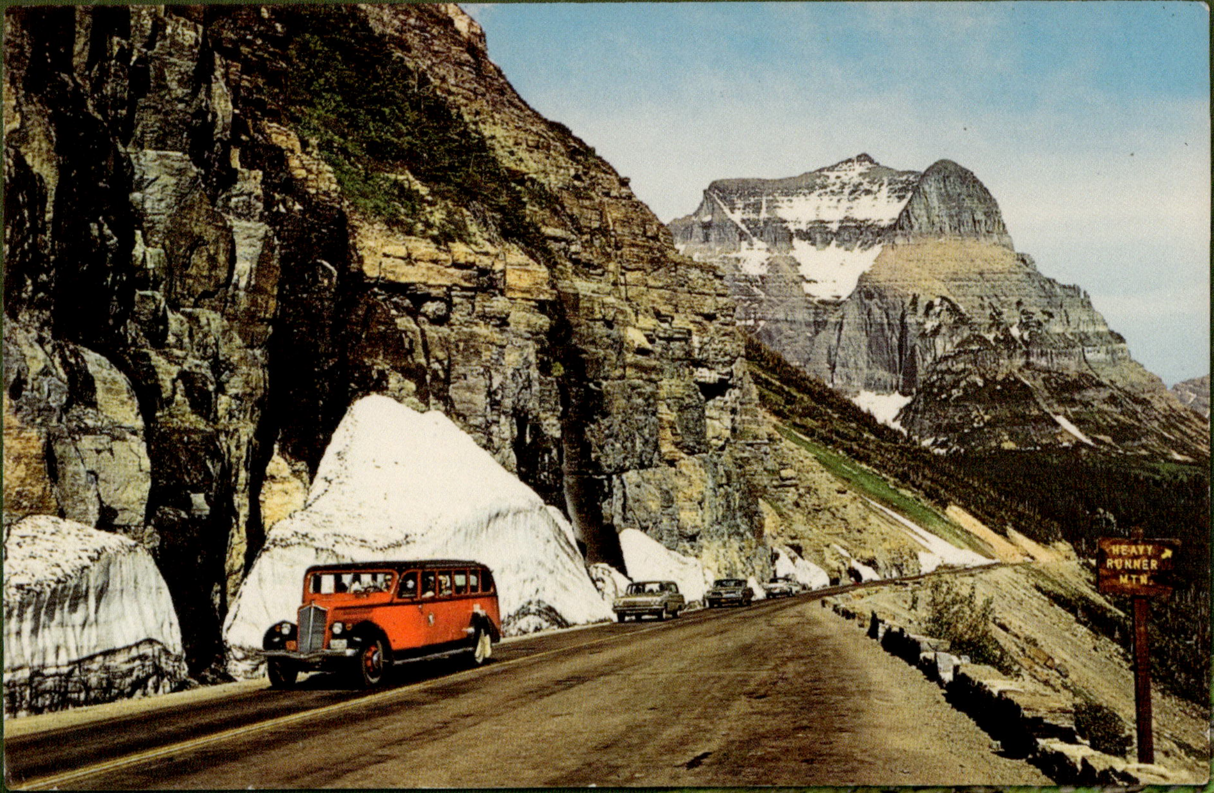

In the late 1930s, the earlier buses were replaced by modern passenger buses also made by the White Motor Co. With its signature roll-back canvas convertible top, passengers could experience all the sights and sounds of a trip through the park. The drivers of the seventeen-passenger tour buses were called "jammers," so named for the jamming of the gears as they traversed the mountain roads. The buses were converted from standard transmissions to automatic transmissions in the late 1980s, silencing the ride, but not the thrill. Plastichrome postcard published by Bob Anderson Postcards.

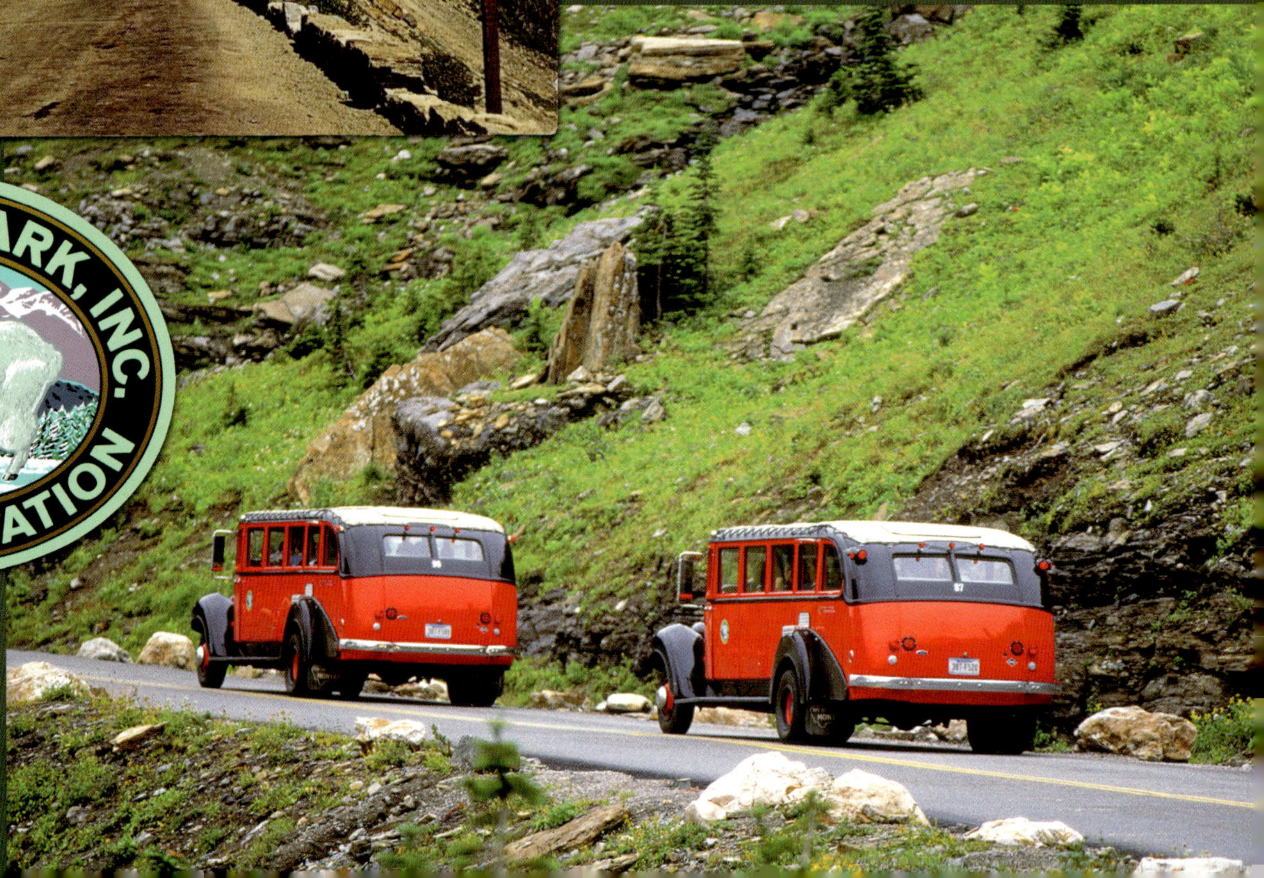

In the 1990s, the buses began to experience safety issues and were removed from the roads. When park visitors expressed disappointment over the loss, the National Park Service and Glacier Park, Inc. arranged for the buses to be refurbished by the Ford Motor Co. and they were returned to use in 2003. The Red Bus Tours are operated by Glacier Park, Inc. *Photo and logo courtesy of Glacier Park, Inc.*

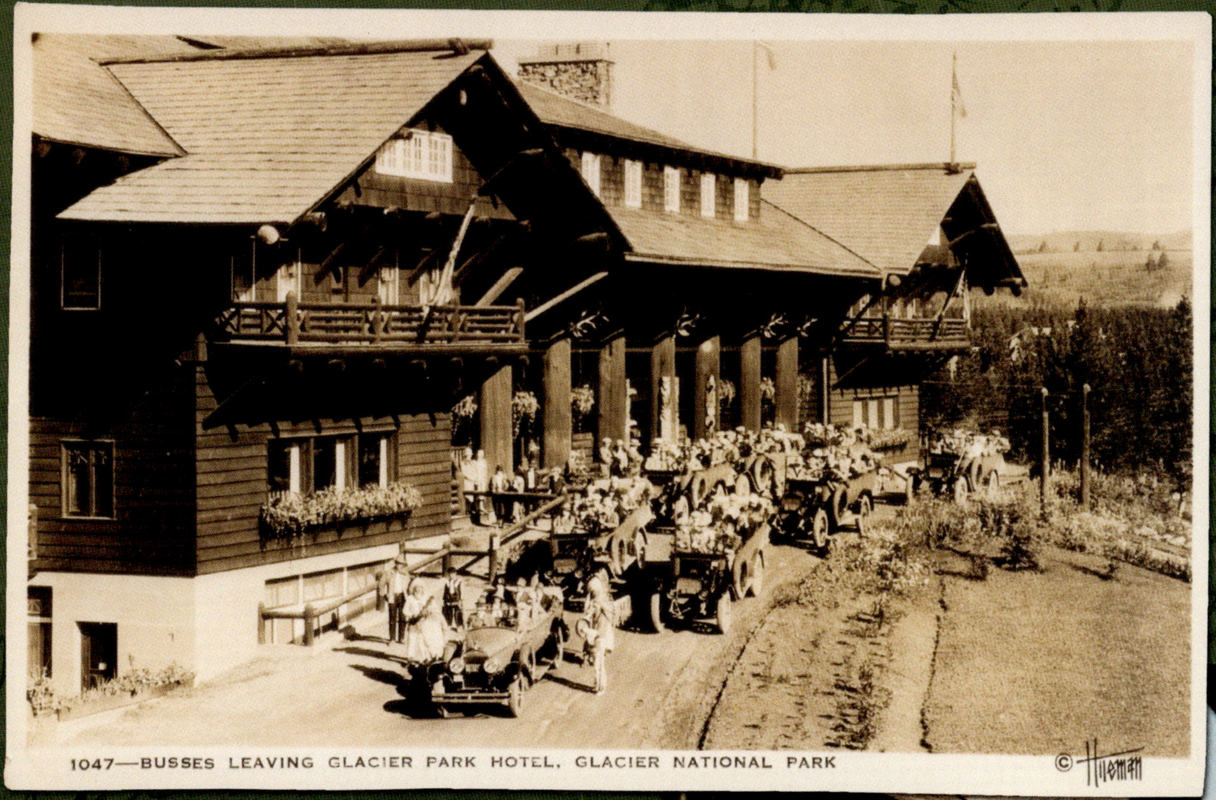

A fleet of touring buses get ready to leave the Glacier Park Hotel. A Blackfeet native bids farewell to tourists in the first bus as they prepare to head for their next destination. This early postcard is by T. J. Hileman, whose name appears on hundreds of Glacier postcards produced from his commercial studio. Many of those images are now part of the park's archives.

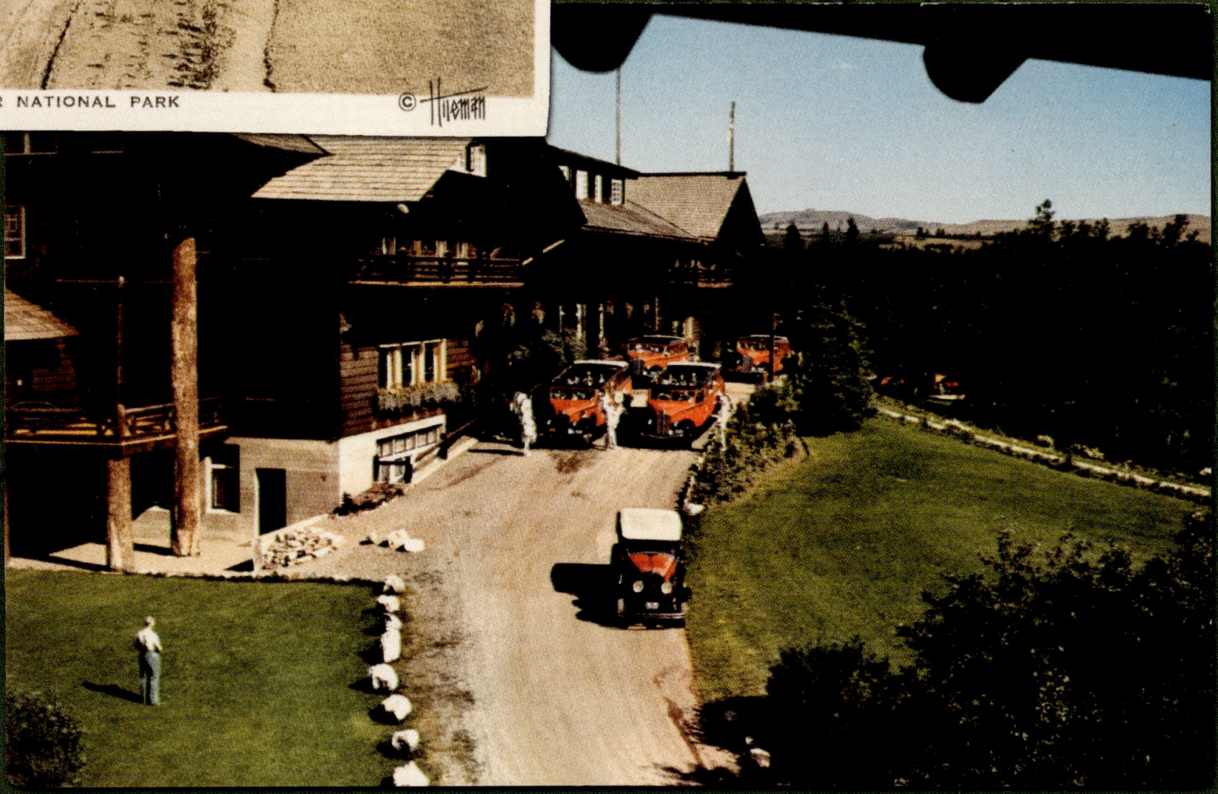

The same scene is taking place in this later H. S. Crocker postcard. In this case the Blackfeet natives are welcoming guests to their hotel instead of bidding them farewell, according to information on the back of the postcard.

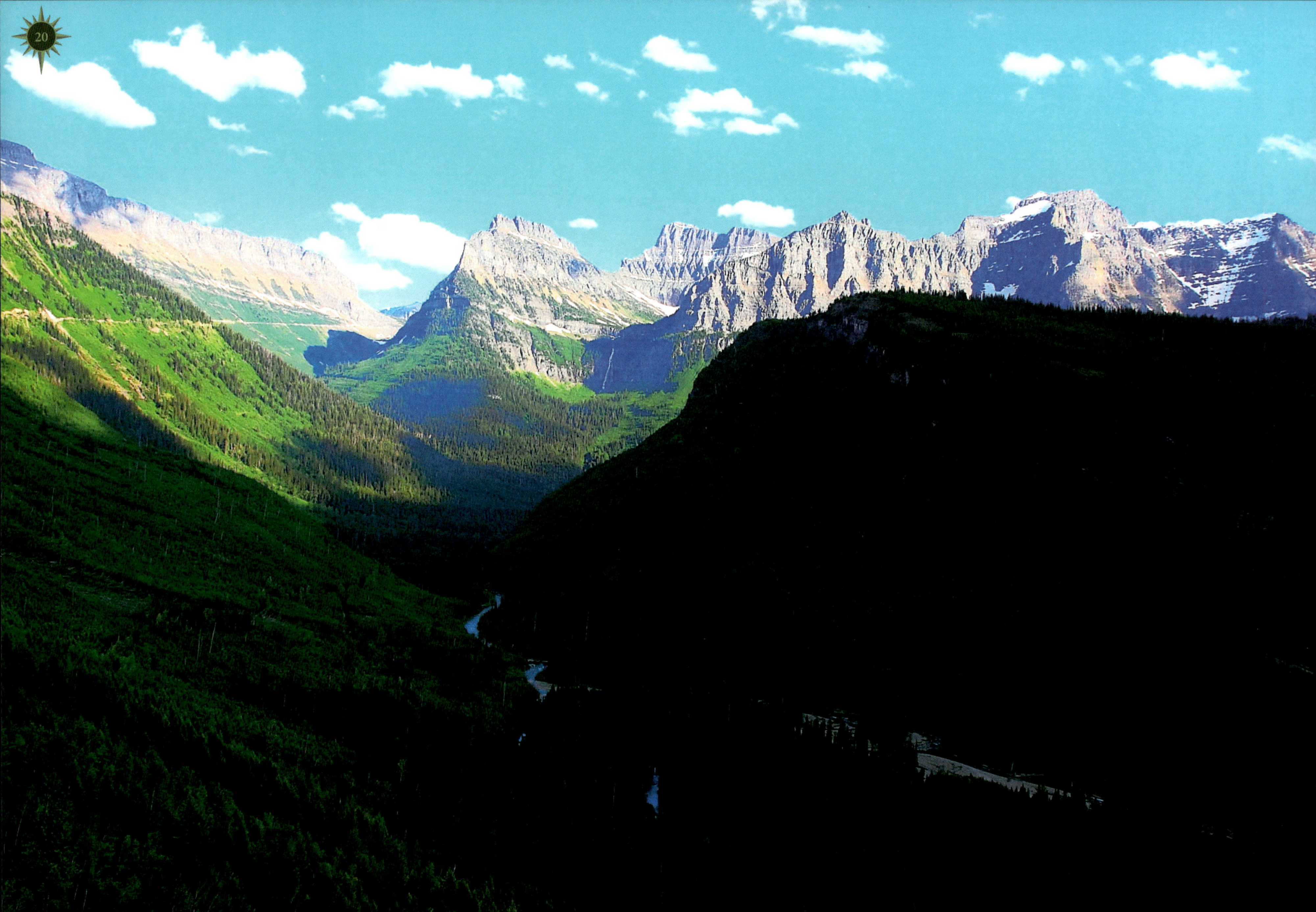

The Going-to-the-Sun Road was named a National Historic Landmark in 1997 and is also a National Civil Engineering Landmark. It is considered to be one of the most scenic highways in the world with numerous opportunities for breathtaking views, including this one of the McDonald Creek Valley. *Courtesy I-Ting Chiang*.

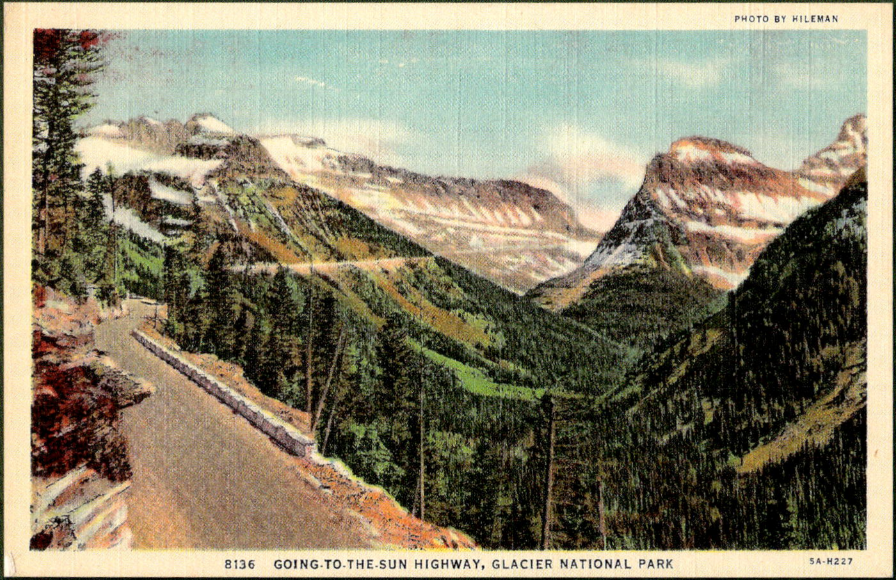

The Going-to-the-Sun Road was named after the 9,642-foot high mountain of the same name. It took more than a decade to build before its dedication was held on July 15, 1933. The road covers fifty miles from West Glacier to St. Mary with its highest elevation of 6,646 feet at Logan Pass, providing travelers with spectacular views. Linen postcard published by C. T. Art-Colortone and photographed by T. J. Hileman.

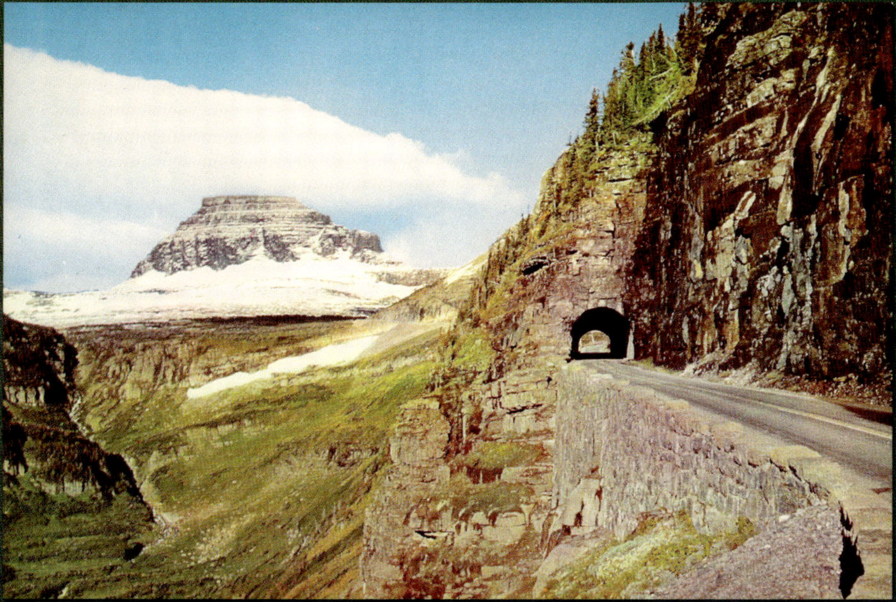

This colorful view featuring the East Side Tunnel and Clements Mountain pays tribute to the engineering skills that made the Going-to-the-Sun Road possible as it "winds through the park and ascends the sheer cliffs of the Continental Divide by way of Logan Pass." Postcard by Northwest Curio & Post Card Co.

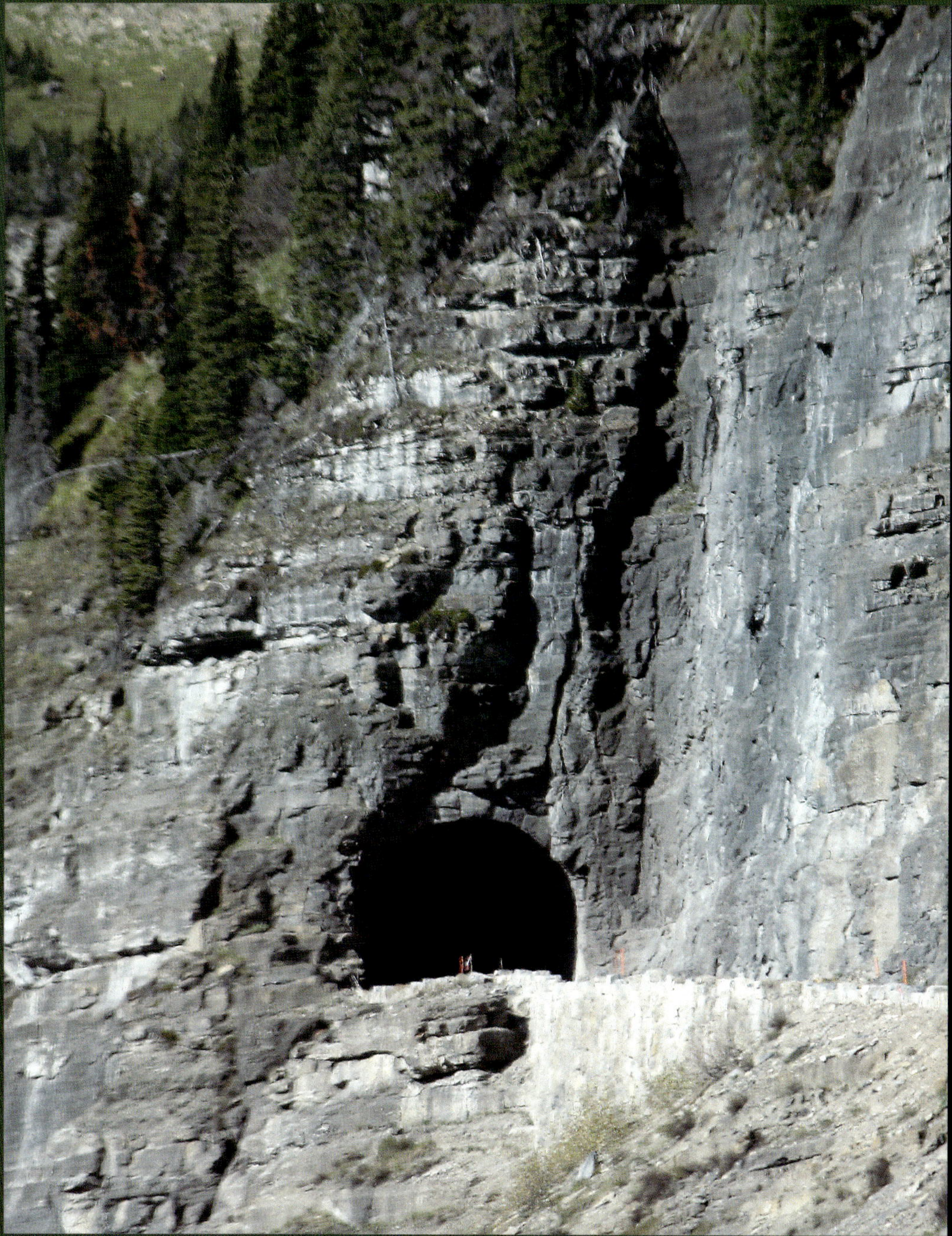

A closer and more recent view of the East Side Tunnel. *Courtesy of Bryan and Nicole Kohrmann.*

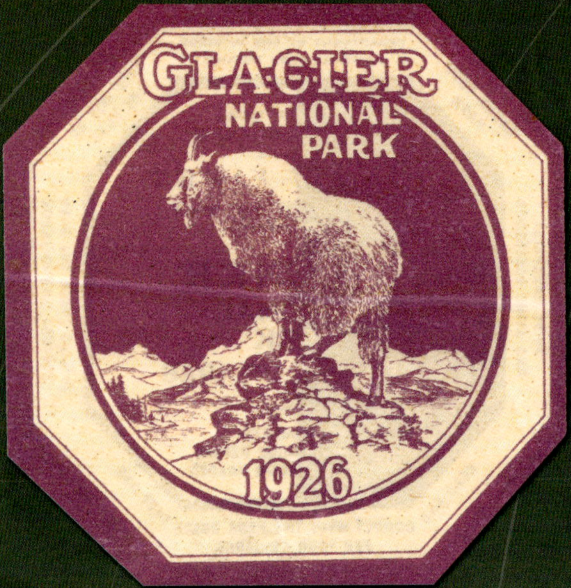

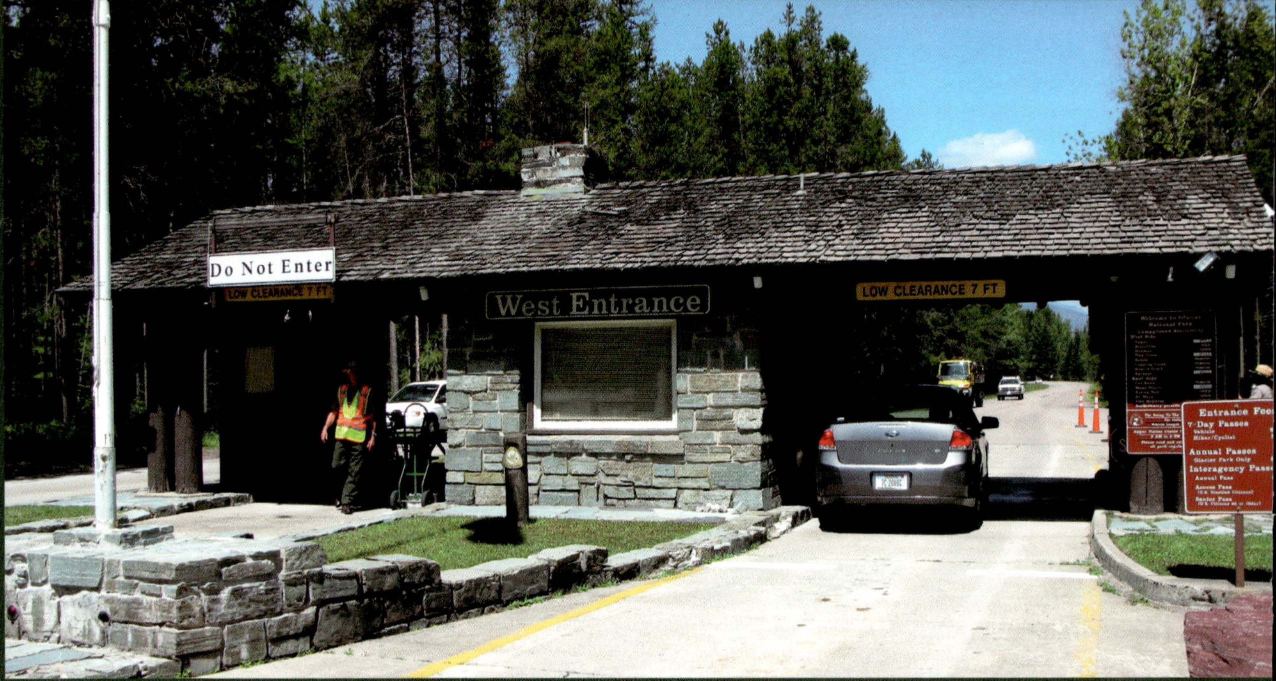

Improvements to the roads in and around Glacier National Park allowed easier access for tourists who came in their own vehicles. This purple decal was issued in 1926 as a souvenir and was to be placed on the windshield. The National Park Service issued a series of such stickers for its most popular parks, each depicting an animal symbolic of that location. In this case, the mountain goat was selected as the featured animal for Glacier. The Glacier Park entry pass was issued on July 10, 1934, at the Belton entrance for a $1.00 fee. The earlier Belton entrance is now called the West Glacier entrance.

The West Glacier entrance marks the beginning of the Going-to-the-Sun Road with access to hiking trails, picnic areas, campgrounds, boating, and other activities at Sprague Creek, Lake McDonald, and Avalanche Creek before reaching the top of Logan Pass.

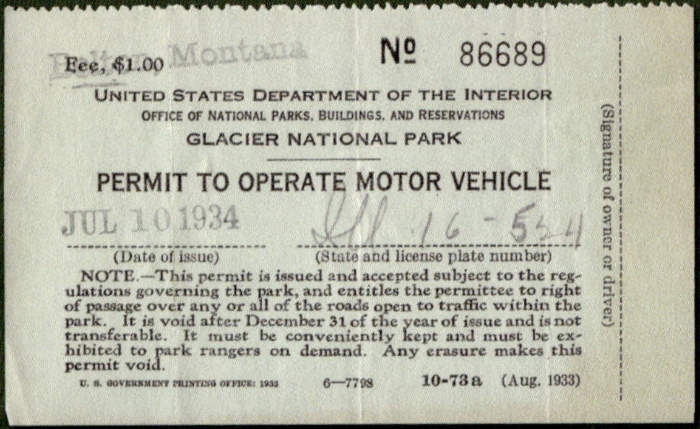

Fee, $1.00 Belton, Montana № 86689

UNITED STATES DEPARTMENT OF THE INTERIOR
OFFICE OF NATIONAL PARKS, BUILDINGS, AND RESERVATIONS
GLACIER NATIONAL PARK

PERMIT TO OPERATE MOTOR VEHICLE

JUL 10 1934 — (Date of issue)

16-534 — (State and license plate number)

NOTE.—This permit is issued and accepted subject to the regulations governing the park, and entitles the permittee to right of passage over any or all of the roads open to traffic within the park. It is void after December 31 of the year of issue and is not transferable. It must be conveniently kept and must be exhibited to park rangers on demand. Any erasure makes this permit void.

U. S. GOVERNMENT PRINTING OFFICE: 1933 6—7798 10-73a (Aug. 1933)

(Signature of owner or driver)

The Apgar Visitor Center is located near the West Glacier entrance.

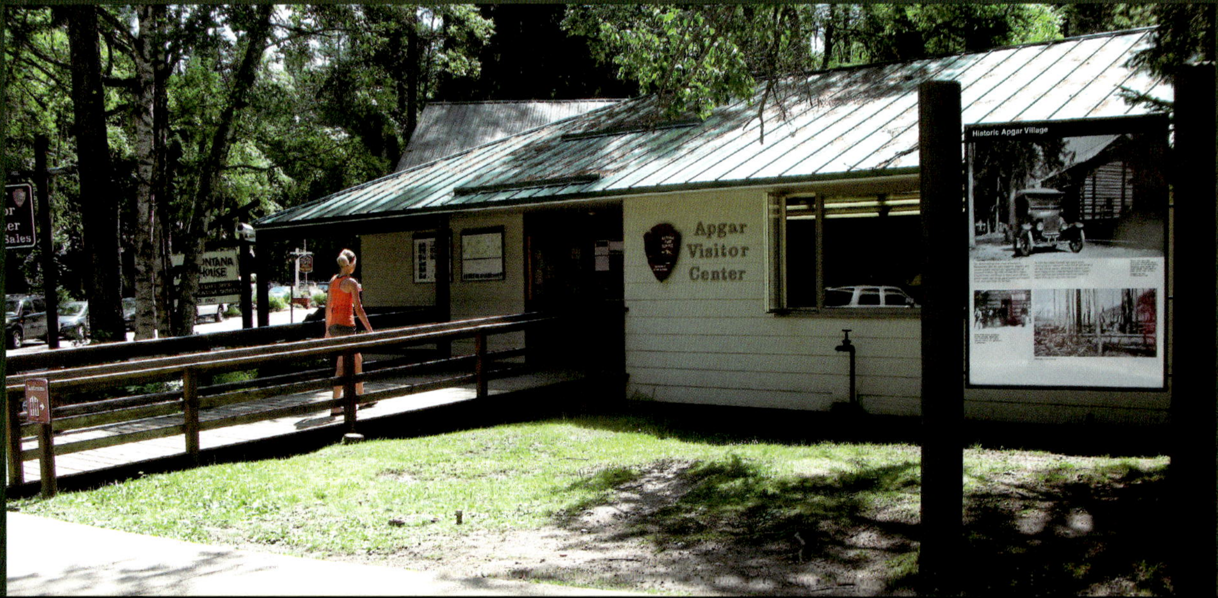

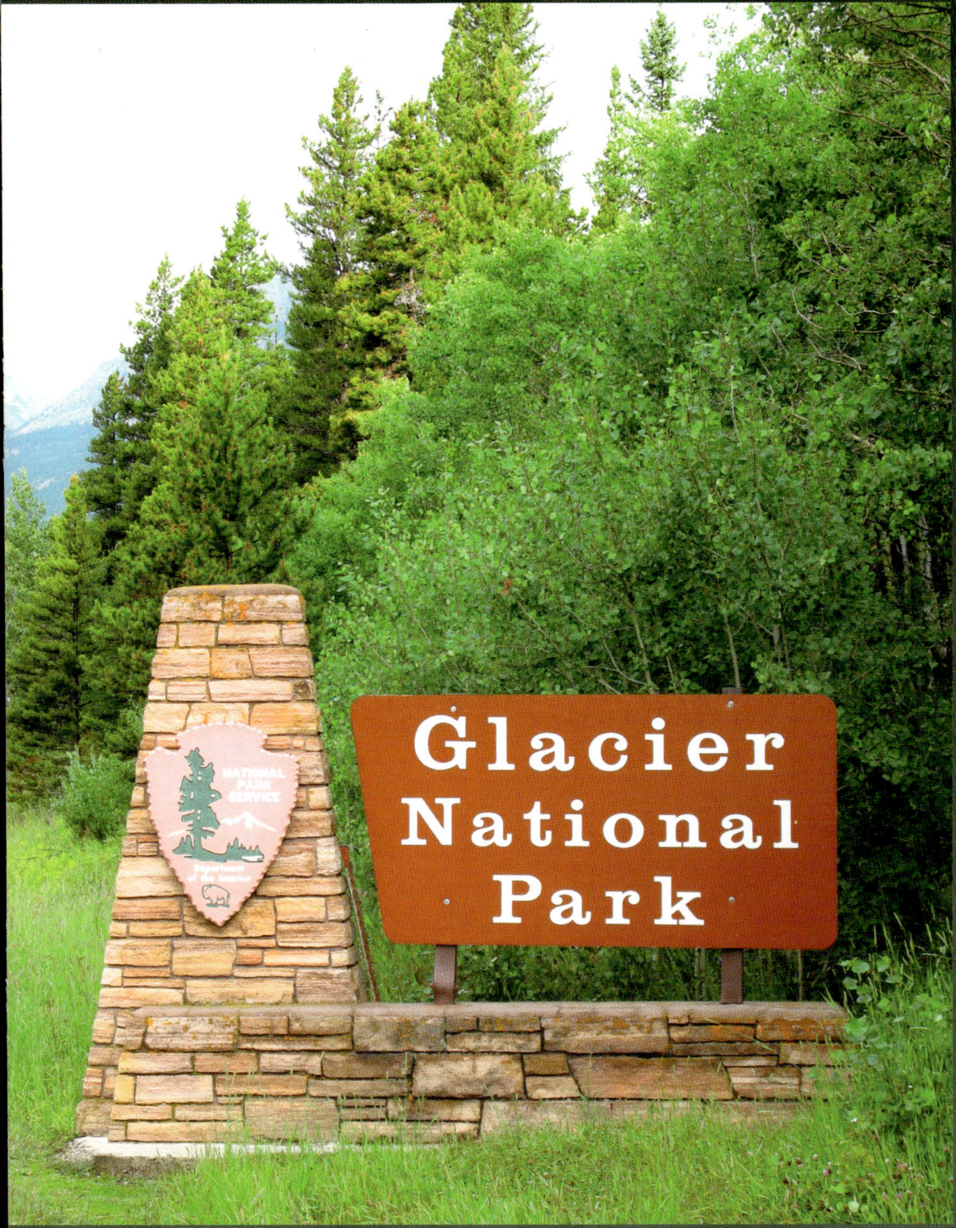

In addition to the West Glacier entrance at Belton, there are four other ways to enter the park. The Many Glacier entrance is for travelers coming from Babb while the St. Mary entrance station serves as the access point from Browning. Another entrance is at Two Medicine in the southeast part of the park near East Glacier Park (pictured here). A less used entry is at Polebridge in the northwest part of the park.

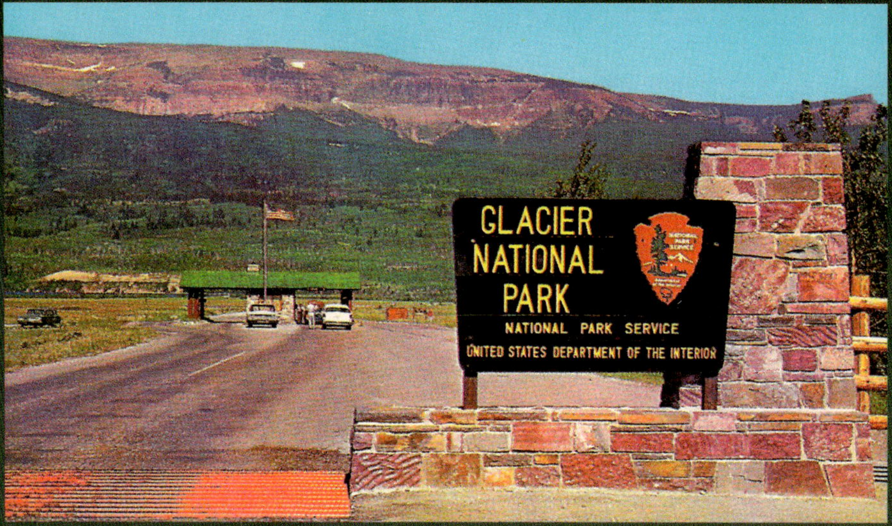

The St. Mary Entrance Station provides access to Going-to-the-Sun Road from the eastern end of the park while following the shoreline of St. Mary Lake. Plastichrome card by Bob Anderson Postcards.

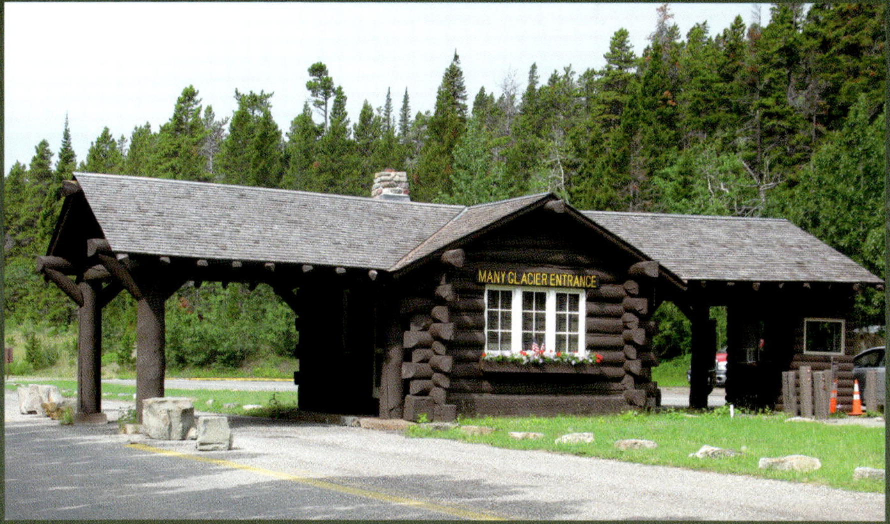

The Many Glacier entrance provides a popular way for tourists to see the sights on the northeast side of the park. Located in this area are Sherburne Lake, Grinnell Glacier, Many Glacier Hotel, and the Swiftcurrent and Josephine lakes.

This map of the Glacier-Waterton International Peace Park is from a circa 1950s Great Northern Railway brochure that shows Going-to-the-Sun Road, dedicated in 1933, and the Chief Mountain Highway to Canada, as well as lodging, lakes, and other tourist information.

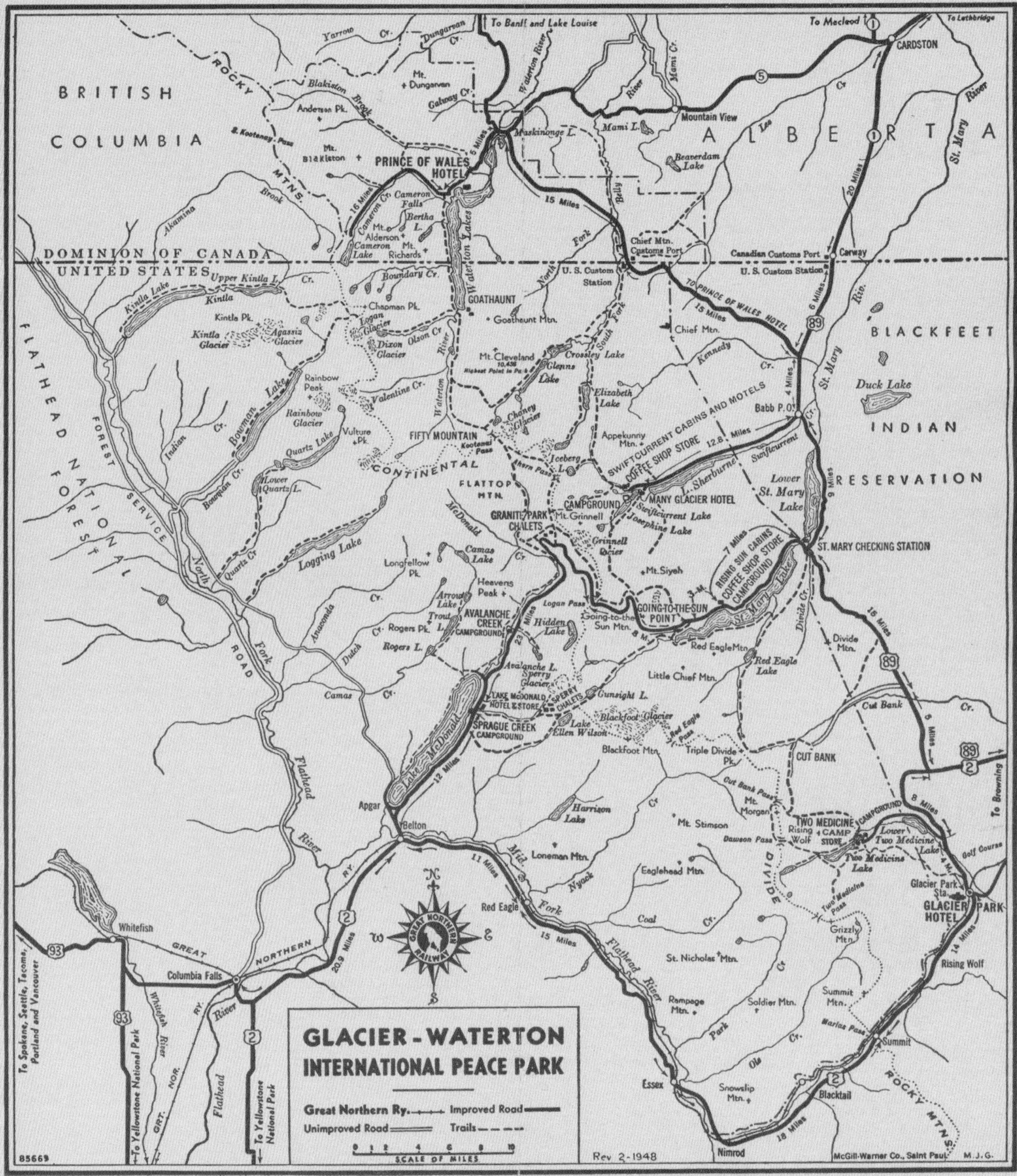

LODGING
WHERE TO STAY

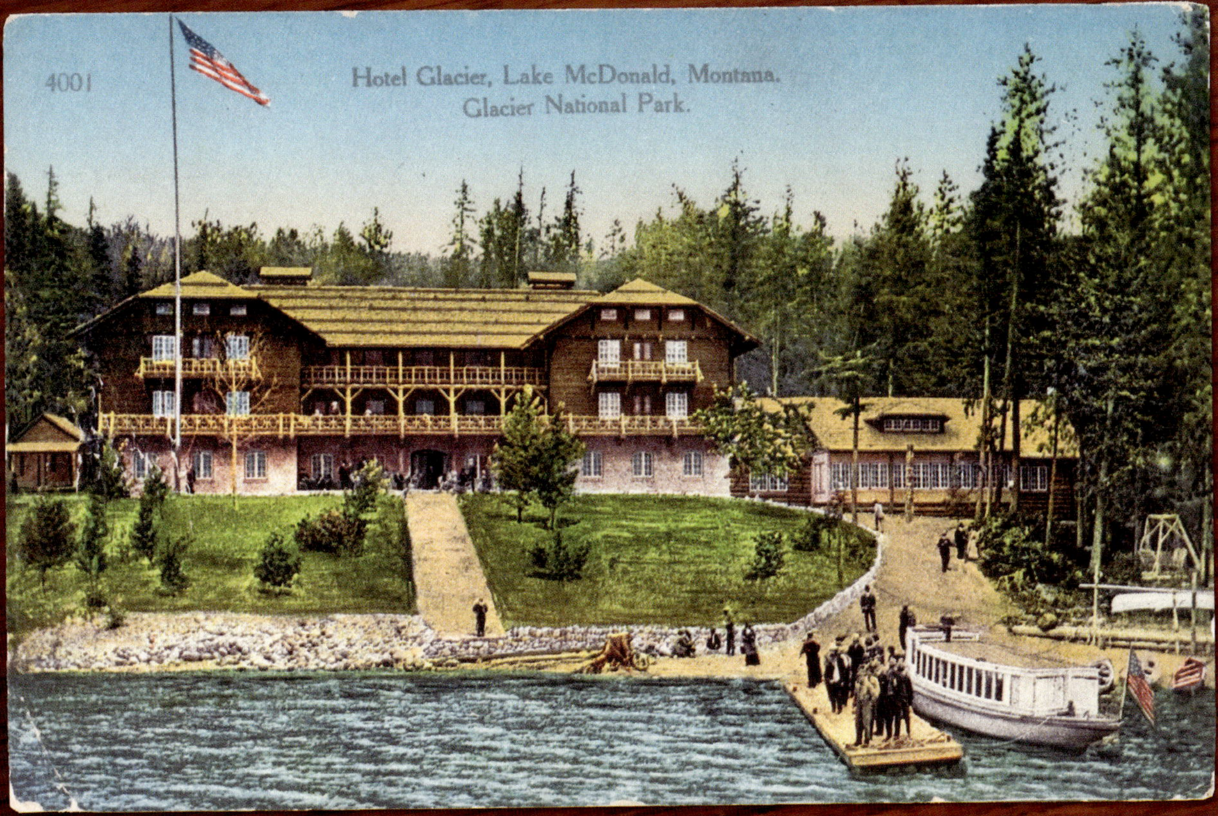

The new Hotel Glacier was built by John Lewis and opened in 1914, replacing an earlier hotel built by George Snyder in 1895. Publisher of postcard unknown.

Before the Belton Chalet was opened by the railroad in 1910, other more primitive establishments had already been built. They included a hotel Ed Dow opened at Belton, some cabins built by Milo Apgar, and George Snyder's Hotel, which was built at the head of Lake McDonald and opened in 1895. Snyder operated the hotel until it was sold to John Lewis in 1906. The hotel was then called the Glacier Hotel. After the railroad opened the Belton Chalet, the company proceeded to build a network of hotels, chalets, and tent camps to serve the park. The enterprises were overseen by Louis Hill, son of the railroad's founder James Hill.

GLACIER PARK LODGE

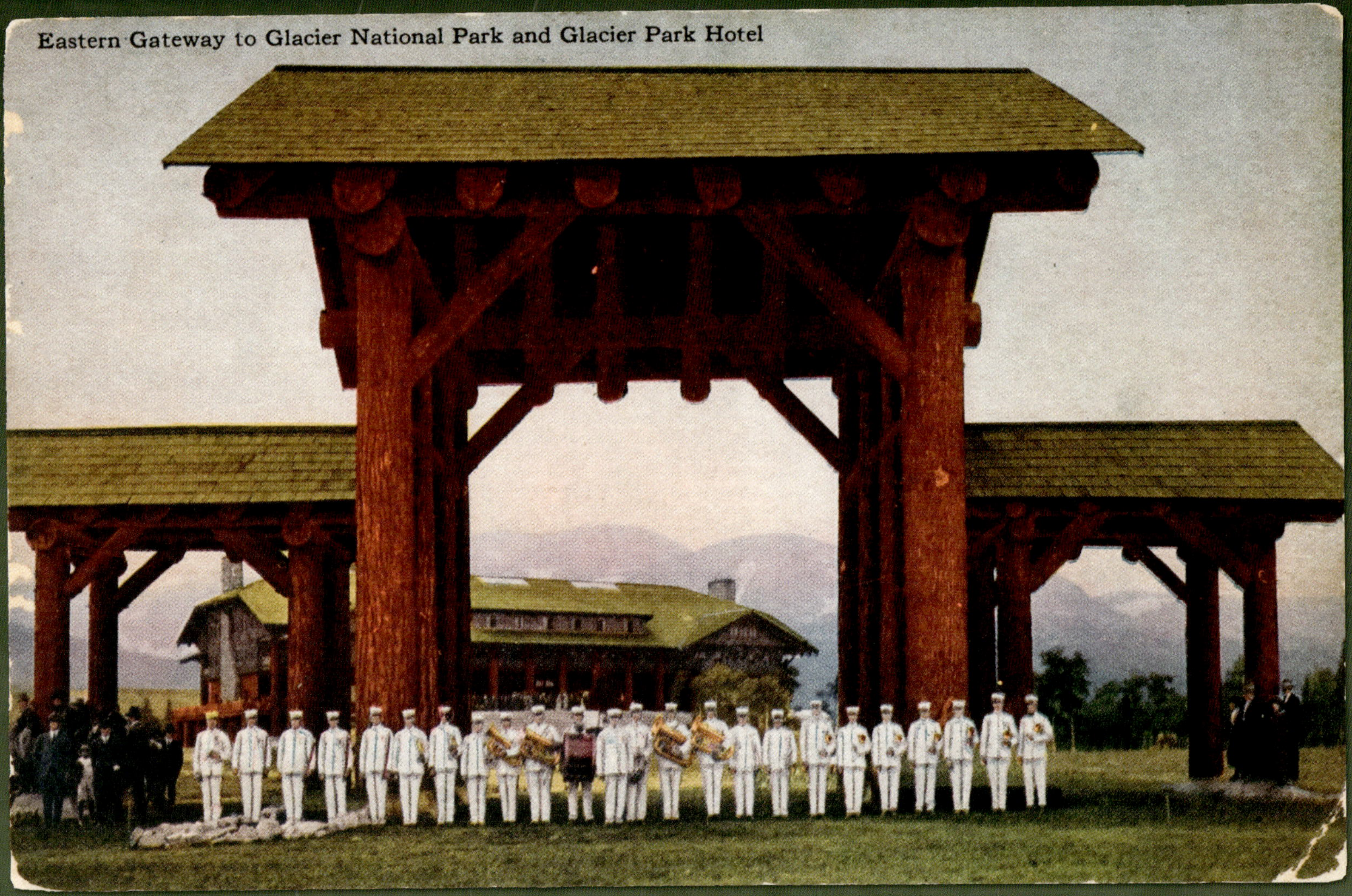

An early view of the "Eastern Gateway to Glacier National Park" and the new Glacier Park Hotel. In 1912, Louis W. Hill, then president of the Great Northern Railway, purchased 160 acres just outside the park from the Blackfeet to build the hotel and nearby train station. The facilities were to be used as a stopover for rail passengers heading into the park. The arch was built in 1913. It was removed in the 1920s after it was damaged in a wind storm. "See America First" Great Northern Railway postcard.

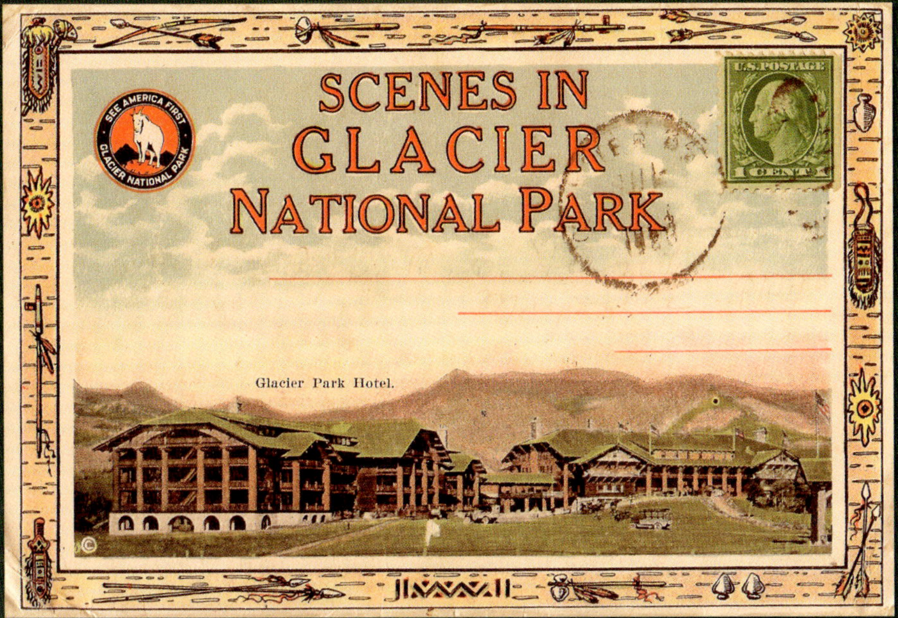

The entry arch can still be seen on the far right of this souvenir folder postmarked 1928. The "See American First" emblem used by the Great Northern Railway to promote the park decorates the outside of the folder, which pictures the expanded Glacier Park Hotel.

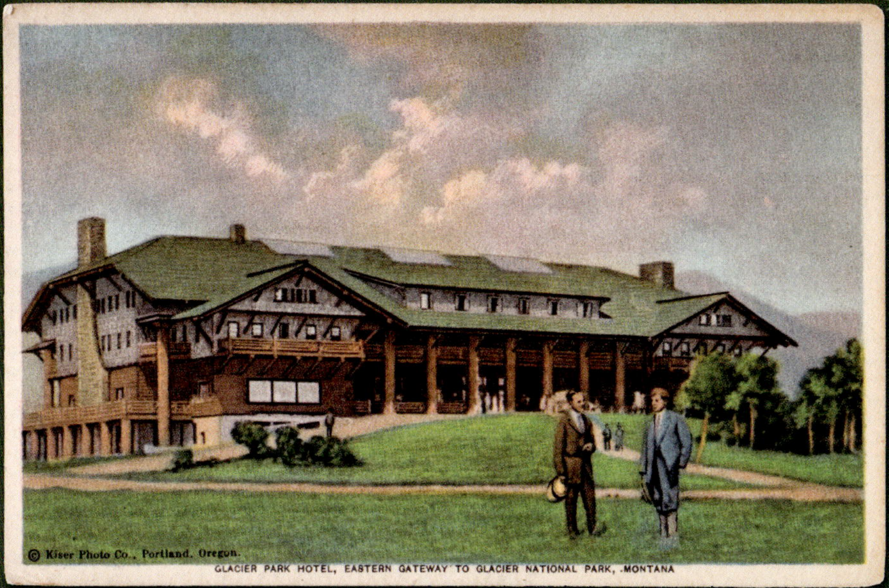

The Glacier Park Hotel opened in 1913 with sixty-one guest rooms following fifteen months of construction. Amenities included beauty and barber shops, a plunge pool in the basement, steam heat, and many private baths. The architect for the Swiss-like chalet was Samuel L. Bartlett of St. Paul, Minnesota, whose design replicated elements of the Forestry Building from the 1905 Lewis and Clark Centennial Exposition in Portland, Oregon, with its use of massive pillars made of unpeeled logs. Postcard by Kiser Photo Co.

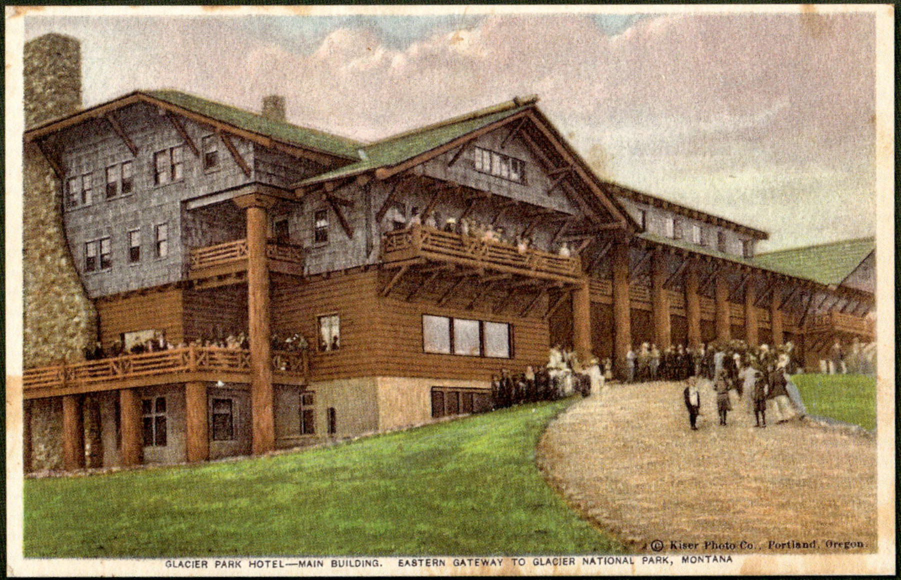

Another view of the hotel on this early Great Northern Railway card, photographed by Kiser, includes the slogan: "Visit Glacier National Park. Where Glaciers of the long ago – lay gleaming 'neath eternal snow."

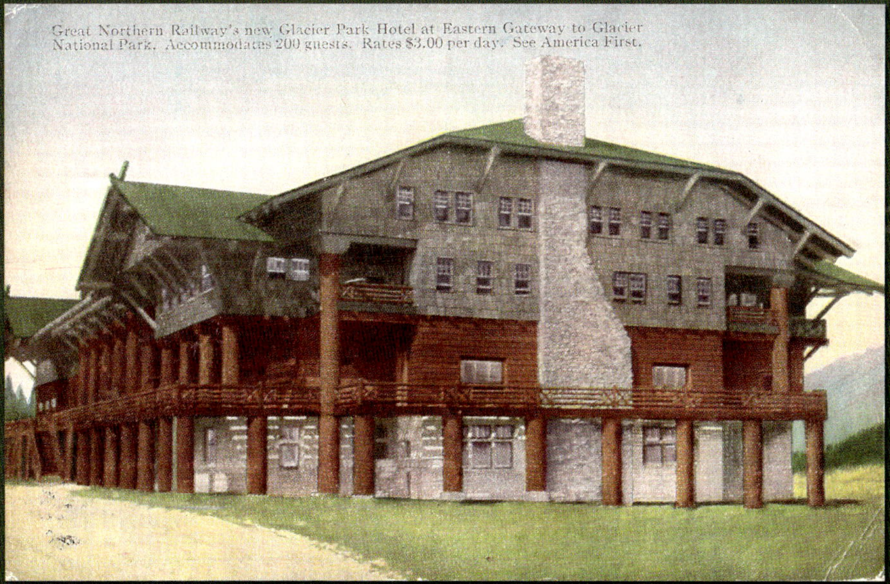

A similar early Great Northern Railway card offers a different view of the Glacier Park Hotel and yet another clever promotional message on the back, "Tour Glacier National Park. Grandeur dwells on every side, see it on a horseback ride." The card was mailed August 21, 1913, during the hotel's inaugural year. At the time, the hotel could accommodate two hundred guests and rates were $3.00 per day.

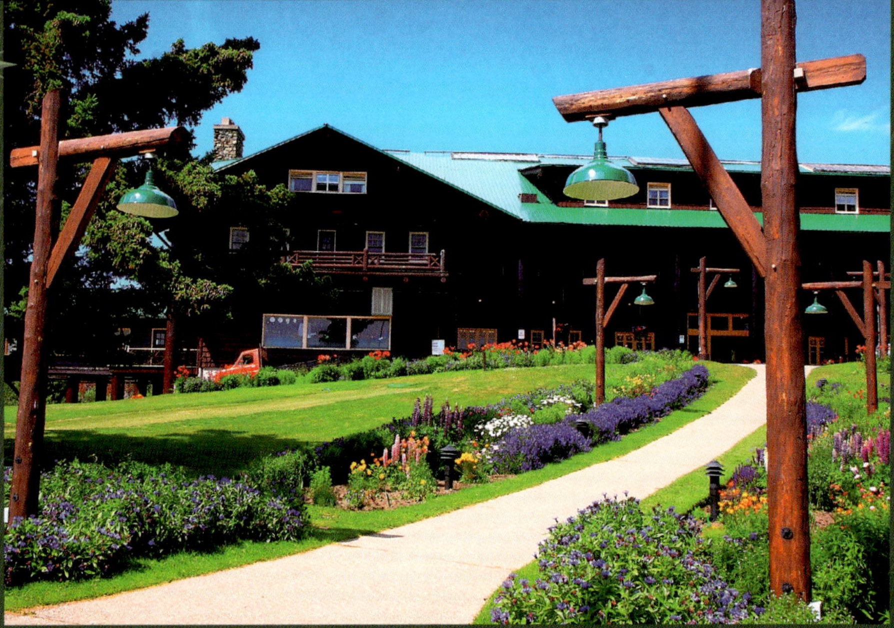

Now known as the Glacier Park Lodge, the property features 161 guest rooms that can accommodate over five hundred guests. Amenities include the Great Northern Dining Room, Empire Bar, Empire Café, gift shop, and day spa, as well as numerous outdoor activities. *Courtesy of I-Ting Chiang*.

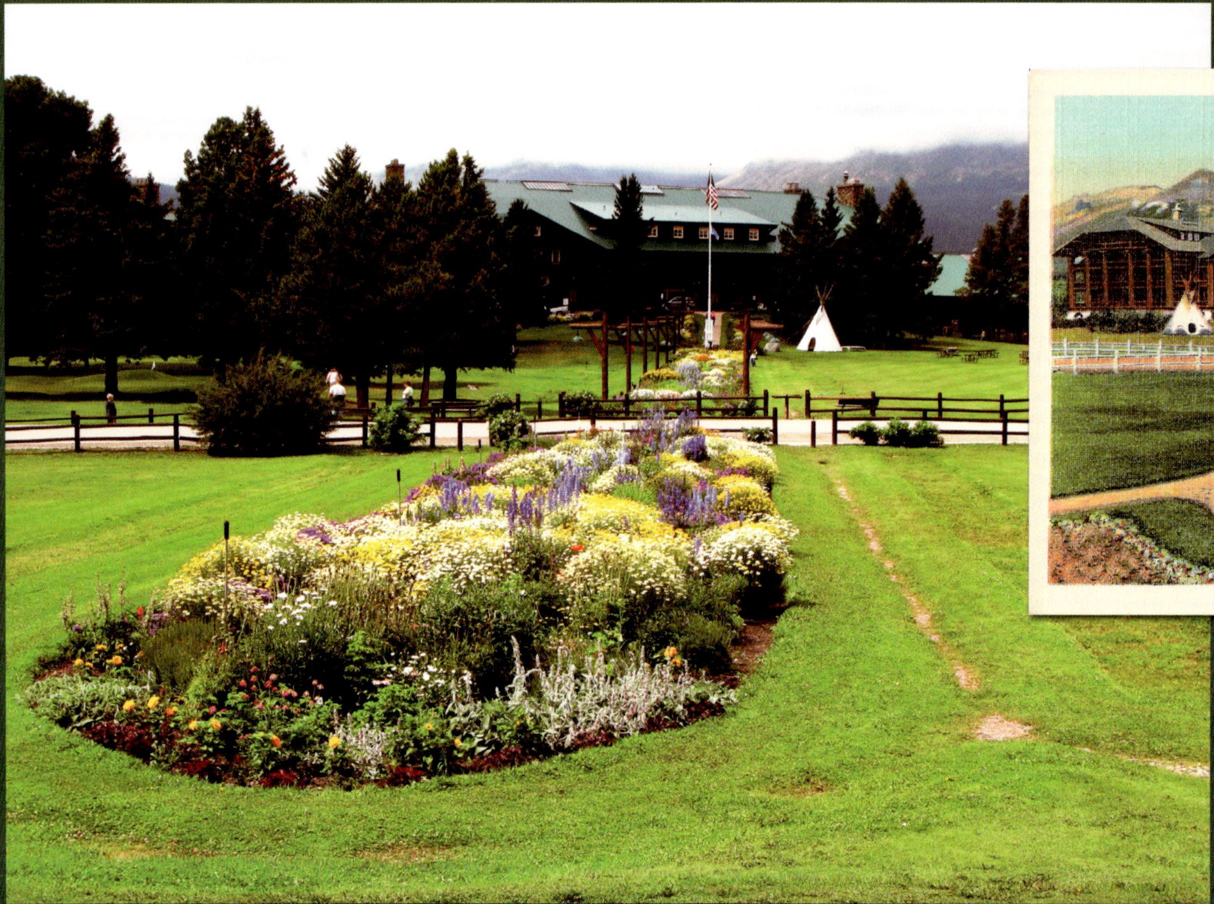

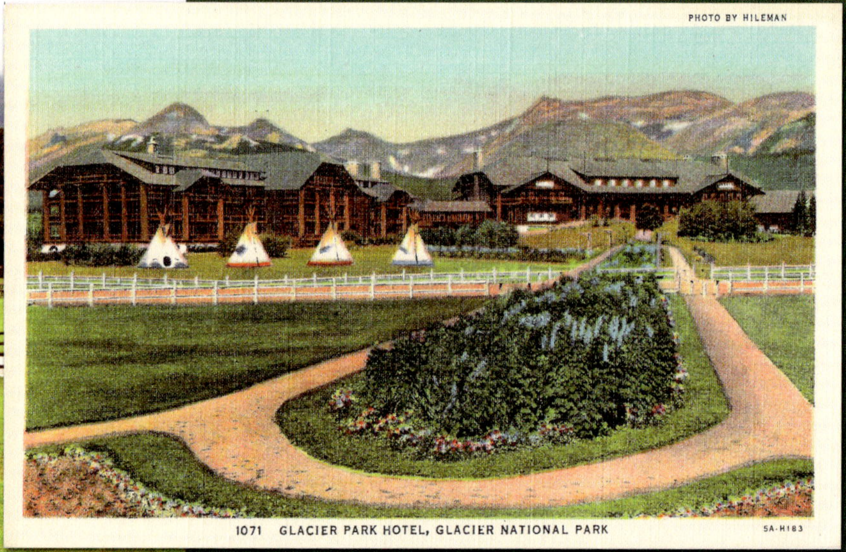

The hotel grounds featured beautiful flower beds and other intricate landscaping to create an impressive sense of arrival. A garden path was used to connect the hotel to the train station. Teepees on the lawn have always provided a special touch. Today, the property has an updated look, though the flowers on the front lawn still retain the beauty planned by Louis Hill shortly after the hotel was built. Postcard is a late 1930s linen by C. T. Art-Colortone with Hileman photo.

Soon after the hotel's opening, Hill recognized the need for expansion to accommodate the hotel's unanticipated popularity. In 1914, he arranged for construction of a four-story annex on the south side of the property. Viewcard by Hileman.

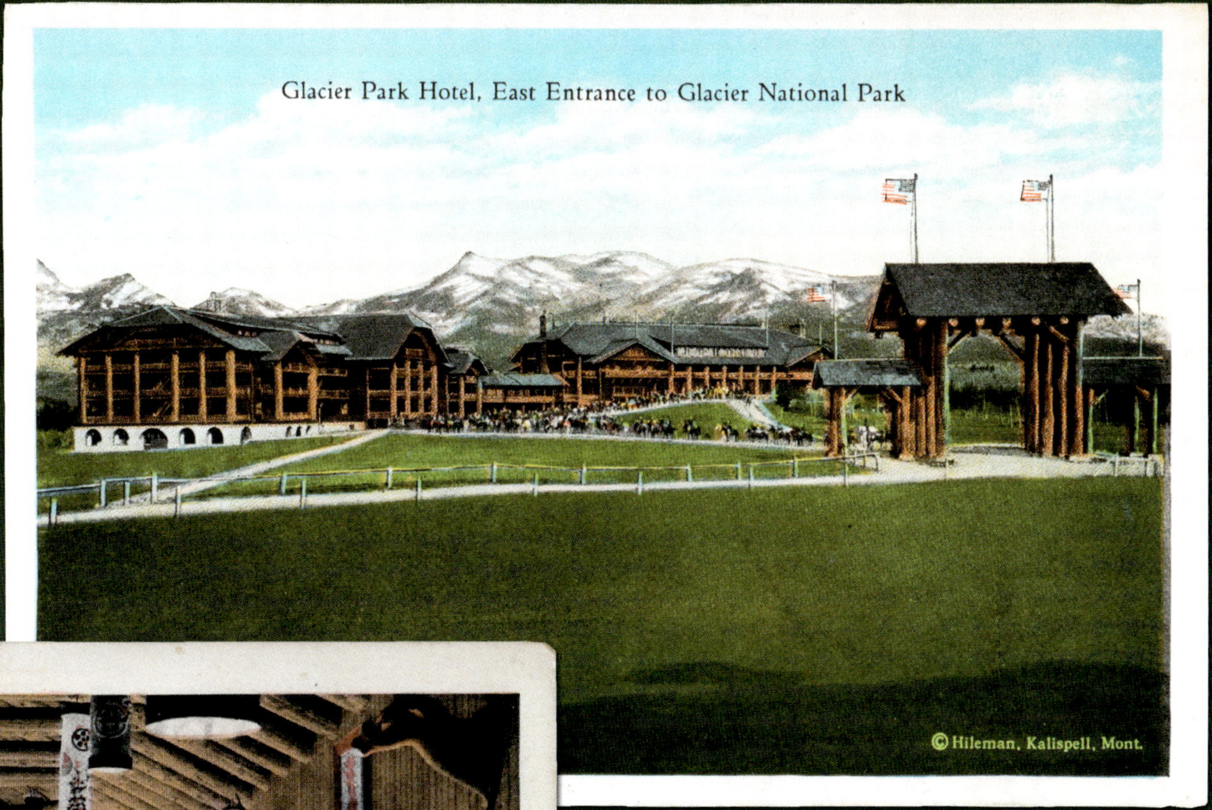

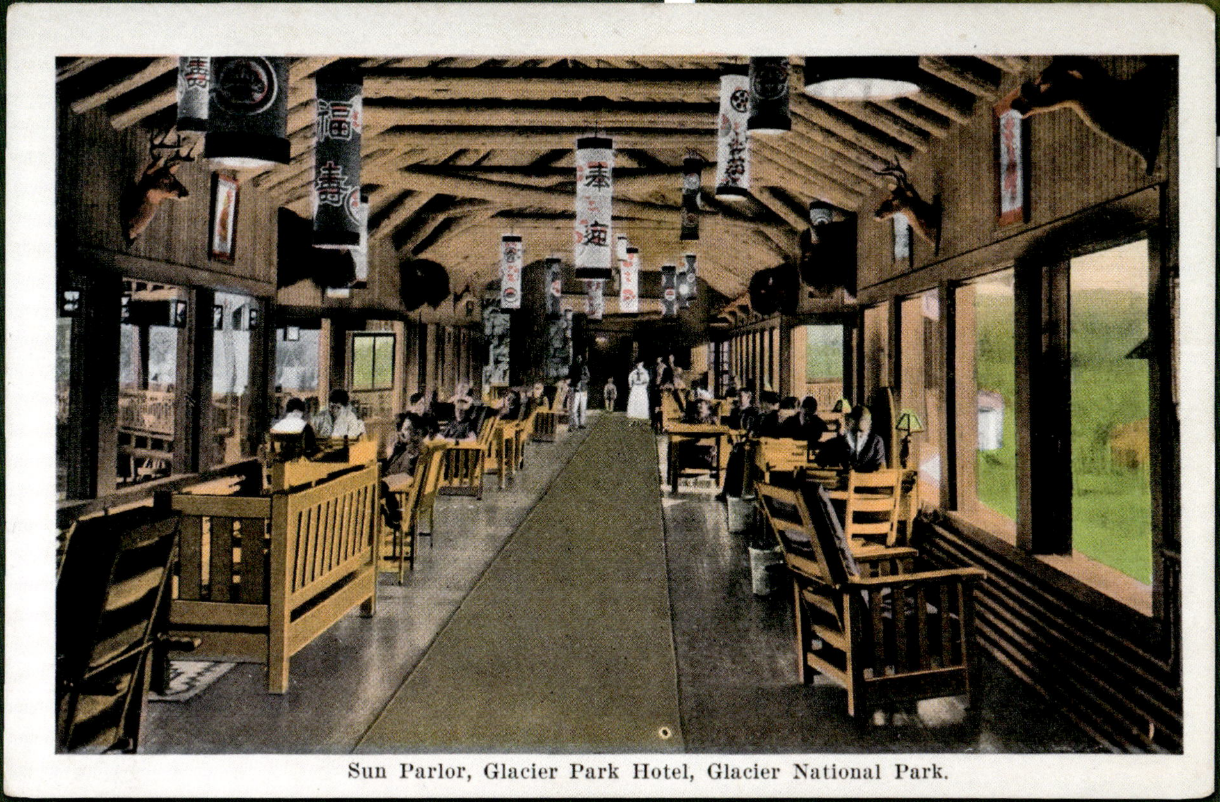

When the annex was built, a connecting breezeway was used as a sun parlor, as shown in this early postcard by E. C. Kropp Co. The area continues to be enjoyed by visitors today.

The annex added 111 guest rooms to the property. This view was photographed from a guest room balcony in the adjoining main lodge. The hotel underwent major changes from 1957 to 1959 when bathrooms were added to each room and the decor was updated. The Great Northern sold the hotel in 1960. It is currently owned and operated by Glacier Park, Inc., a subsidiary of Viad Corp.

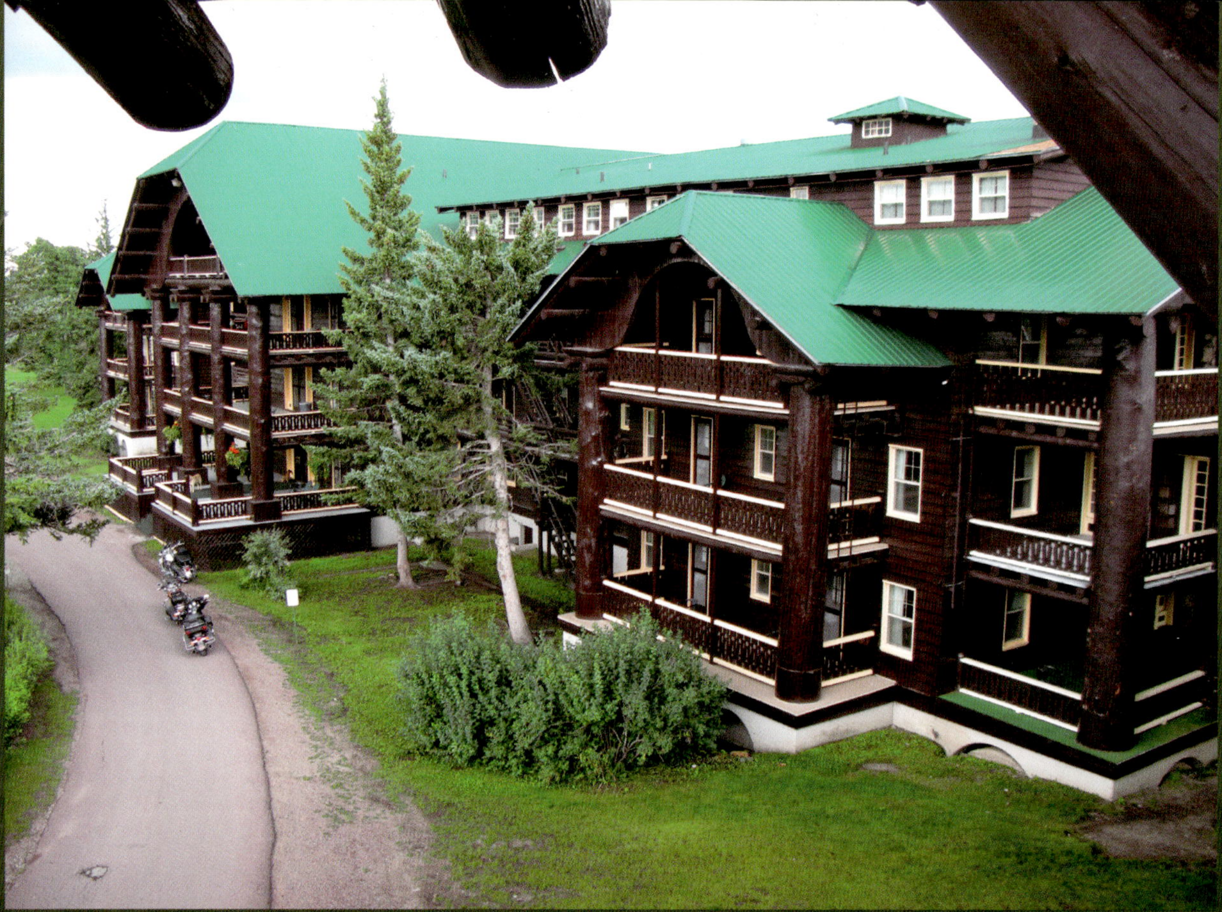

Another recent view of the annex shows the massive timbers used in its construction.

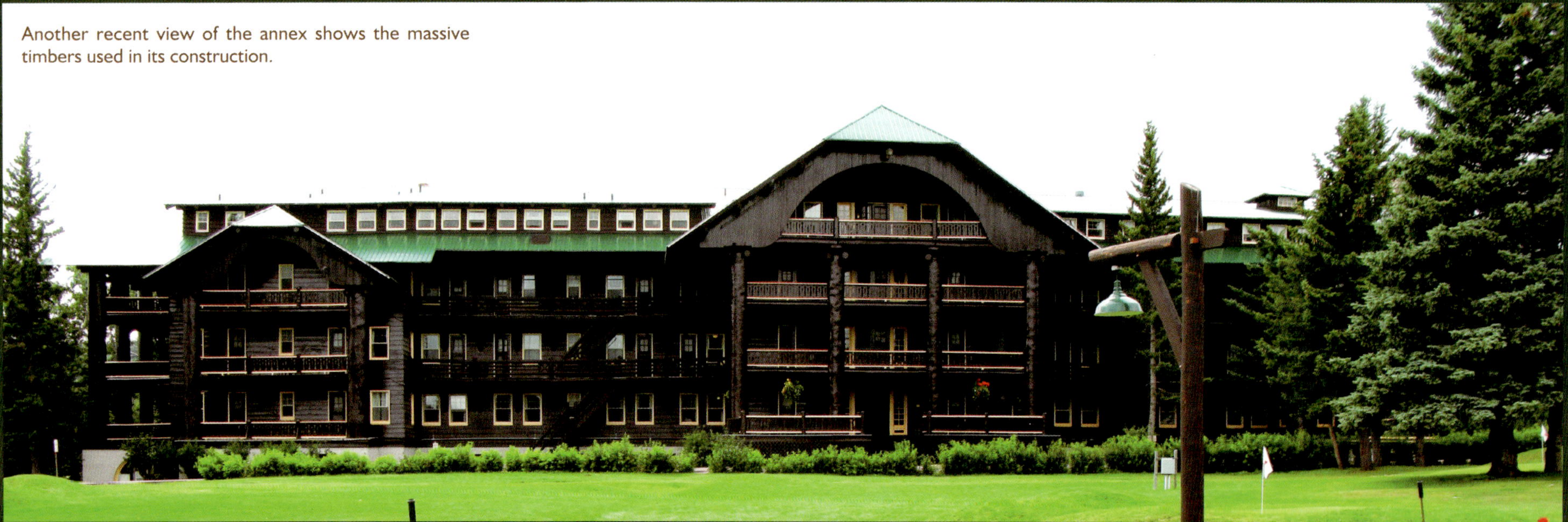

By the late 1930s, when this linen postcard was made, Hill's Japanese lanterns had been replaced by Arts and Crafts-style lighting, which is still in place. C. T. Art Colortone postcard.

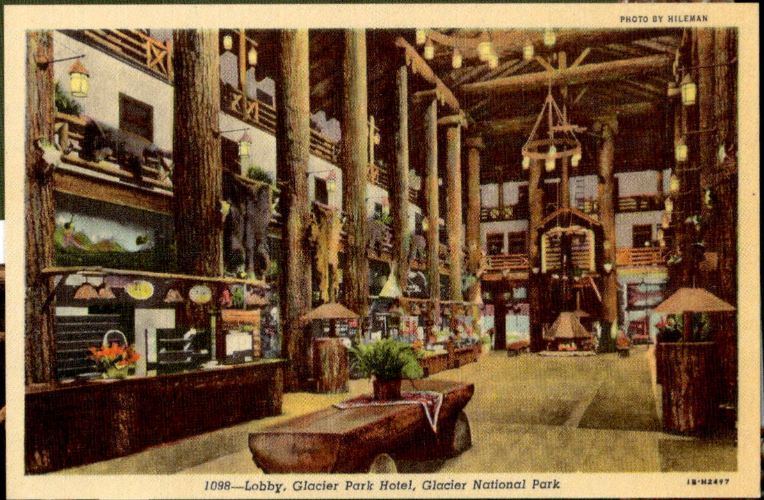

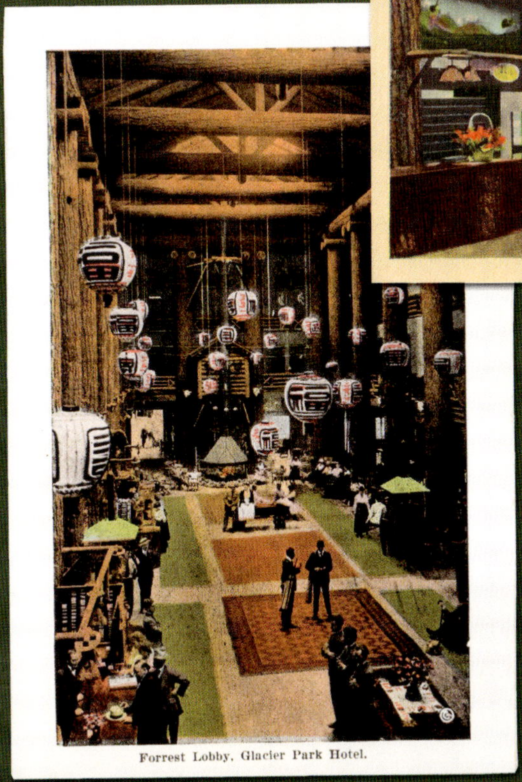

The Glacier Park Hotel lobby as it looked originally. The cathedral-like space uses large Douglas firs shipped from the Pacific Northwest as supports to provide the forest look. Surprisingly, the lobby was also decorated with Japanese lanterns, a touch added by Louis Hill to remind visitors of the Oriental Limited train then offered by the railroad. The lobby featured a copper-hooded open fireplace on one end and a large stone fireplace at the other. It spans 200 feet long by 100 feet wide. From an early railroad folder called "Scenes in Glacier National Park."

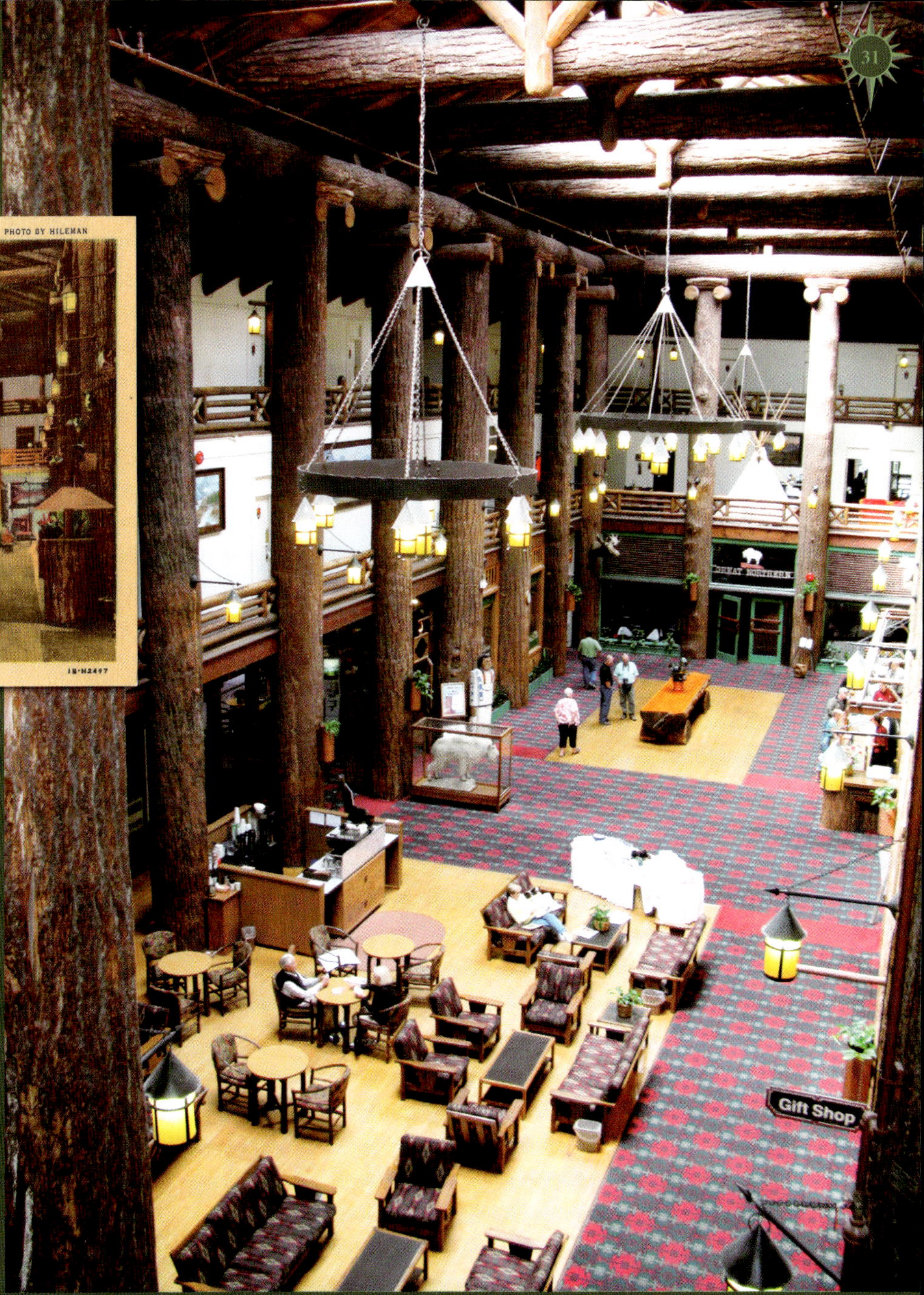

The lobby has continued to be updated through the years. The open fireplace has been removed at the far end. The half log table pictured near the restaurant entry is the only original furnishing still used in the lobby today.

The dining room of the Glacier Park Hotel was furnished with Windsor type chairs. The same type chairs are still used today. The lunch menu is dated June 18, 1957, and is pictured alongside a view of Josephine Lake and Mt. Gould.

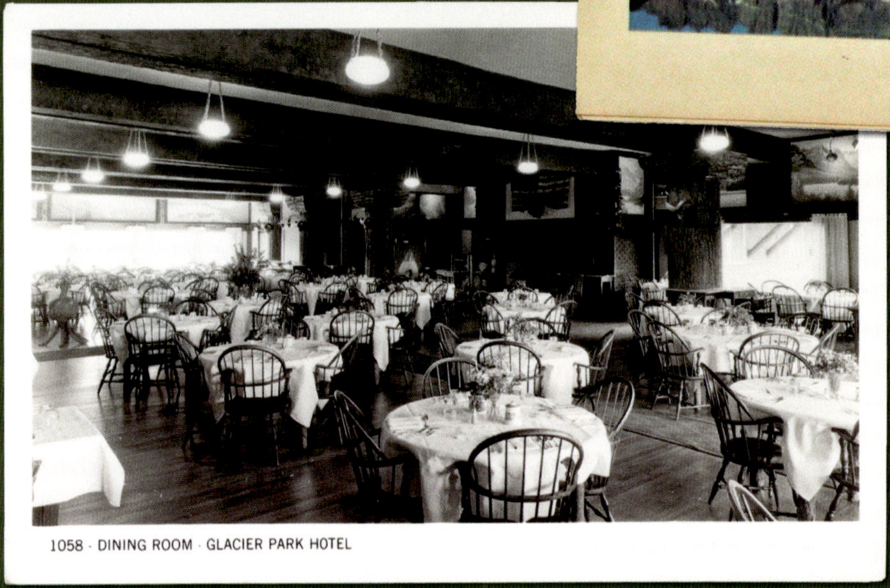

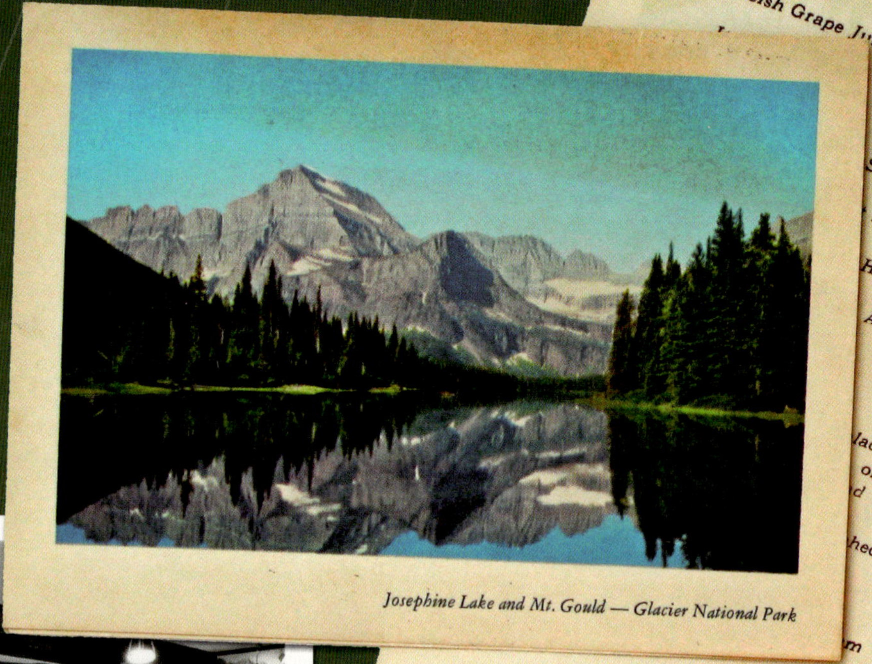

GLACIER PARK LODGE
GLACIER NATIONAL PARK
MONTANA

WEDNESDAY, JUNE 19, 1957

LUNCHEON

Welsh Grape Juice

Apple Juice

Relish Tray

Spears Hollandaise Canadian Bacon

Ribs of Beef Braised Vegetables

Ham Hocks Fresh Cabbage

Avocado Tomato Wedges Boiled Egg

Buttered Green Beans

lad Mayonnaise

or

d French Dressing

heon Rolls

m Strawberry Ice Cream

Gold Cake

Beverages Pineapple Sherbet

Cocktails Will be Served at Your Table if You Wish

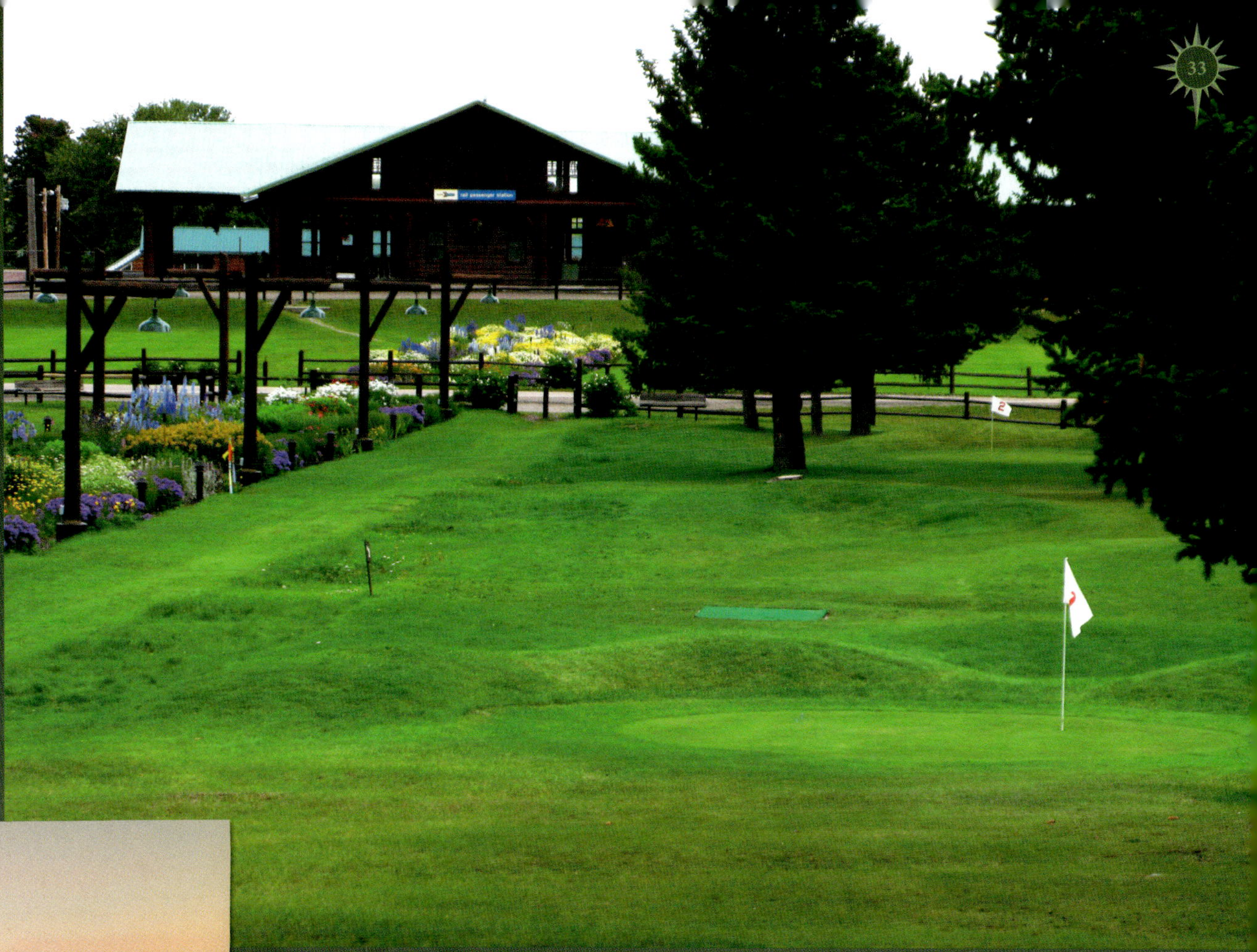

Guests can still play golf on the original golf course or on a pitch and putt course on the front grounds. The train station can be seen in the background.

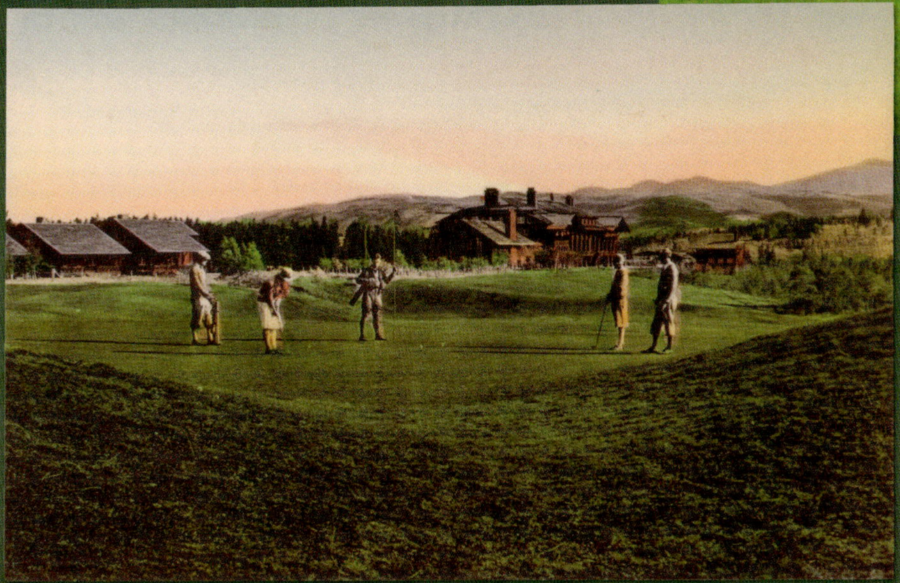

From the beginning, the hotel has offered more amenities than any of the other Great Northern properties, including swimming, horseback riding, and golfing. The nine-hole golf course, pictured on this hand-colored postcard by Albertype Co., was added in 1927 and is still in use. Each hole was named for a chief of the Blackfeet Nation. The course was built on land that had originally been part of the Blackfeet Indian Reservation.

LAKE MCDONALD LODGE

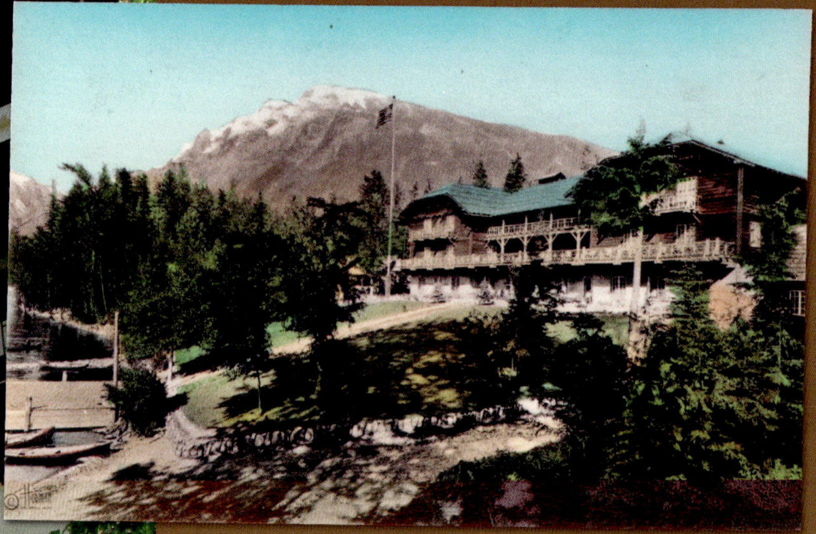

Built by John Lewis and opened in 1914, Lake McDonald Lodge was originally known as the Lewis Glacier Hotel as well as Hotel Glacier. In the early years the only way guests could reach the 65-room hunting lodge was by crossing the lake by boat until a primitive road was opened in 1921. The Great Northern Railway bought the hotel in 1930. In 1932, the hotel was purchased by the National Park Service with a provision that allowed the railroad to retain a twenty-year lease on the property. It was renamed Lake McDonald Hotel and later Lake McDonald Lodge. This hand-colored postcard was made by the Albertype Co. circa 1930s.

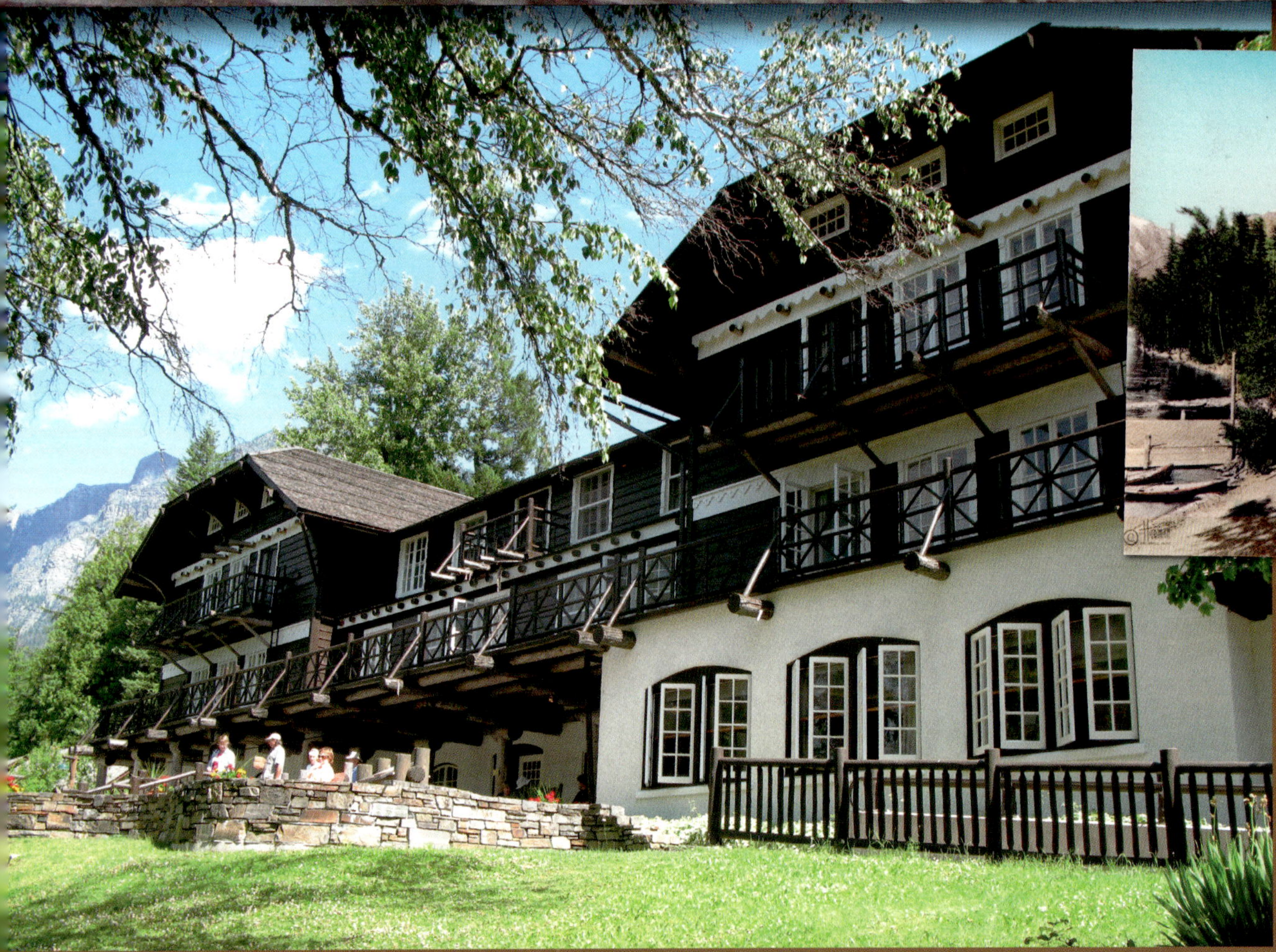

Lake McDonald Lodge was renovated in the late 1980s, preserving architect Kirtland Cutter's Swiss chalet motif and interior Arts and Crafts touches. The work included significant restoration and infrastructure upgrades. The lodge was named a National Historic Landmark in 1987. In addition to the main lodge (pictured), the grounds include rental cabins and a motor inn that combine to offer one hundred guest rooms managed by Glacier Park, Inc.

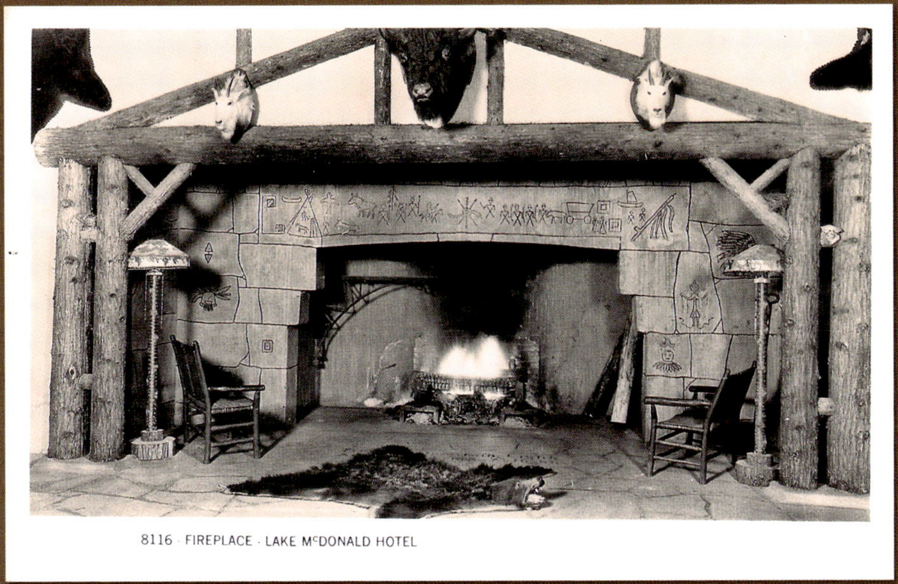

The original fireplace was decorated with Native American designs. Postcard by Hileman.

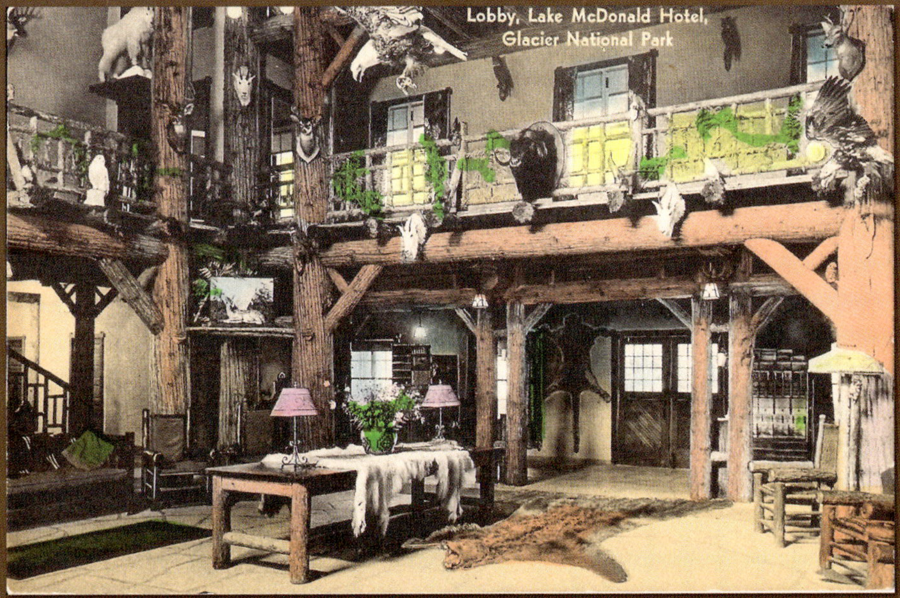

Balconies decorate the sides of the lobby as well as the outside walls of the lodge. Hand-colored by the Meriden Gravure Co., this postcard was published by the Glacier Park Hotel Co.

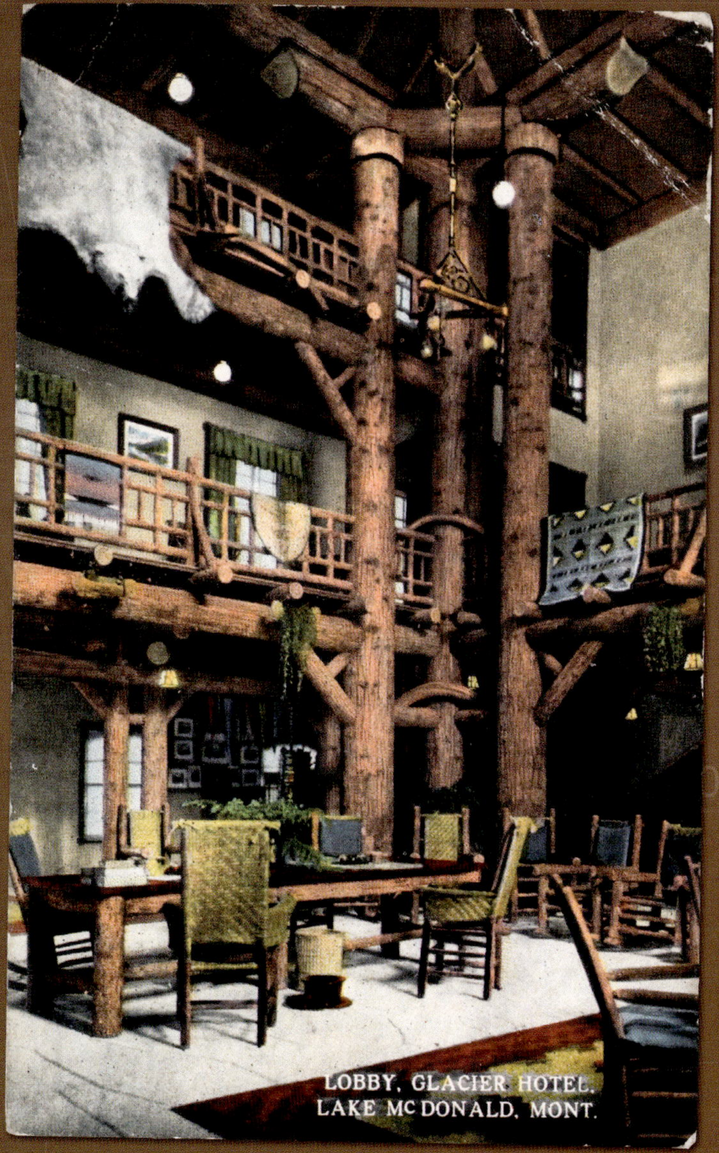

The three-story lobby features supports made of native cedar trees with the bark still intact. It was decorated with taxidermy mounts and animal hides from area wildlife. Early postcard by Bloom Bros. Co.

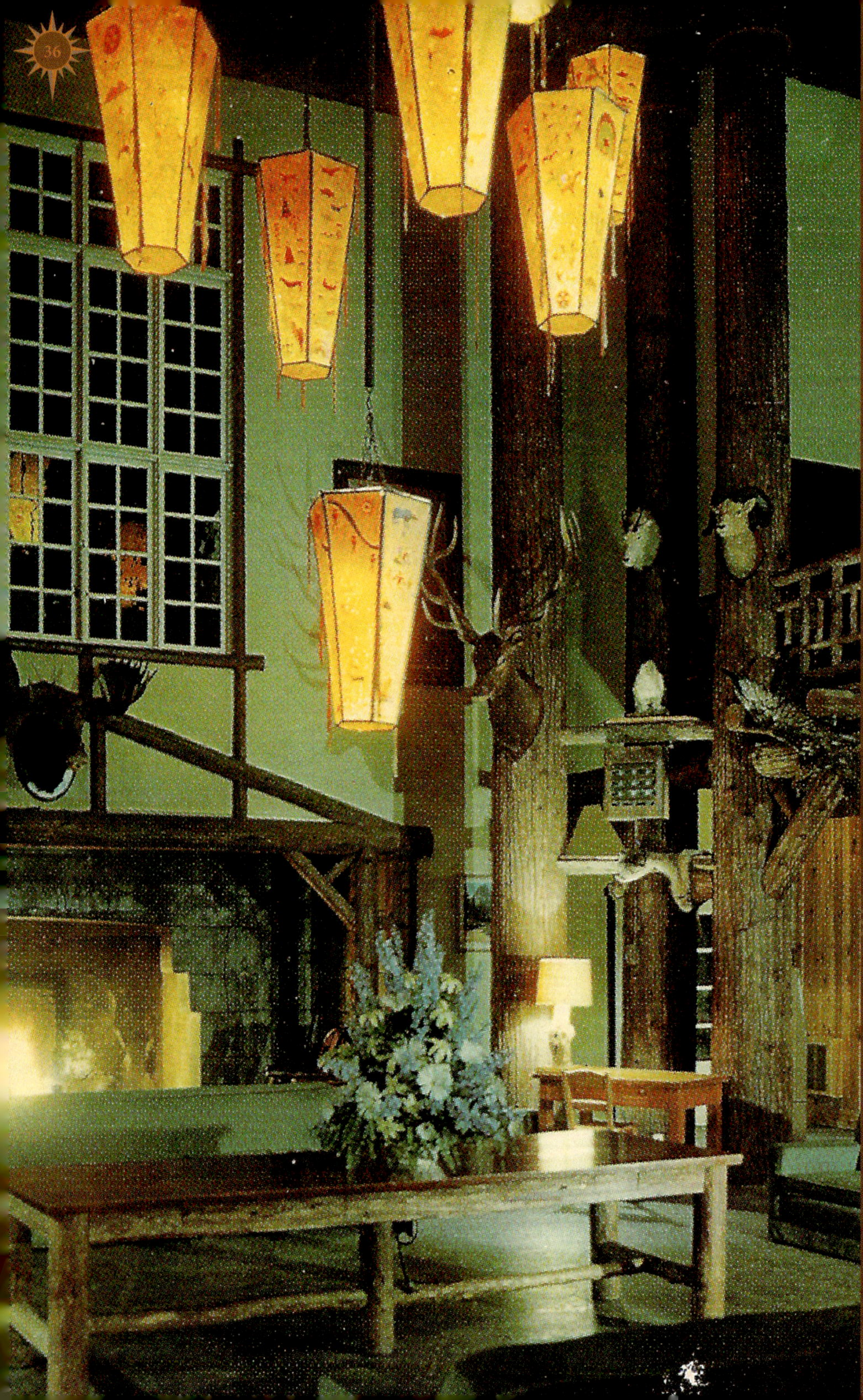

The light fixtures in the lobby were relocated to the lodge from the Prince of Wales Hotel in Waterton Lakes National Park in the 1960s. The shades were originally painted by the Blood natives. This postcard, published by Glacier Park Inc., features the newly installed light shades, the fireplace, and an original slab table as well as several trophy mounts that were original to the hotel.

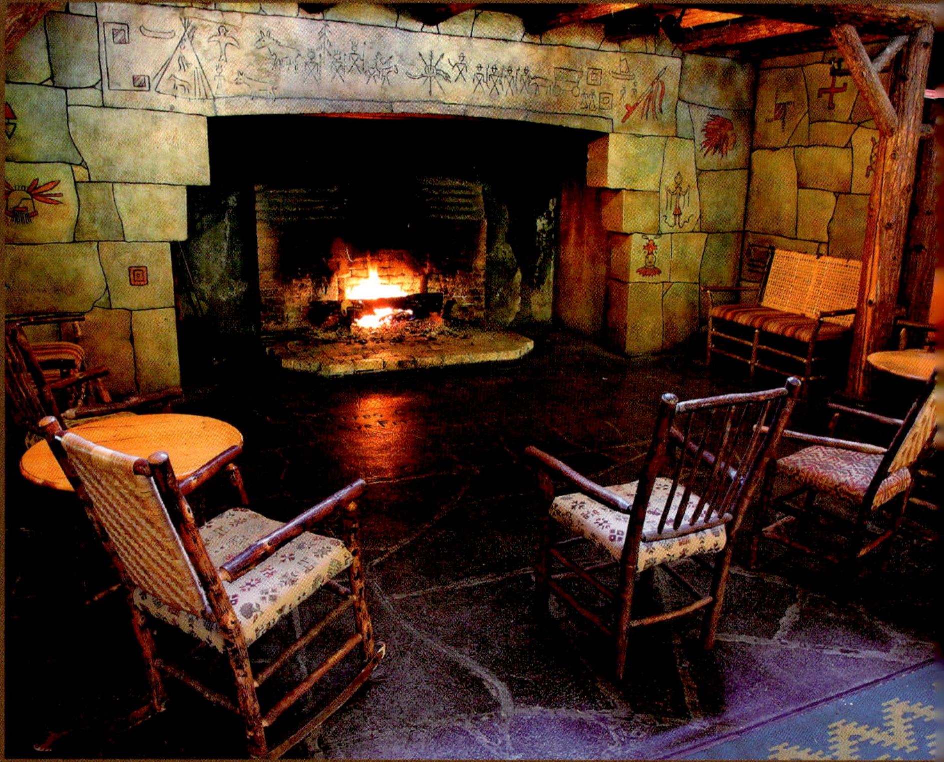

As the evening temperatures drop, guests are drawn to the lobby to enjoy the warmth of a comforting fire. The fireplace was restored during the building's renovation. *Courtesy of I-Ting Chiang*.

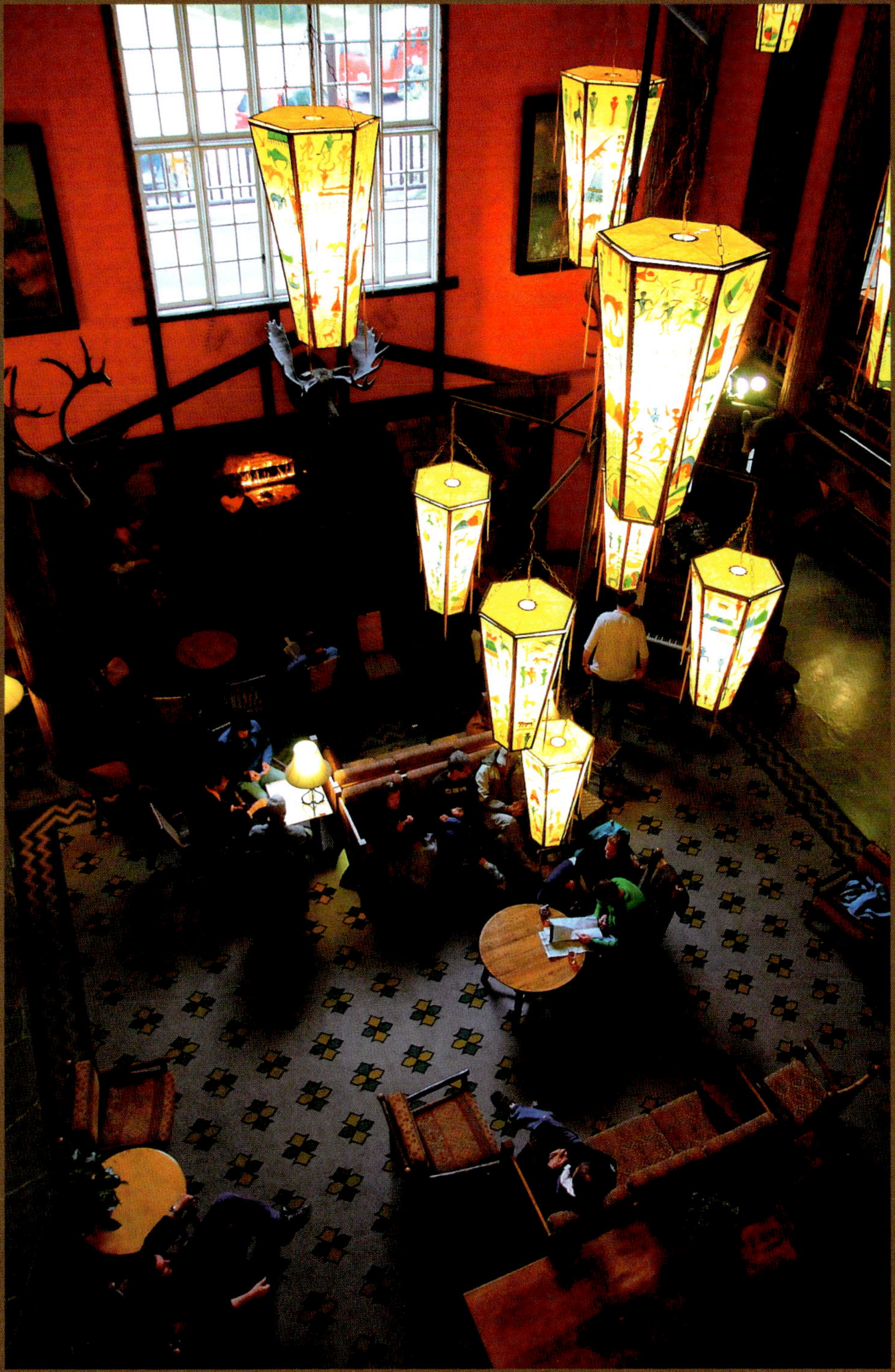

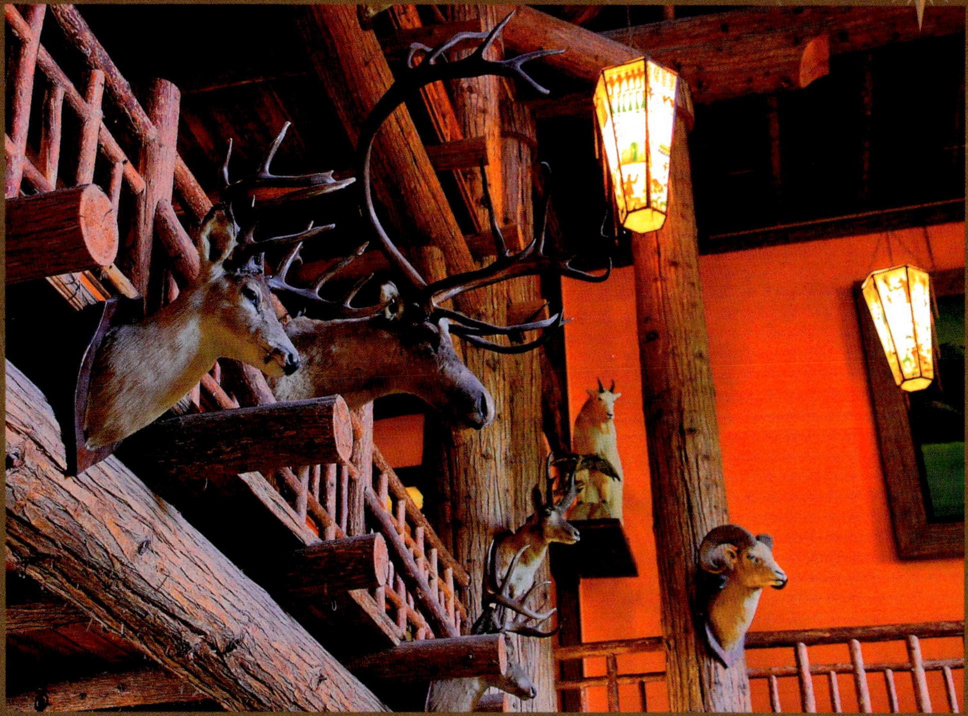

Because of wear, new light shades were made using the original frames in 1982. The light shades, period trophy mounts, and the fireplace combine to create an authentic setting for today's visitors. *Courtesy of I-Ting Chiang*.

75° 90° 105° 120° 135°

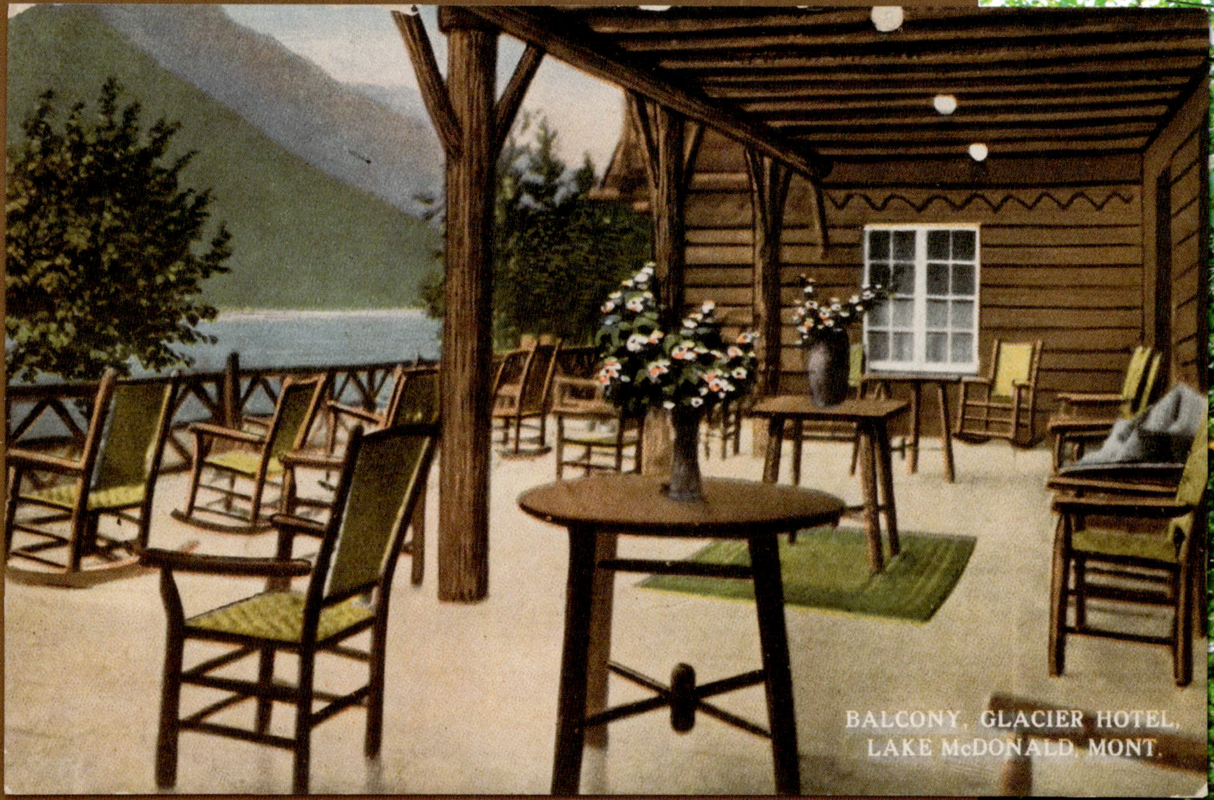

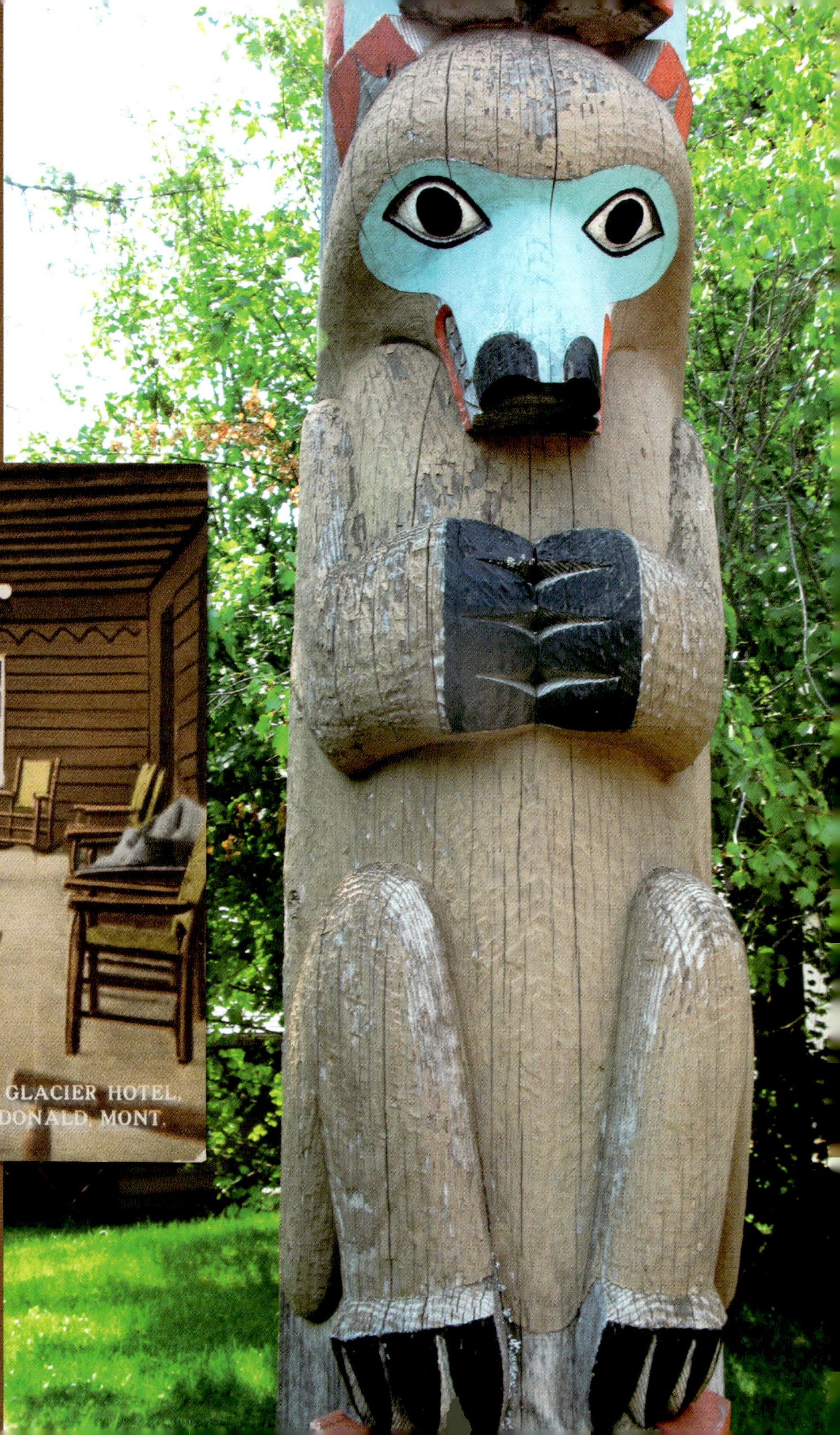

This early postcard, published for J. E. Lewis, shows outside seating at the hotel in its early days. Hickory furniture is still used to furnish the area. John Lewis had installed a totem pole outside the hotel when it was first built. It had disappeared over the years so a replica was carved during renovations. Photos of the original were used to make it as authentic as possible and it is now in place for visitors to enjoy.

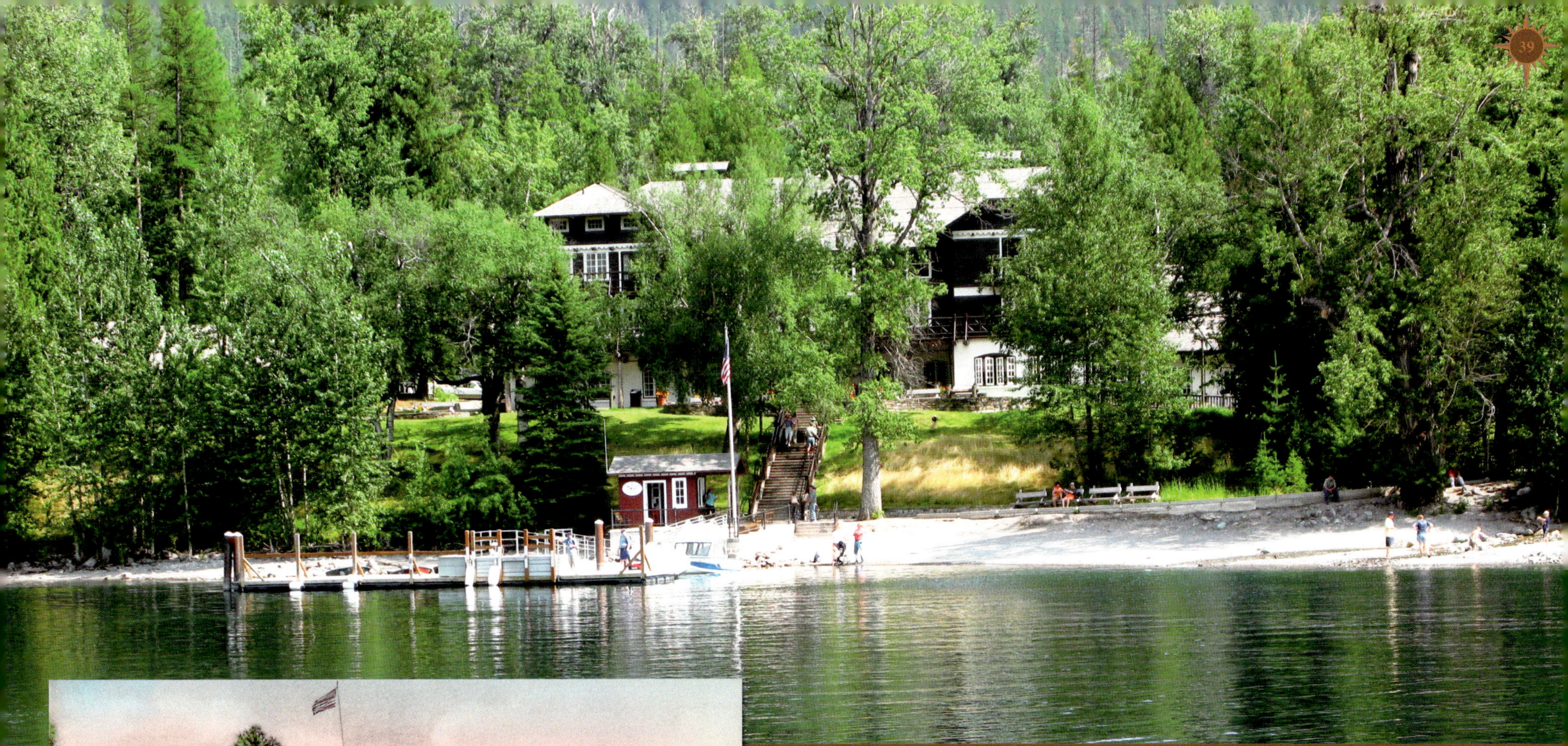

This recent photograph shows the same scene, although slightly hidden by the mature trees. The grounds provide easy access to fishing, wading, and a scenic boat tour that uses the dock to service passengers.

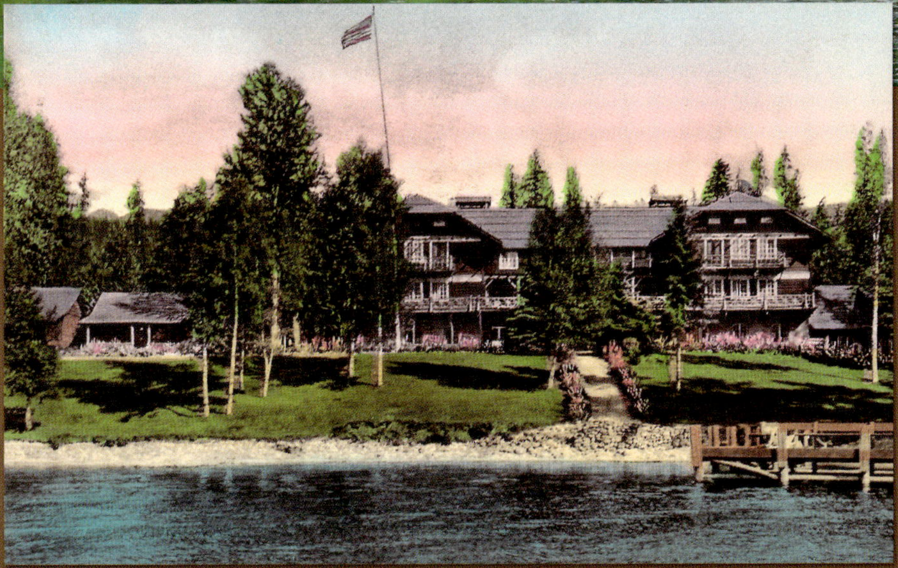

In this image, the lodge is identified as the McDonald Hotel. The facility has had several name changes throughout its long history. This early scene pictures the hotel as well as rental cabins on the left. Hand-colored Albertype Co. postcard; published by the Glacier Park Hotel Co.

Early postcard of the Glacier Hotel dining room published for J. E. Lewis by Bloom Bros. Co. The luncheon menu is circa 1950s.

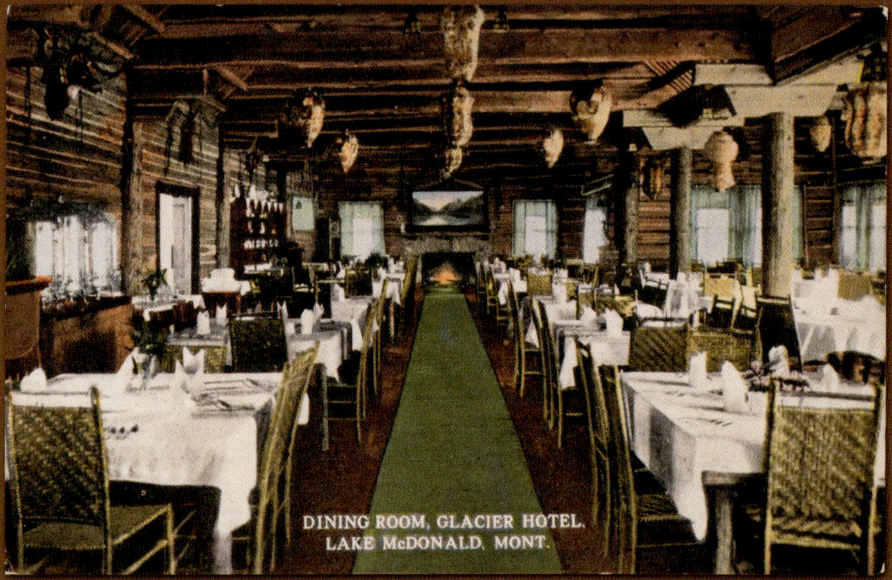

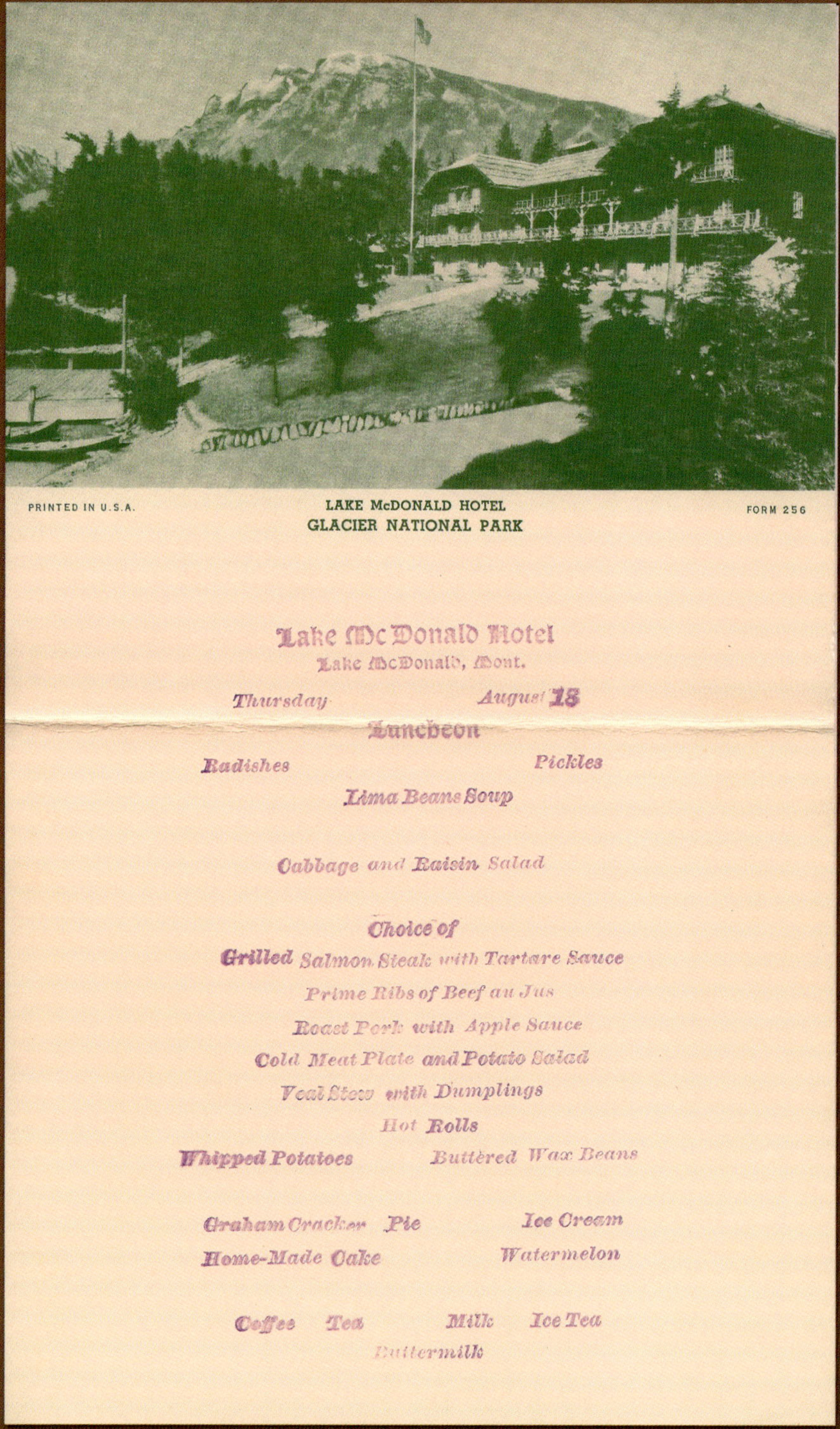

PRINTED IN U.S.A. | LAKE McDONALD HOTEL | GLACIER NATIONAL PARK | FORM 256

Lake McDonald Hotel
Lake McDonald, Mont.

Thursday August 18

Luncheon

Radishes Pickles

Lima Beans Soup

Cabbage and Raisin Salad

Choice of

Grilled Salmon Steak with Tartare Sauce

Prime Ribs of Beef au Jus

Roast Pork with Apple Sauce

Cold Meat Plate and Potato Salad

Veal Stew with Dumplings

Hot Rolls

Whipped Potatoes Buttered Wax Beans

Graham Cracker Pie Ice Cream

Home-Made Cake Watermelon

Coffee Tea Milk Ice Tea

Buttermilk

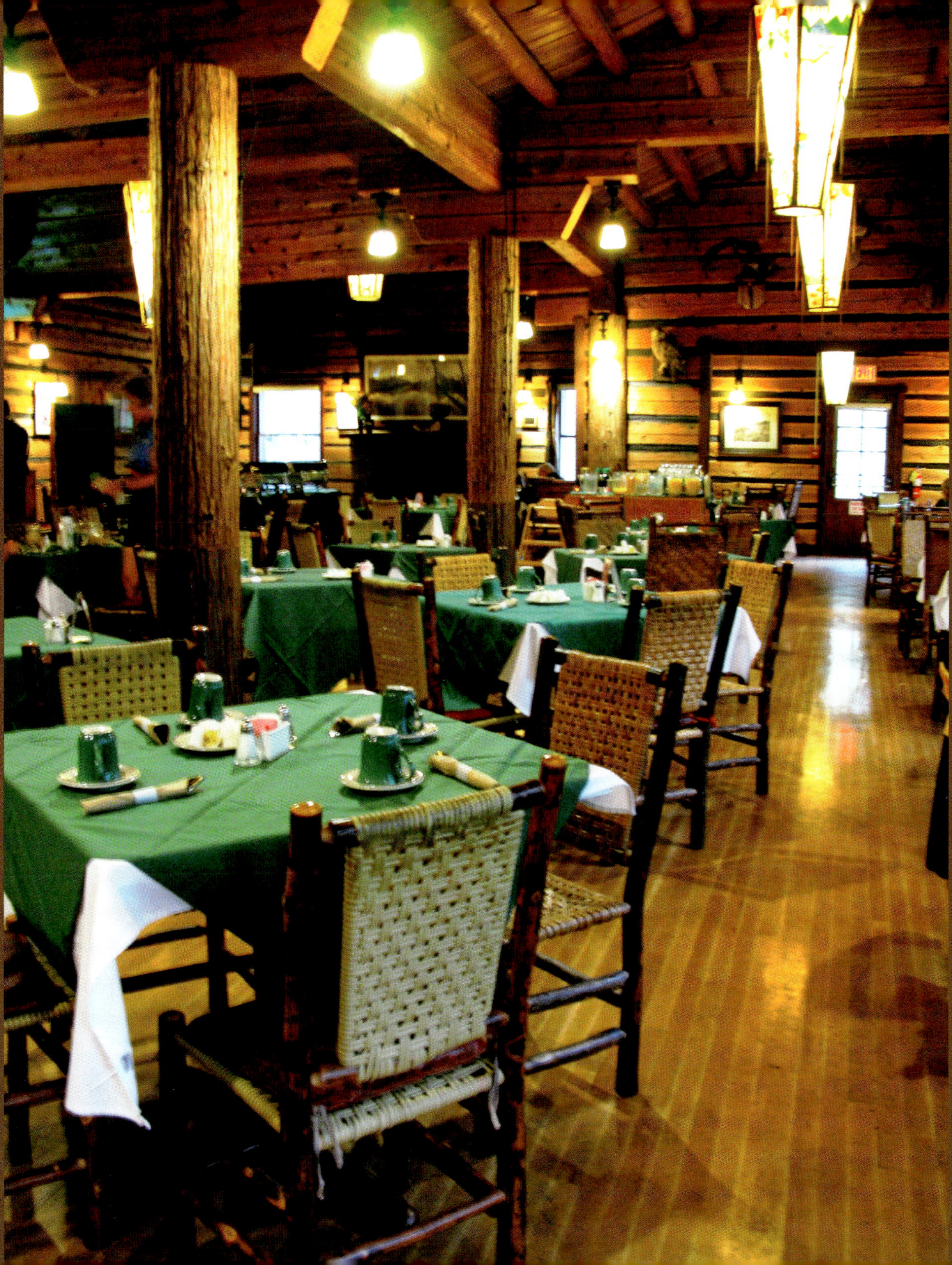

During the restoration, contractors discovered the dining room had been made by connecting several smaller buildings. Much work and expense was spent on this area to bring the building up to code. The dining room still contains hickory furnishings and looks much as it did in the early days.

MANY GLACIER HOTEL

The four-and-a-half story Many Glacier Hotel was the railroad's crown jewel when it opened in 1915. Much needed restoration of the hotel has been underway by the National Park Service, including significant structural repairs to protect the building from the harsh winters. This recent photograph shows how the property continues to reflect the grandeur of its earlier days.

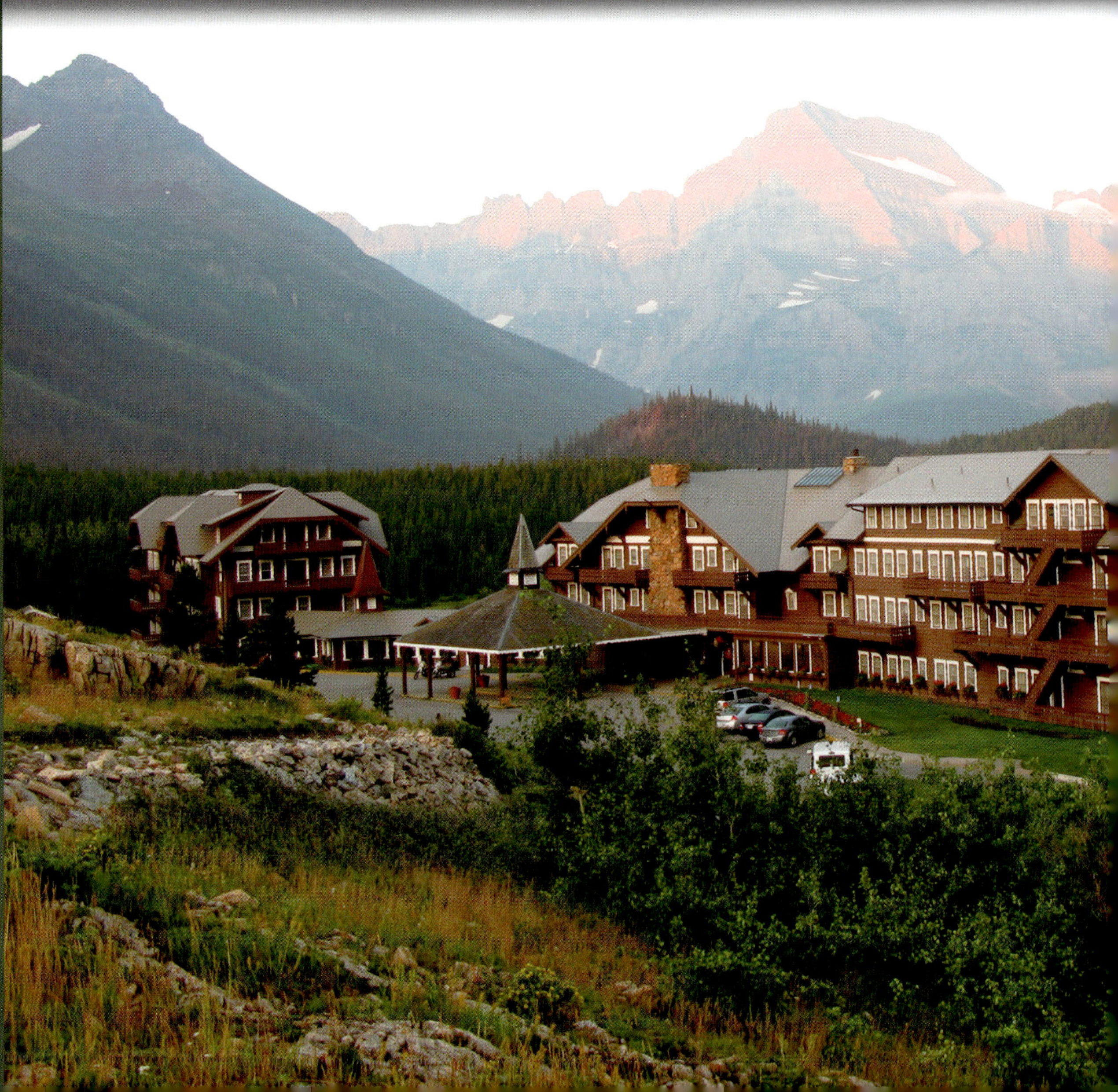

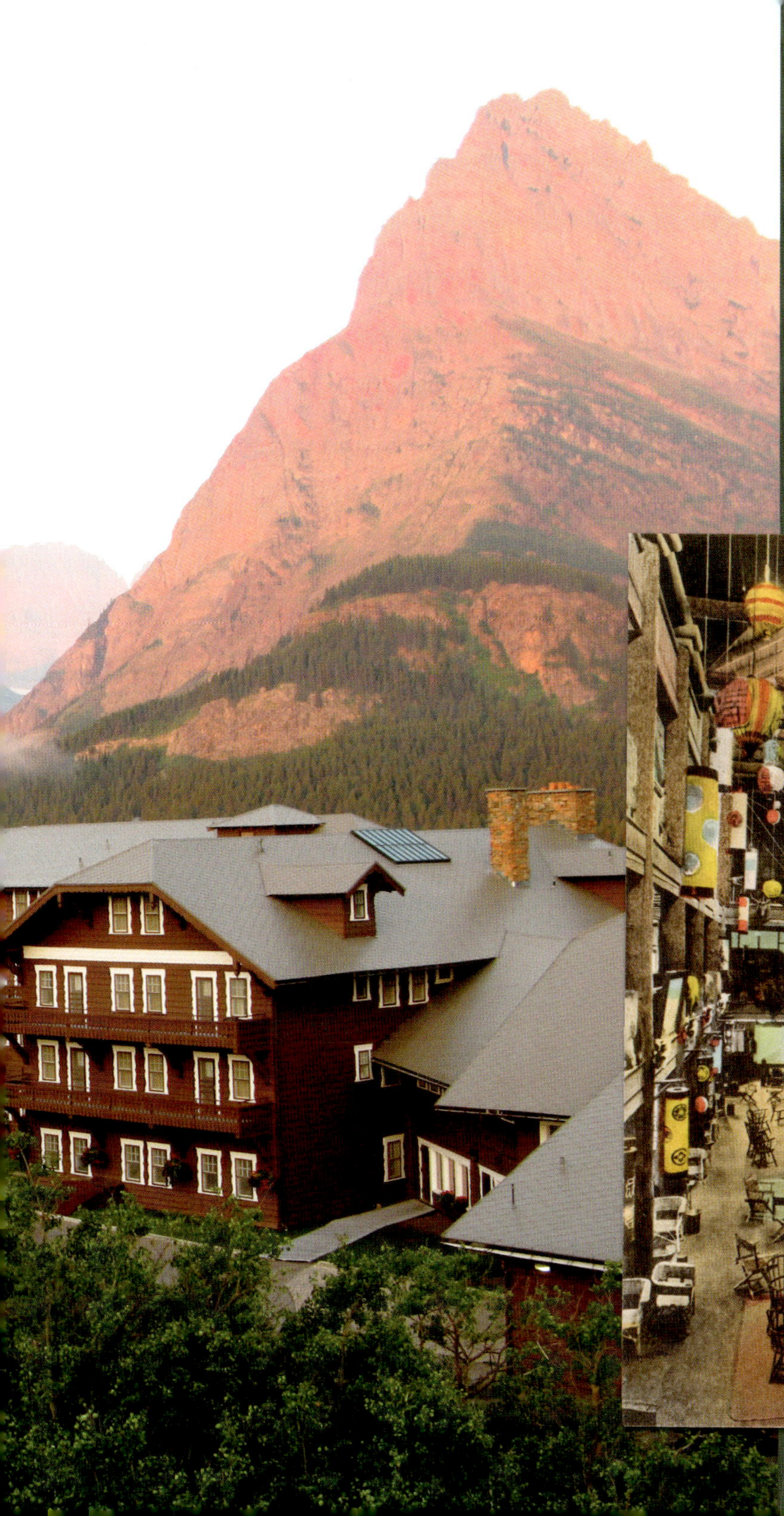

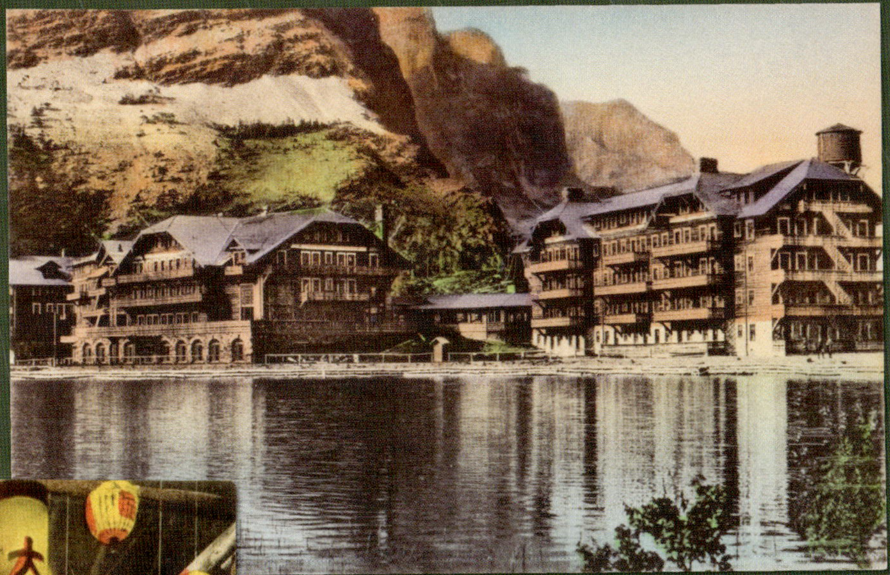

Designed by Thomas D. McMahon to reflect a series of Swiss chalets, Many Glacier Hotel is the largest and most remote of the railroad's hotels. It is located on the shore of Swiftcurrent Lake, formerly called McDermott Lake. The hotel includes three sections and is six hundred feet in length. An annex was added in 1917 and is connected to the main building by a breezeway with a cupola on the roof. The hotel was designated a National Historic Landmark in 1987. Hand-colored postcard made by Albertype Co. circa 1930.

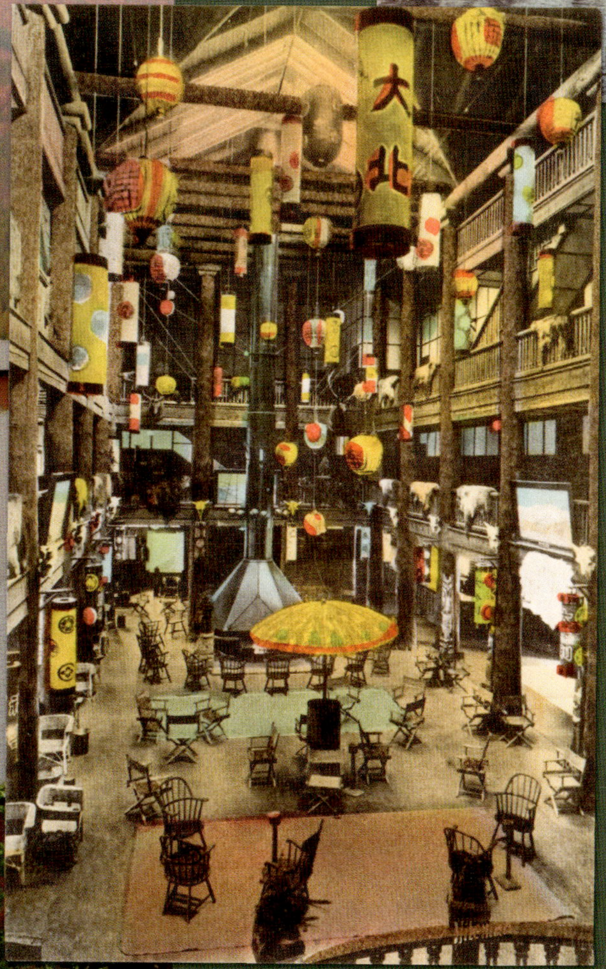

The lobby of the Many Glacier Hotel is four stories tall, was made with peeled log columns, and included two fireplaces, one of which was a hooded free-standing model. This hand-colored postcard by the Albertype Co. shows the lobby in its early days decorated with Hill's Oriental lanterns.

The lobby after the oriental decorations have been removed. This image also provides a view of the railing around the double helix staircase. Linen postcard by C. T. Art-Colortone, late 1930s.

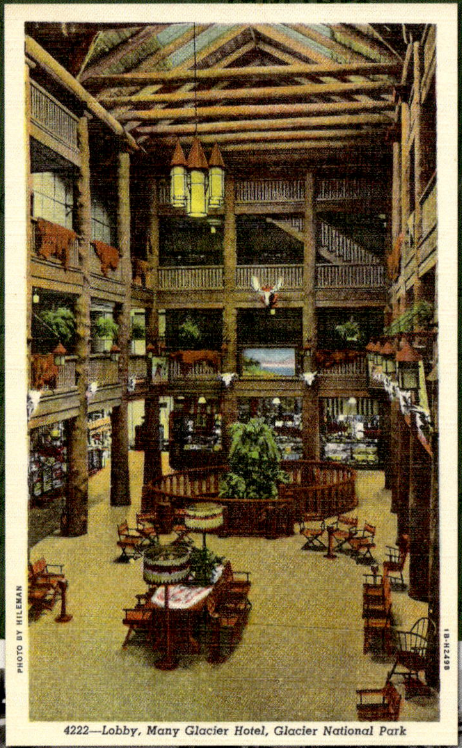

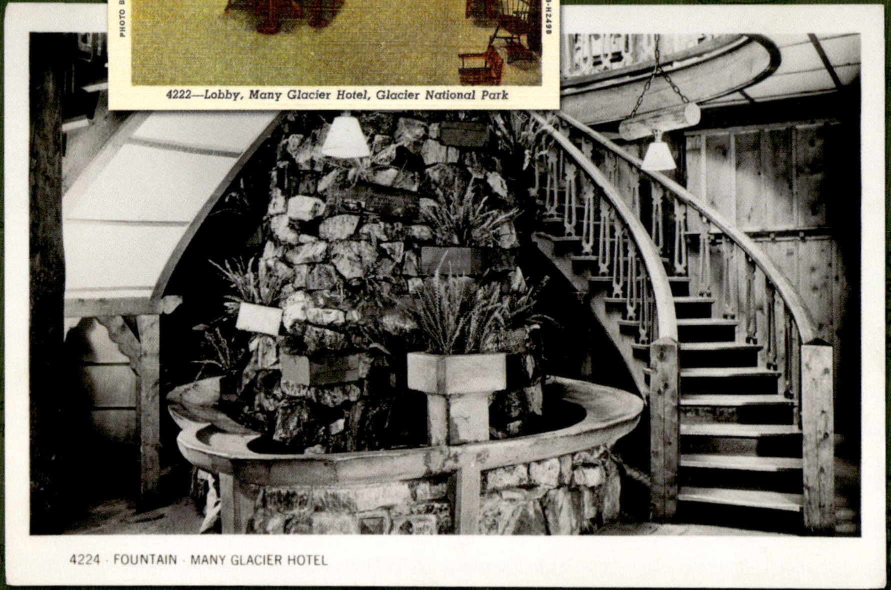

This unmarked real photo postcard provides a view of the double helix staircase and fountain that led from the lobby to the lower level of the building.

The staircase and fountain were removed in the late 1950s to allow for expansion of the gift shop. One of the highlights of the original lobby was a 180-foot mural painted by Chief Medicine Owl and others illustrating the history of the Blackfeet. It, too, was removed during the modernization of the hotel. This photograph shows the lobby as it has looked in recent years with the fireplace on the lower right.

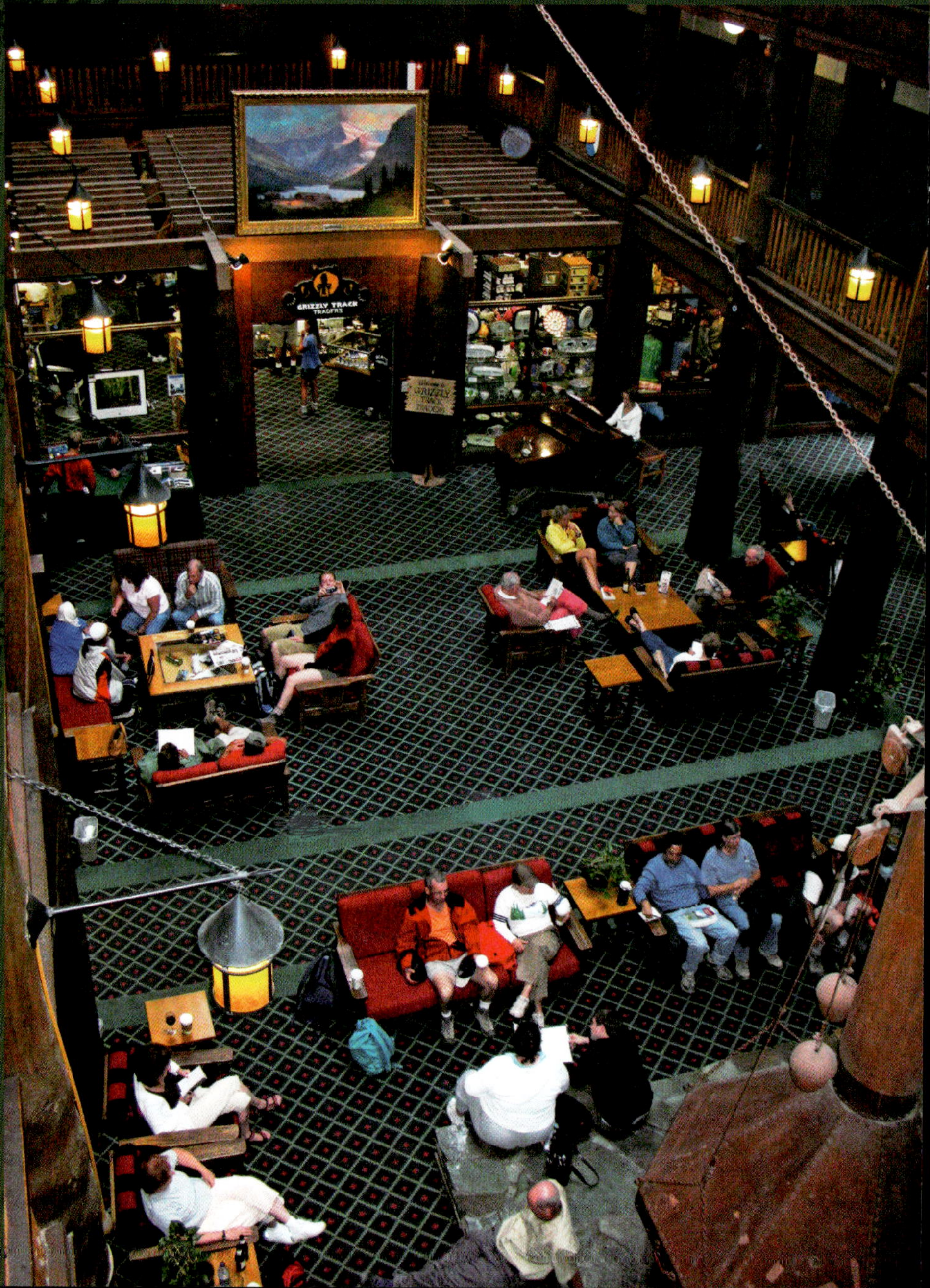

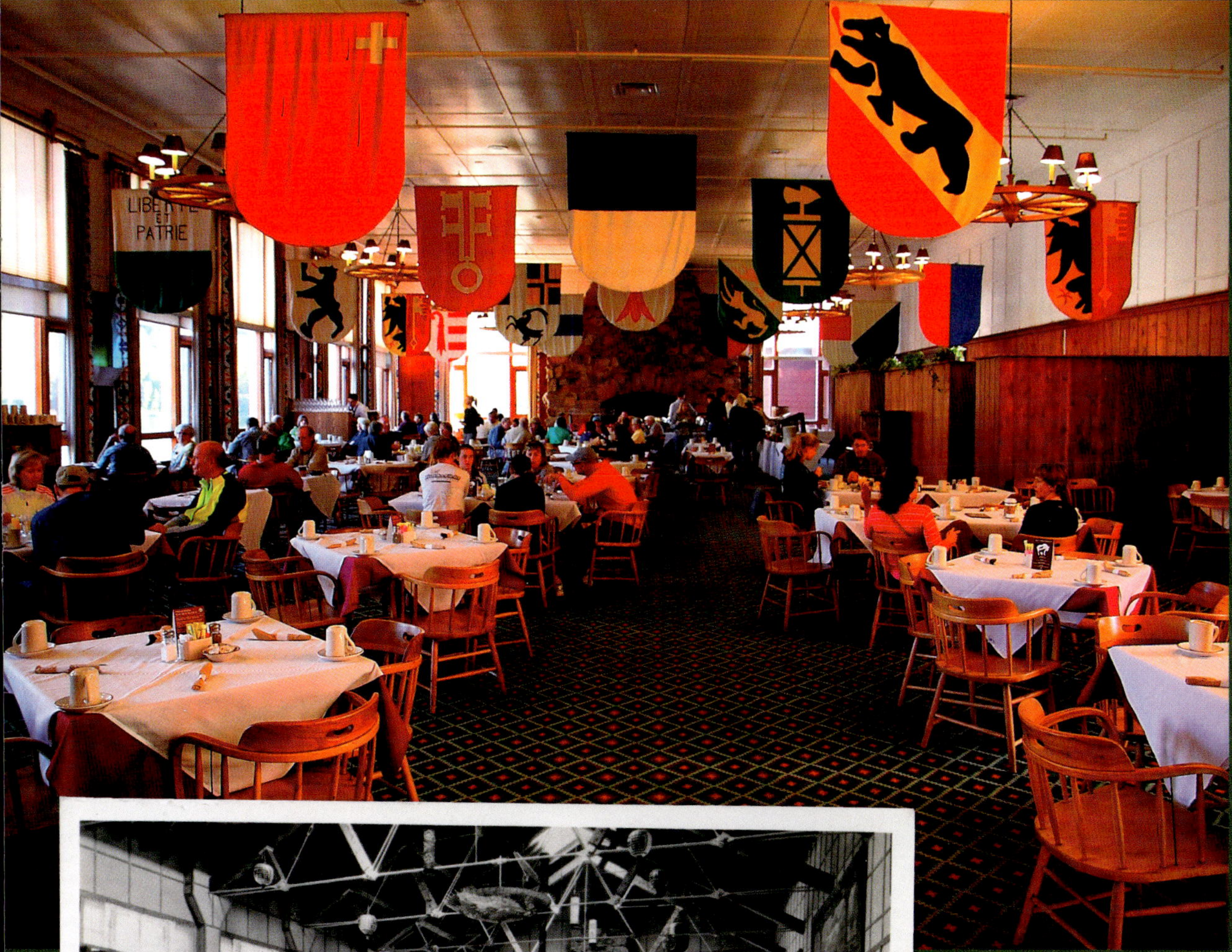

In later years, the Ptarmigan dining room took on a Swiss theme and was modernized to include a dropped ceiling. The ceiling line and window configuration are being returned to their original state along with the fireplace during renovations. The Many Glacier breakfast menu pictures Swiftcurrent Falls and dates from August 1954. Many of these menus were taken home as souvenirs. *Dining room photograph courtesy of I-Ting Chiang.*

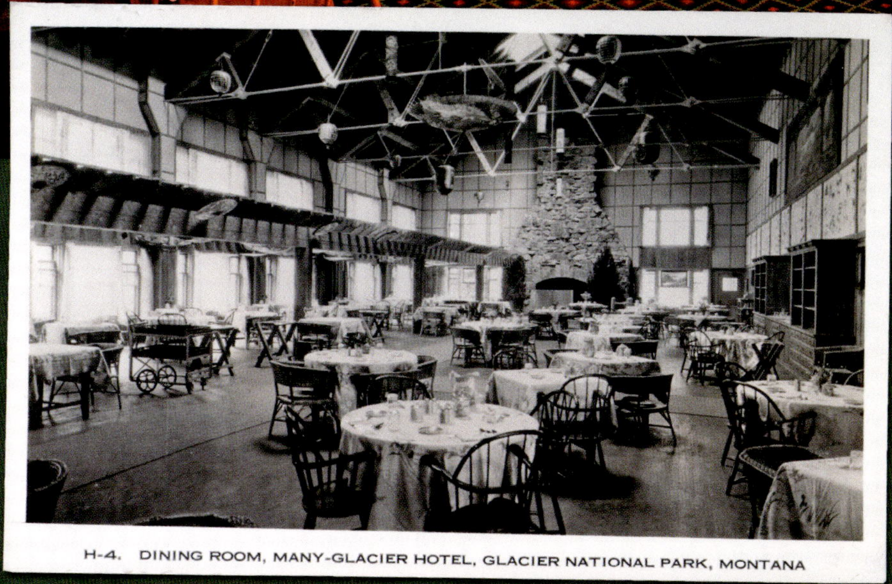

In addition to the lobby, the Many Glacier Hotel dining room also featured Oriental lantern decor in the early days. The hotel was sold by the railroad in 1960. The property is now owned by the National Park Service and is operated by Glacier Park, Inc. It includes 214 guest rooms. Unmarked real photo postcard.

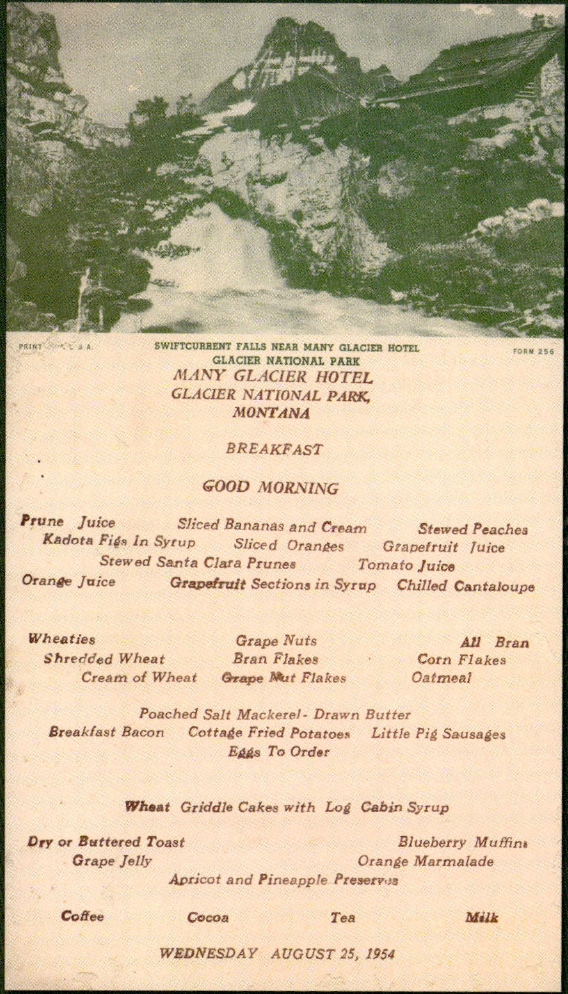

SWIFTCURRENT FALLS NEAR MANY GLACIER HOTEL
GLACIER NATIONAL PARK

FORM 256

MANY GLACIER HOTEL
GLACIER NATIONAL PARK,
MONTANA

BREAKFAST

GOOD MORNING

Prune Juice — Sliced Bananas and Cream — Stewed Peaches
Kadota Figs In Syrup — Sliced Oranges — Grapefruit Juice
Stewed Santa Clara Prunes — Tomato Juice
Orange Juice — Grapefruit Sections in Syrup — Chilled Cantaloupe

Wheaties — Grape Nuts — All Bran
Shredded Wheat — Bran Flakes — Corn Flakes
Cream of Wheat — Grape Nut Flakes — Oatmeal

Poached Salt Mackerel - Drawn Butter
Breakfast Bacon — Cottage Fried Potatoes — Little Pig Sausages
Eggs To Order

Wheat Griddle Cakes with Log Cabin Syrup

Dry or Buttered Toast — Blueberry Muffins
Grape Jelly — Orange Marmalade
Apricot and Pineapple Preserves

Coffee — Cocoa — Tea — Milk

WEDNESDAY AUGUST 25, 1954

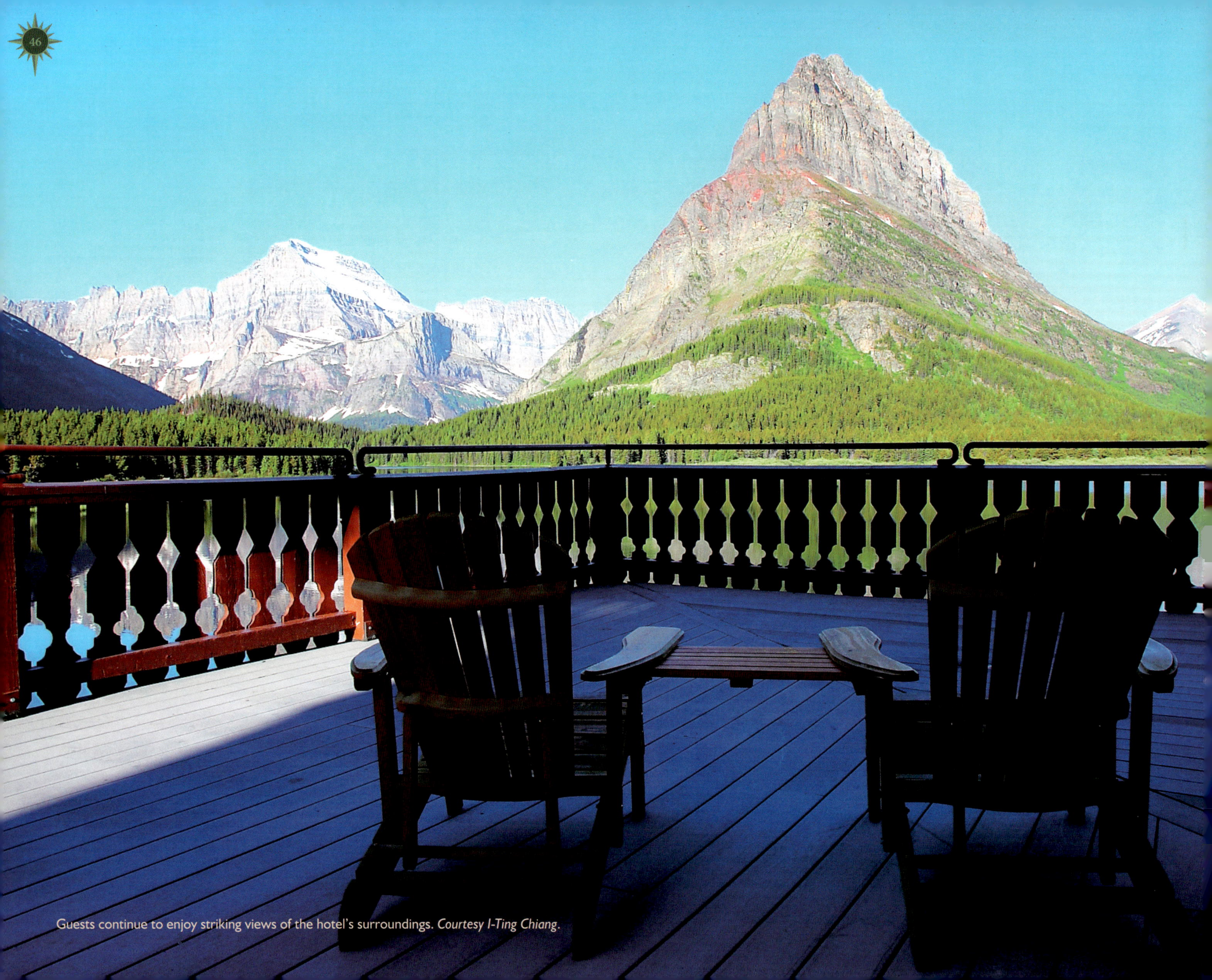

Guests continue to enjoy striking views of the hotel's surroundings. *Courtesy I-Ting Chiang*.

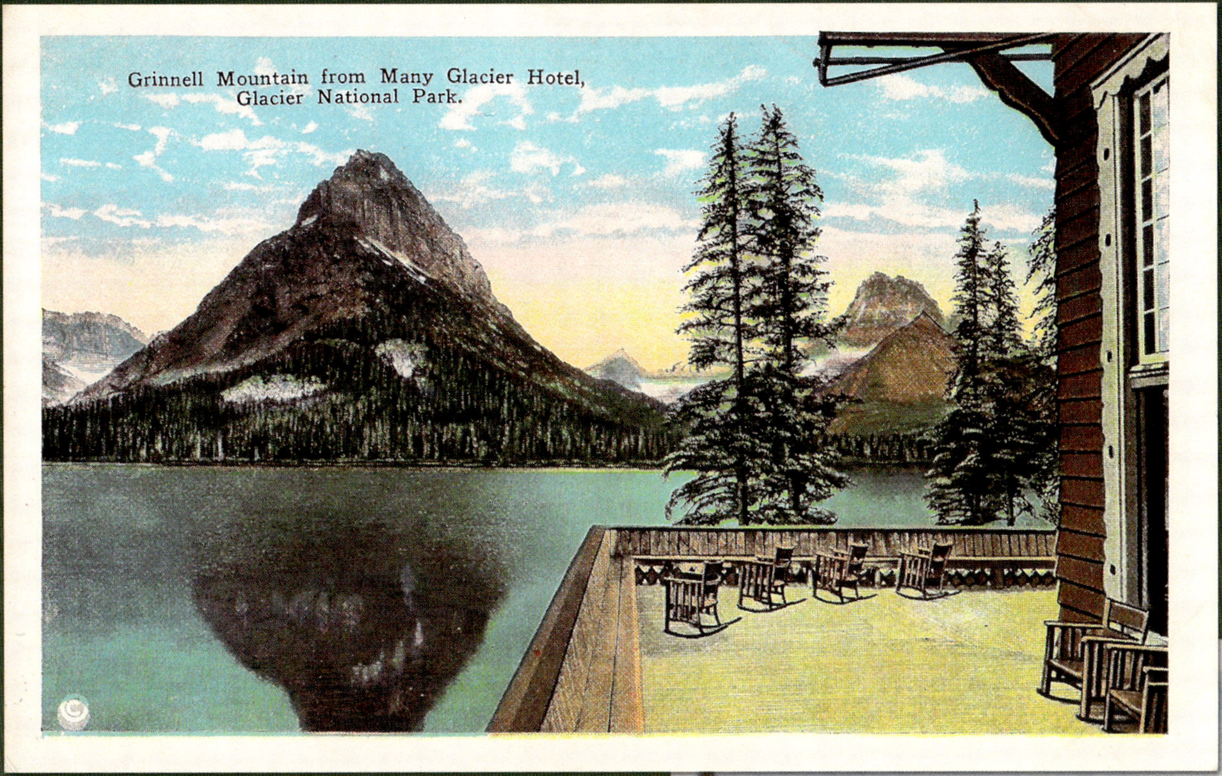

This early postcard offers views of Grinnell Mountain from the hotel deck. Published by the Glacier Park Hotel Co. with a Hileman photo.

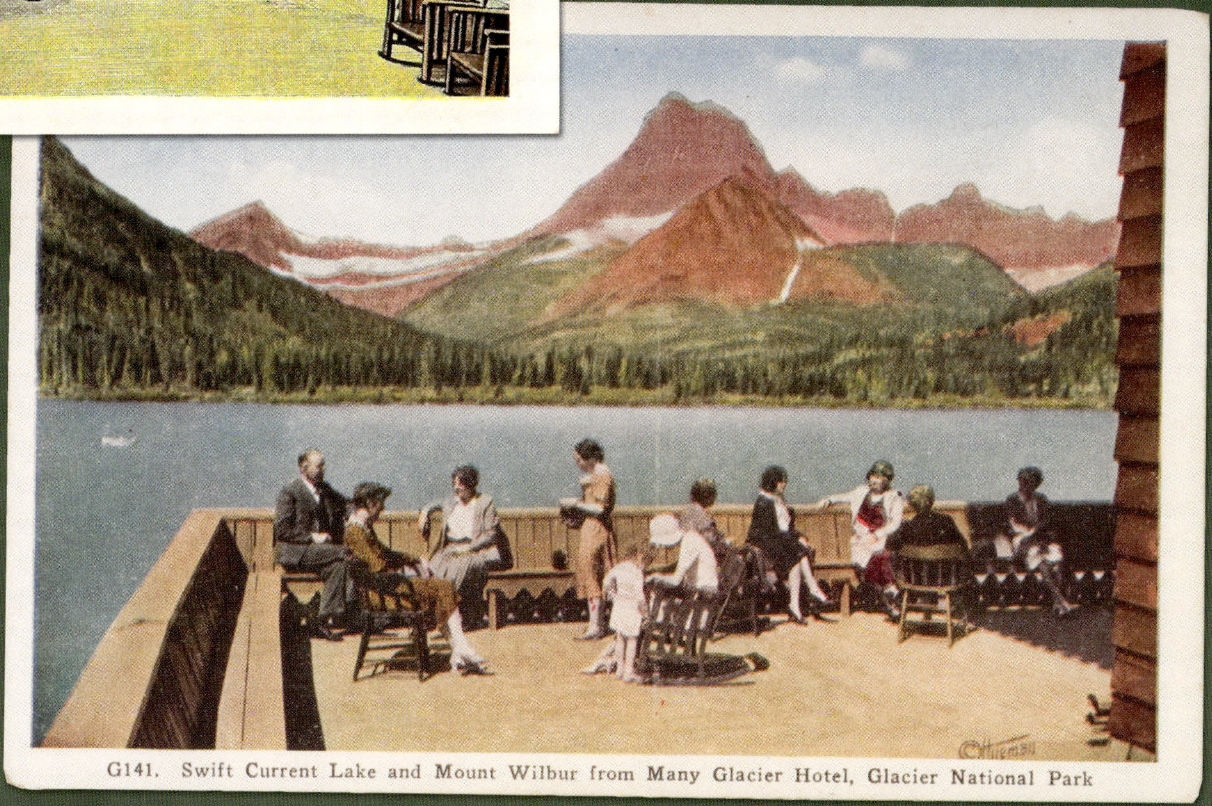

This circa 1920s postcard, published for the Glacier Park Hotel Co. by Hileman, shows guests enjoying the scenic views of Swiftcurrent Lake and Mt. Wilbur as seen from the hotel's wraparound balcony, which offers 180-degree views.

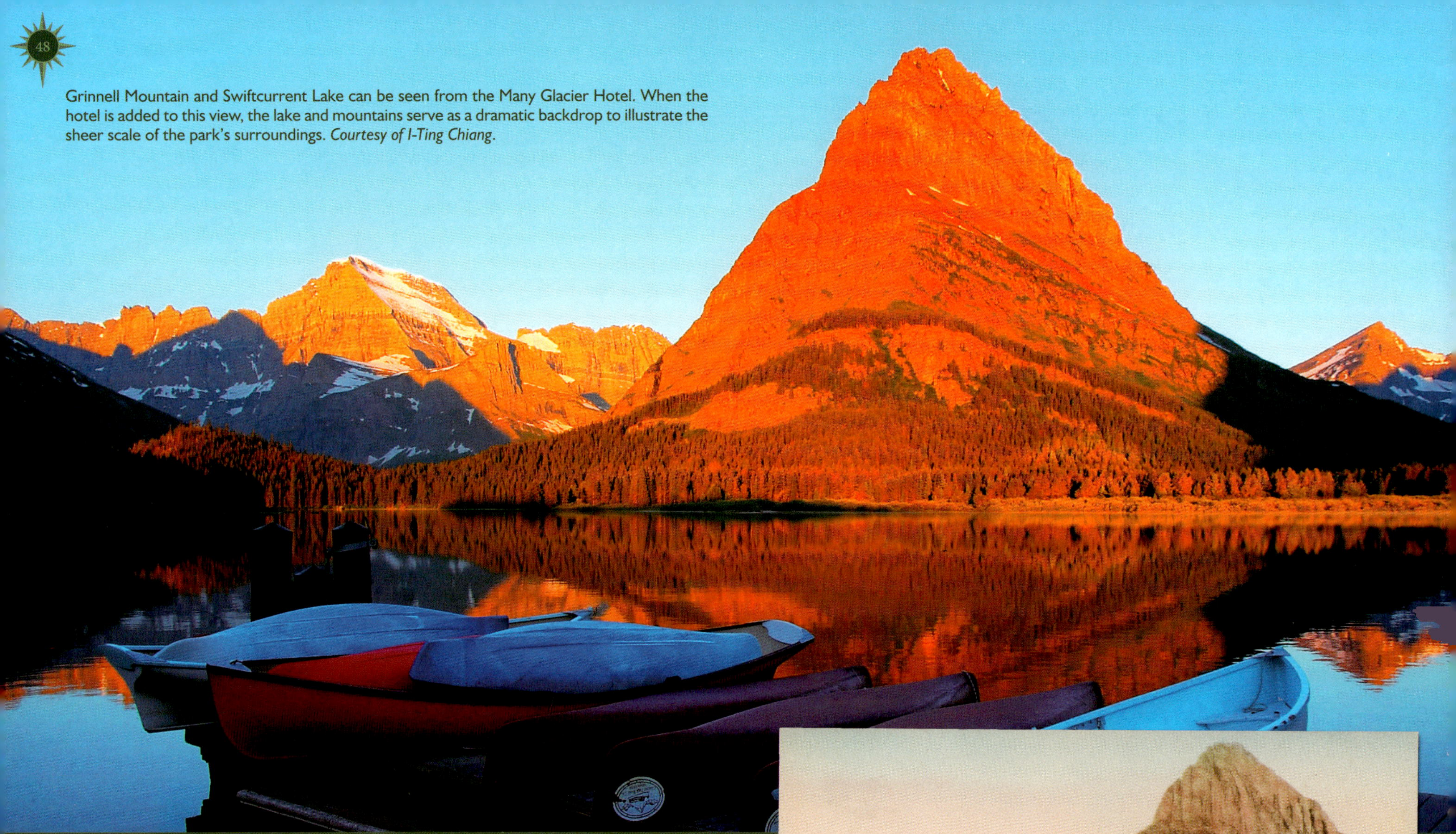

Grinnell Mountain and Swiftcurrent Lake can be seen from the Many Glacier Hotel. When the hotel is added to this view, the lake and mountains serve as a dramatic backdrop to illustrate the sheer scale of the park's surroundings. *Courtesy of I-Ting Chiang*.

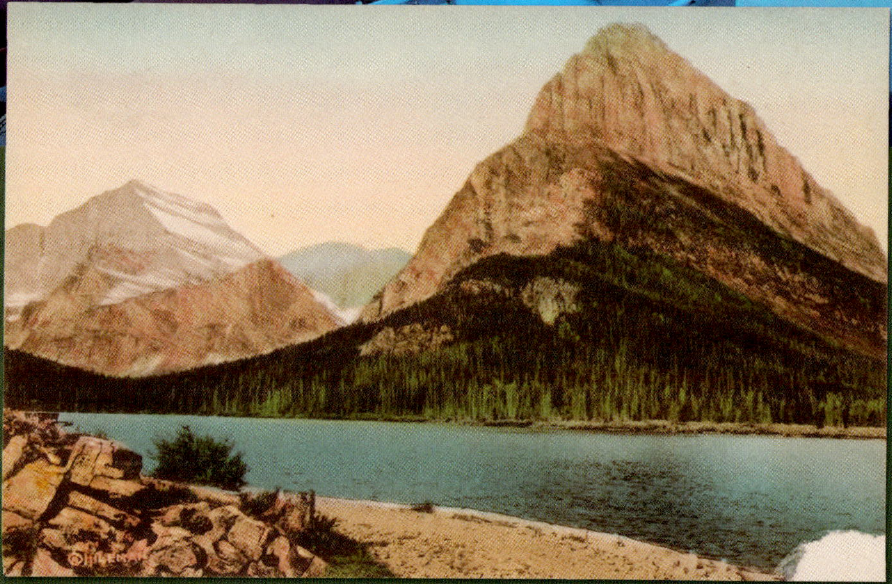

Grinnell Mountain is named for George Bird Grinnell, a prominent naturalist and writer who helped lobby Congress to establish the park. Hand-colored postcard published by Glacier Park Hotel Co. and made by the Albertype Co., circa 1930.

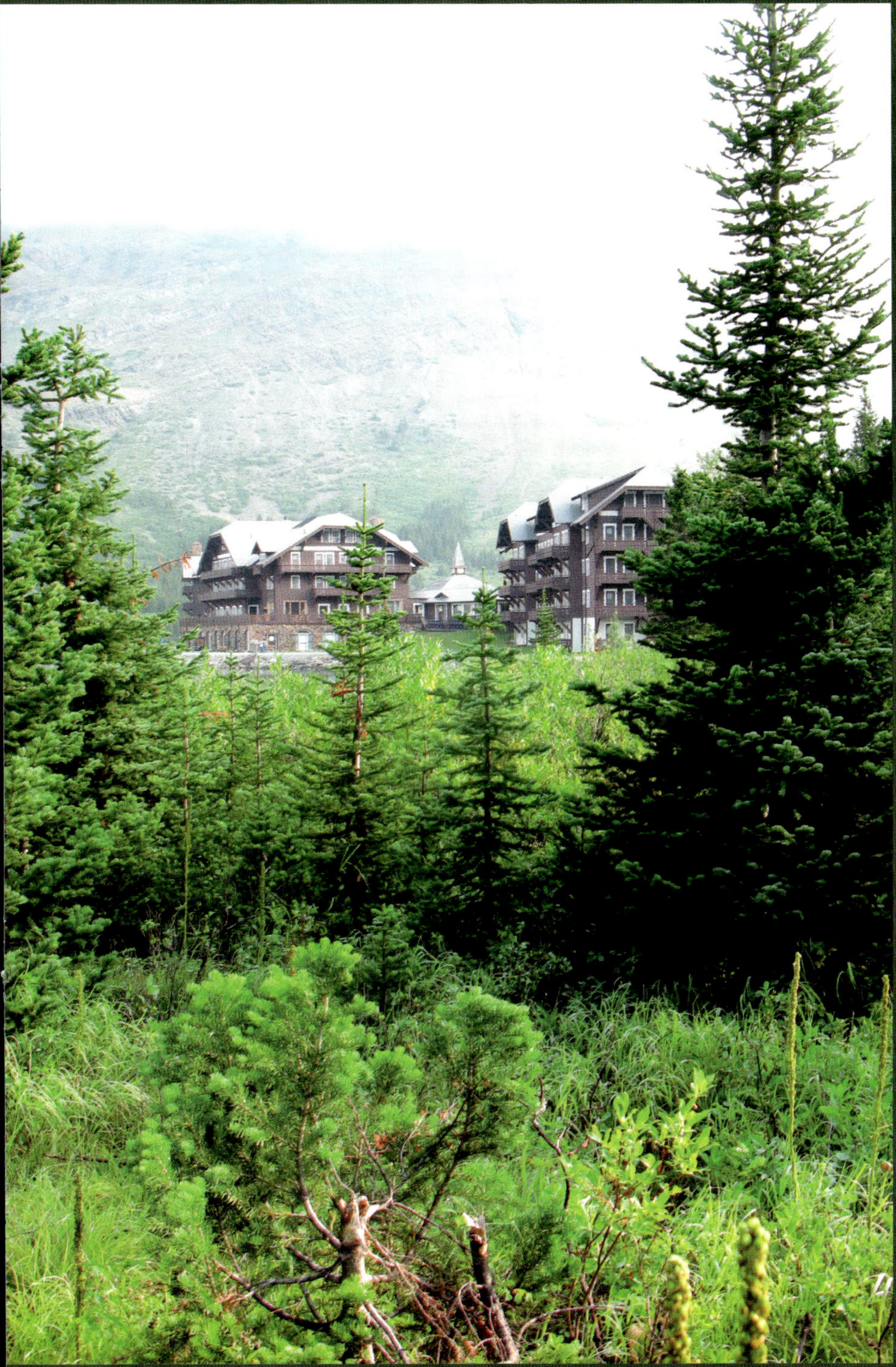

Views of Swiftcurrent Lake can be found by following the Swiftcurrent Nature Trail, a two-and-a-half mile loop around the lake. The trail keeps the hotel in close proximity, yet allows for a scenic adventure in the woods.

The *Chief Two Guns* launch can be seen from the trail as it readies to make its journey across the lake to pick up passengers from the hotel.

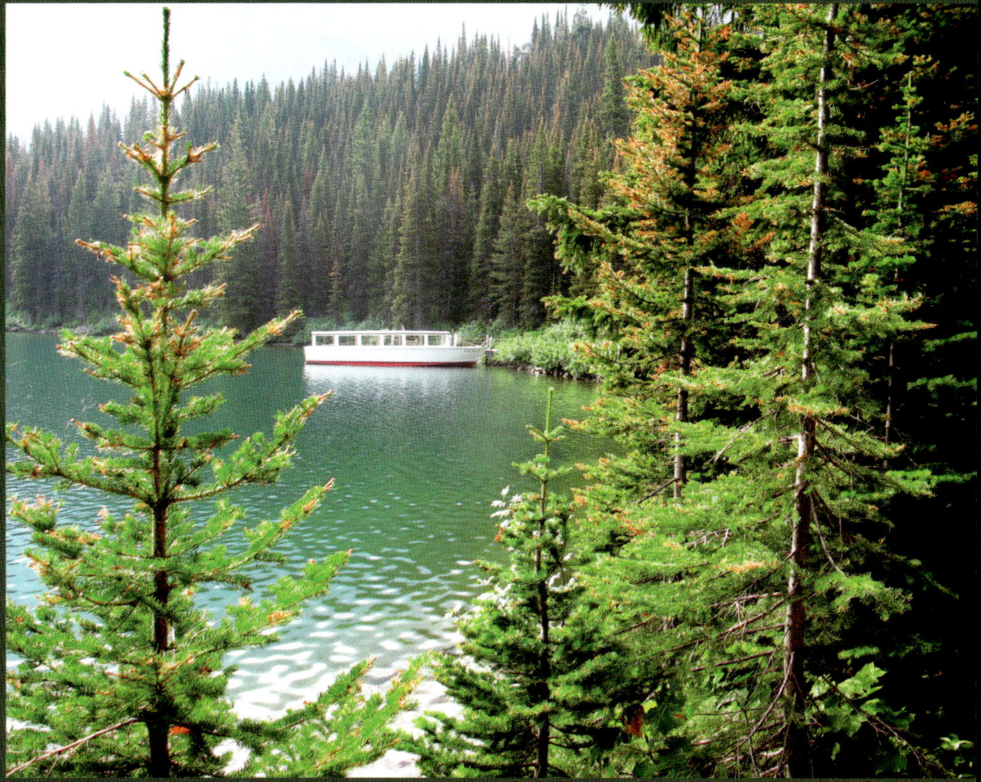

TWO MEDICINE CHALETS

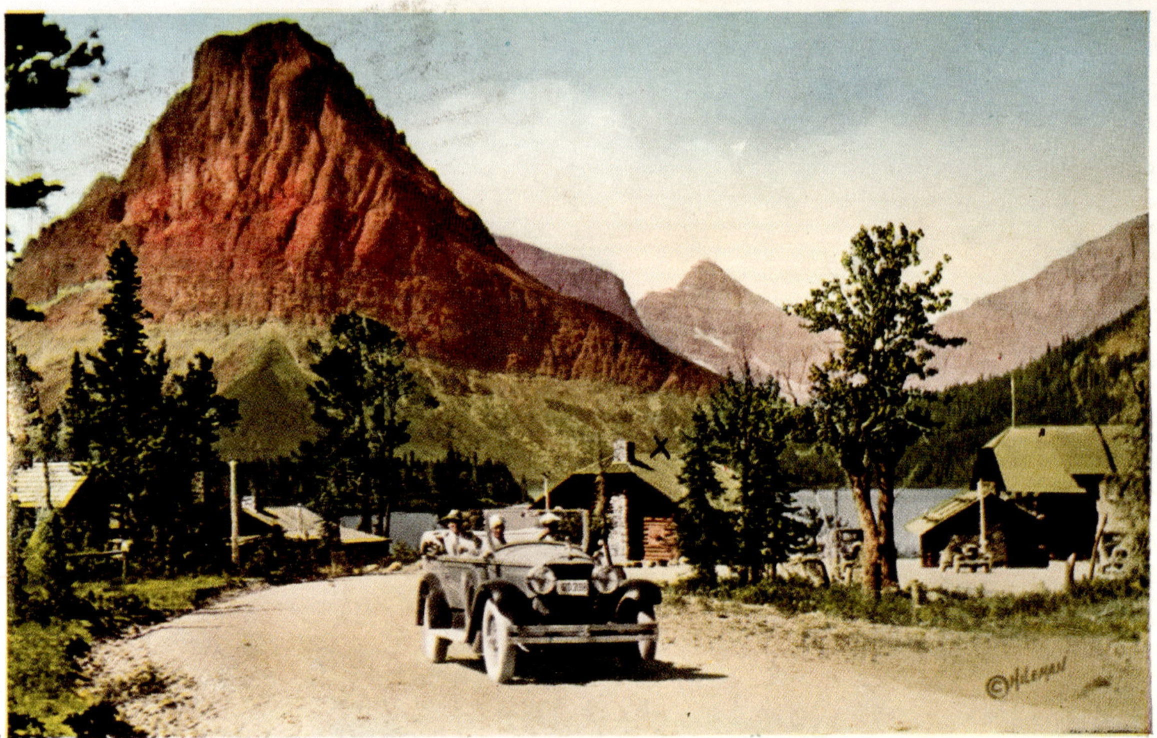

x shows our Chalet. G120. Two Medicine Chalets and Mt. Rockwell, Glacier National Park

The Two Medicine Lake area, located about thirteen miles from East Glacier, was first used as a tepee camp in 1911. The Two Medicine Lake name came from ceremonial double Medicine Lodges that had been set up by the Blackfeet for an earlier Sun Dance. In 1912, two log chalets were built and in 1913 a large cabin and a dormitory were added. These buildings were located around the lakeshore offering views of Mt. Rockwell. The dining room and kitchen were built in 1915. This Hileman postcard was published for the Glacier Park Hotel Co. It was mailed in 1934 and is addressed to a woman in Arlington, Virginia, with the message: "This is where President Roosevelt will spend his vacation – lovely spot."

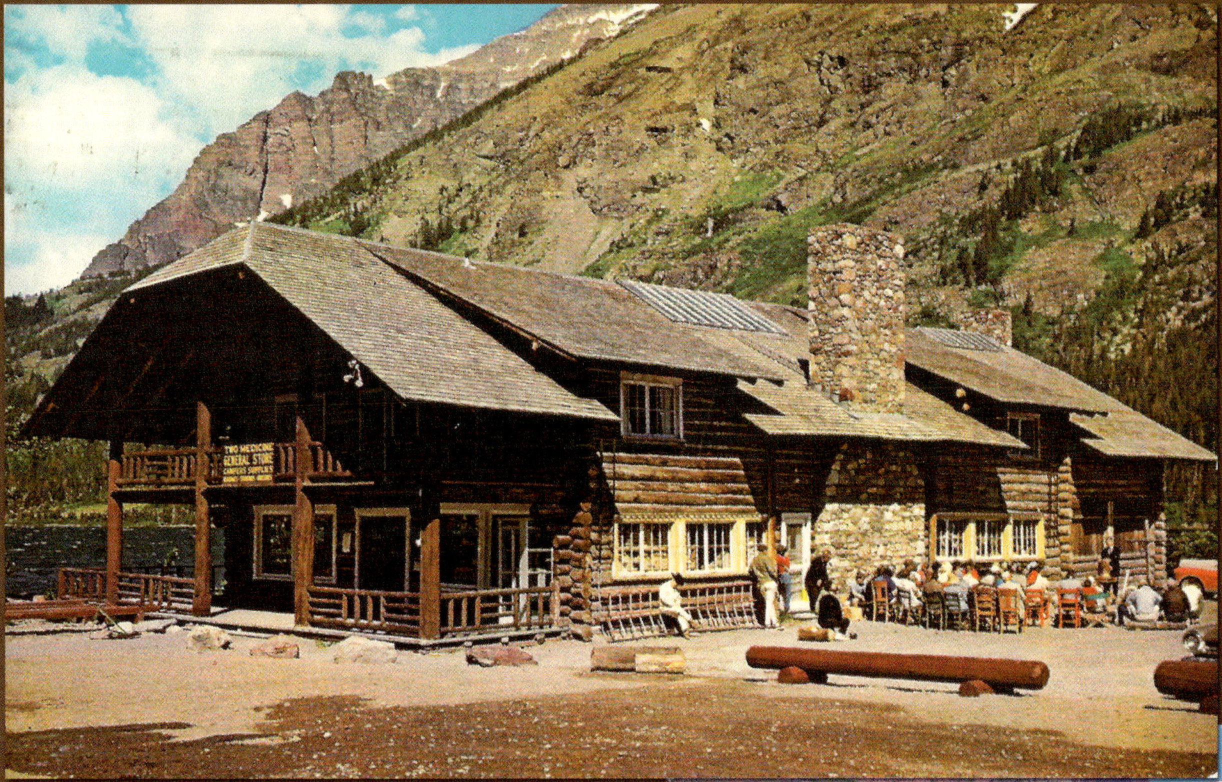

Business at the chalets never fully recovered after being closed from 1944-46 during World War II and the buildings were in need of repair. The facility was closed permanently in the early 1950s and by 1956 most of the buildings had been destroyed by fire. The dining hall was saved to be used as a camp store, as shown on this Plastichrome postcard distributed by Glacier Park, Inc. Information on the card states that a church service was held every Sunday morning and one was in progress when the photo was taken.

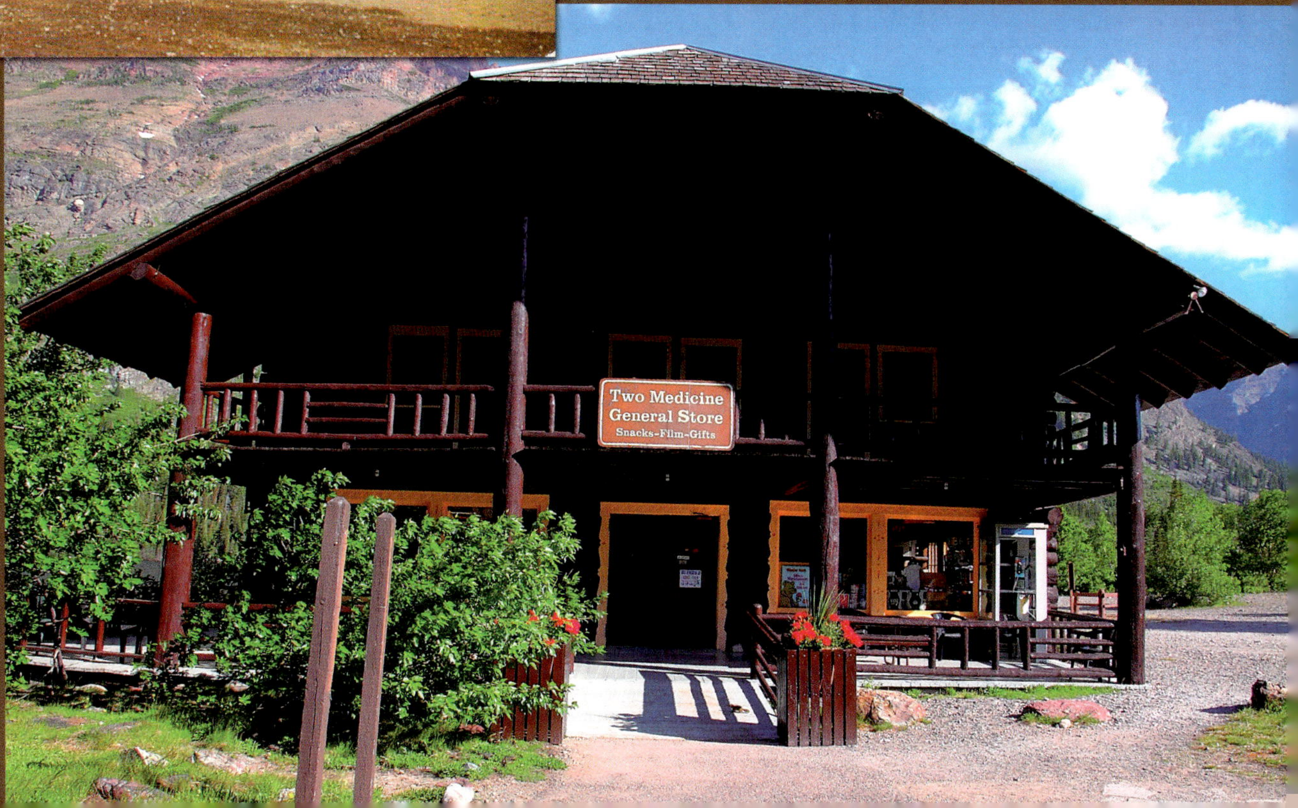

The Two Medicine Camp Store is still in use today. It is a registered historic landmark and is the only log-constructed chalet remaining in the park. It is operated by Glacier Park, Inc. *Courtesy of I-Ting Chiang*.

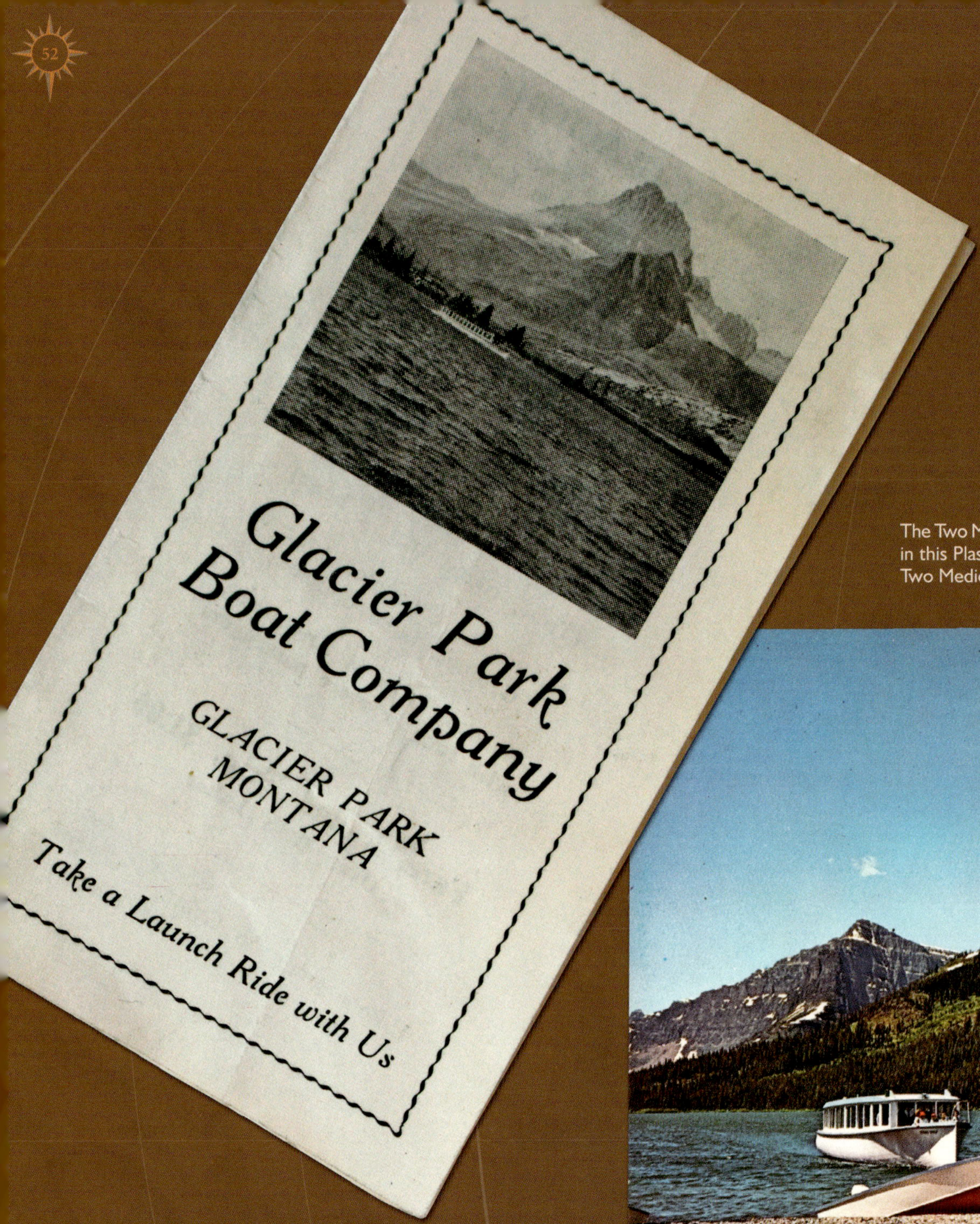

The Two Medicine Lake boat launch, located near the southeastern entrance to the park, is shown in this Plastichrome postcard distributed by Glacier Park, Inc. The earlier brochure prices the Two Medicine Lake scenic round-trip boat tour at seventy-five cents per person.

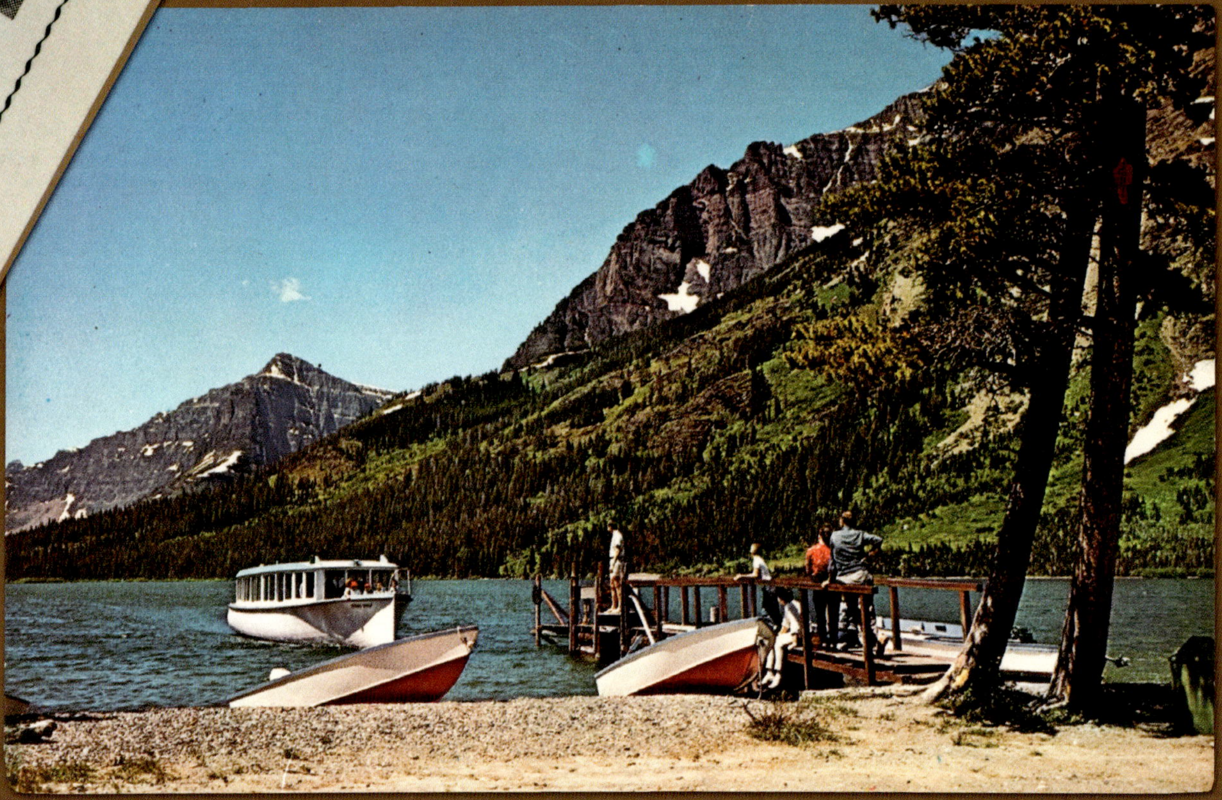

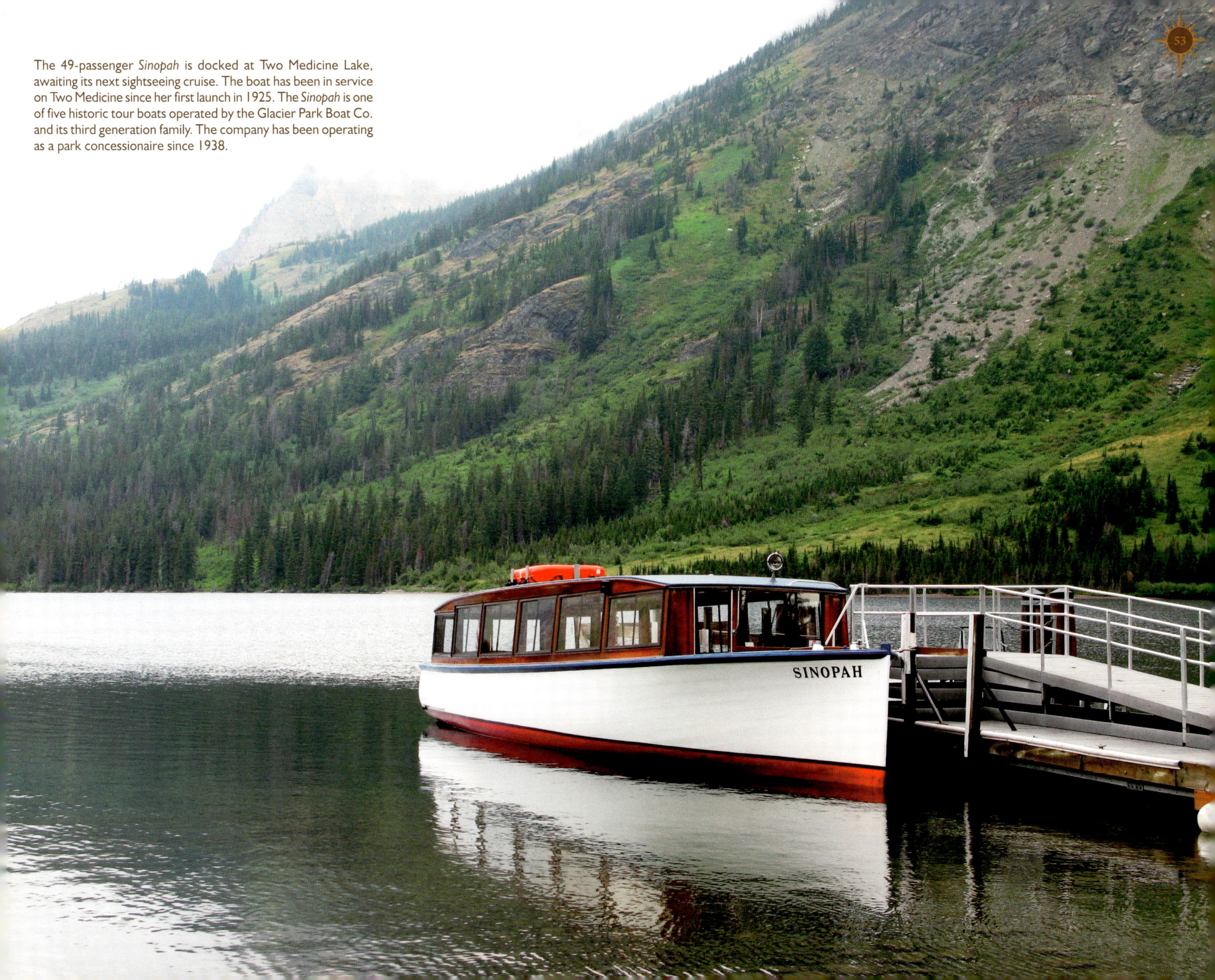

The 49-passenger *Sinopah* is docked at Two Medicine Lake, awaiting its next sightseeing cruise. The boat has been in service on Two Medicine since her first launch in 1925. The *Sinopah* is one of five historic tour boats operated by the Glacier Park Boat Co. and its third generation family. The company has been operating as a park concessionaire since 1938.

ST. MARY CHALETS

The St. Mary Chalets were located at the foot of St. Mary Lake on the park's east side. It began as a tepee camp in 1911 and the chalets opened in 1913. Included were a kitchen, dining room, dormitories, recreation building, and cabins. After the Going-to-the Sun Road opened, the chalets were eventually closed since it had been used mostly as a transportation hub. The buildings were removed during the 1940s. Postcard published by Glacier Park Hotel Co. Also pictured is a luggage decal circa 1930s. *Courtesy Glacier National Park Archives.*

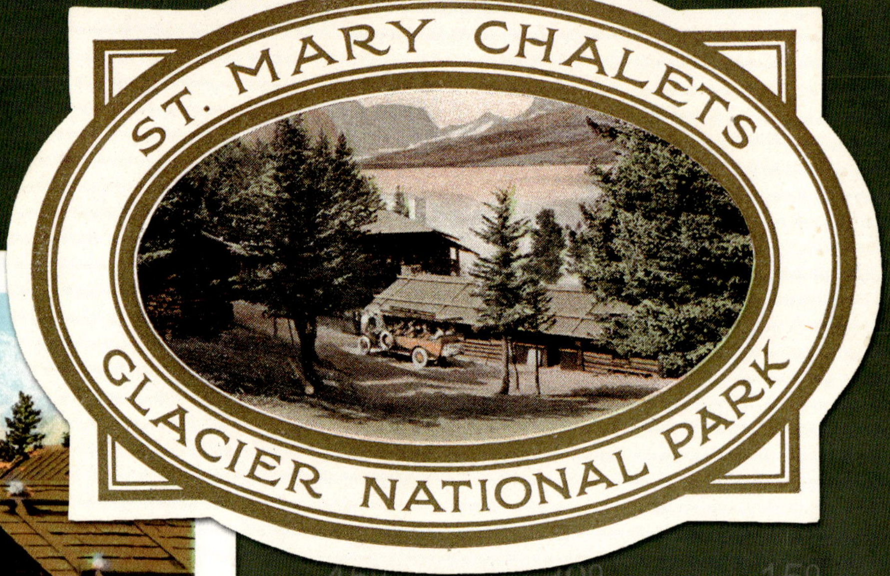

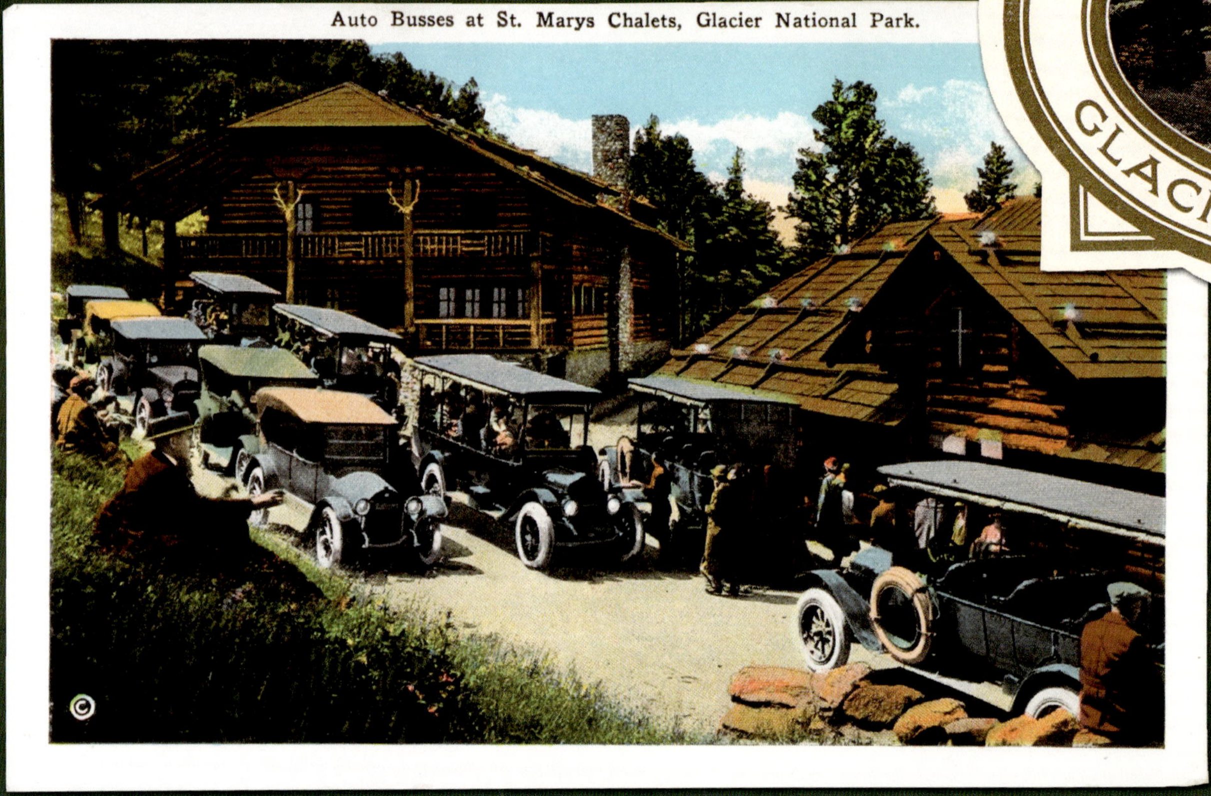

An earlier view shows visitors who were most likely on a "stopover" at St. Mary Chalets and were waiting for their next transportation connection. Albertype Co. postcard published by Glacier Park Hotel Co.

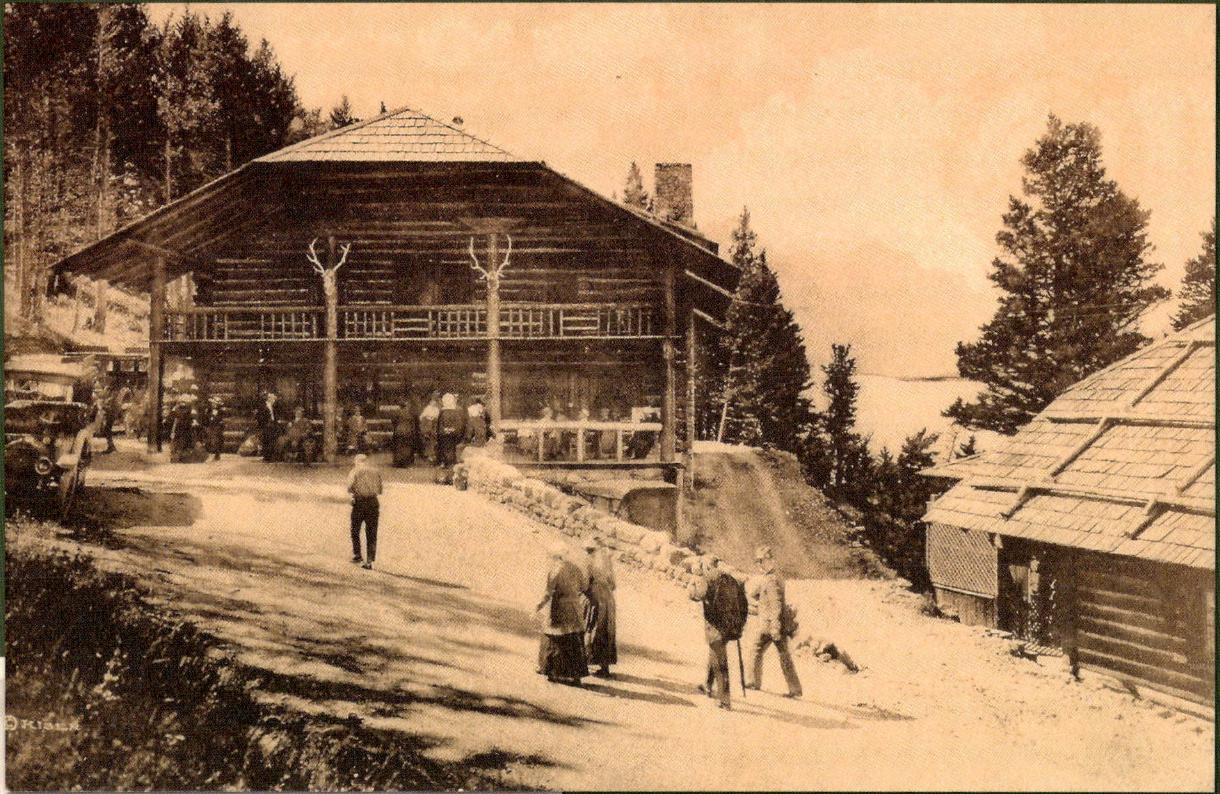

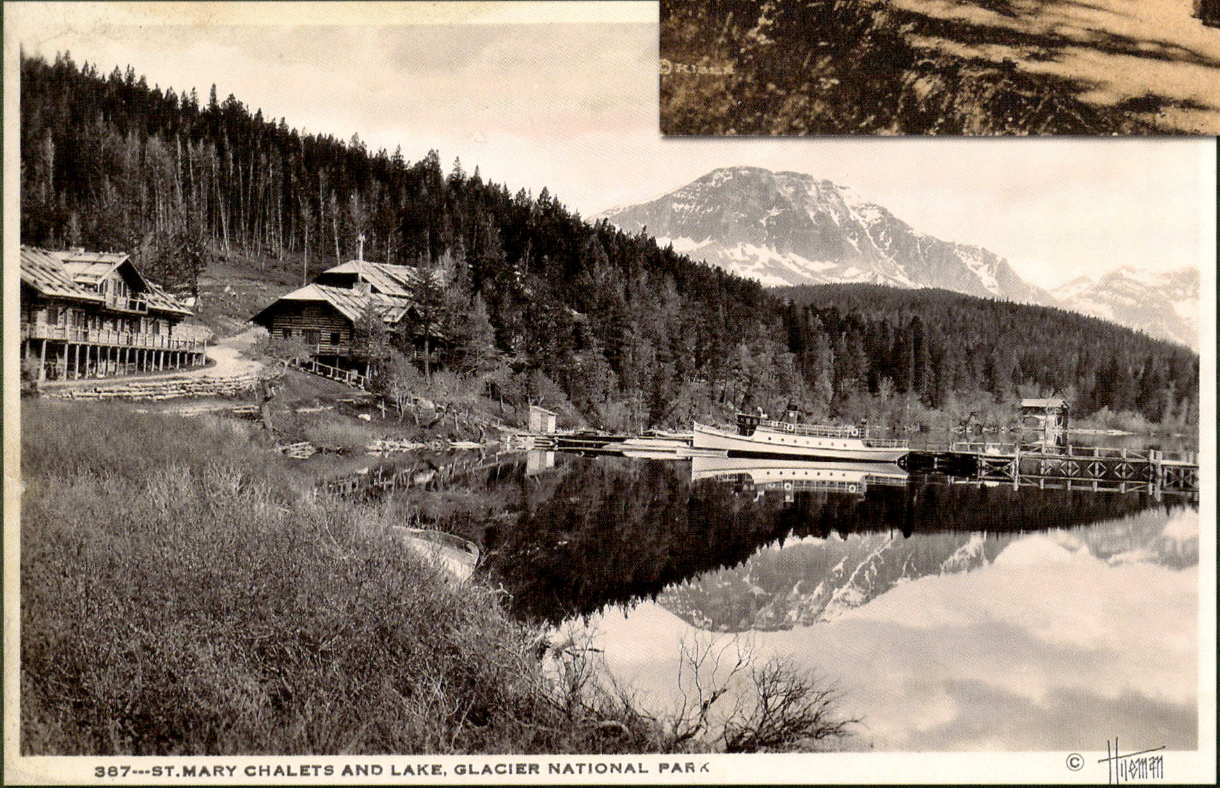

This later real photo Hileman postcard provides another view of St. Mary Chalets, the lake and boat dock, and the launch, which was ready for passengers.

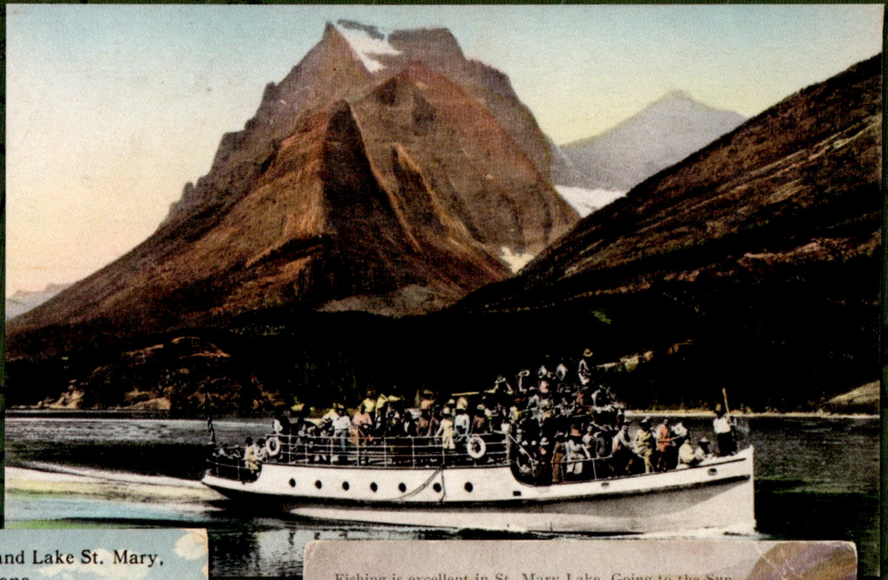

Captain William Swanson built the *St. Mary* launch in 1913. It was operated between the St. Mary and Going-to-the-Sun chalets. Hand-colored postcard published by Glacier Park Hotel Co. and made by Albertype Co.

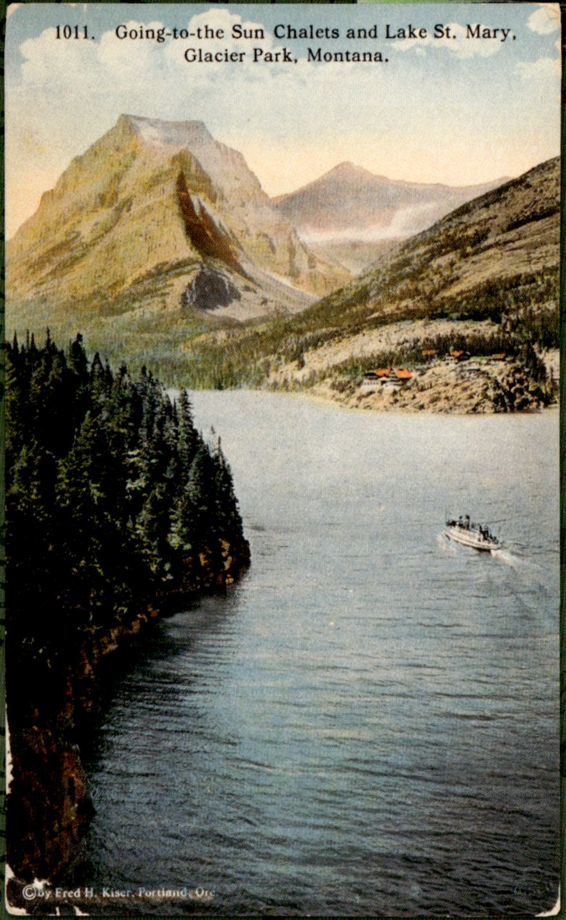

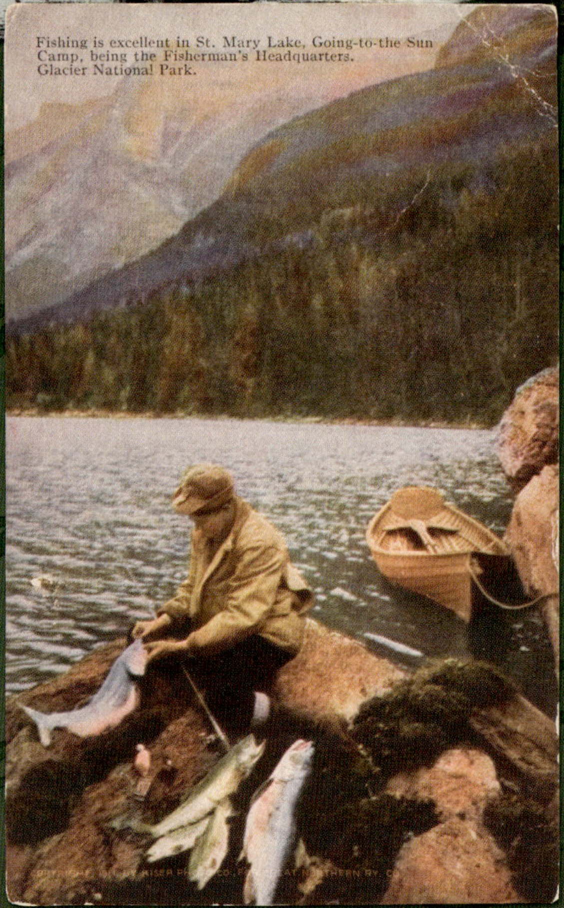

FAR LEFT : This early Kiser postcard of St. Mary Lake shows the launch heading to the Going-to-the-Sun Chalets.

IMMEDIATE LEFT : This fishing scene on St. Mary Lake was produced by the Great Northern Railway. No fishing license is required of visitors who fish in any of the hundreds of lakes and streams in the park.

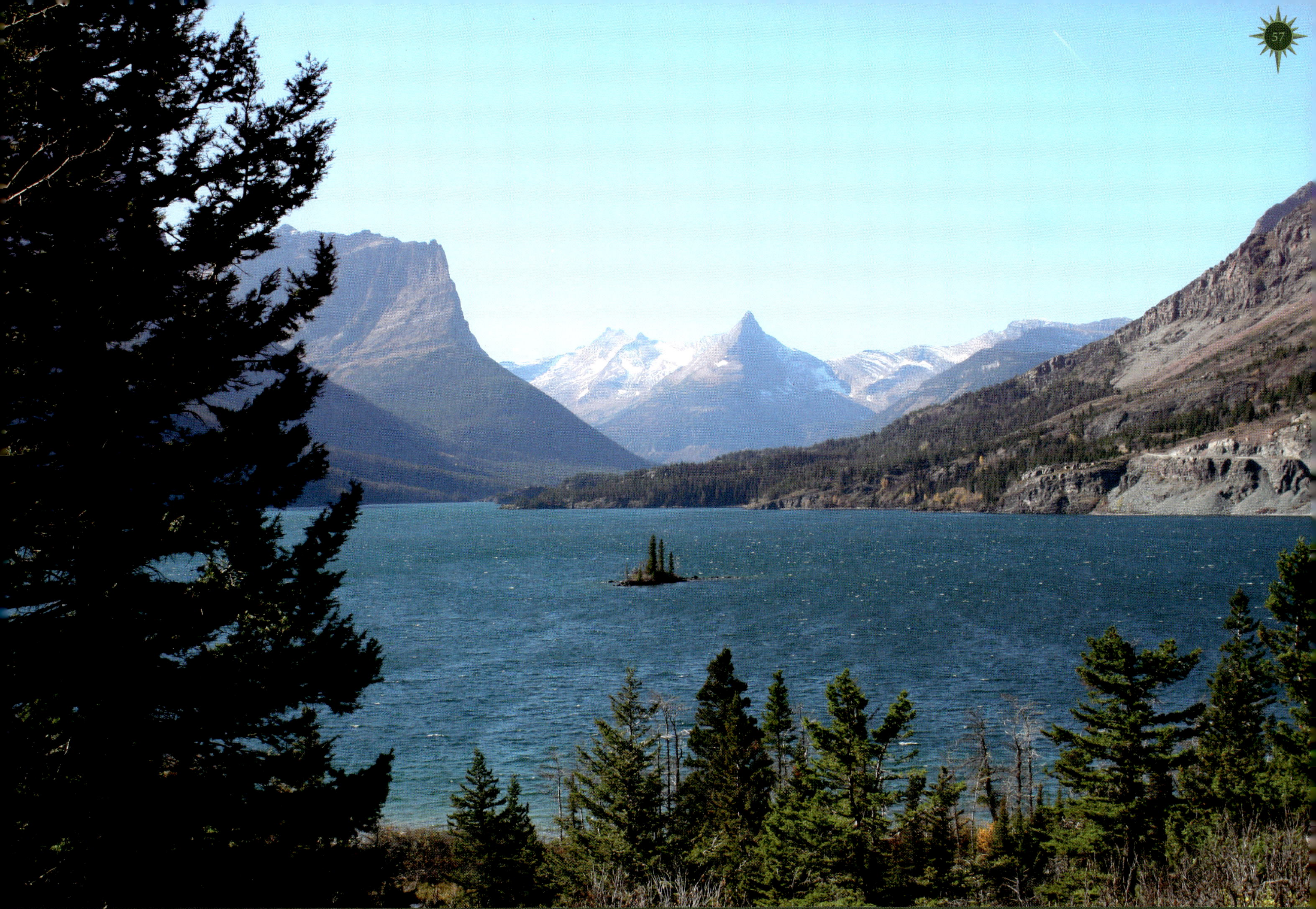

This recent view of St. Mary Lake features Wild Goose Island, with Jackson Glacier in the distance. *Courtesy of Bryan and Nicole Kohrmann.*

The first people to camp in the area were the Blackfeet natives. Although they were still camping in the park until the 1950s, it was done at the request of railroad officials to promote tourism. HHT Co. postcard picture by Kiser.

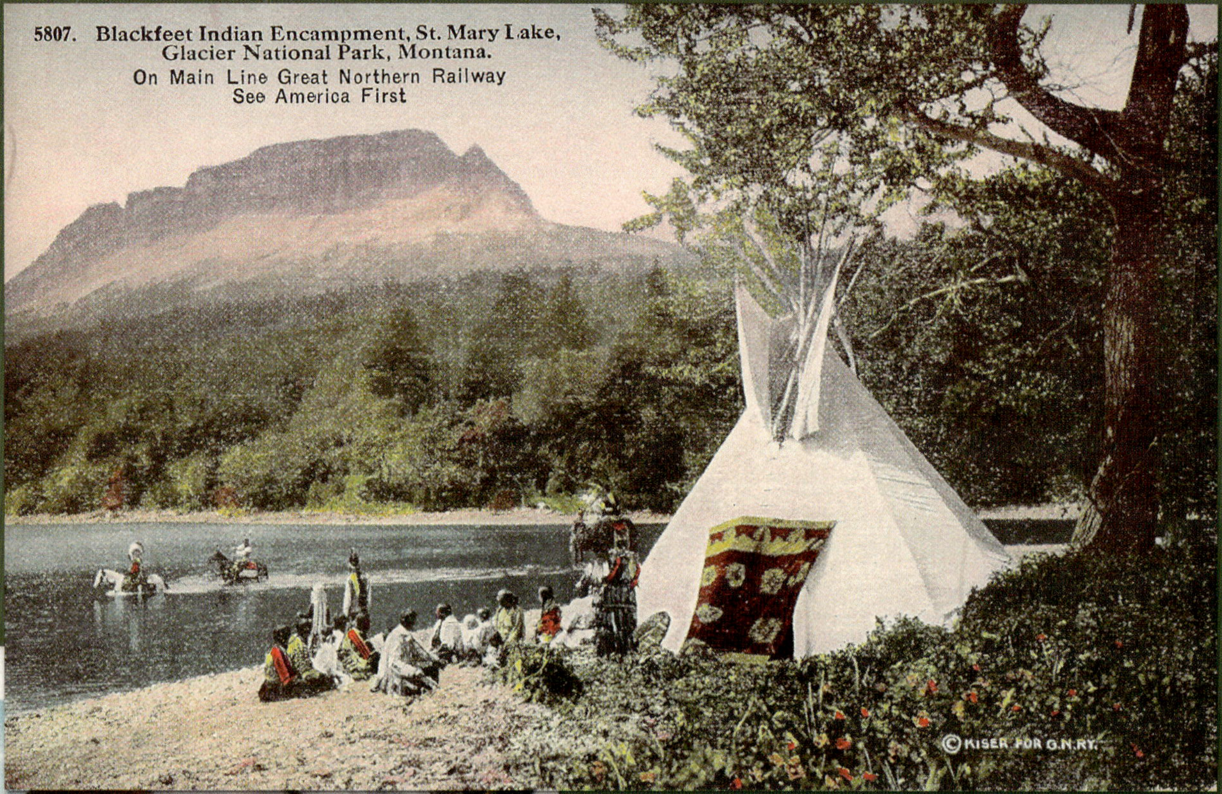

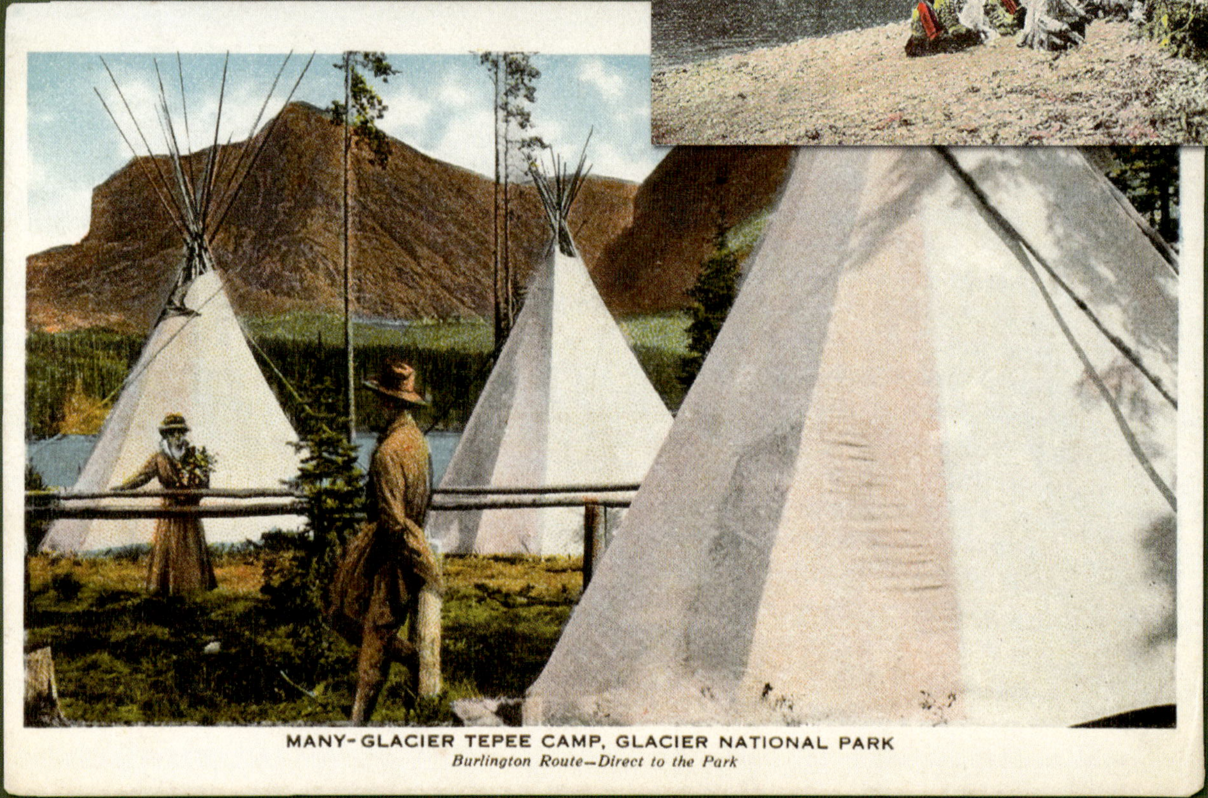

The earliest commercial camping facilities available for visitors were tepee camps located throughout the park. These areas included Lake McDonald, Cut Bank Camp, Two Medicine Chalets, St. Mary Chalets, Sperry, and Many Glacier. The tepees each held four beds and rented for fifty cents per night. Featured is the tepee camp at Many Glacier, circa 1911. A chalet was added in 1912 and included twelve cabins. Burlington Route postcard.

At ten miles long, St. Mary Lake is the second largest lake in the park and remains a visitor favorite. The Rising Sun Campground is located in the same general area that once was occupied by the St. Mary Chalets. It is along the lake and has eighty-three sites, toilets, showers, fire grates, picnic tables, and food service. Other Glacier Park Campgrounds include: Apgar, located at the southern shore of Lake McDonald; Avalanche Creek, along Going-to-the-Sun Road; Bowman Lake, at the northwest corner of Glacier; Fish Creek, on Lake McDonald; Kintla Lake, a remote site; Many Glacier, on Many Glacier Road; Sprague Creek, at Lake McDonald; Two Medicine, at Two Medicine Lake; and the Waterton Town Site in Canada. *Courtesy of Bryan and Nicole Kohrmann.*

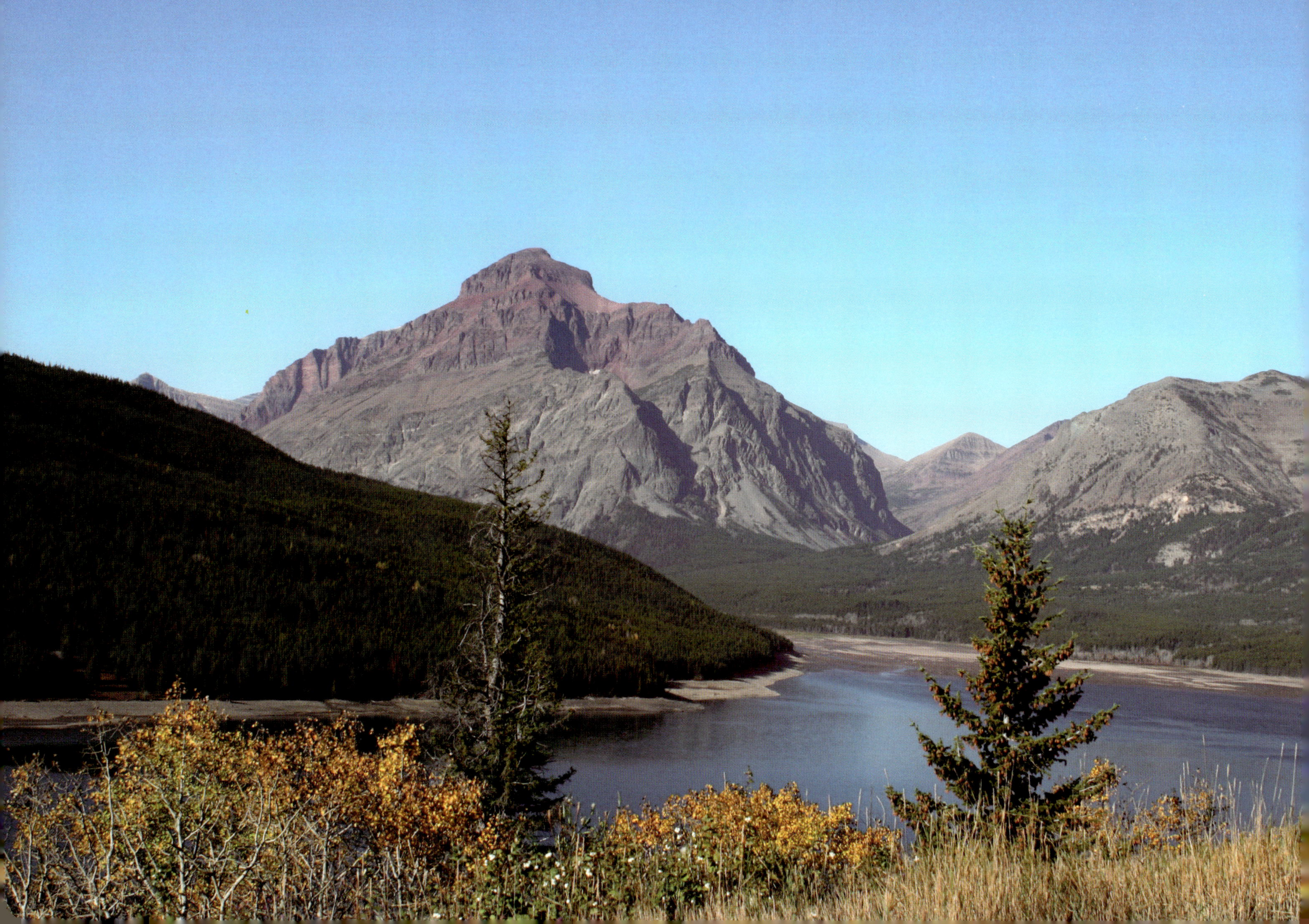

GOING-TO-THE-SUN CHALETS

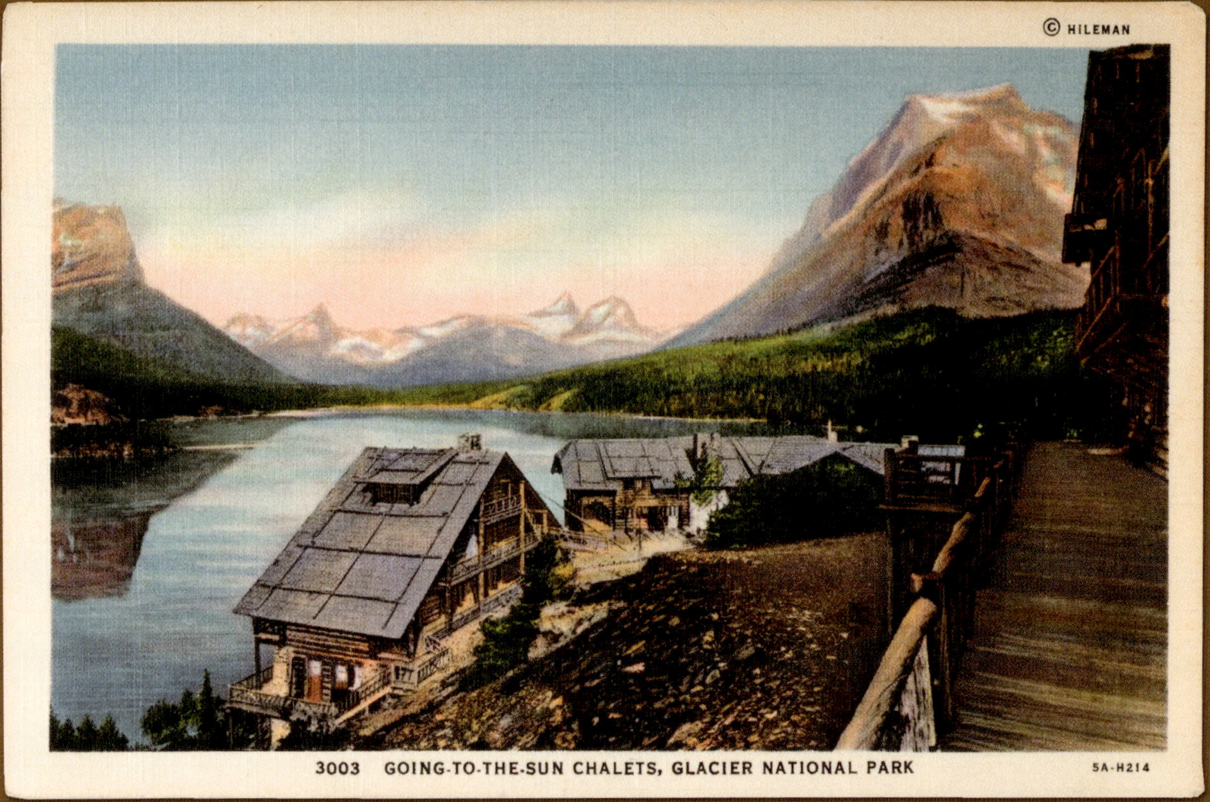

Going-to-the-Sun Chalets was the most popular of the railroad's chalets during its initial years and could only be reached by boat. It began as a temporary camp in 1911. By 1912, a kitchen, dining room, five cabins, and a two-story log building had been constructed. Hileman linen postcard for Glacier Park Hotel Co. by C. T. Art-Colortone.

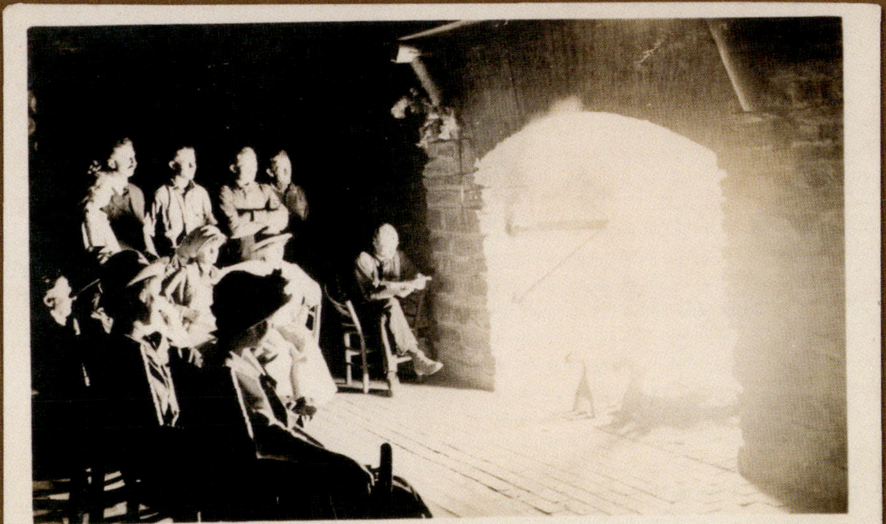
Evening around the fire-place, Going-to-the-Sun Chalets, Glacier National Park.

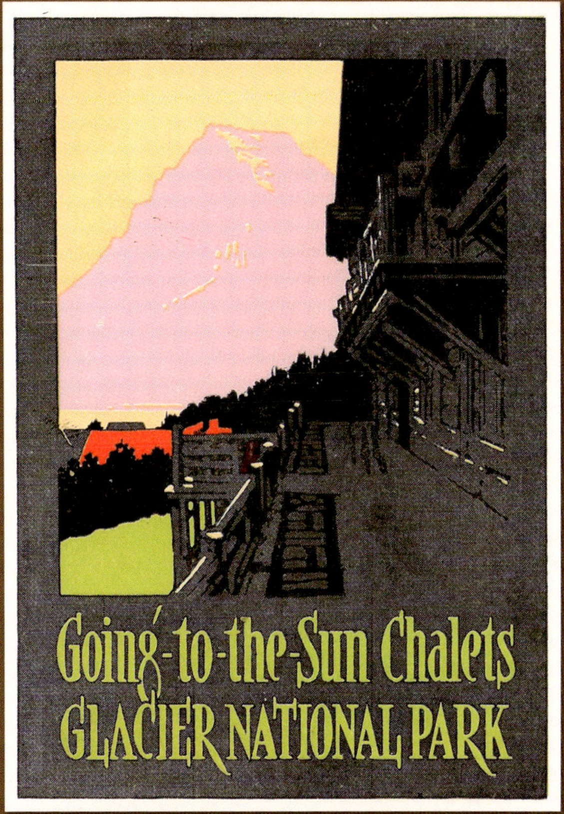

The chalets were expanded in 1915 and a large lobby was added where visitors could sit in front of the fire in the evening. Unmarked real photo postcard. **RIGHT**: Unmarked vintage decal.

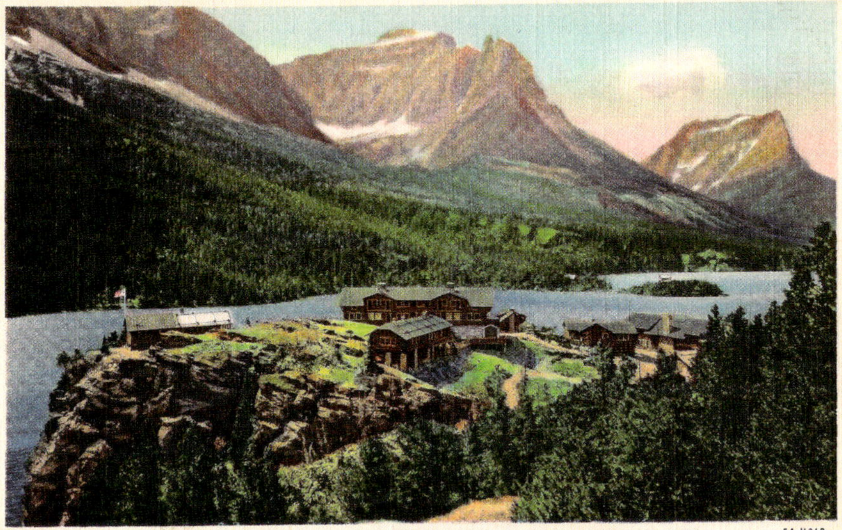
PHOTO BY HILEMAN

3104 GOING-TO-THE-SUN CHALETS, ST. MARY LAKE, GLACIER NATIONAL PARK 5A-H218

The popularity of the chalets declined following the convenience of the new Going-to-the-Sun Road and they were eventually closed. The area had been a hub for horse riders for decades. Postmarked 1937, this linen postcard offers a view of St. Mary Lake from Going-to-the-Sun Chalets. Several of the chalet buildings are featured, but by 1948 the buildings had been removed. C. T. Art-Colortone card published by the Glacier Park Hotel Co.

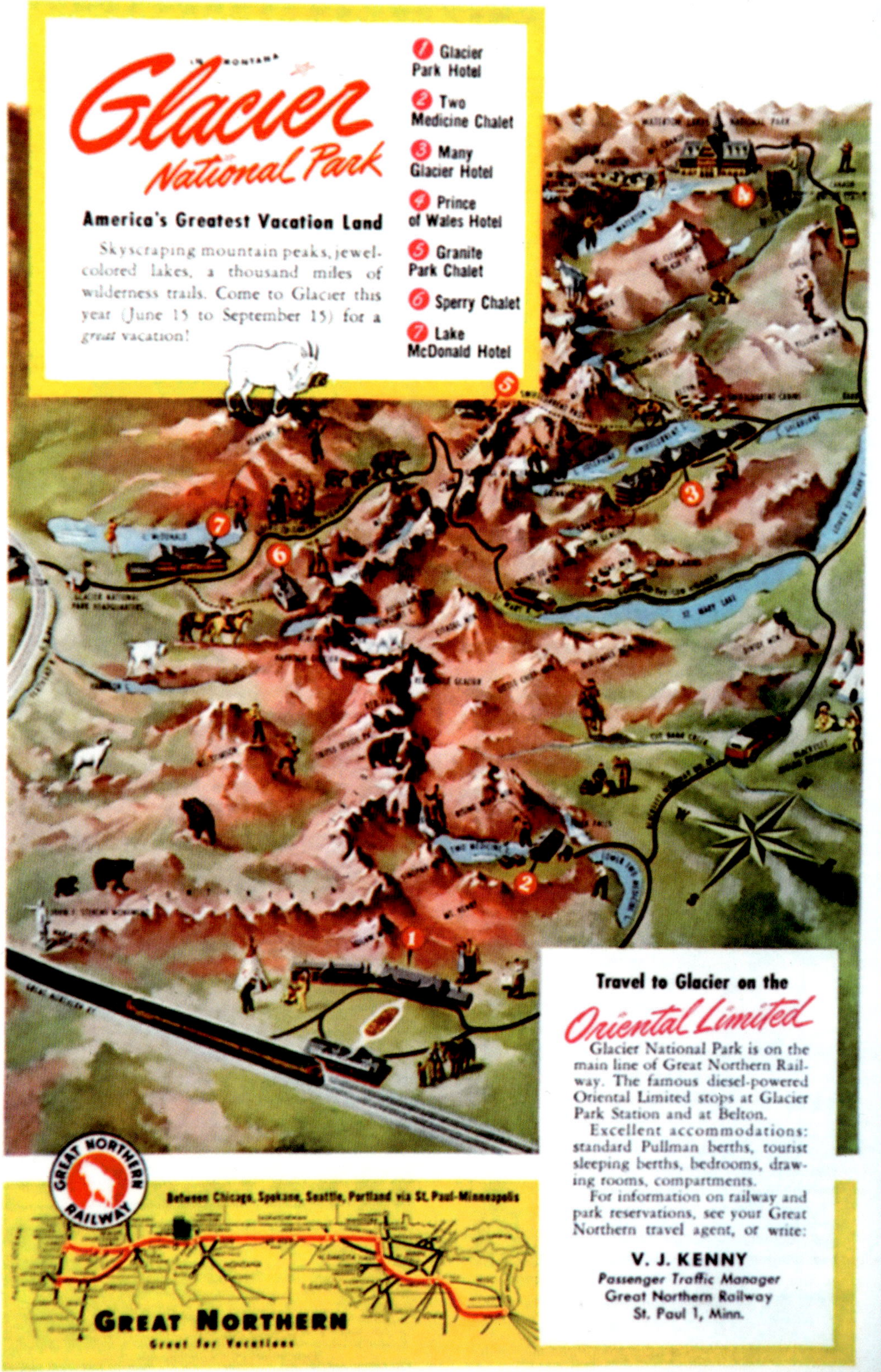

This Great Northern Railway map of Glacier Park features the various lodging facilities in the park circa 1948. Besides the large hotels, the Two Medicine, Granite Park, and Sperry chalets were included. The accompanying ad was promoting the famous diesel-powered Oriental Limited train that stopped at Glacier Park Station and Belton. The Oriental line was revived in 1947 after a sixteen-year absence.

GRANITE PARK CHALETS

The Granite Park Chalets sit at an altitude of 6,690 feet, the highest of all the chalets built by the railroad. They are reached only by trail. Built of stone from the area, the first chalet was opened in 1915. A larger two-story building was soon added. It included a combination lobby-dining room, kitchen, and storage area on the first floor and guest rooms on the second floor. Great Northern Railway "See America First" postcard. Also pictured is a luggage decal circa 1930s. *Courtesy Glacier National Park Archives.*

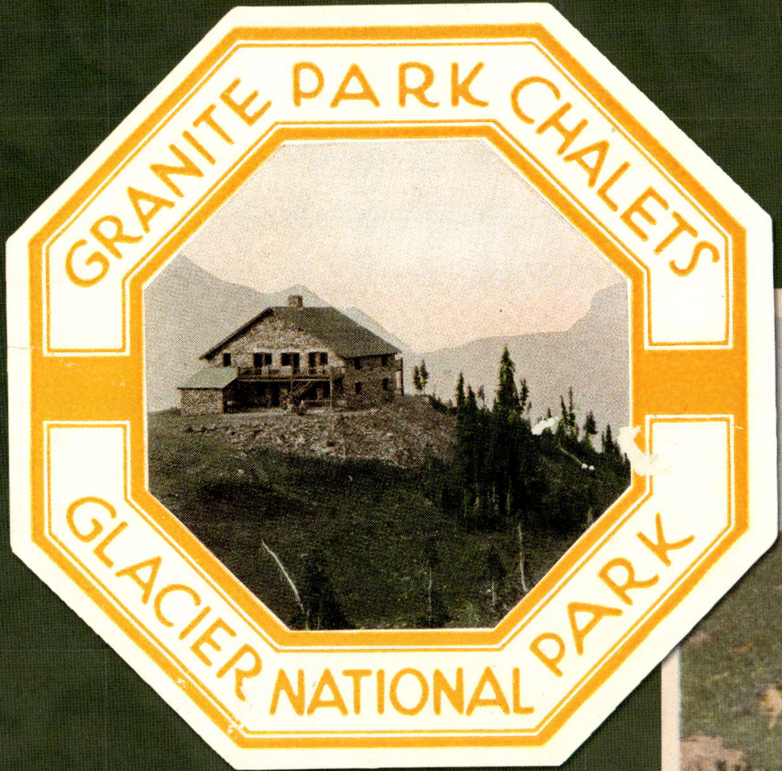

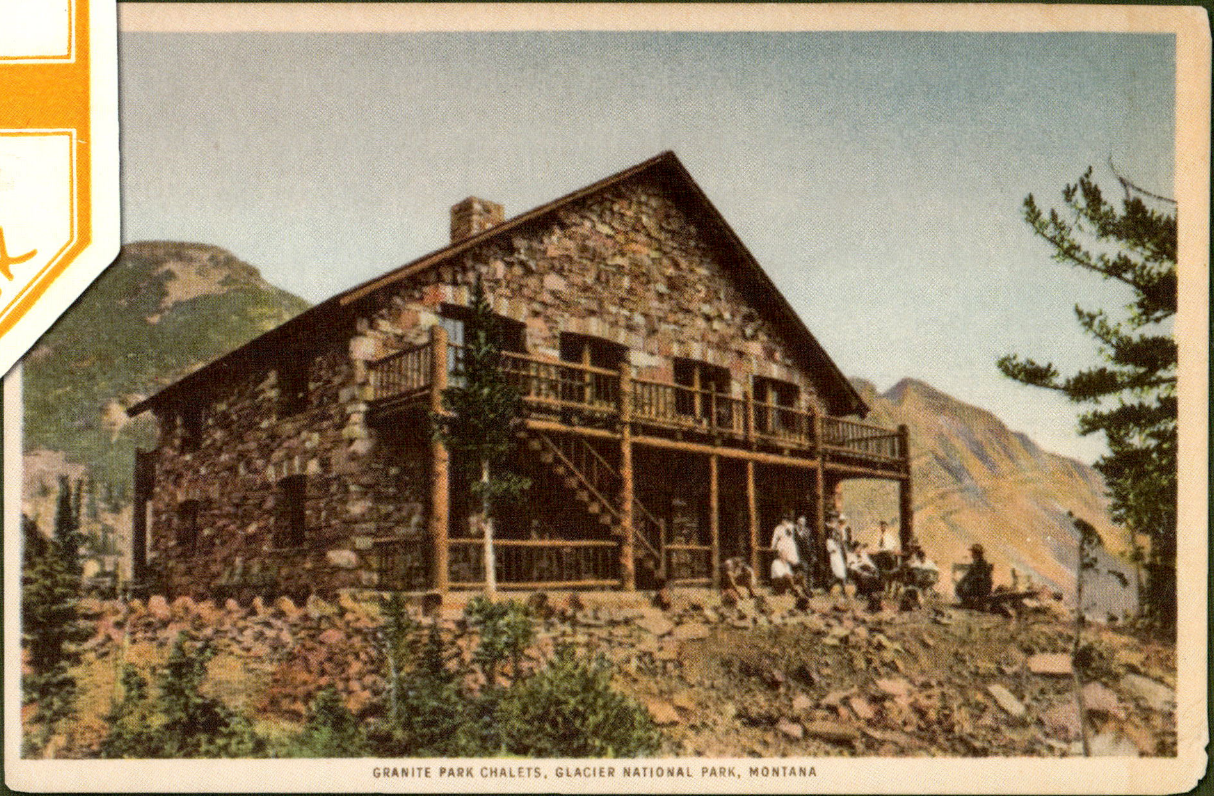

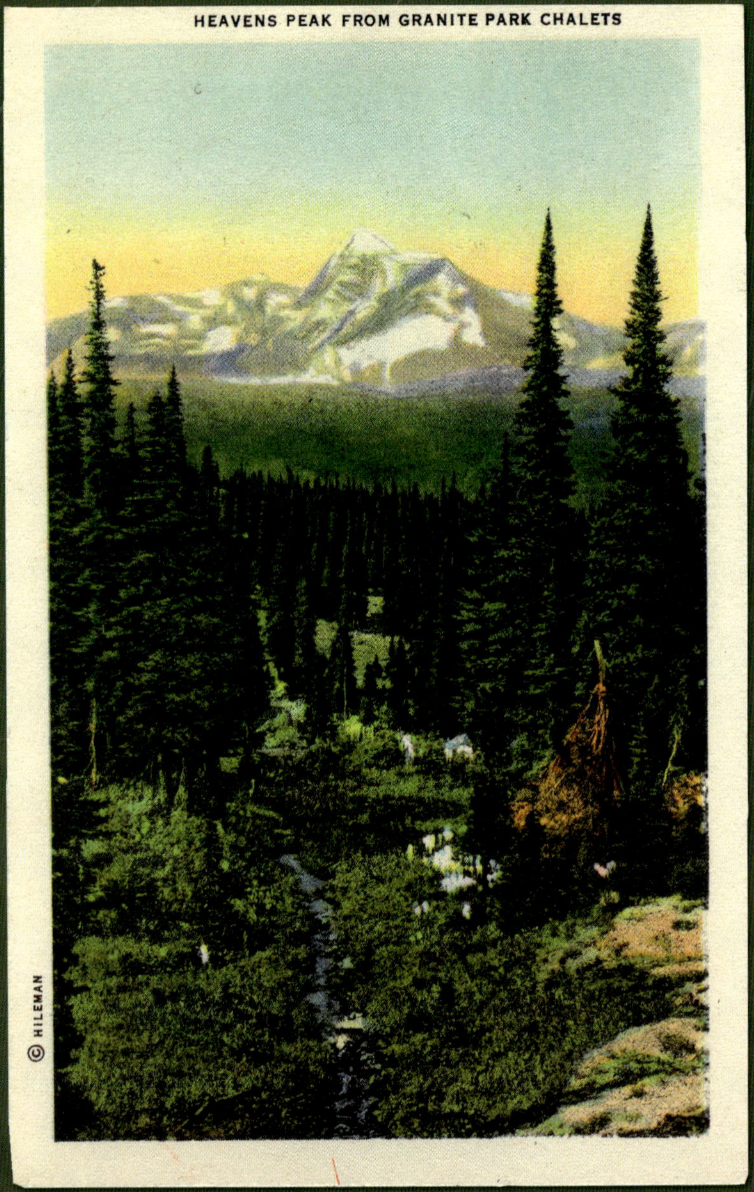

This early Hileman postcard shows the view from the Granite Park Chalets.

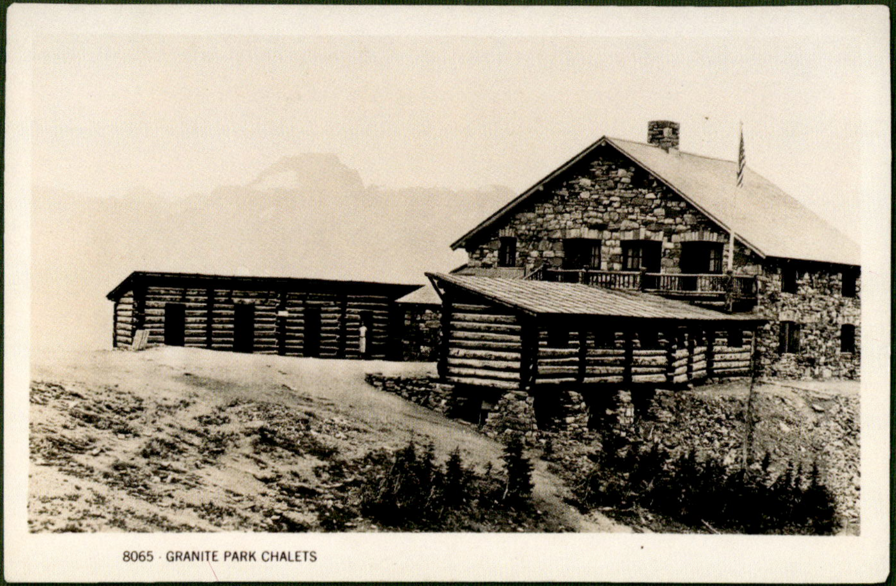

Twelve additional guest rooms, called "cribs," were added to the facility in the 1920s. The National Park Service purchased the chalets from the railroad in 1954 for $1.00. The chalets were closed in 1992 because of inadequate waste facilities. After repairs and upgrades, the chalets reopened in 1996 as an overnight shelter for hikers. It became a National Historical Landmark in 1987 and is operated by a private concessionaire.

75°

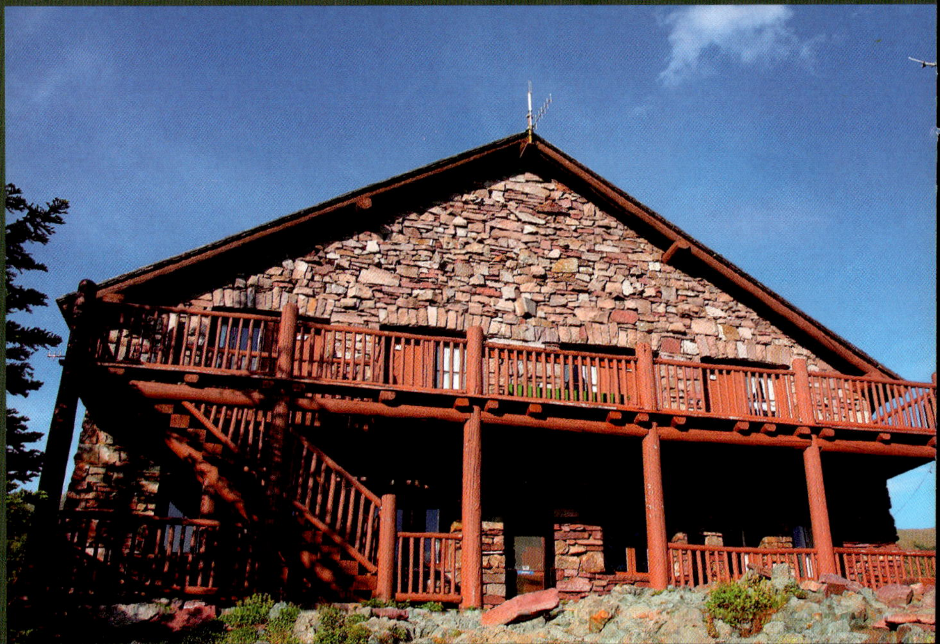

Granite Park Chalets as it looks today. *Courtesy I-Ting Chiang.*

SPERRY CHALETS

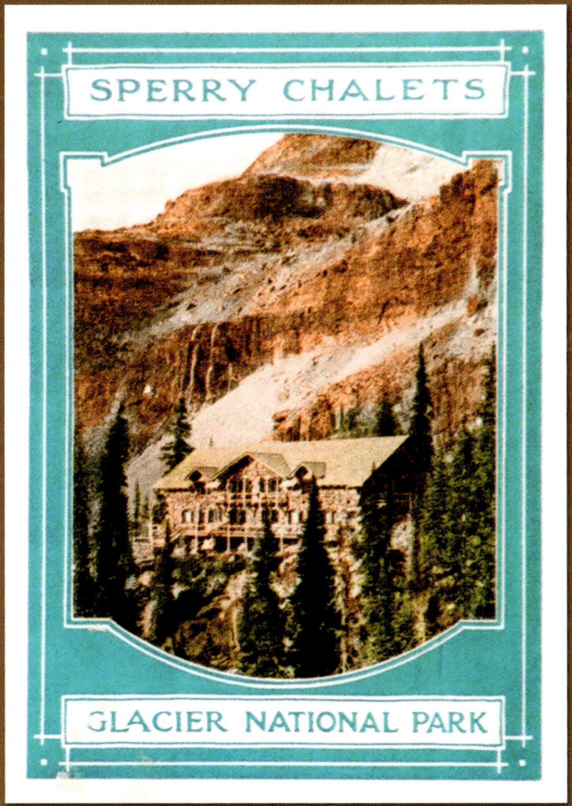

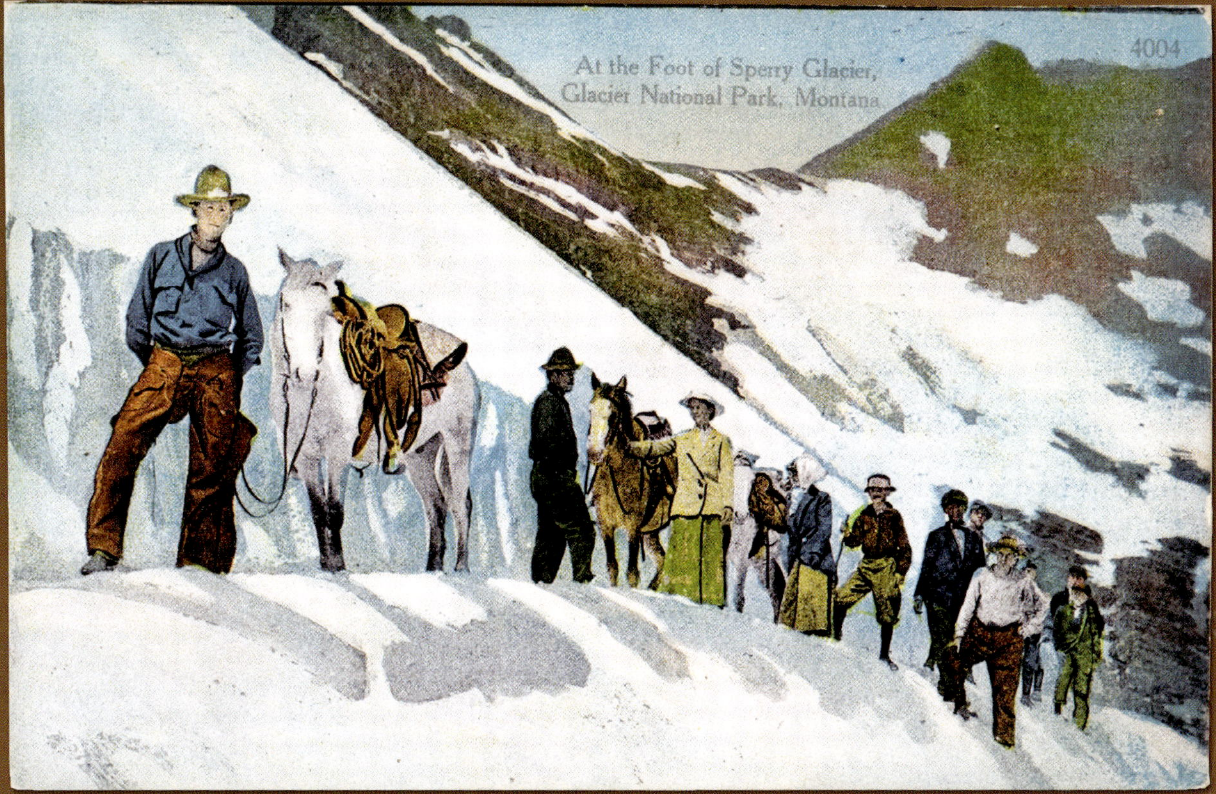

Sperry Glacier was named after Lyman B. Sperry, who explored it in 1896. It can be seen in the background of this luggage decal of the Sperry Chalets picturing the front of the dormitory building. The trip to the glacier is made easier by an overnight stay at the Sperry Chalets, which is about four miles away. Early postcard by HHT Co. pictures a riding party on the way to Sperry Glacier.

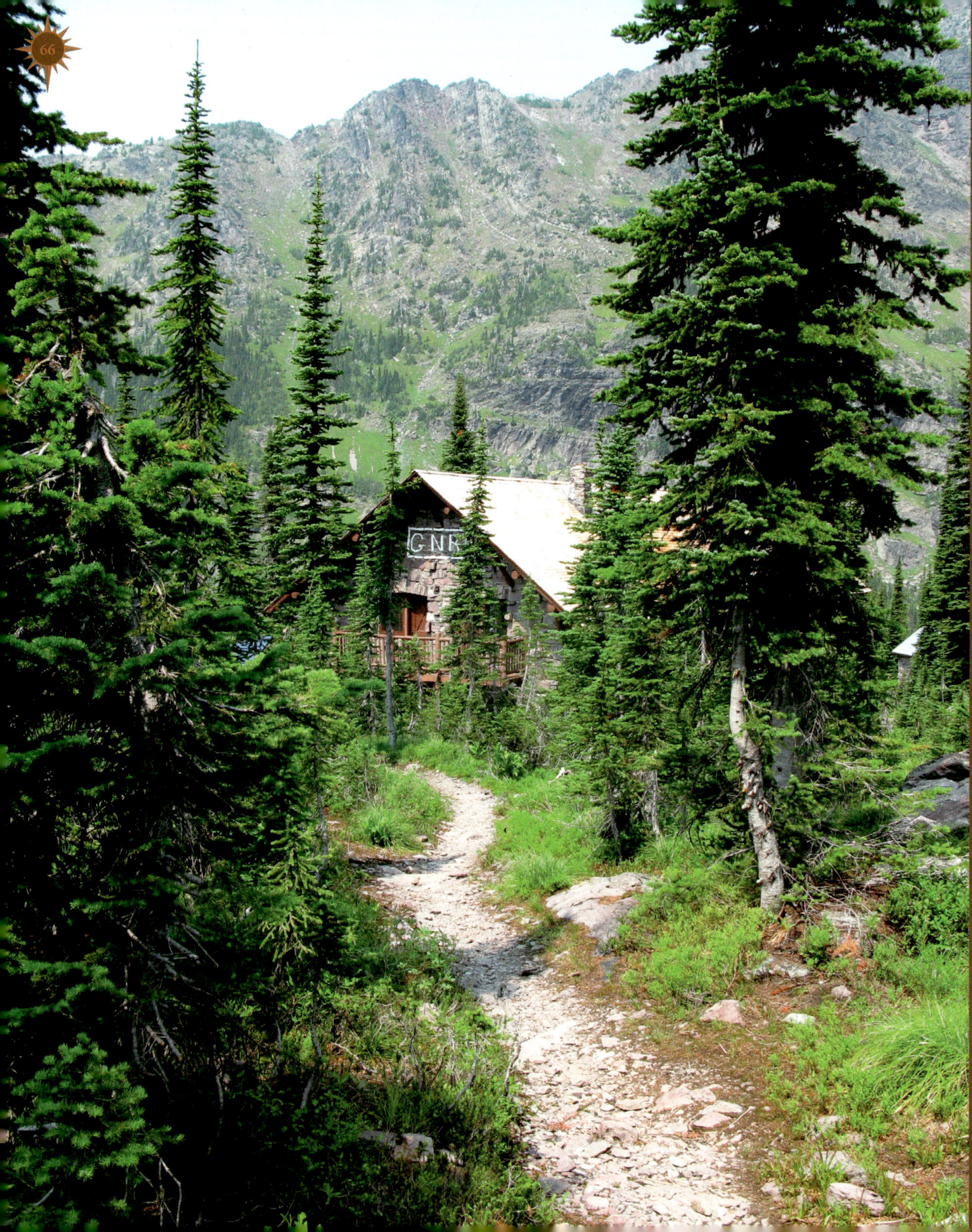

A 3,300-foot climb from Lake McDonald Lodge is one of the routes used to reach the remote setting of the Sperry Chalets, where hikers and riders are rewarded with wondrous views amid a peaceful setting.

OPPOSITE PAGE : The dormitory building for Sperry Chalets opened in 1914. Neither the Granite nor Sperry chalets has ever had electricity, hot water, inside toilets, or automobile access. When the dormitory was built, the building was marked "GNRY" for Great Northern Railway (pictured). One of the many mountain goats that inhabit the chalets is also shown.

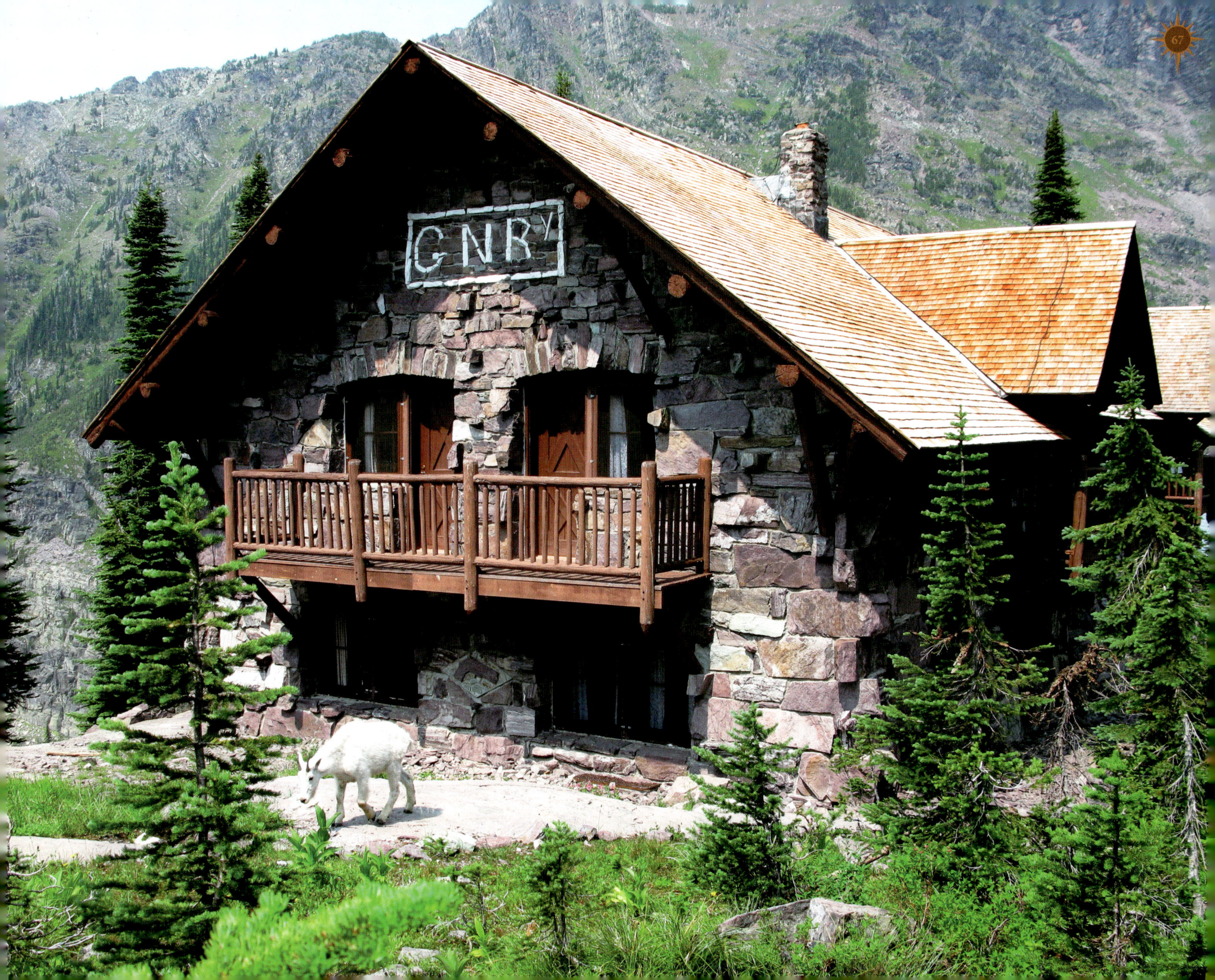
GNRY

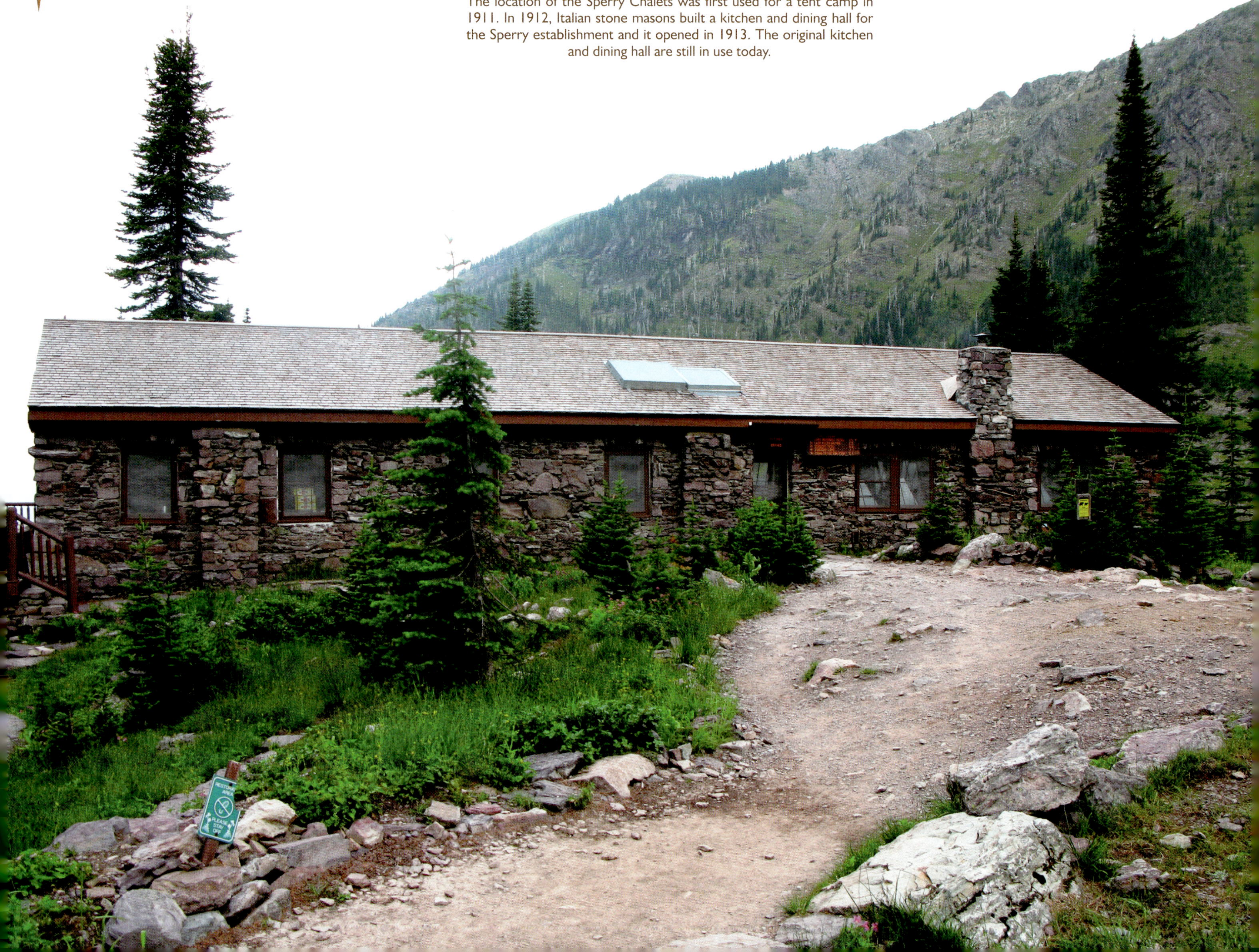

The location of the Sperry Chalets was first used for a tent camp in 1911. In 1912, Italian stone masons built a kitchen and dining hall for the Sperry establishment and it opened in 1913. The original kitchen and dining hall are still in use today.

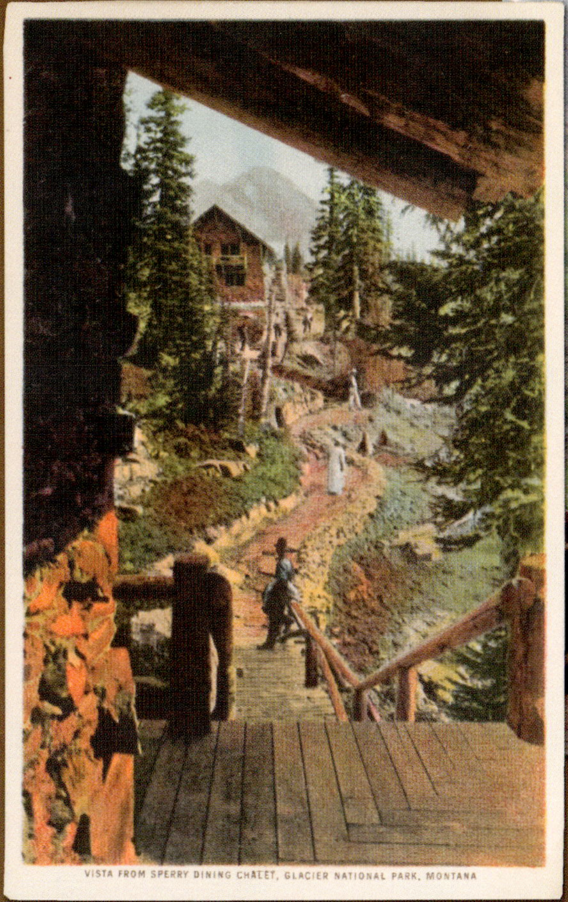

VISTA FROM SPERRY DINING CHALET, GLACIER NATIONAL PARK, MONTANA

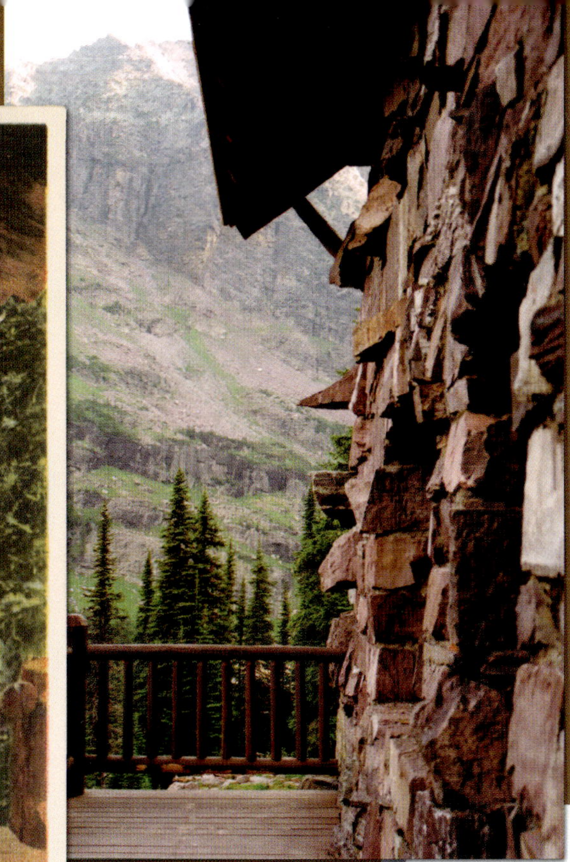

The Great Northern Railway sold the Sperry Chalets to the National Park Service in 1954 for $1.00 in a transaction that paralleled the transfer of ownership of the Granite Park Chalets. Sperry was also closed in 1992 to fix the inadequate sewer facilities. This "See America First" postcard shows the dormitory building from the dining chalet. Also pictured is a recent view from the dormitory balcony.

Sperry reopened in 1999 as a full-service chalet and can be reached by foot or horseback. The chalets and its surrounding area are pictured in this early postcard photographed by Hileman for the Glacier Park Hotel Co. Also shown is a recent photograph capturing a similar scene.

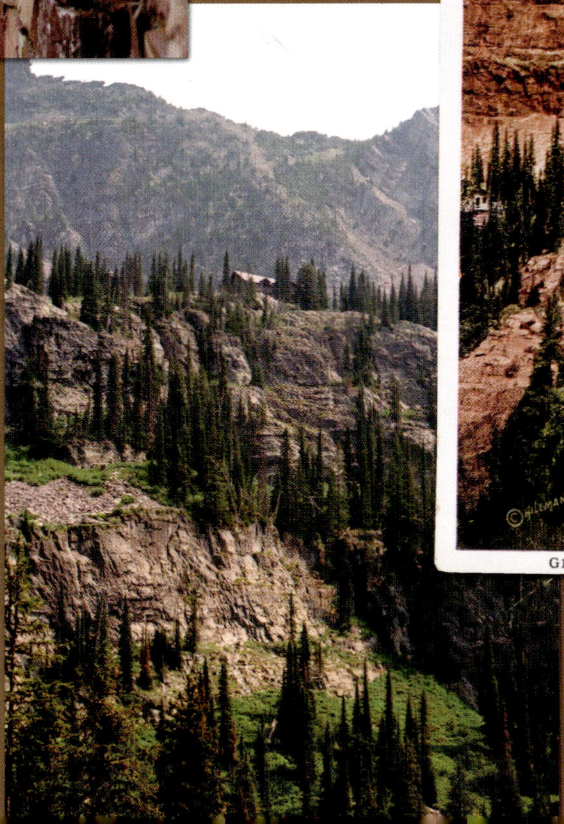

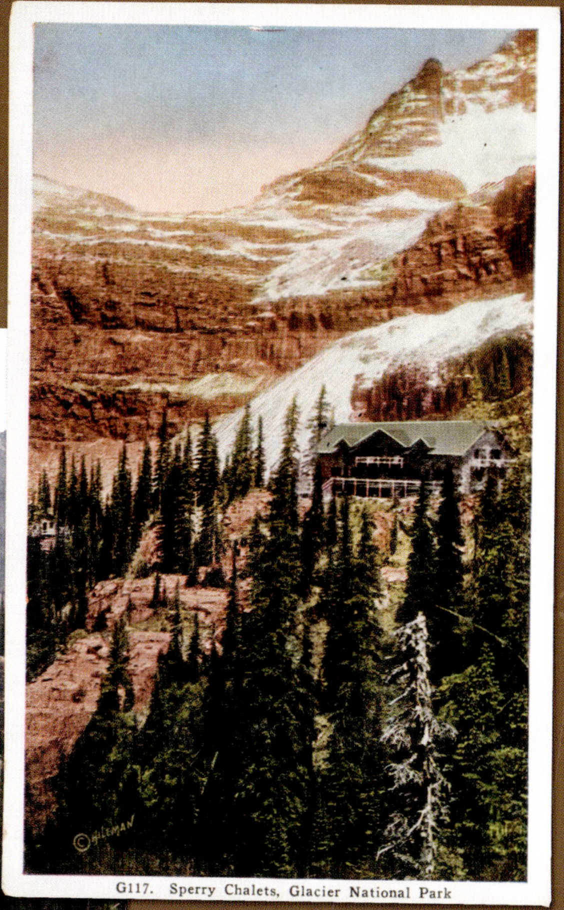

G117. Sperry Chalets, Glacier National Park

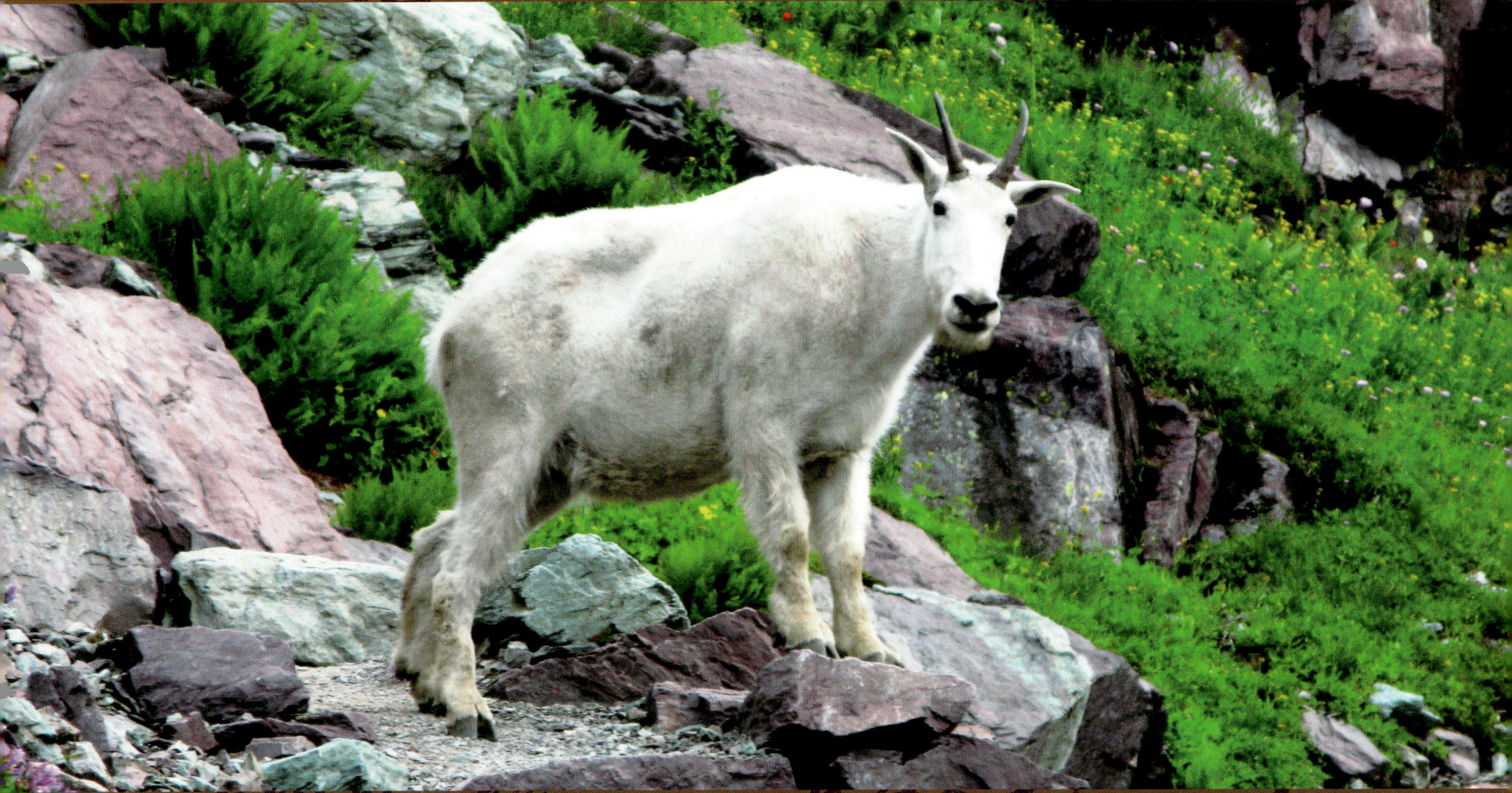

Mountain goats have been entertaining Sperry Chalet visitors for decades and their sightings are among the trip's highlights. The chalet is a National Historic Landmark and is operated by a private concessionaire.

BELTON CHALETS

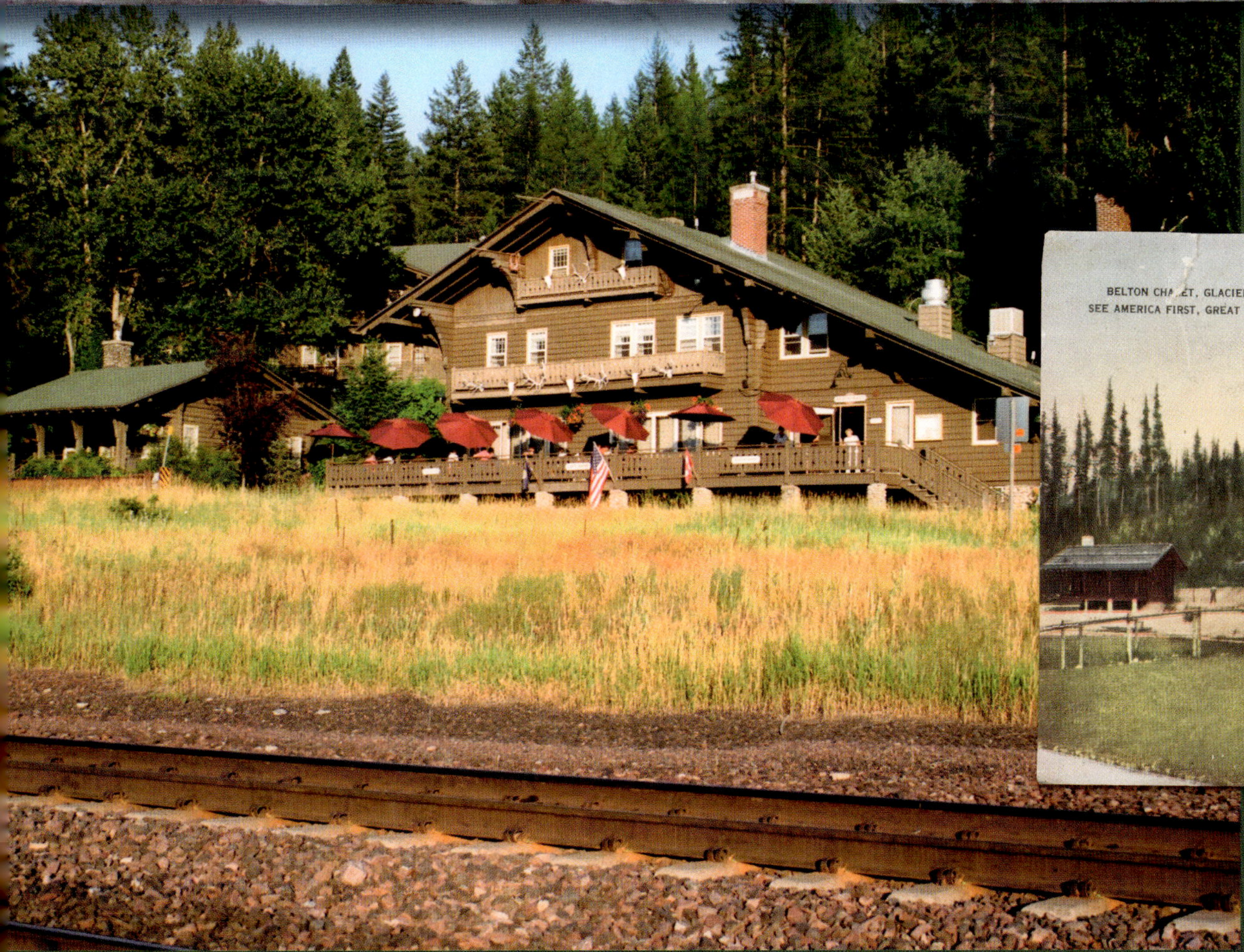

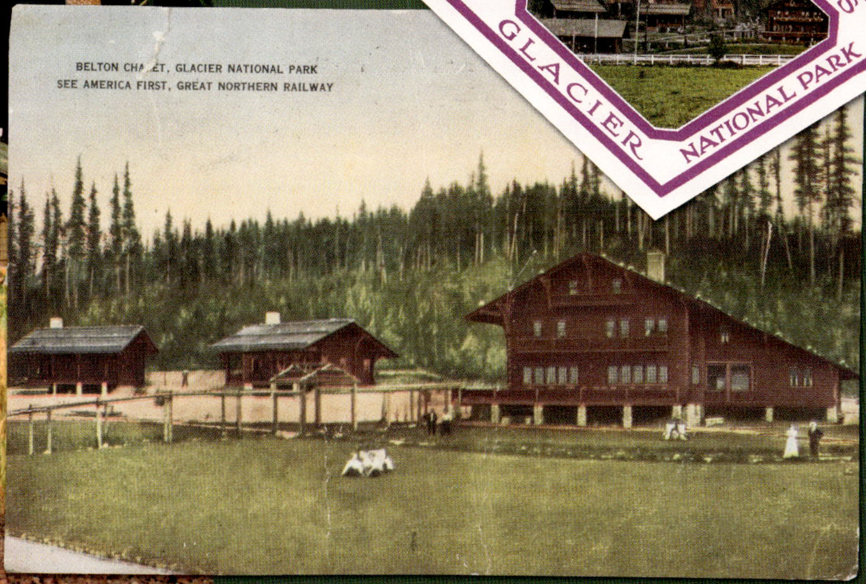

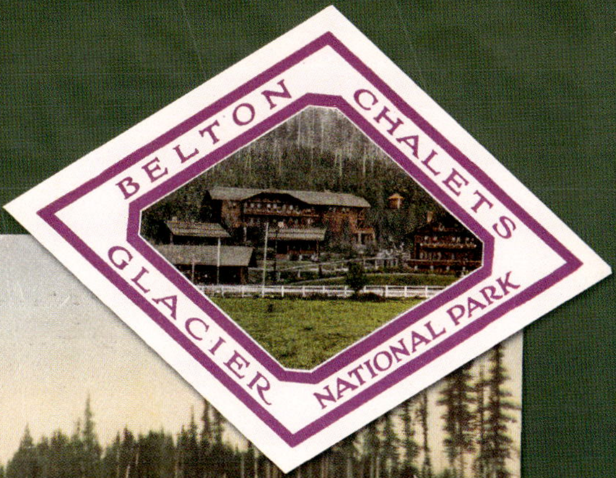

The first Great Northern Railway enterprise built to accommodate early train visitors to Glacier National Park was the depot and the Chalet at Belton, both of which were opened by 1910. Influenced by initial designs by Cutter and Malmgren Architects of Spokane, Washington, Belton Chalet features an unmistakable Swiss design that would be repeated in other railroad pursuits to reinforce its "American Alps" theme. During the next several years the building was enlarged and three others were added. This early postcard was postmarked 1914 and is marked "See America First." Great Northern Railway. Also pictured is a luggage decal circa 1930s. *Courtesy Glacier National Park Archives.*

Great Northern Railway sold the Belton Chalet in 1946 after the railroad's focus shifted to other areas of the park. The chalet was eventually purchased by Andy Baxter and Cas Still in 1997 and has undergone significant restoration.

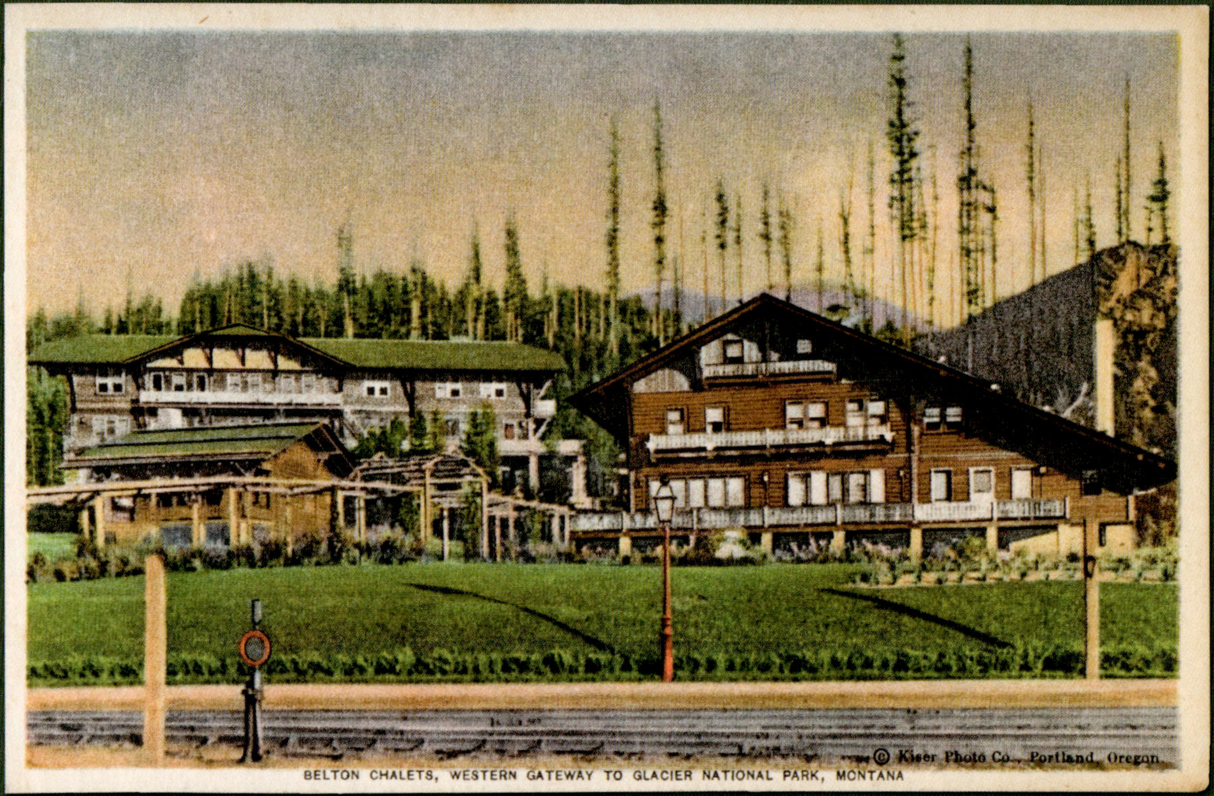

This Great Northern Railway Kiser Photo Co. postcard shows additional buildings of the Belton Chalet, which included two cottages and a dormitory. All four Belton Chalet buildings are listed on the National Register of Historic Places and as National Historic Landmarks. Today its handsome charm beckons guests who relish in the simple pleasures of the Arts and Craft décor and the ever-present sounds of trains rumbling down the tracks nearby. A restaurant now occupies the original chalet building.

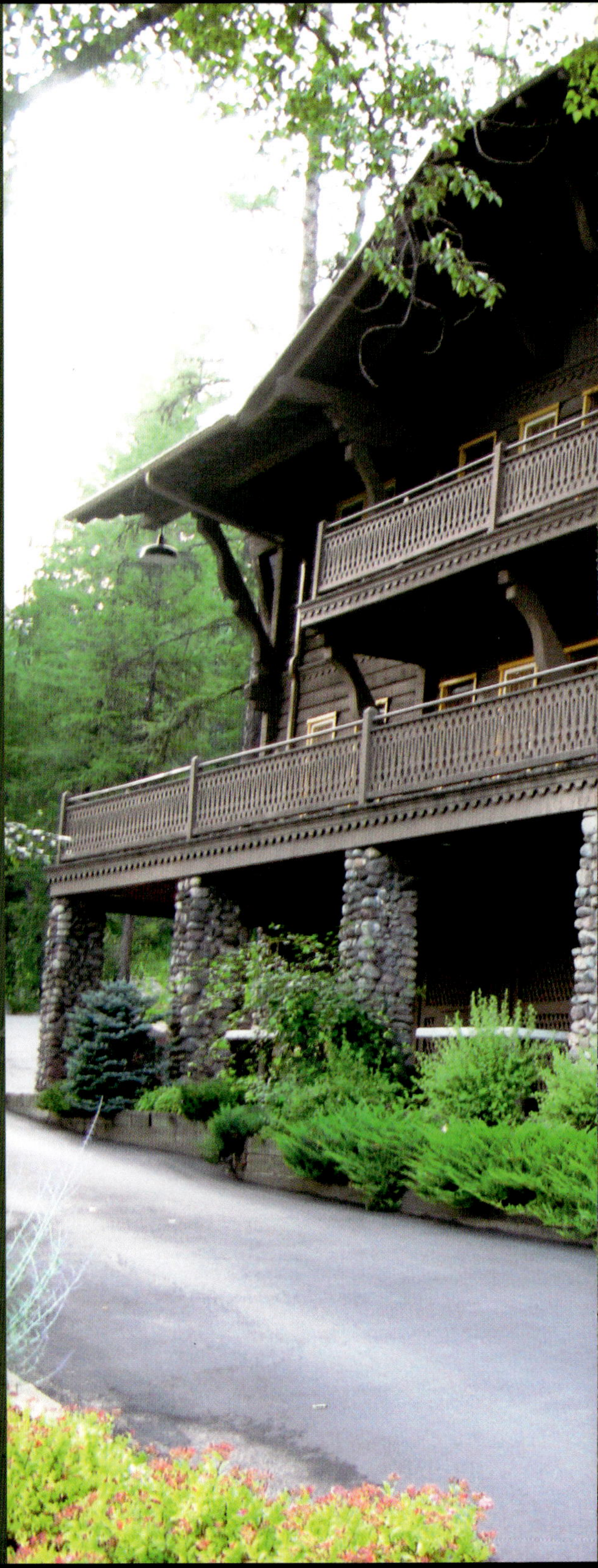

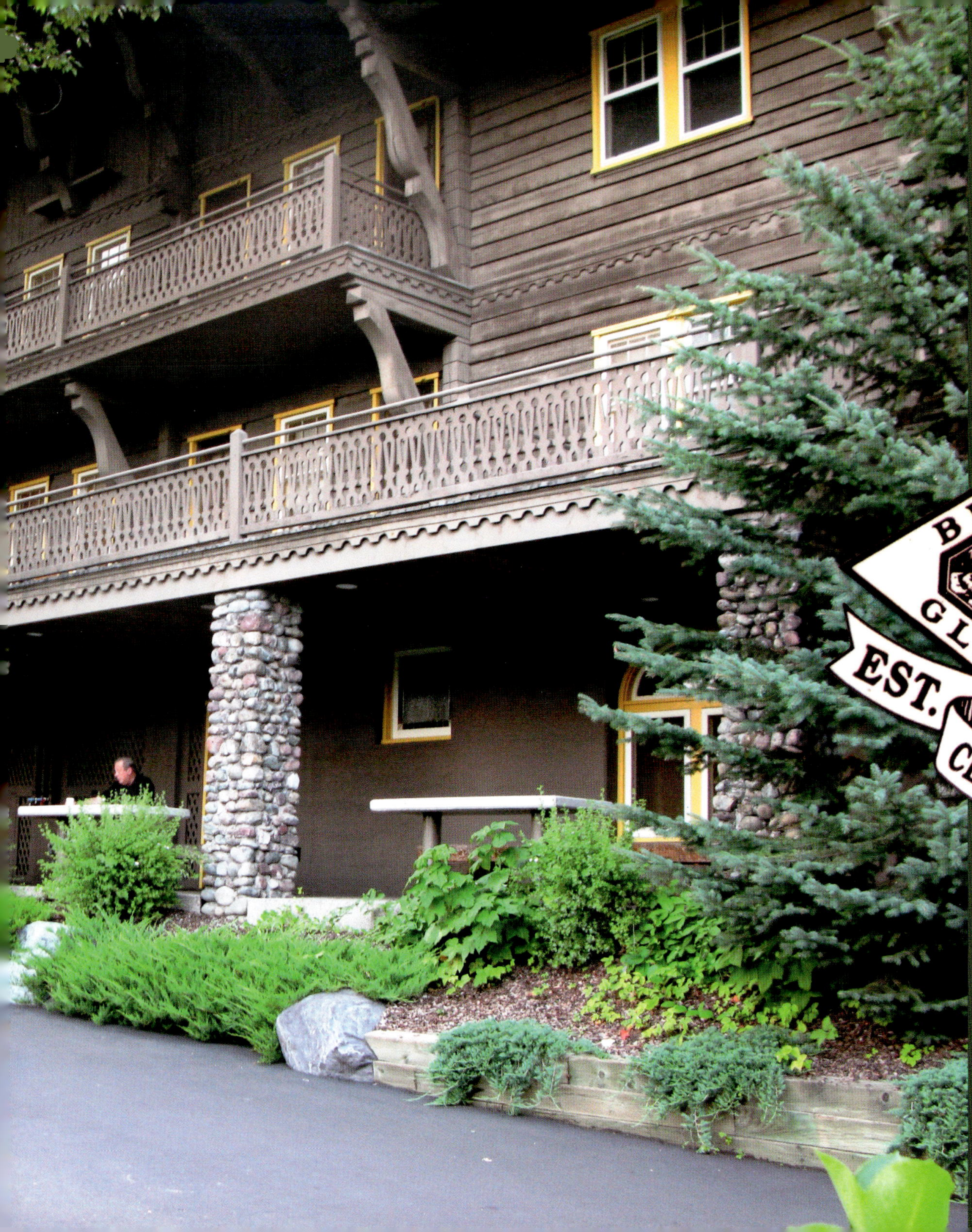

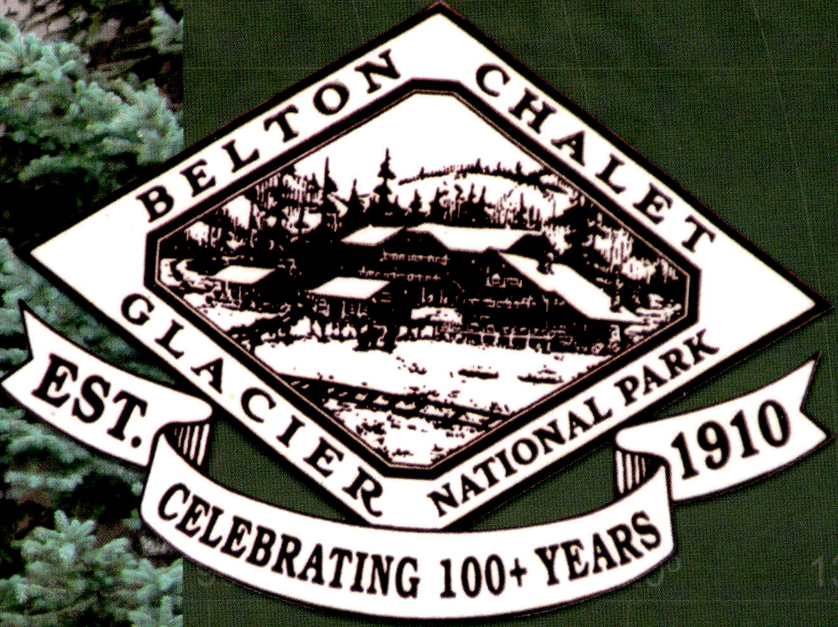

The lodge and lobby are now located in the original dormitory building and includes twenty-five period guest rooms with bathrooms and a lower level rec room. *Anniversary sticker courtesy of Belton Chalet.*

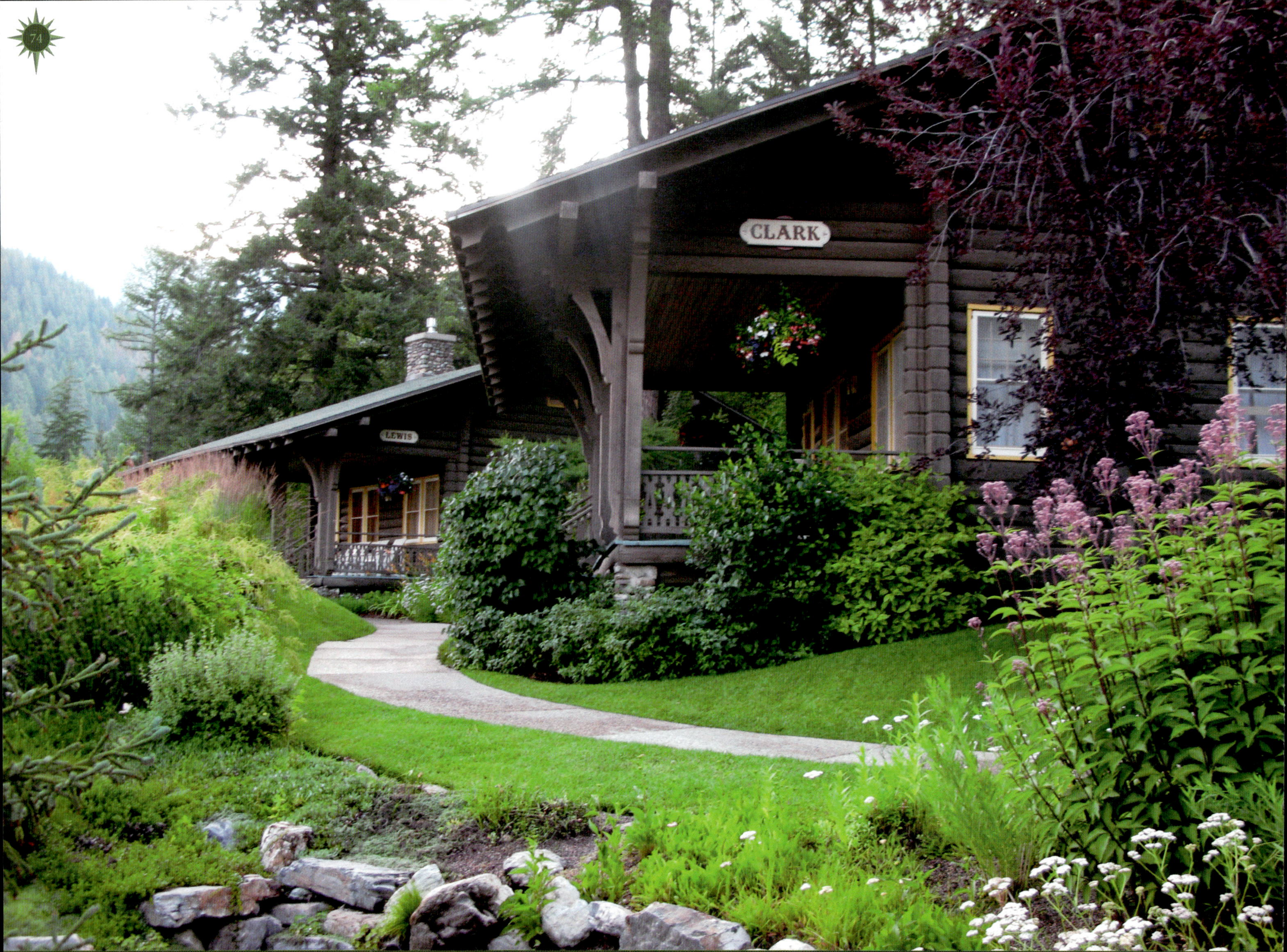

The Belton Cottages, Lewis and Clark, are surrounded by beautiful gardens. Each cottage has three bedrooms and can accommodate up to six guests.

ADDITIONAL LODGING

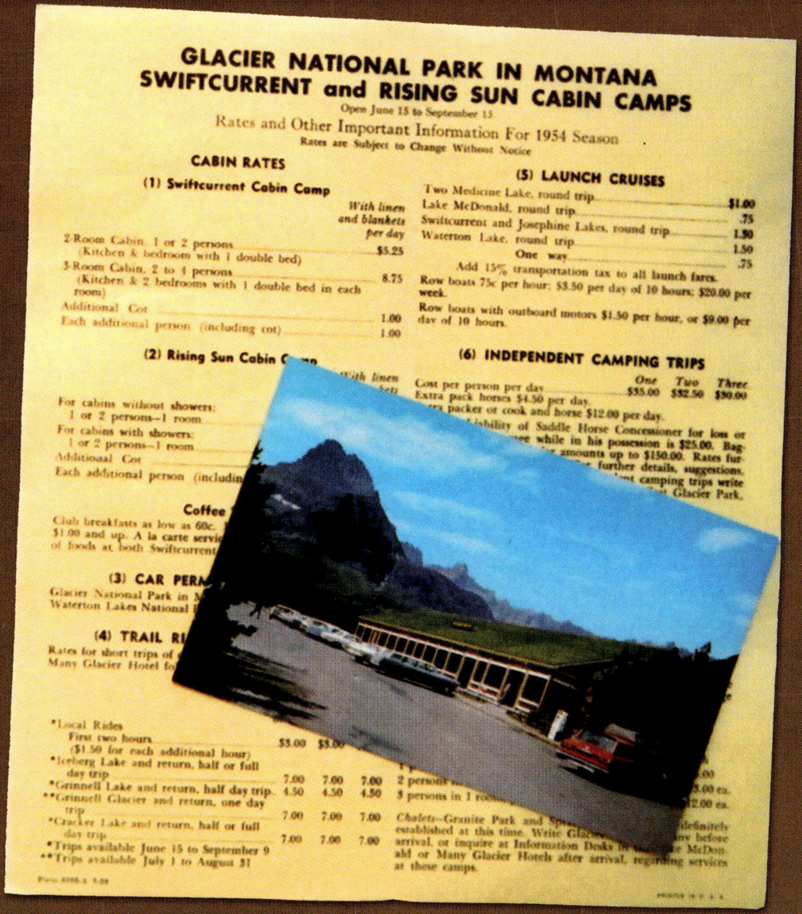

GLACIER NATIONAL PARK IN MONTANA
SWIFTCURRENT and RISING SUN CABIN CAMPS
Open June 15 to September 15
Rates and Other Important Information For 1954 Season
Rates are Subject to Change Without Notice

CABIN RATES

(1) Swiftcurrent Cabin Camp

	With linen and blankets per day
2-Room Cabin, 1 or 2 persons (Kitchen & bedroom with 1 double bed)	$5.25
3-Room Cabin, 2 to 4 persons (Kitchen & 2 bedrooms with 1 double bed in each room)	8.75
Additional Cot	1.00
Each additional person (including cot)	1.00

(2) Rising Sun Cabin C...

For cabins without showers:
1 or 2 persons—1 room
For cabins with showers:
1 or 2 persons—1 room
Additional Cot
Each additional person (includin...

Coffee ...

Club breakfasts as low as 60c. ...
$1.00 and up. A la carte servi...
of foods at both Swiftcurrent...

(3) CAR PERM...

Glacier National Park in M...
Waterton Lakes National ...

(4) TRAIL RI...

Rates for short trips of ...
Many Glacier Hotel fo...

*Local Rides First two hours ($1.50 for each additional hour)	$5.00	$5.00	
*Iceberg Lake and return, half or full day trip	7.00	7.00	7.00
*Grinnell Lake and return, half day trip	4.50	4.50	4.50
**Grinnell Glacier and return, one day trip	7.00	7.00	7.00
*Cracker Lake and return, half or full day trip	7.00	7.00	7.00

*Trips available June 15 to September 9
**Trips available July 1 to August 31

(5) LAUNCH CRUISES

Two Medicine Lake, round trip	$1.00
Lake McDonald, round trip	.75
Swiftcurrent and Josephine Lakes, round trip	1.50
Waterton Lake, round trip	1.50
One way	.75

Add 15% transportation tax to all launch fares.
Row boats 75c per hour; $3.50 per day of 10 hours; $20.00 per week.
Row boats with outboard motors $1.50 per hour, or $9.00 per day of 10 hours.

(6) INDEPENDENT CAMPING TRIPS

	One	Two	Three
Cost per person per day	$55.00	$52.50	$50.00

Extra pack horses $4.50 per day.
...packer or cook and horse $12.00 per day.
...iability of Saddle Horse Concessioner for loss or ...re while in his possession is $25.00. Bag... amounts up to $150.00. Rates fur... further details, suggestions, ...t camping trips write ... Glacier Park.

2 persons ...
3 persons in 1 ro...

Chalets—Granite Park and Sp... ...definitely established at this time. Write Glac... ...y before arrival, or inquire at Information Desks ... McDonald or Many Glacier Hotels after arrival, regarding services at these camps.

Visitors have also enjoyed motel-like accommodations that can be found at Swiftcurrent Motor Inn. Originally called Swiftcurrent Auto Cabins, it was built in the mid-1930s after the National Park Service pressured the railroad to offer inexpensive lodging. Twenty-seven cabins were constructed about a mile from Many Glacier Hotel. Additional cabins and motel-type units were later added. A brochure and a vintage postcard by H. S. Crocker, Inc. are shown. The pictured property is listed on the National Register of Historic Places and is operated by Glacier Park, Inc.

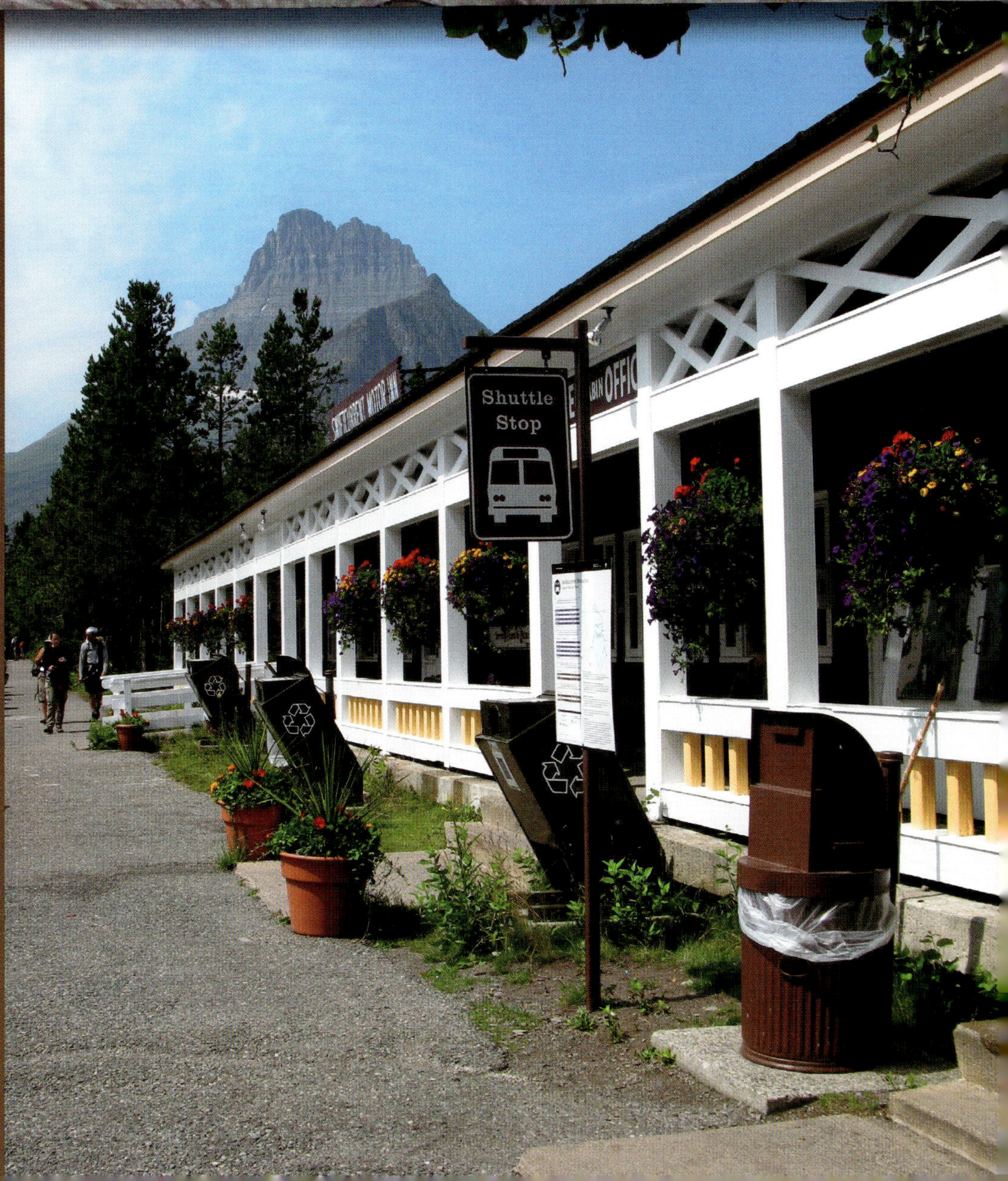

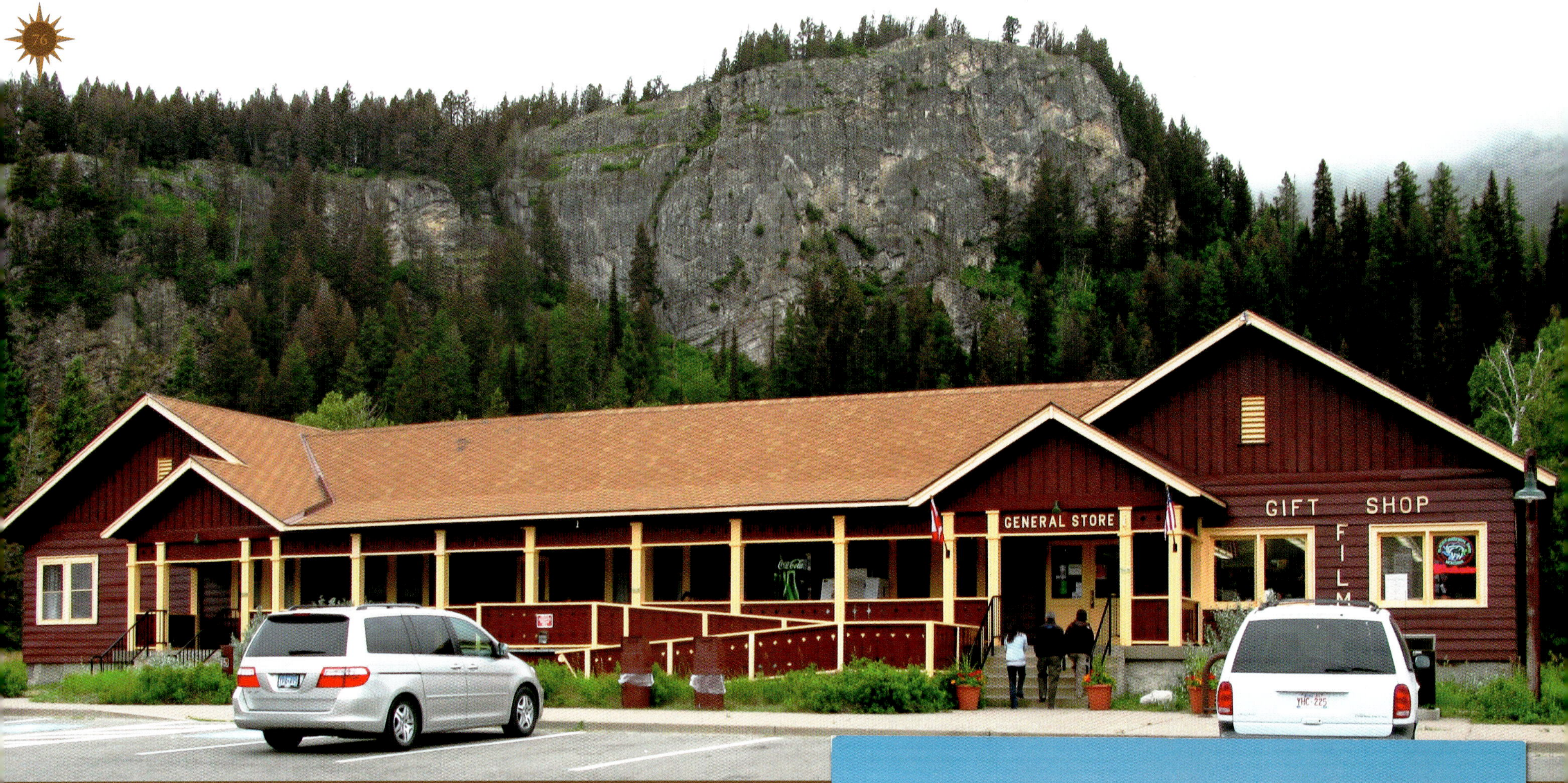

Rising Sun Motor Inn was first called East Glacier Auto Cabins when it was built in 1940 in the northeast section of the park at St. Mary Lake. It now includes cabins and motel units, which are among six concession properties managed by Glacier Park, Inc., authorized by the National Park Service. It was added to the National Register of Historic Places in 1996.

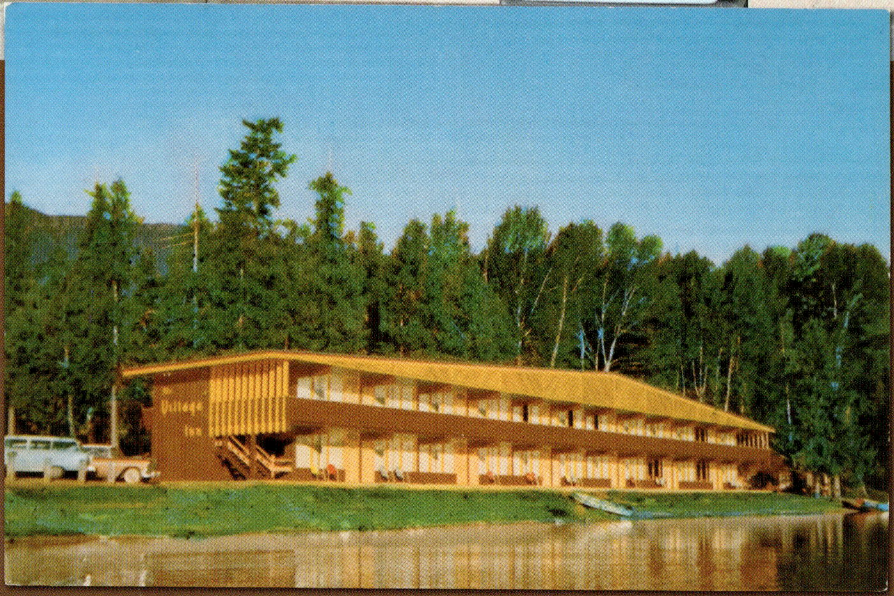

The Village Inn at Apgar was built on the shore of Lake McDonald in 1956 by Bill Mackin. He sold the property to the National Park Service in 1959. It was added to the National Register of Historic Places in 1987. Postcard by Security Lithograph Co.

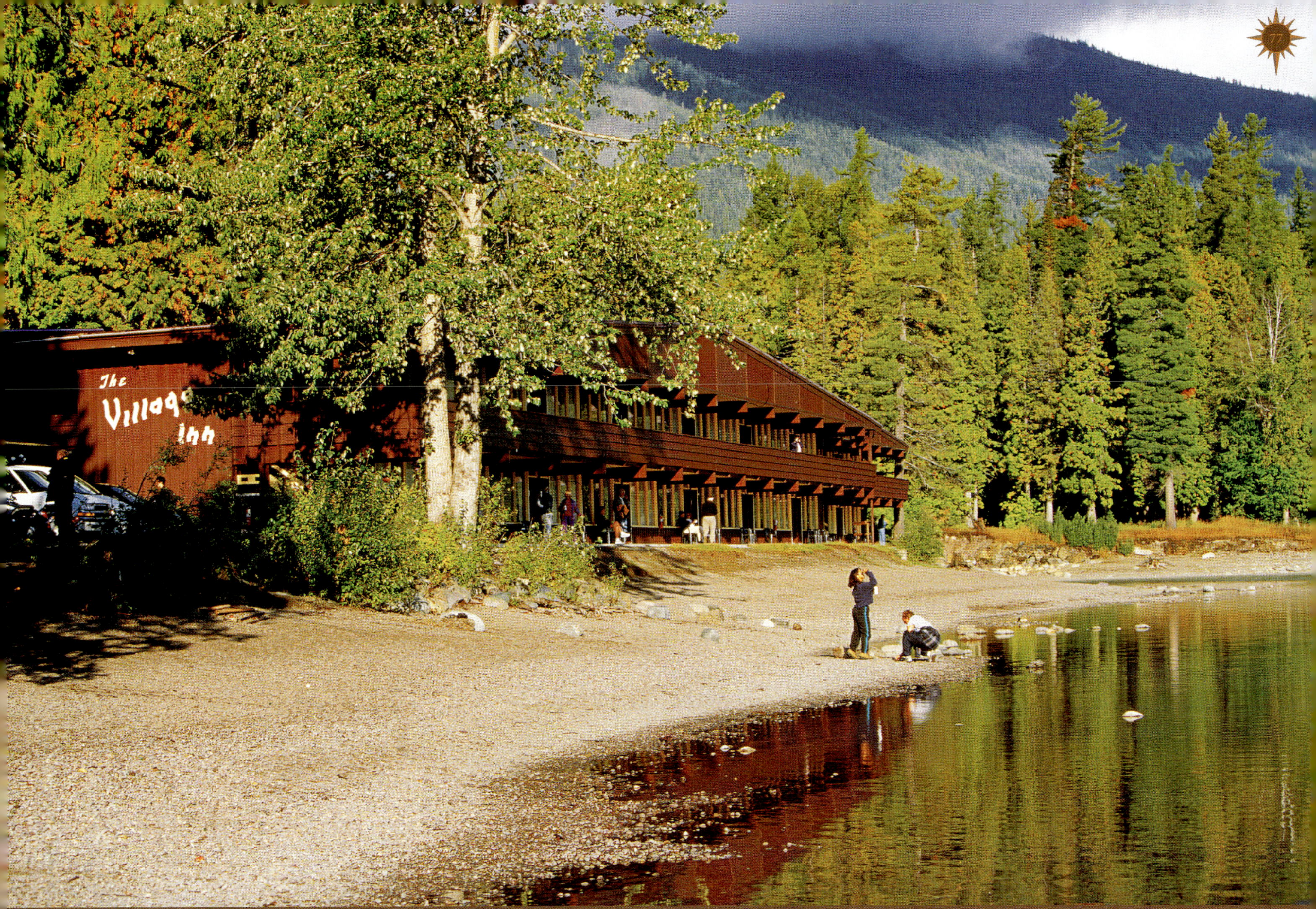

Today, the Village Inn looks much as it did when it was built. The two-story property is managed by Glacier Park, Inc., and includes thirty-six rooms. The Apgar Village Lodge, located nearby, includes historic cabins built by Milo Apgar in the early 1900s. The lodge has been owned and operated by the Lundgrens family since 1938. *Photo of the Village Inn courtesy of Glacier Park Inc.*

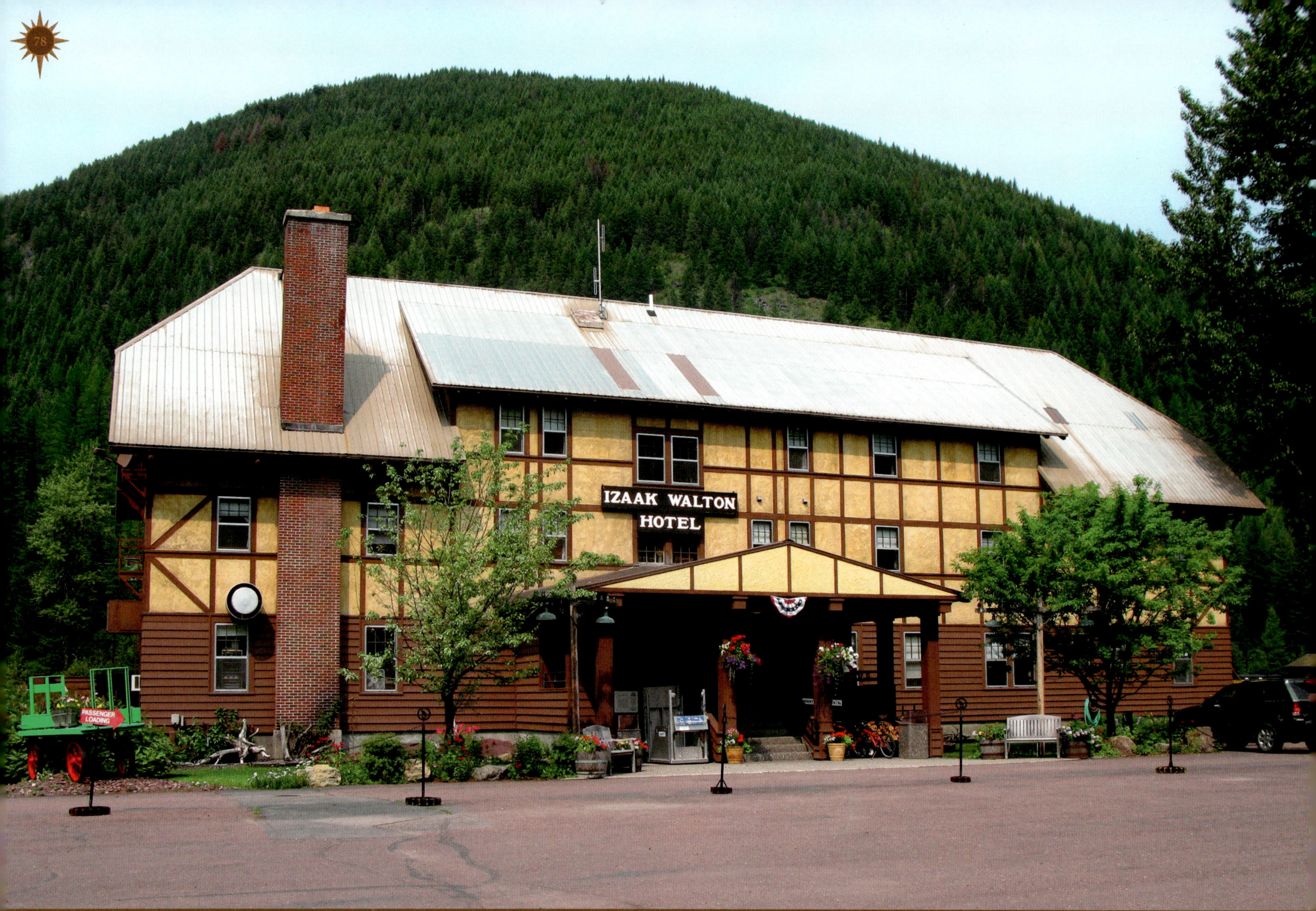

Another interesting vintage lodging property is the Izaak Walton Inn, located at the southern edge of Glacier. Amtrak stops at its back door near Essex, Montana. It was built in 1939 to be used by railroad personnel and also as a resort at a proposed new entrance to Glacier National Park, which never materialized. Guests can stay in hotel rooms or in refurbished train cabooses. It is also open in the winter for skiing or snowshoeing. The St. Mary Lodge & Resort, located at the East Gateway to Glacier Park near Going-to-the-Sun Road, offers additional lodging alternatives.

WILDLIFE

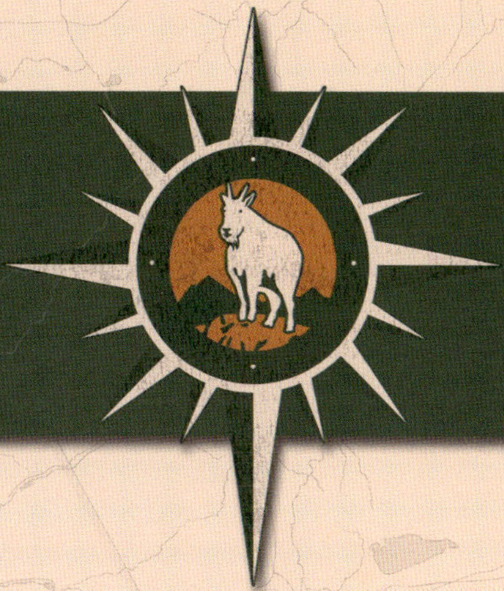

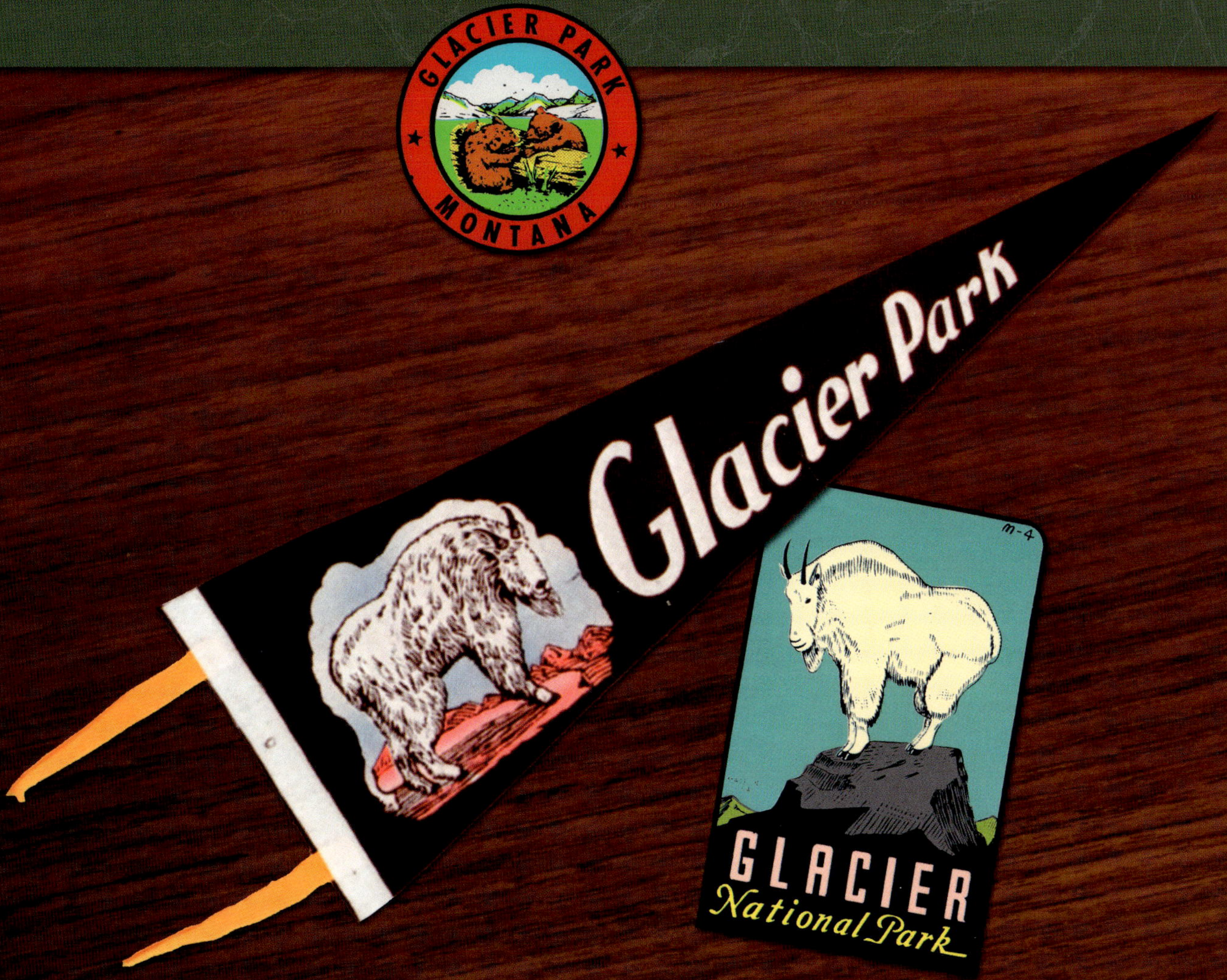

Decals by Lindgren-Turner Co. and Enco Inc.

Taking time to view the vast wildlife is a must for visitors of the park. Whether on a hike, a trail ride, or even along the road, sightings of mountain goats or bighorn sheep are frequent occurrences. Black bears, grizzly bears, and mountain lions can be seen on occasion, causing park officials to monitor their whereabouts to keep visitors safe. The park is home to nearly seventy species of mammals. Others include the white-tailed deer, mule deer, wolves, moose, elk, lynx, and coyotes. Smaller animals like the ground squirrels that can be found in the alpine meadows at Logan Pass, plus beavers, marmots, pikas, wolverines, and chipmunks, also inhabit the park. Among the 270 species of birds, visitor favorites are the bald eagles, golden eagles, harlequin ducks, ospreys, and hummingbirds.

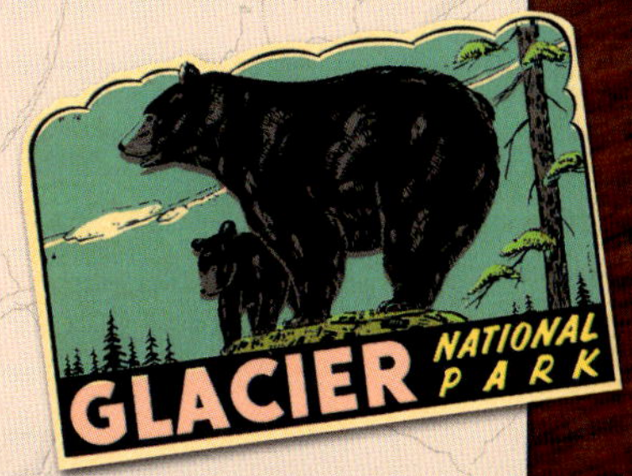

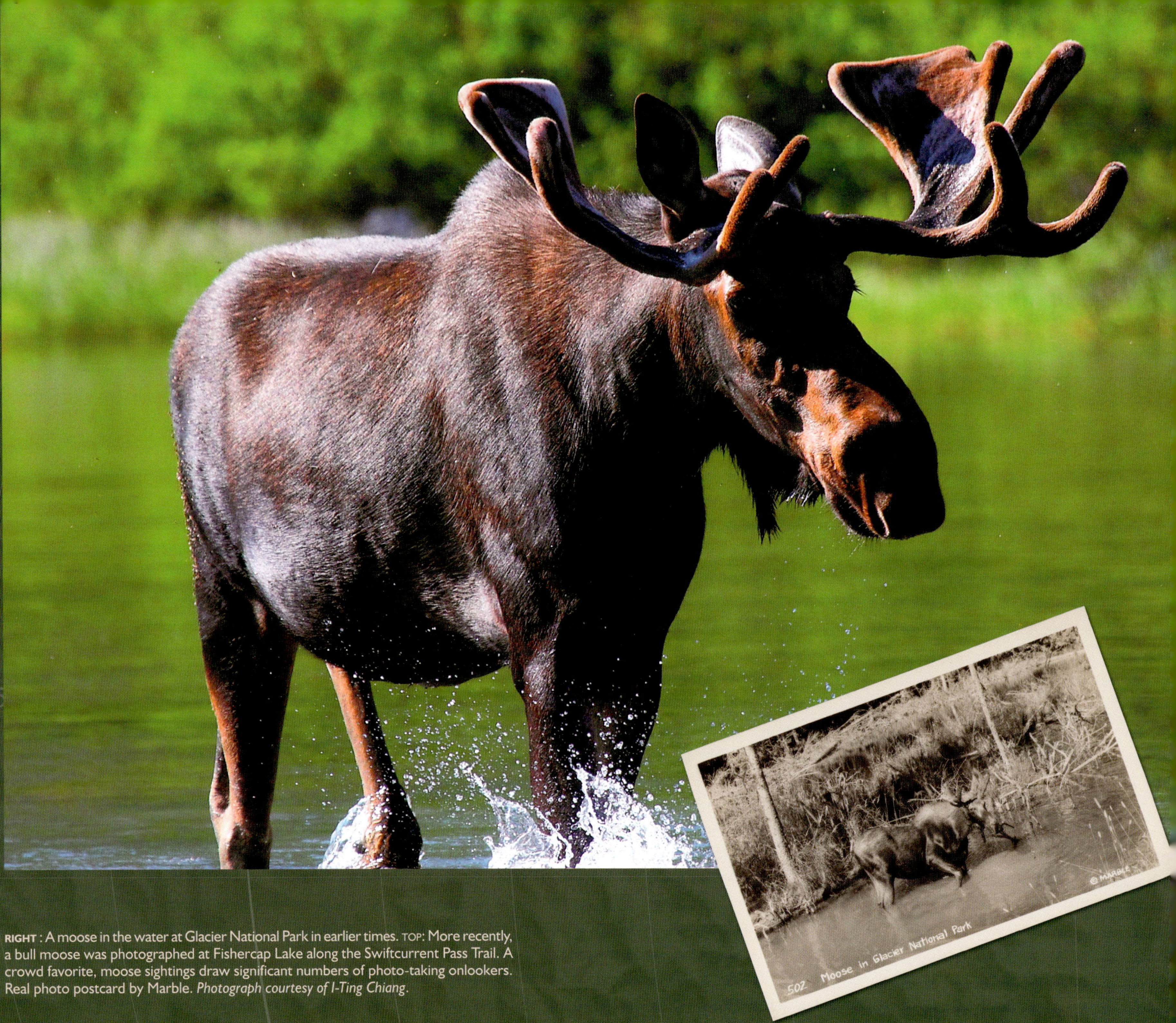

RIGHT : A moose in the water at Glacier National Park in earlier times. TOP: More recently, a bull moose was photographed at Fishercap Lake along the Swiftcurrent Pass Trail. A crowd favorite, moose sightings draw significant numbers of photo-taking onlookers. Real photo postcard by Marble. *Photograph courtesy of I-Ting Chiang*.

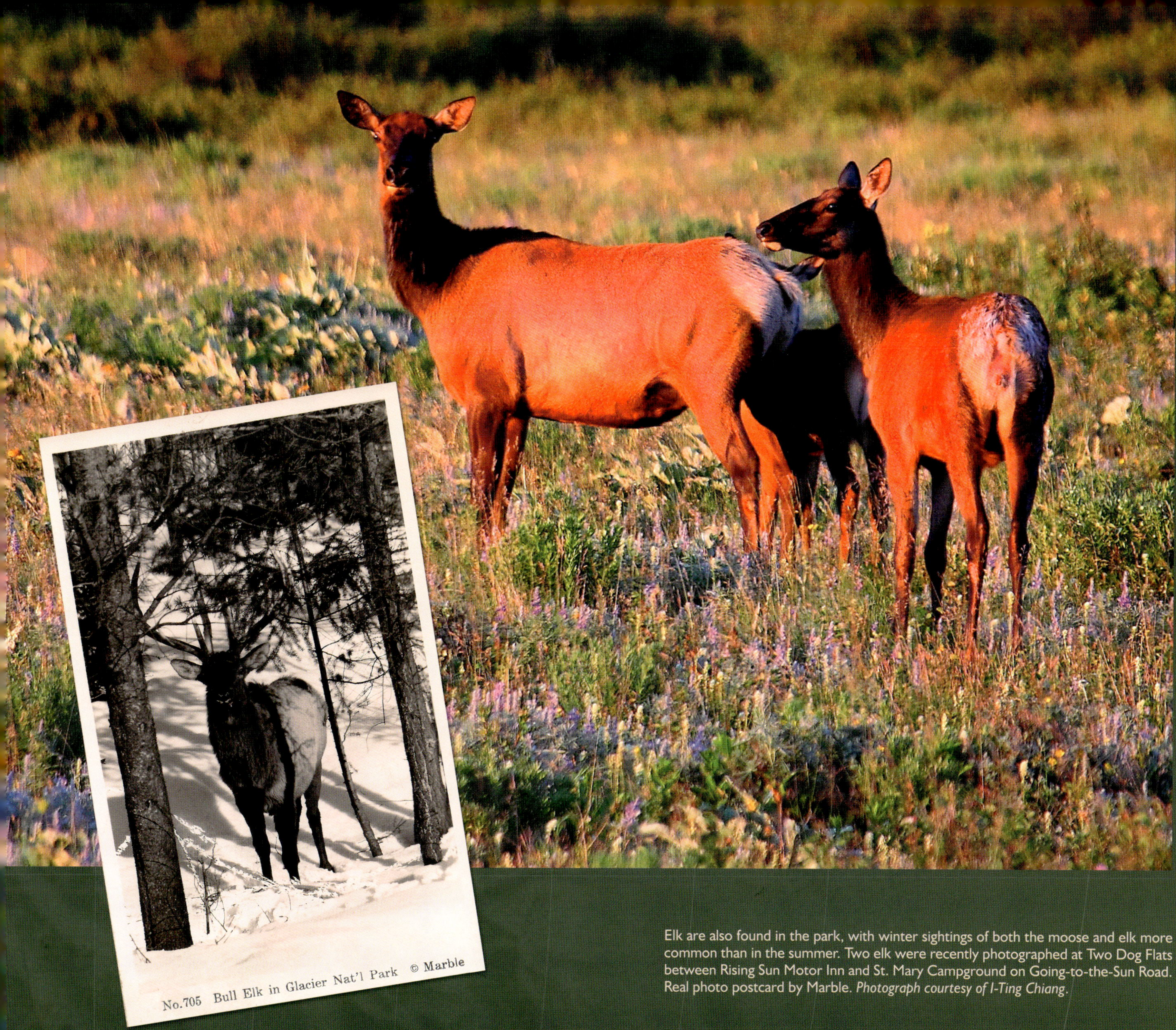

Elk are also found in the park, with winter sightings of both the moose and elk more common than in the summer. Two elk were recently photographed at Two Dog Flats between Rising Sun Motor Inn and St. Mary Campground on Going-to-the-Sun Road. Real photo postcard by Marble. *Photograph courtesy of I-Ting Chiang.*

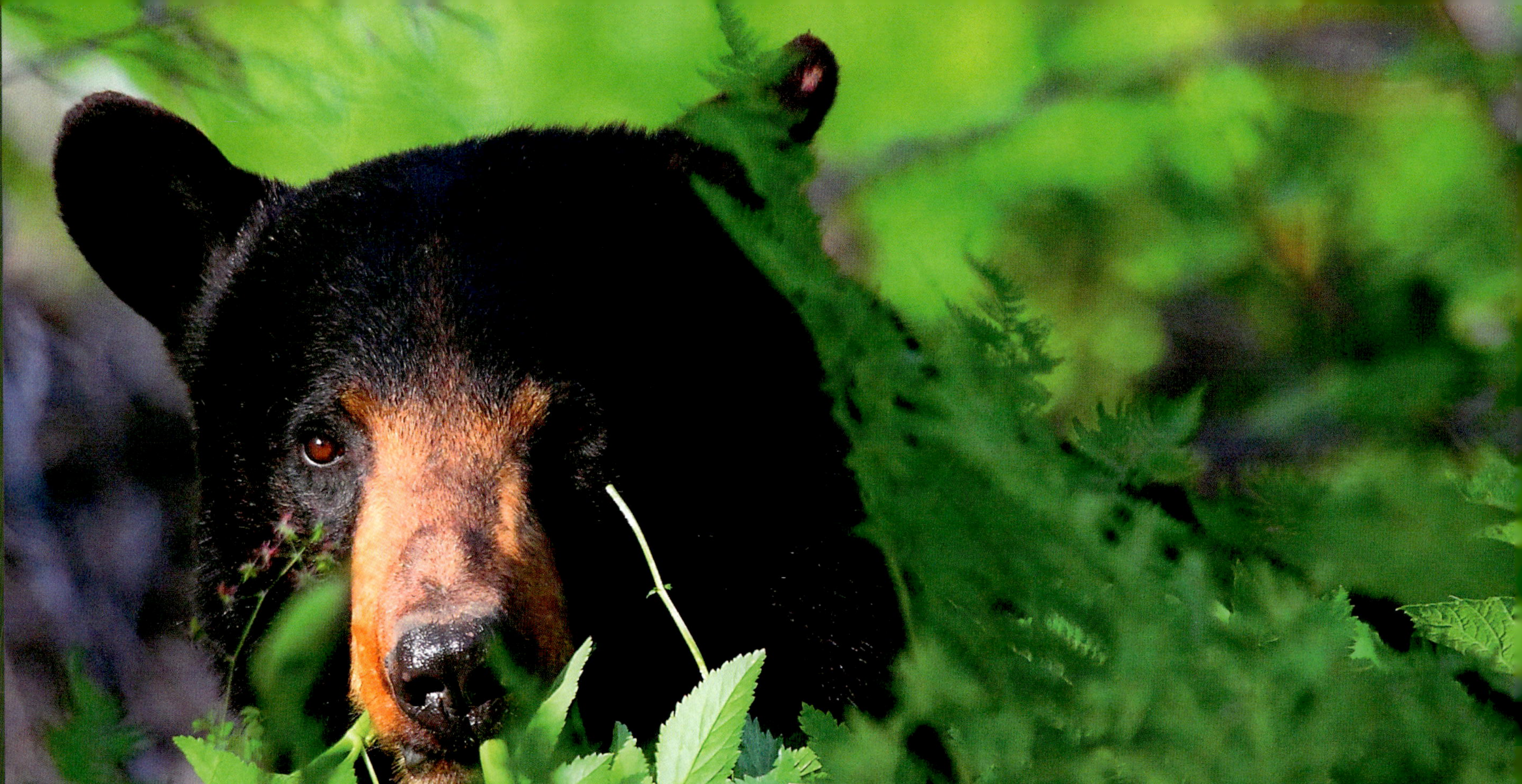

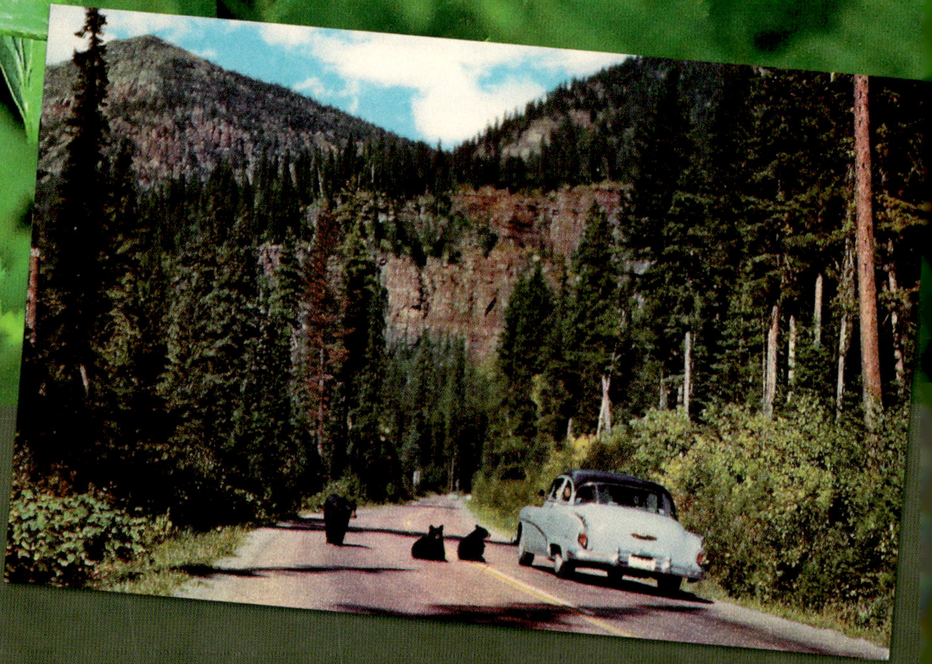

RIGHT : This view of a roadside sow and her cubs in the McDonald Valley is among the many examples of postcard images issued in previous decades showing the common practice of visitors feeding and interacting with bears and other wildlife in the national parks. Today, visitors are discouraged from such interactions. Postcard published by W. R. Mackin and Hugh Black.

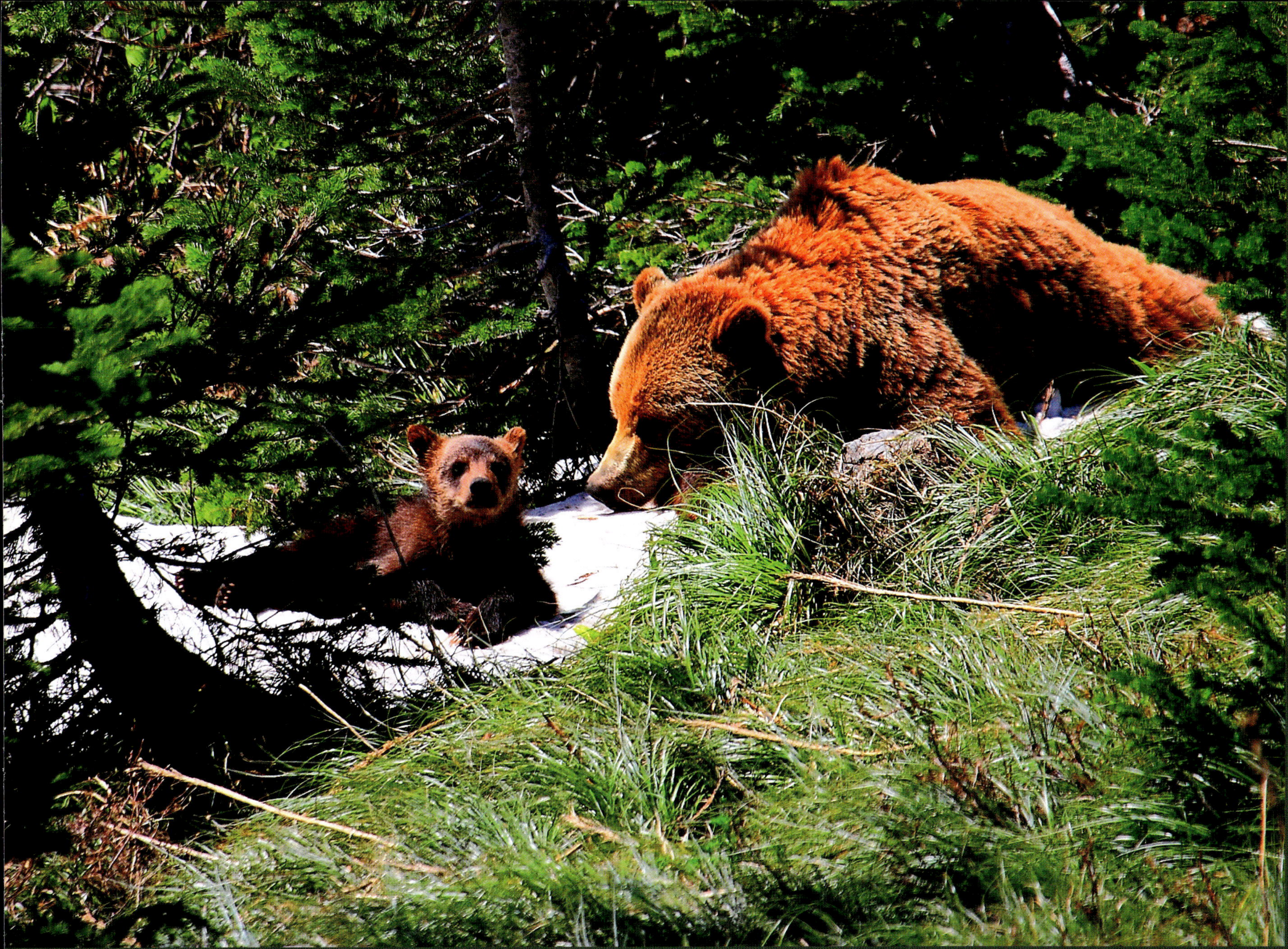

Black bears (opposite page) and grizzly bears both inhabit the park and their movements are carefully monitored by researchers. Warning signs and safety messages are prevalent throughout the area to help keep visitors safe. The black bear was photographed near Sun Point along Going-to-the-Sun Road while the grizzly bears were found along the Iceberg Lake Trail. In both cases, the bears were photographed from a respectful distance so as not to disturb their activities. *Courtesy of I-Ting Chiang*.

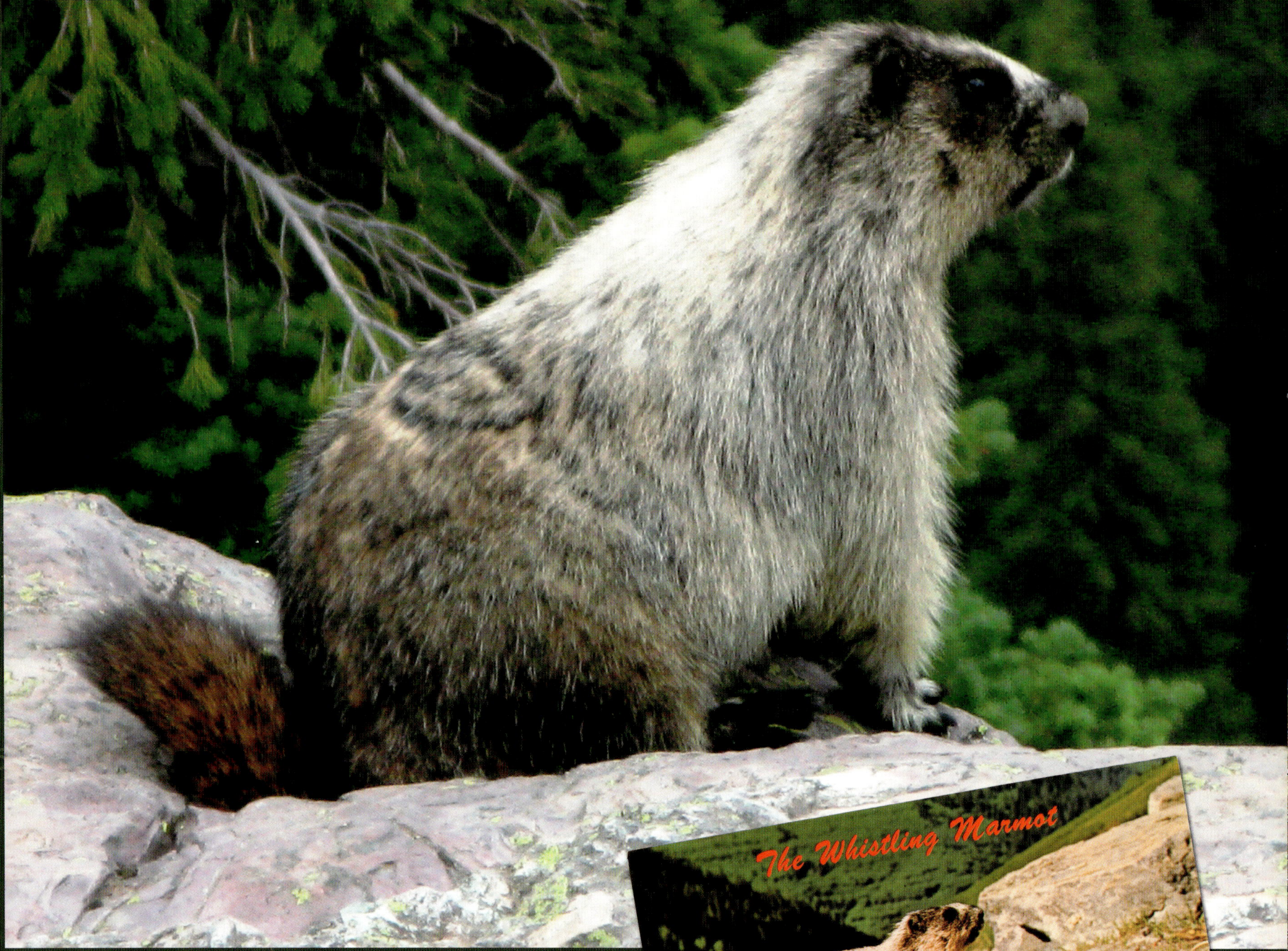

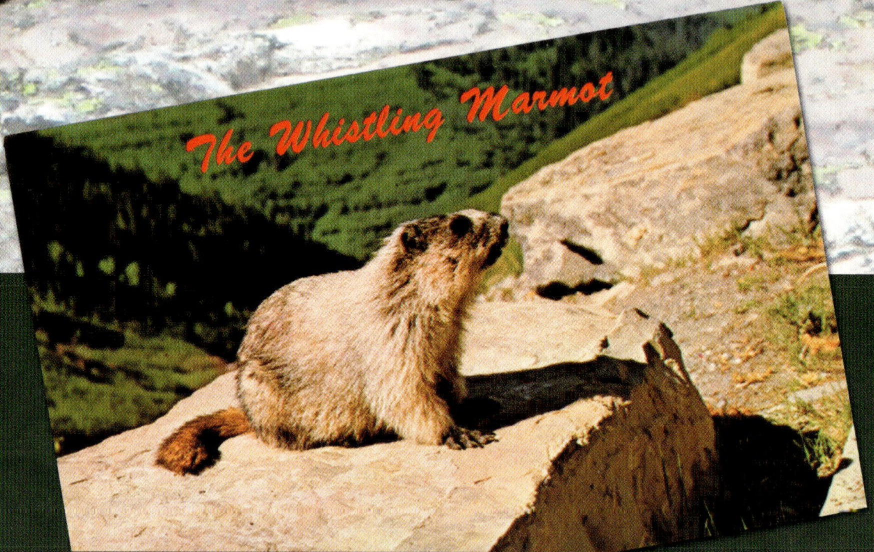

The hoary marmot, also called the whistling marmot, or whistle pig, lives near the tree line and blends into its surroundings. It "whistles" by sounding a high-pitched warning when danger abounds. The marmot hibernates for seven to eight months during the long winter season. The marmot above was photographed while basking on the sun-warmed rocks at the Sperry Chalets on a summer afternoon. Postcard published by Bob Anderson Postcards.

BIGHORN SHEEP

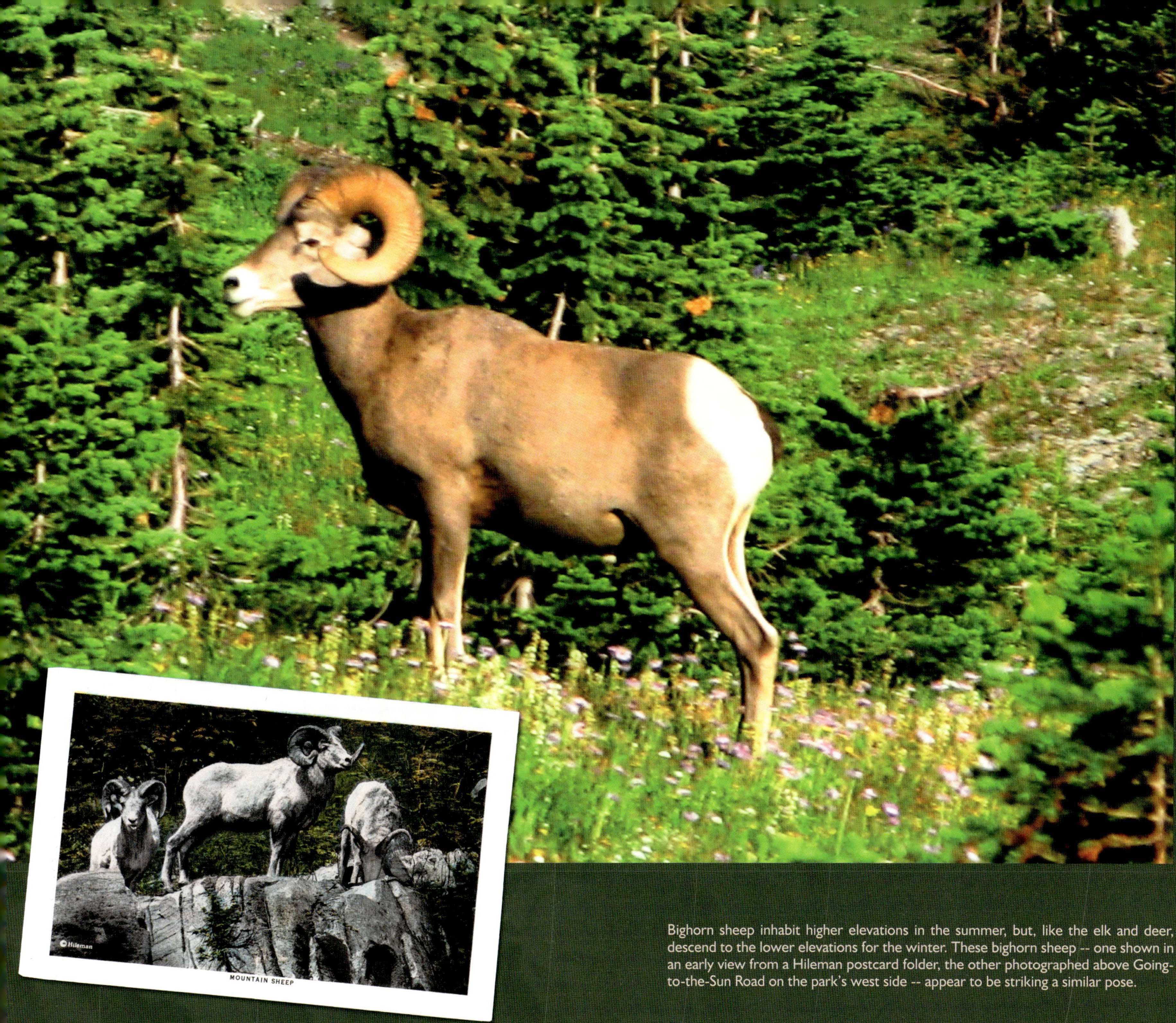

135°

Bighorn sheep inhabit higher elevations in the summer, but, like the elk and deer, descend to the lower elevations for the winter. These bighorn sheep -- one shown in an early view from a Hileman postcard folder, the other photographed above Going-to-the-Sun Road on the park's west side -- appear to be striking a similar pose.

MOUNTAIN GOAT

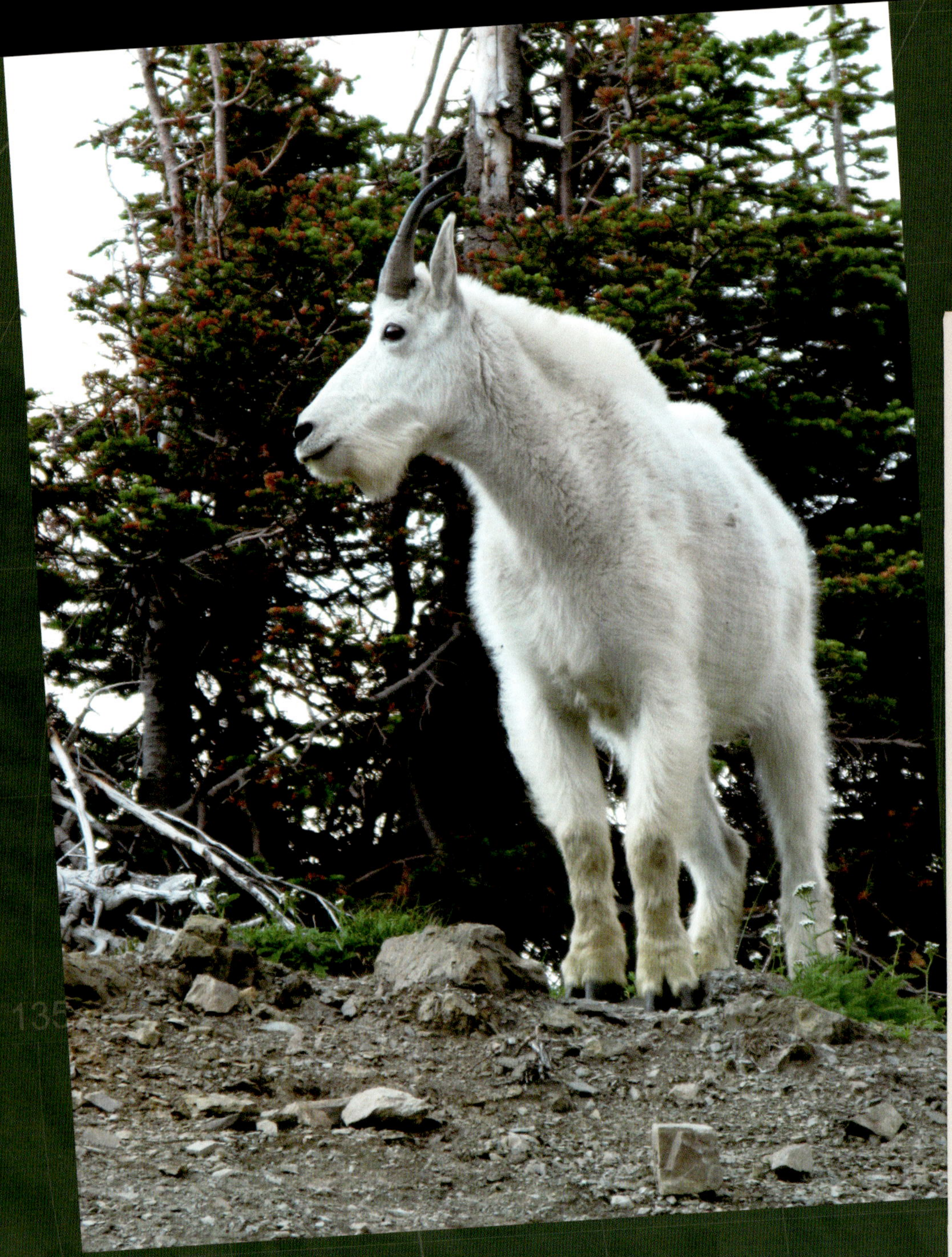

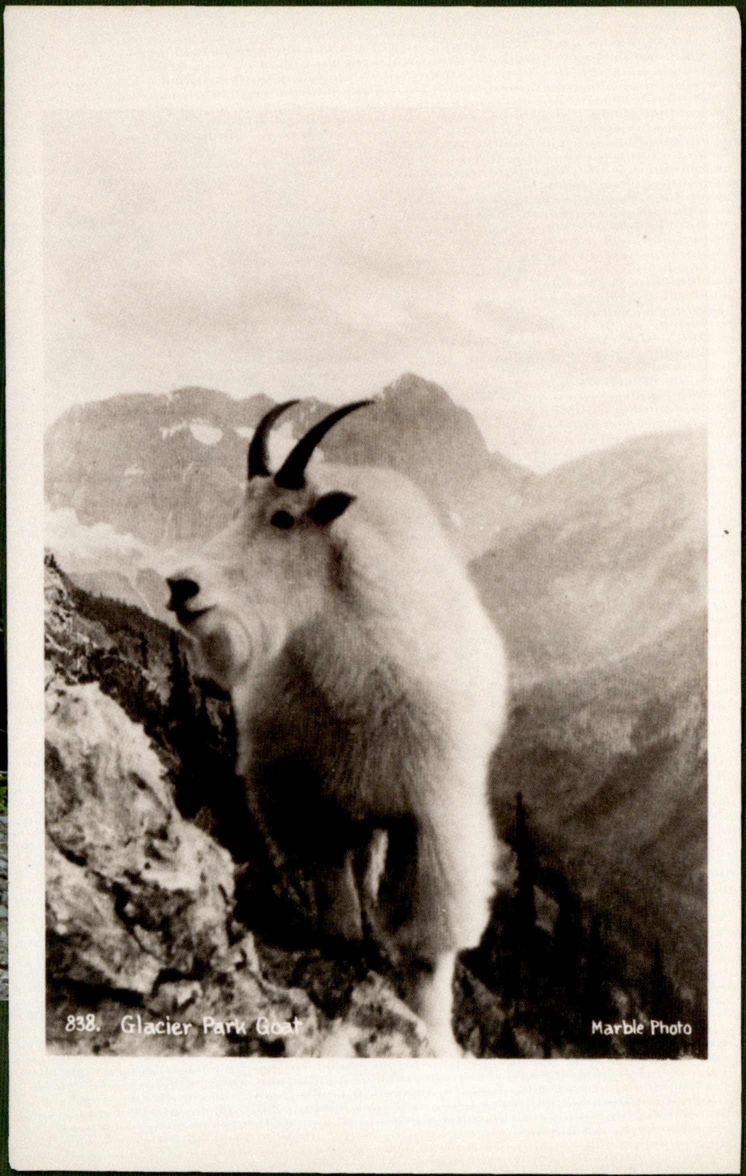

This early real photo postcard by Marble shows a mountain goat at home in the park. Mountain goats can be easily seen along the Continental Divide on the steepest slopes. They are accustomed to visitors and will continue eating along the trails as people ... recent photo captures the majestic qualities of the park's most

OUT AND ABOUT

Hikers on the Grinnell Glacier Viewpoint Trail.
Courtesy of I-Ting Chiang.

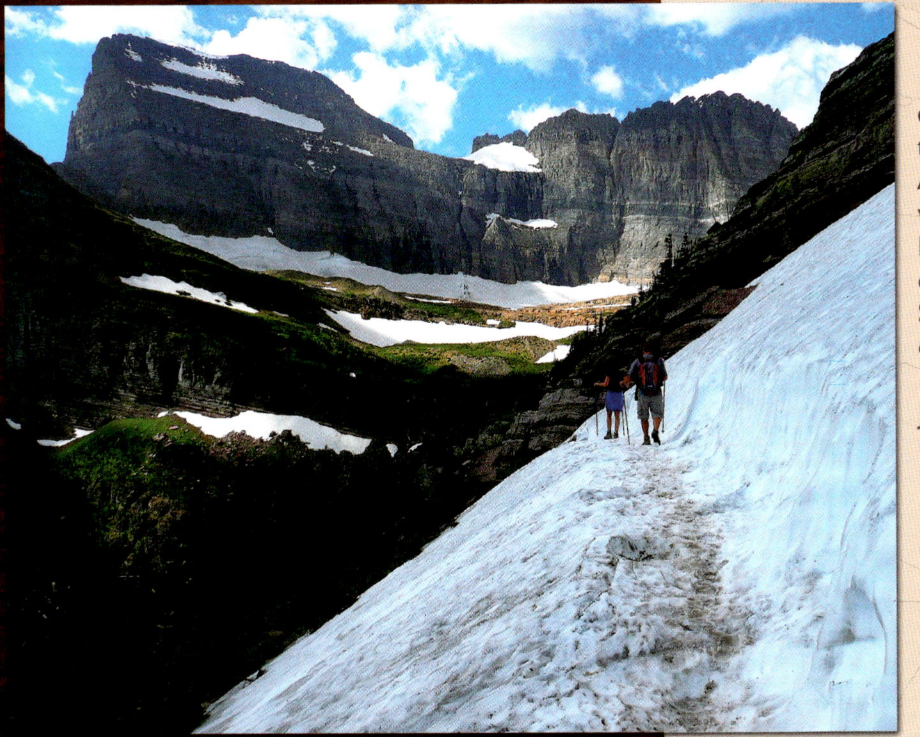

Exploring the park can be as relaxing or as strenuous as visitors prefer. Maps and recommended outings are available at the ranger stations showcasing the park's diverse ecosystem on the west and east sides. From the west entry near Lake McDonald, the Avalanche Creek area offers an easy hike through the cedar-hemlock forest along the Trail of the Cedars and on to the glacier-fed Avalanche Lake. A stop at nearby McDonald Falls is also recommended; it's where the oldest layered rock is found. In the Two Medicine area, a brief stop at Running Eagle Falls to see the "two-in-one" waterfalls leaves plenty of time for other outings. Visitors to the Many Glacier area can take a short stroll around Swiftcurrent Lake or indulge in a day-long hike to Iceberg Lake or Grinnell Glacier, one of the largest of the remaining glaciers.

Also, guided boat tours are offered on McDonald, Two Medicine, Swiftcurrent, Josephine, and St. Mary lakes. These trips have been visitor favorites for decades. Plus, a trip across the Going-to-the-Sun Road over Logan Pass at the Continental Divide is not to be missed with views of the Garden Wall and Jackson Glacier.

The park also offers fishing, boating, backpacking, bicycling, and horseback rides and, in the winter, cross-country skiing and snowshoeing.

For visitors with more time, a trip to Canada's Waterton Lakes National Park is also a treat while history buffs can enjoy a visit to the historical lodges and surviving chalets on both sides of the border. Glacier Park contains 375 historic properties, six of which are National Historic Landmarks.

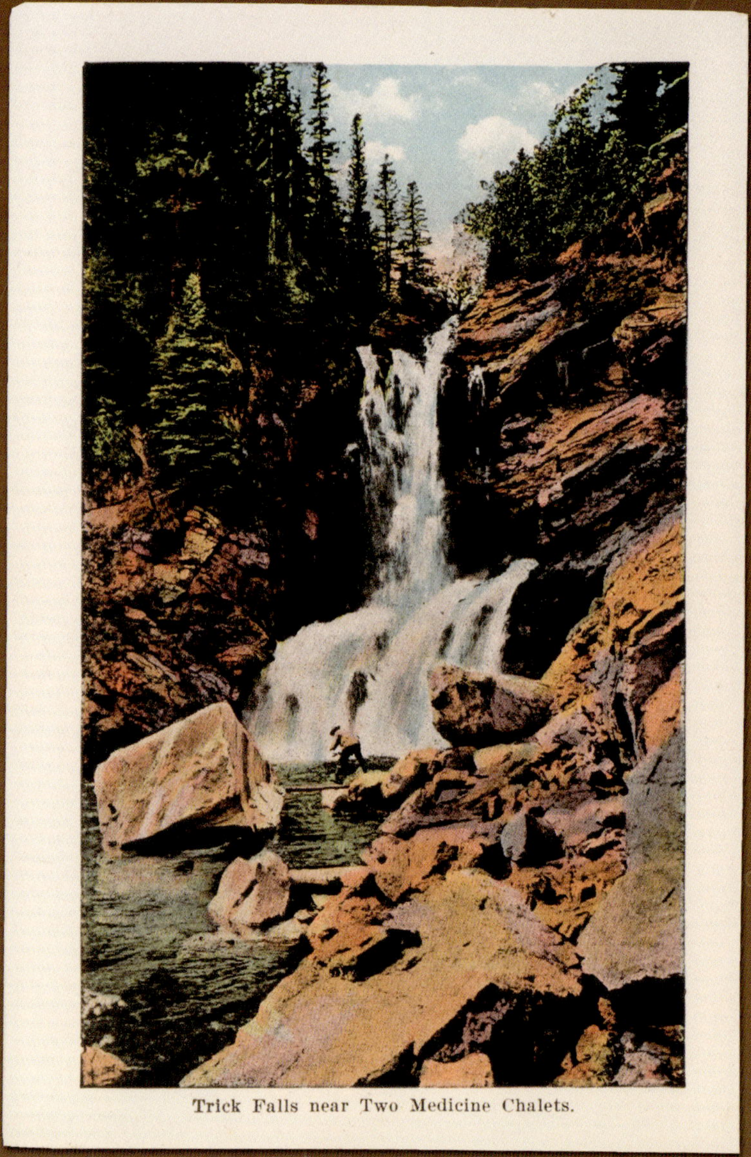

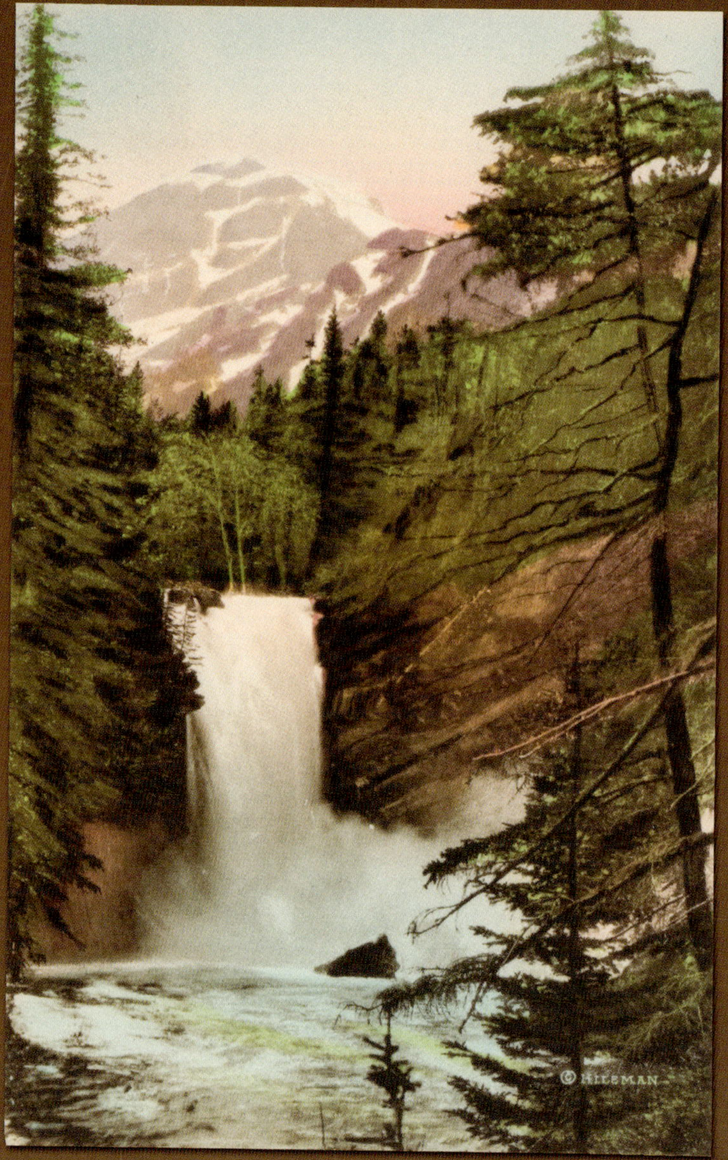

This early view of Trick Falls on the Two Medicine River shows the "two in one" falls with water cascading from both the upper falls and lower falls. The postcard is one of the scenes included in a folder published for the Glacier Park Hotel Co. The other postcard shows the falls during the spring snowmelt, when water is flowing at such a high rate the lower falls become hidden. Hand-colored postcard by the Albertype Co.

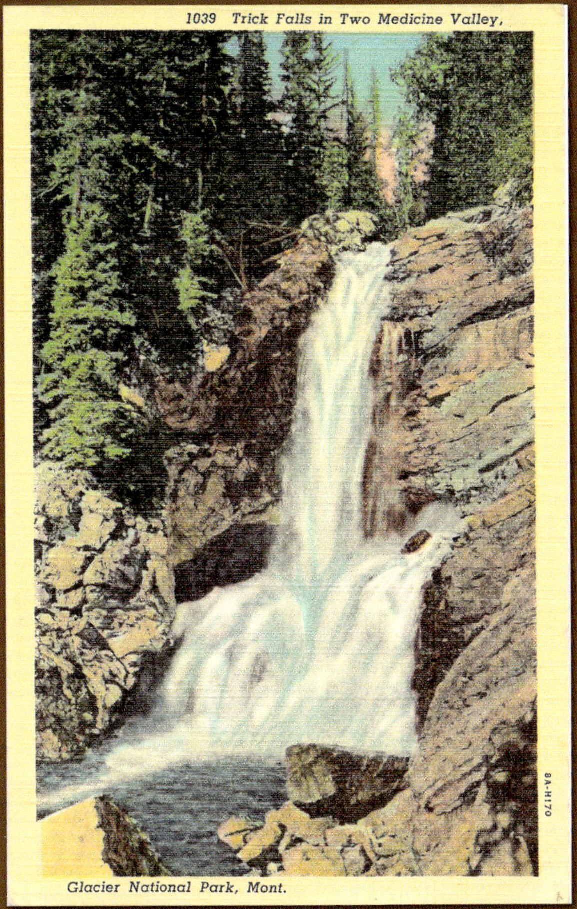

Water from the Two Medicine River flows from the upper and lower falls. C. T. Art-Colortone linen postcard, late 1930s.

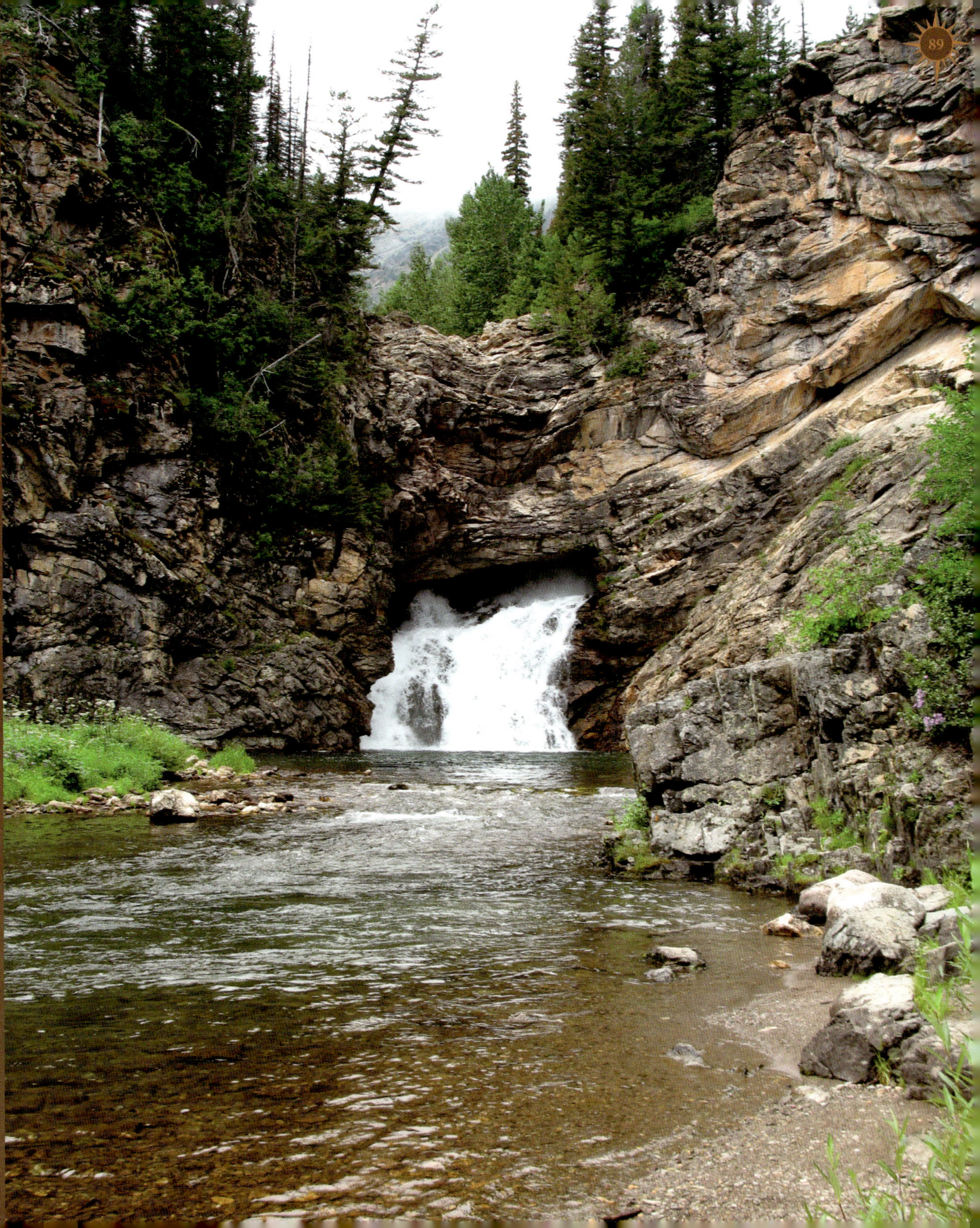

Trick Falls has had a name change and is now called Running Eagle Falls. The falls are considered to be a rare geologic oddity. This photograph shows the falls as they look in July following the snowmelt. The water appears to pour out of the face of the rock rather than above it. The Running Eagle Falls Trailhead is located one mile west of the Two Medicine entrance station at the park's southeastern border. The hike is an easy three-tenths of a mile stroll with a rise in elevation of sixty feet.

One of the most popular stops for visitors in the Lake McDonald area is a hike along the Trail of the Cedars. The ADA-accessible trailhead is located along the Going-to-the-Sun Road just east of the Avalanche Creek campground. Hikers begin by using an elevated boardwalk to make their way through the giant cedar-hemlock forest. *Courtesy of Bryan and Nicole Kohrmann.*

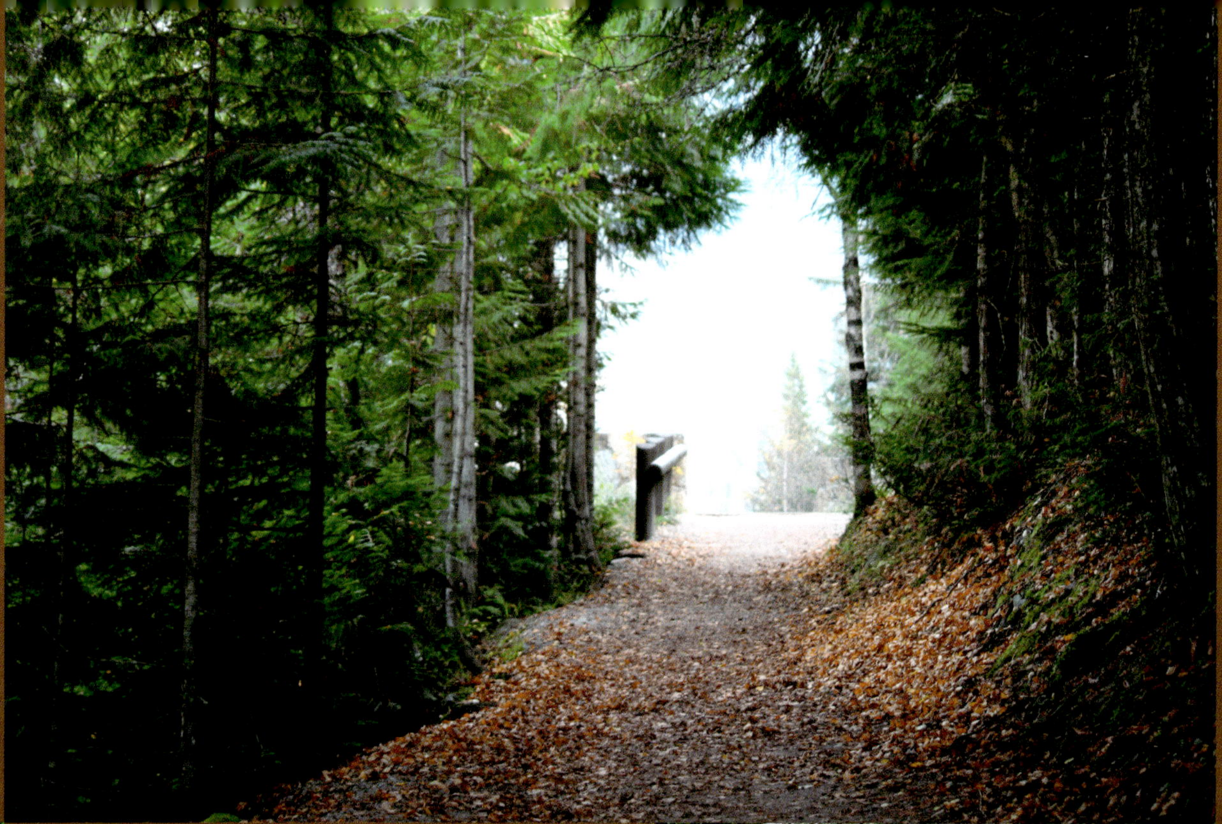

A bridge along the trail offers exquisite views of the Avalanche Gorge and its mossy rocks. The self-guided tour includes information about the diverse ecosystem of the park with its moist Pacific influence on the western side and the dry prairie influence on the eastern side. Ranger-led tours also are available.

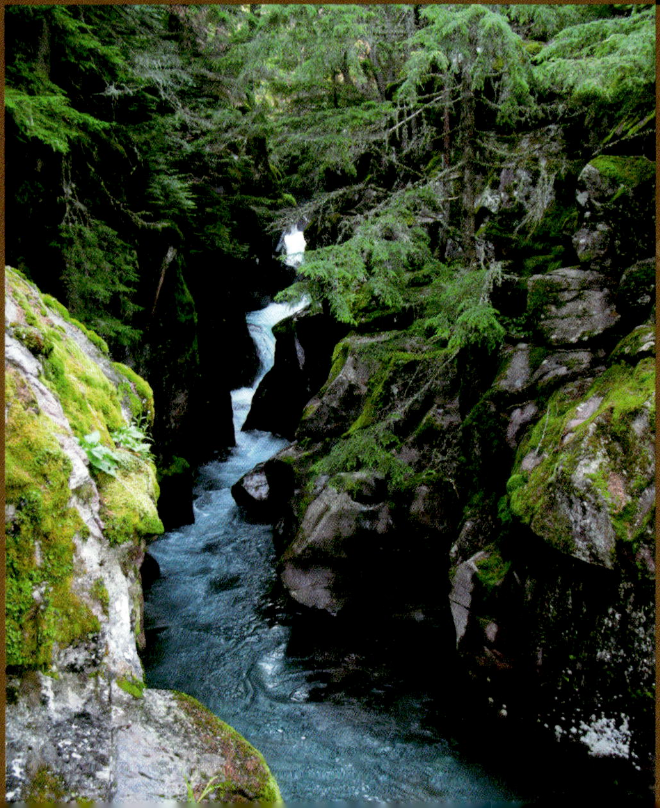

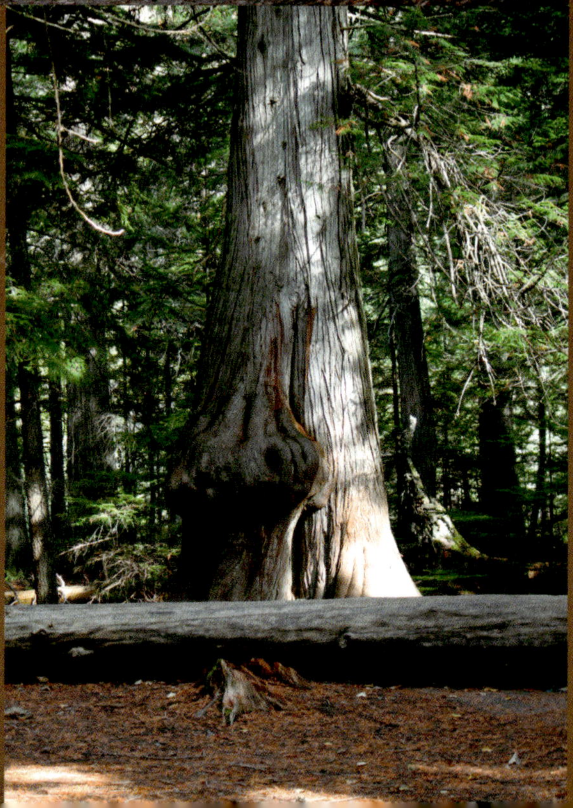

Sights along the Trail of the Cedars include trees nearly five hundred years old and some as tall as eighty feet. *Courtesy of Bryan and Nicole Kohrmann.*

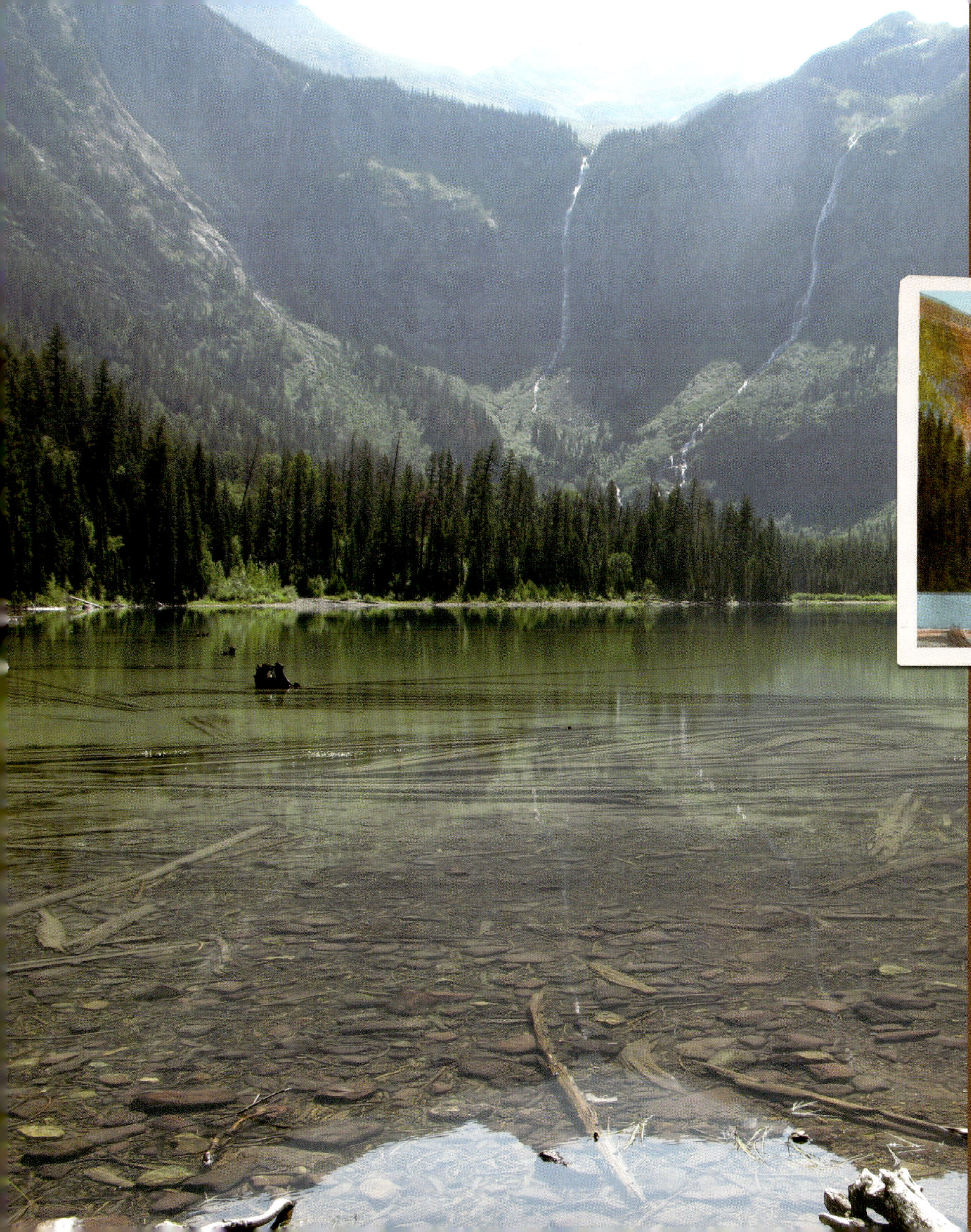

A postcard view of this setting mailed in 1950 provided a vivid description of a visitor's travels through the park, "We spent Aug. 29 driving from Great Falls to St. Mary's at the eastern entrance to Glacier National Park. We stayed that night in a log cabin motel, which we enjoyed. On the 30th, we drove through the park whose grandeur almost overwhelmed us. Rushing waters, towering mountains, indigo lakes, cliffs, gores, hanging valleys, glaciers, forests, wildlife all combined in an awesome panorama." A current photograph repeats the view.

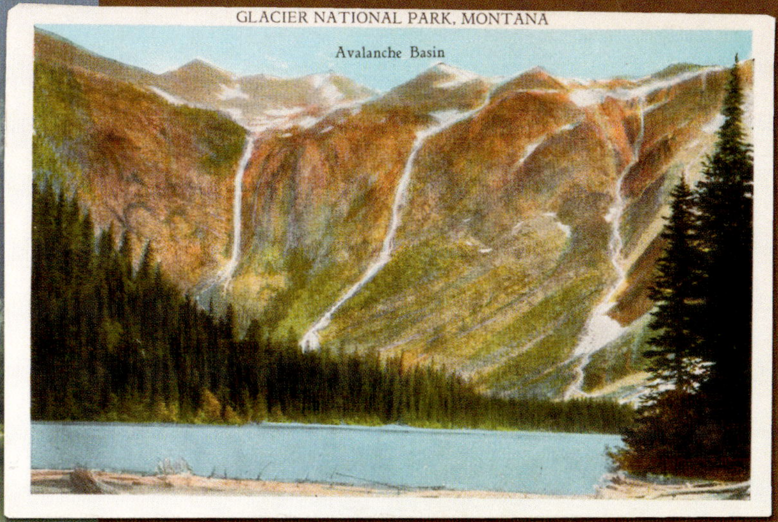

After crossing the bridge at Avalanche Gorge, the trail continues with a two-mile hike to Avalanche Lake with an elevation rise of five hundred feet. This view of the area shows waterfalls cascading down the steep grades. Early postcard is from a folder by Hileman and published by the Glacier Park Hotel Co.

The *DeSmet* launch has provided tourists with scenic views from Lake McDonald since it was built in 1930 while a brochure issued by the Glacier Park Boat Co. contains tour information for the *DeSmet* and the other excursion boats used in the park: *Little Chief* and *Red Eagle* on St. Mary Lake, *Rising Wolf* on Two Medicine Lake, and *Chief Two Guns* on Swiftcurrent Lake. Vintage Plastichrome postcard.

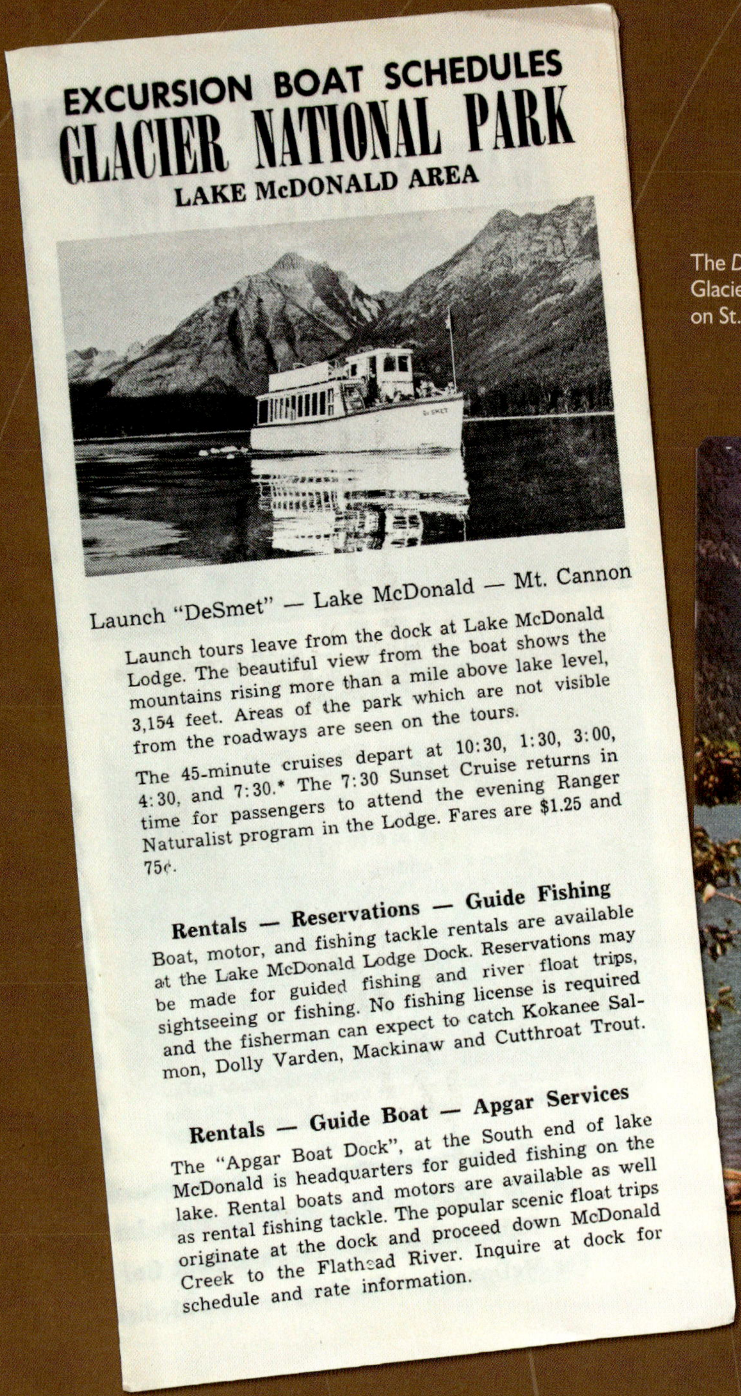

EXCURSION BOAT SCHEDULES

GLACIER NATIONAL PARK

LAKE McDONALD AREA

Launch "DeSmet" — Lake McDonald — Mt. Cannon

Launch tours leave from the dock at Lake McDonald Lodge. The beautiful view from the boat shows the mountains rising more than a mile above lake level, 3,154 feet. Areas of the park which are not visible from the roadways are seen on the tours.

The 45-minute cruises depart at 10:30, 1:30, 3:00, 4:30, and 7:30.* The 7:30 Sunset Cruise returns in time for passengers to attend the evening Ranger Naturalist program in the Lodge. Fares are $1.25 and 75¢.

Rentals — Reservations — Guide Fishing

Boat, motor, and fishing tackle rentals are available at the Lake McDonald Lodge Dock. Reservations may be made for guided fishing and river float trips, sightseeing or fishing. No fishing license is required and the fisherman can expect to catch Kokanee Salmon, Dolly Varden, Mackinaw and Cutthroat Trout.

Rentals — Guide Boat — Apgar Services

The "Apgar Boat Dock", at the South end of lake McDonald is headquarters for guided fishing on the lake. Rental boats and motors are available as well as rental fishing tackle. The popular scenic float trips originate at the dock and proceed down McDonald Creek to the Flathead River. Inquire at dock for schedule and rate information.

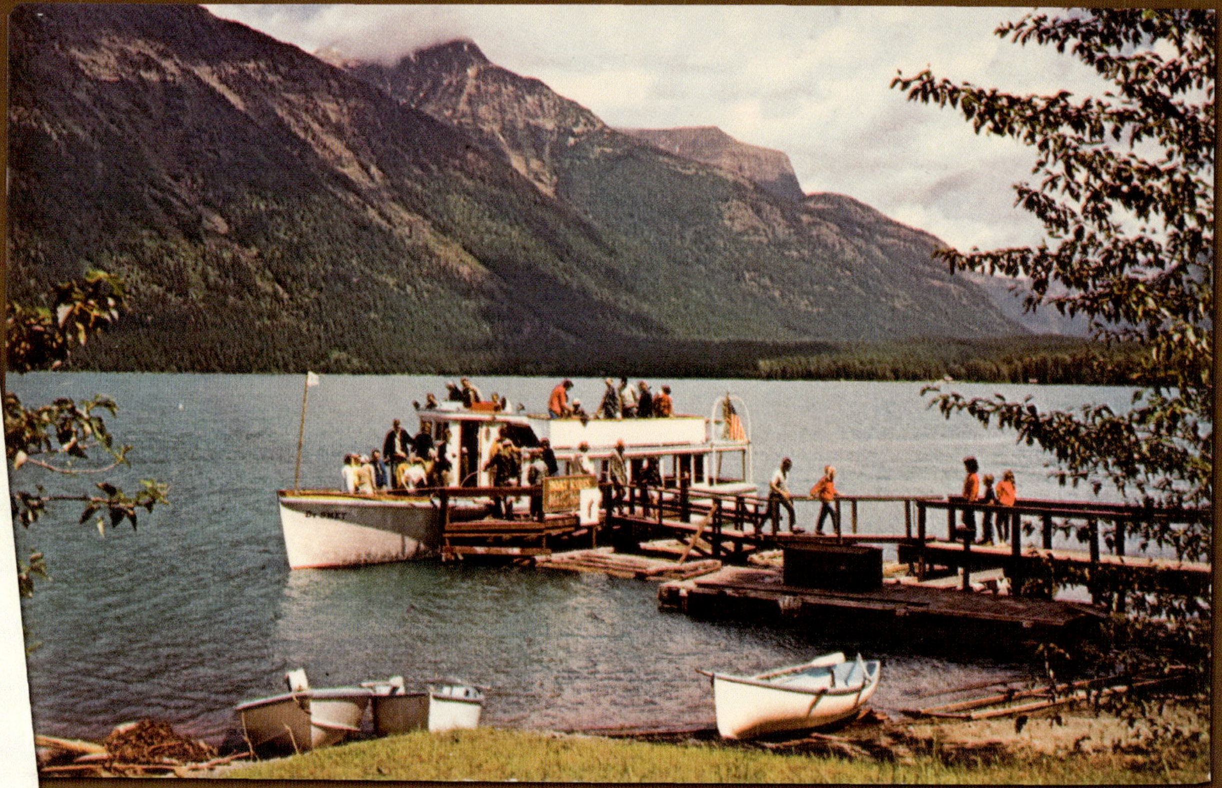

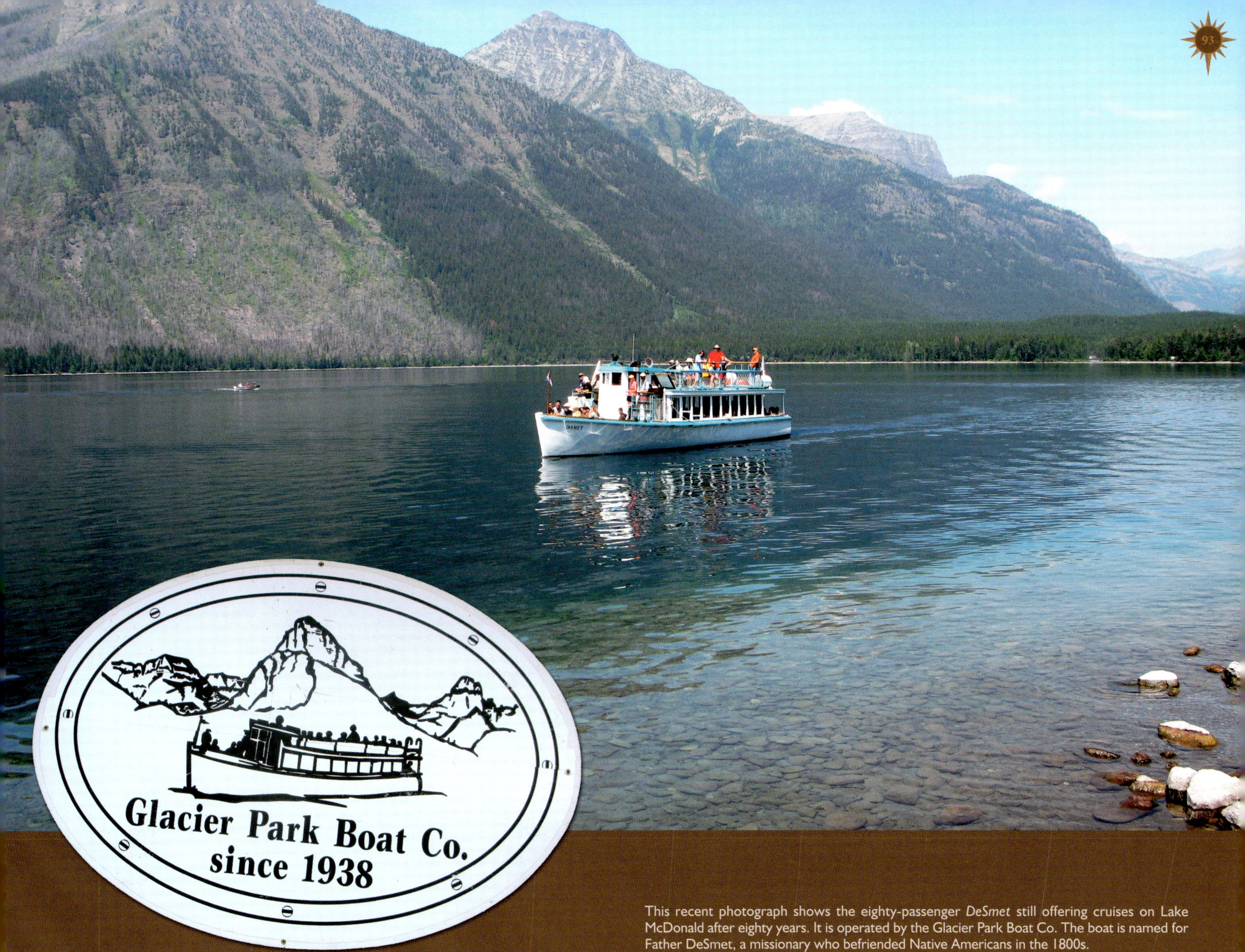

This recent photograph shows the eighty-passenger *DeSmet* still offering cruises on Lake McDonald after eighty years. It is operated by the Glacier Park Boat Co. The boat is named for Father DeSmet, a missionary who befriended Native Americans in the 1800s.

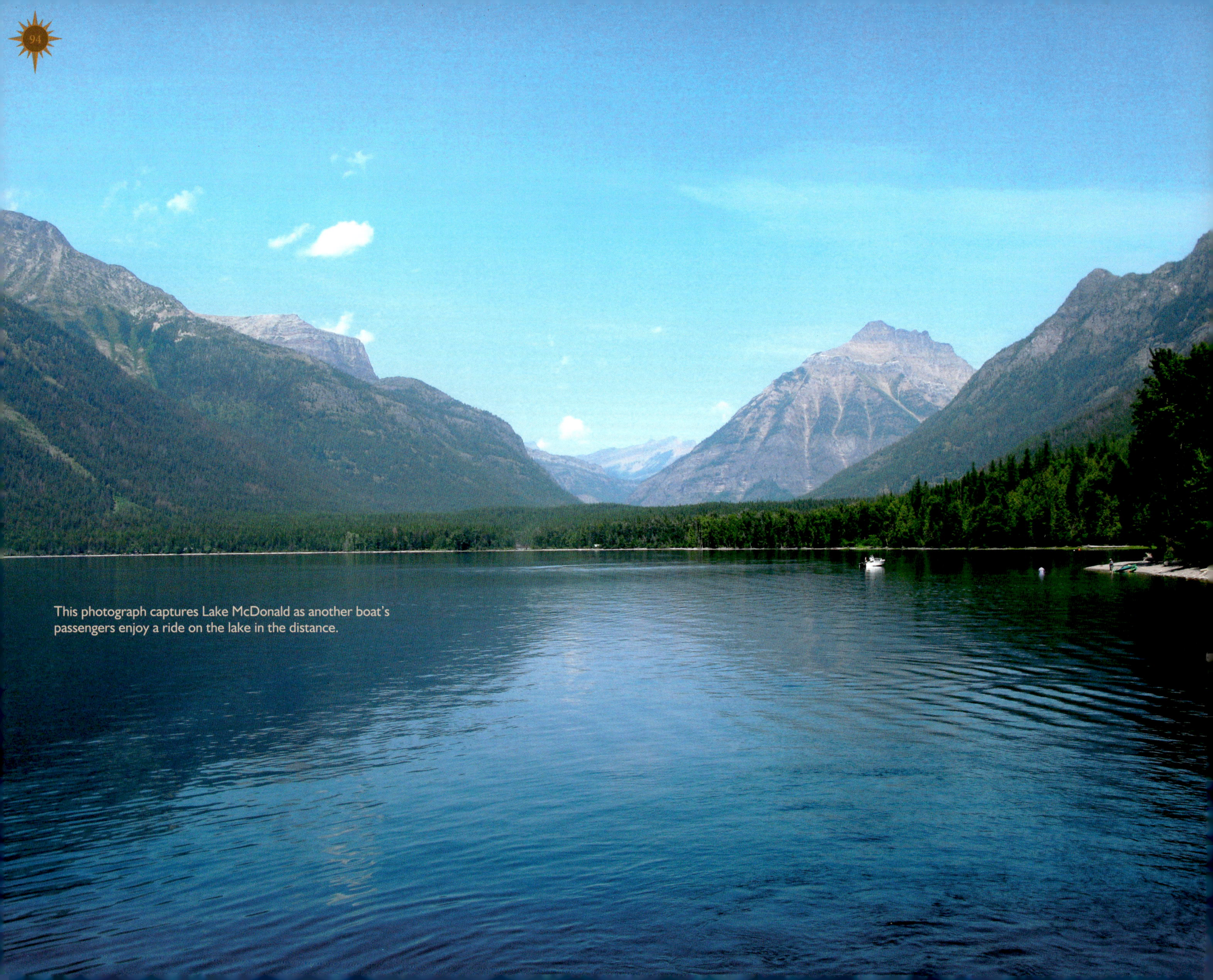

This photograph captures Lake McDonald as another boat's passengers enjoy a ride on the lake in the distance.

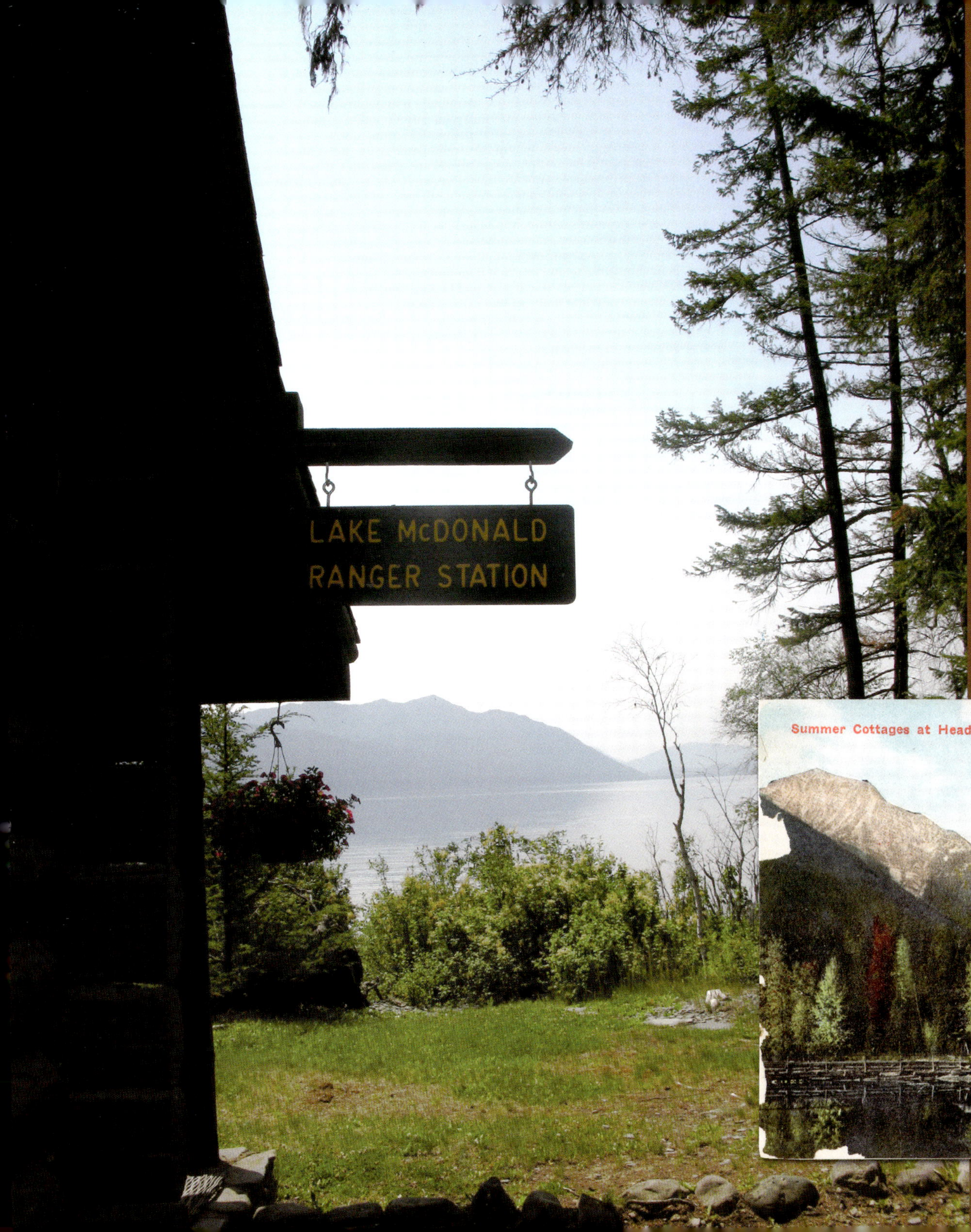

The historic Upper Lake McDonald Ranger station is located on the north shore of the lake. It was built in 1924 to be used as an administrative center with the opening of the Going-to-the-Sun Road. The building is listed on the National Register of Historic Places as a well-preserved example of rustic, park service-designed log architecture. A portion of the infrequently staffed station is shown along with Lake McDonald. Ranger stations with full-time staffing are located at Two Medicine Lake, St. Mary, Apgar, West Entrance area, Goat Haunt, Polebridge, and Many Glacier.

Private cottages on Lake McDonald have existed for many years. The properties were acquired from early land owners or have been retained by the families of the original homesteaders. Private in-holdings have been reduced from 3,000 acres to fewer than five hundred following continuing efforts by the National Park Service to acquire the properties. Postcard by James R. White.

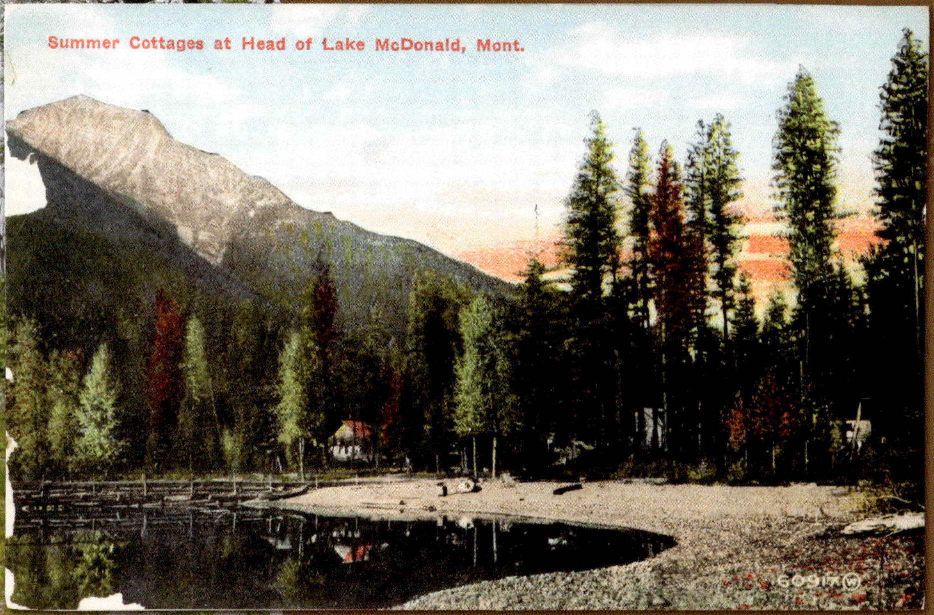

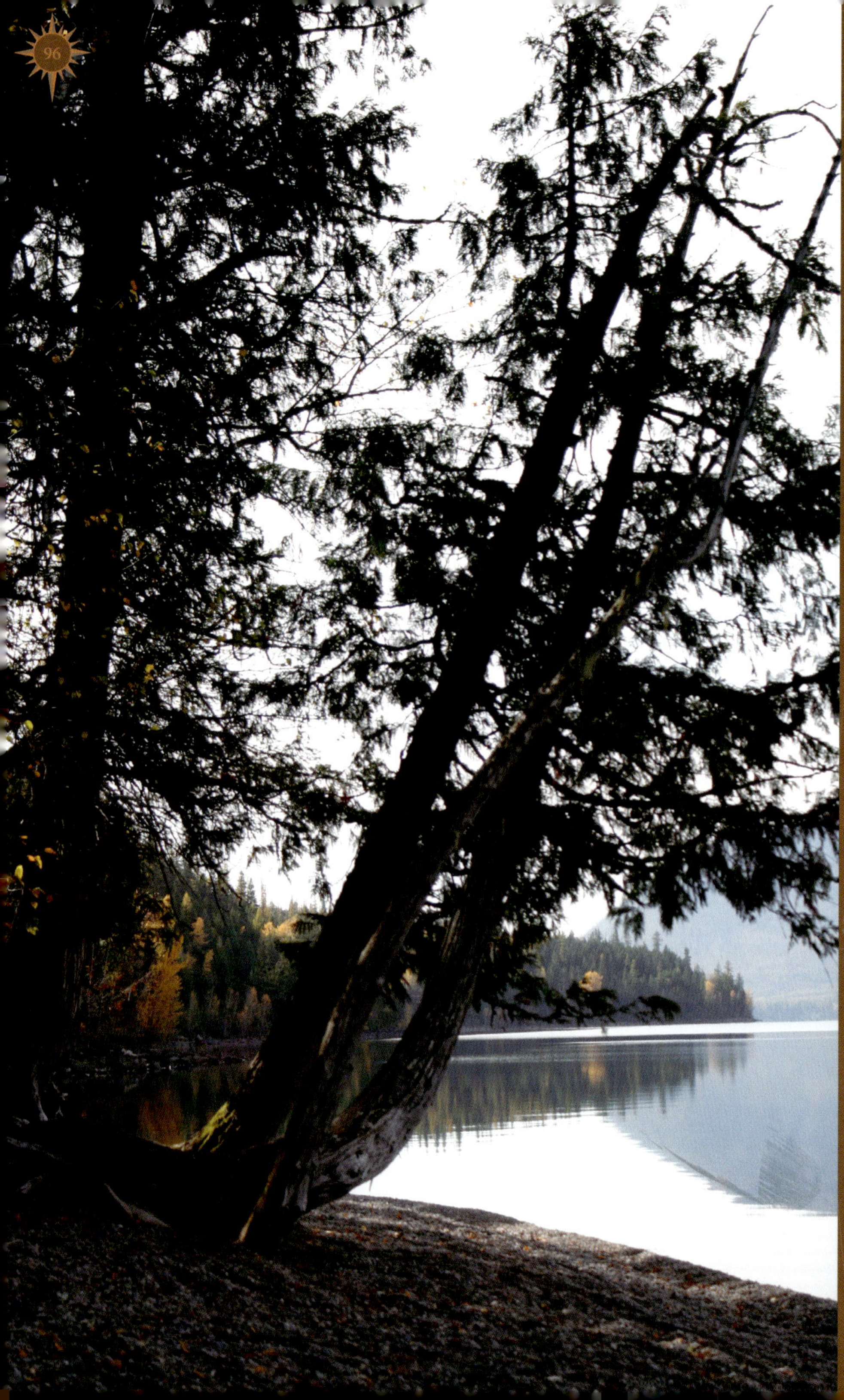

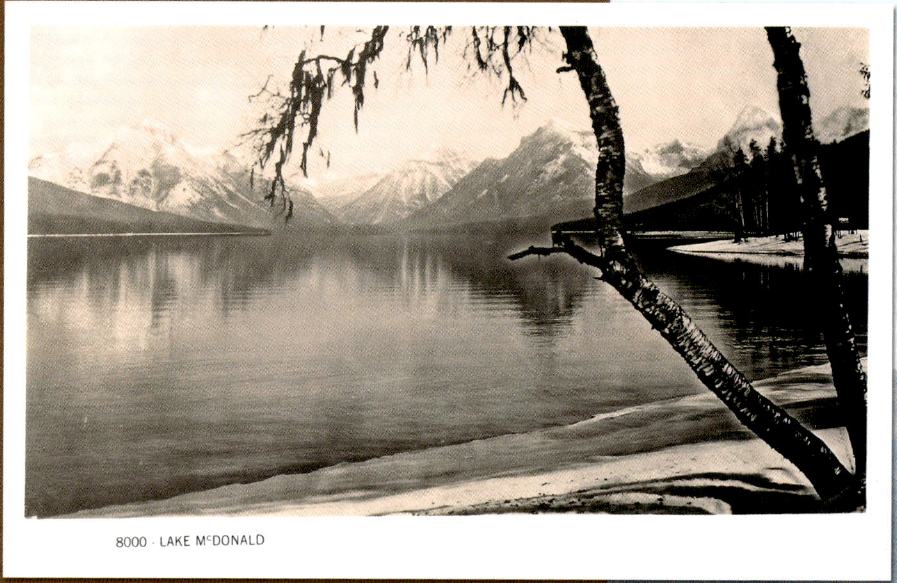

This real photo postcard captures a view of Lake McDonald with a shoreline tree in the foreground.

This contemporary photograph also uses trees to draw upon the beauty of Lake McDonald. *Courtesy of Bryan and Nicole Kohrmann.*

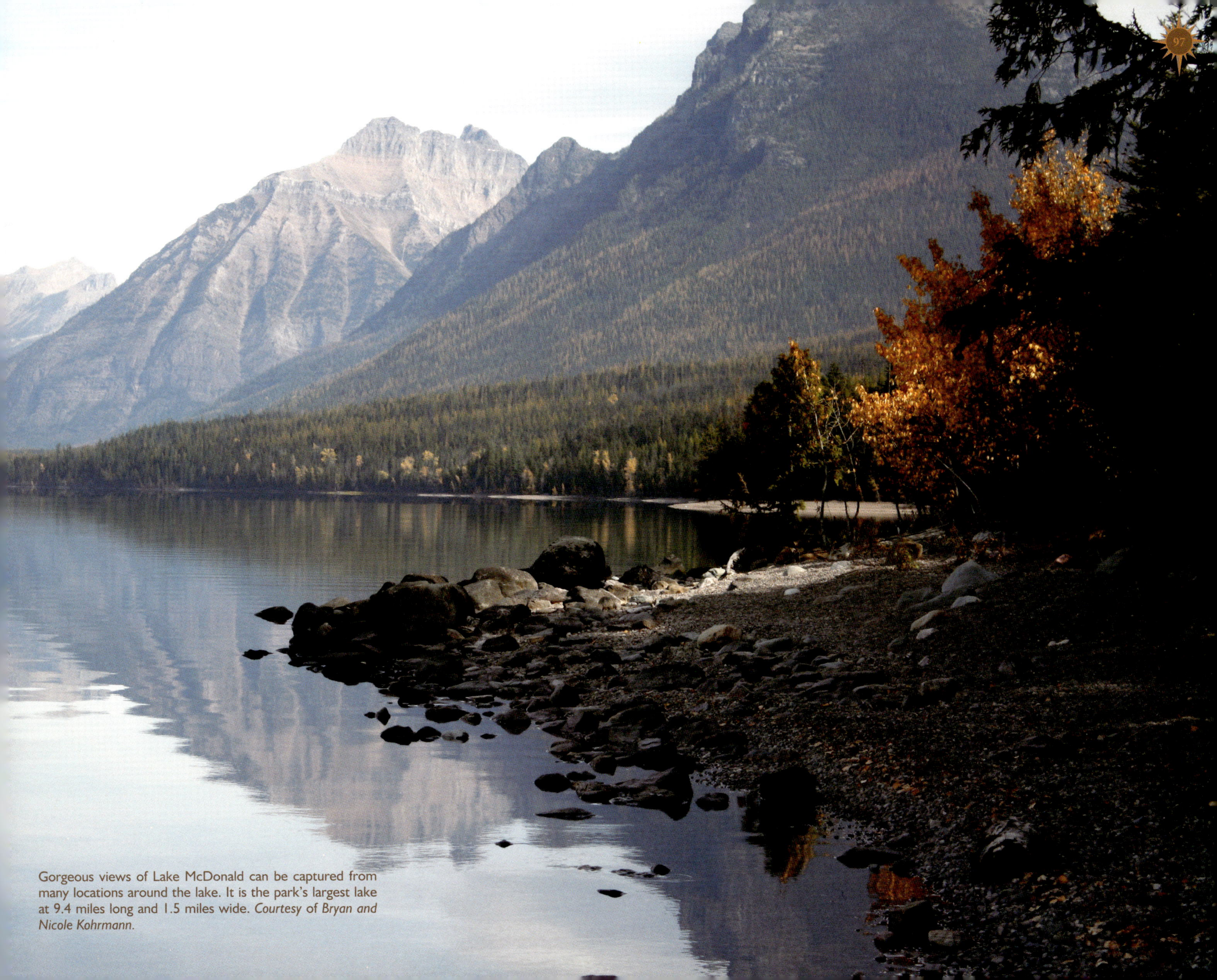

Gorgeous views of Lake McDonald can be captured from many locations around the lake. It is the park's largest lake at 9.4 miles long and 1.5 miles wide. *Courtesy of Bryan and Nicole Kohrmann.*

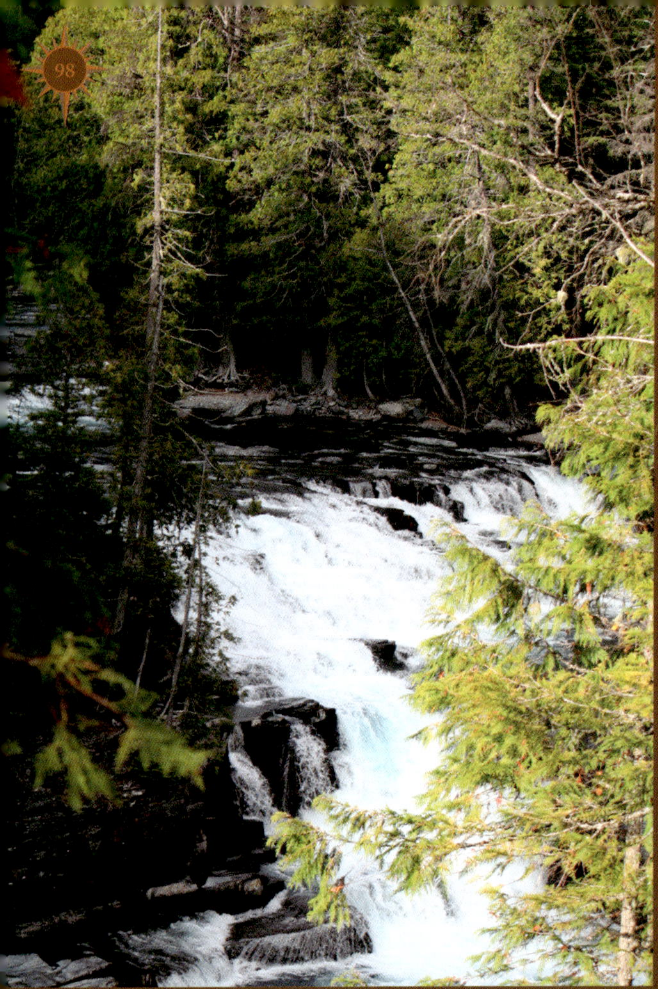

McDonald Falls is a well-traveled roadside waterfall on McDonald Creek along the Going-to-the-Sun Road. The layered rock exposed by the waterfall is thought to be among the oldest in the park. *Courtesy of Bryan and Nicole Kohrmann.*

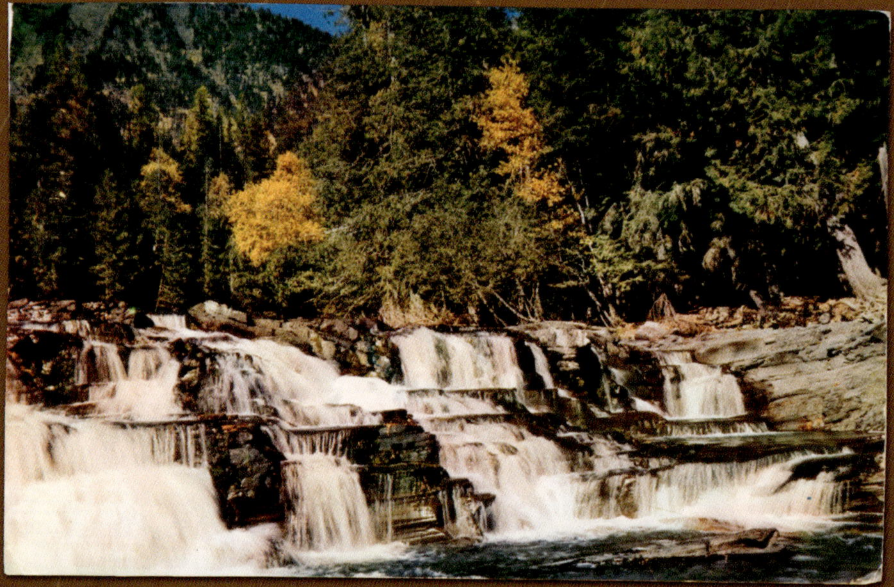

This autumn view of McDonald Falls is from a postcard published by Western Souvenirs. At over twenty-five miles in length, McDonald Creek is the longest stream within the boundaries of the park.

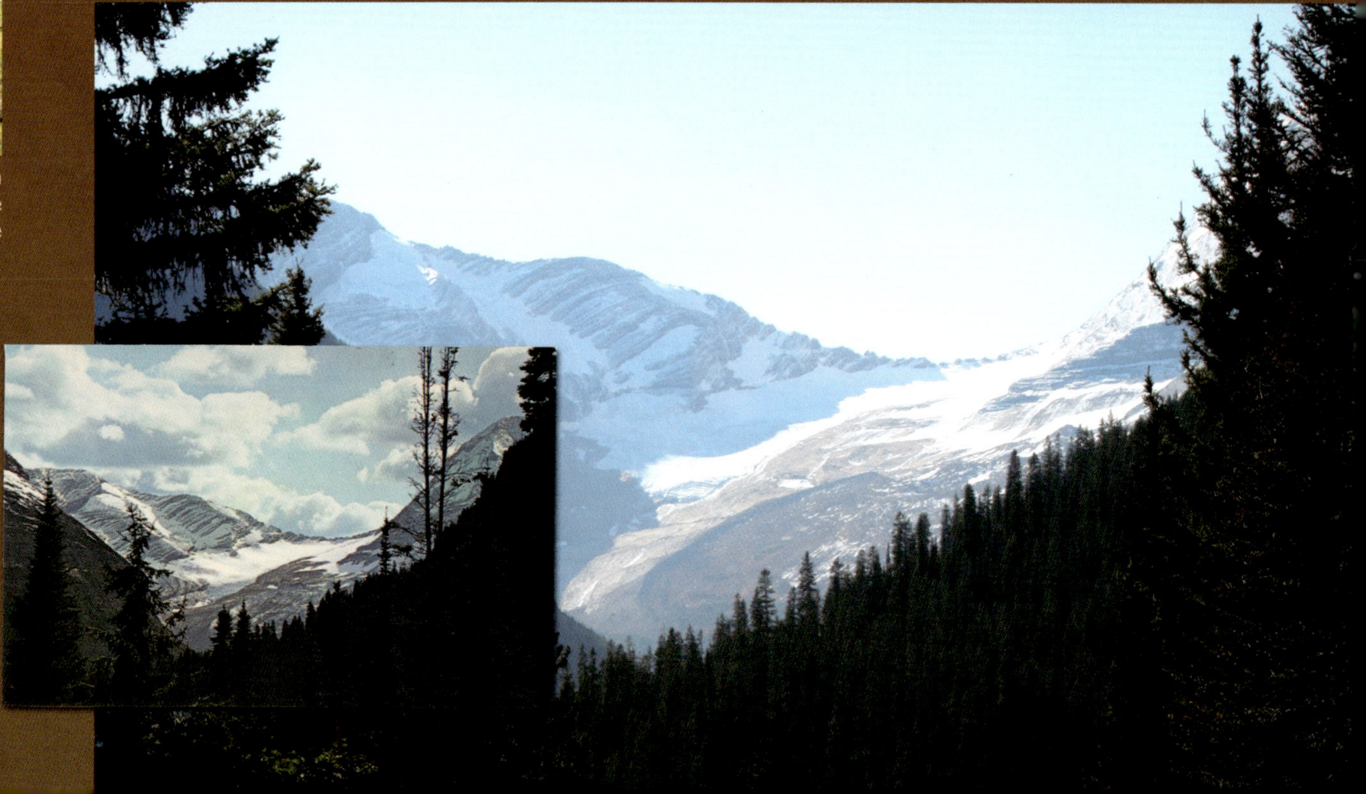

Visitors can stop at the Jackson Glacier Overlook and view the famous Jackson Glacier. The information on the back of the postcard (IMMEDIATE RIGHT) states that this glacier was once part of the ice area of Blackfoot Glacier. The more recent photograph was taken from the overlook on Going-to-the-Sun Road. Plastichrome postcard published by Bob Anderson Postcards. *Photograph courtesy of Bryan and Nicole Kohrmann.*

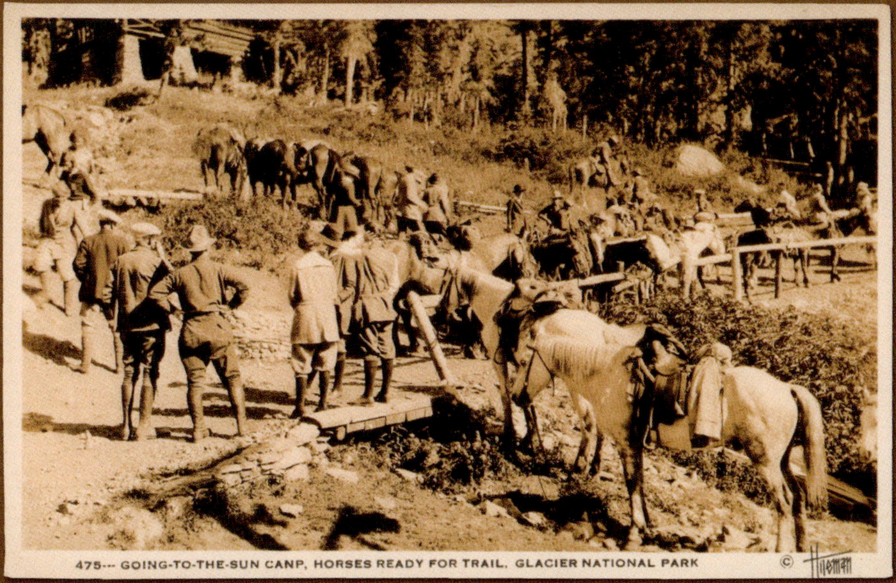

Going-to-the-Sun Chalets was a hub for trail riders and hikers until the new Going-to-the-Sun Road opened in 1933. Visitors then found it easier to tour the park by automobile. Hileman real photo postcard circa 1920s.

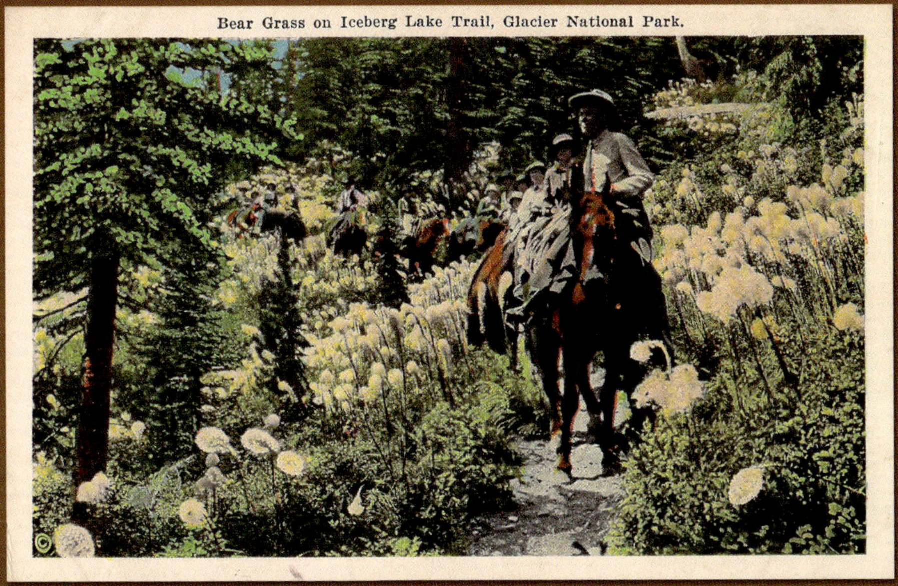

For early visitors who were ambitious, a horseback ride to the Grinnell Glacier or Iceberg Lake could be arranged. The postcard from the era shows such a group on the Iceberg Lake Trail. Hileman photo published by Glacier Park Hotel Co.

When horse travel was the primary mode of transportation, the Park Saddle Horse Co. became an integral part of the business at Many Glacier Hotel when the concession was opened in 1915. Three kinds of horse activity were supplied by the company: local rides, camping pack tours, and escorted trail rides. By the 1920s, the company had six hundred saddle horses available throughout the park to meet the demand. The firm went out of business in 1943 following the increased popularity of motor vehicle travel. Horse rides are still available in the park. Unmarked vintage decal.

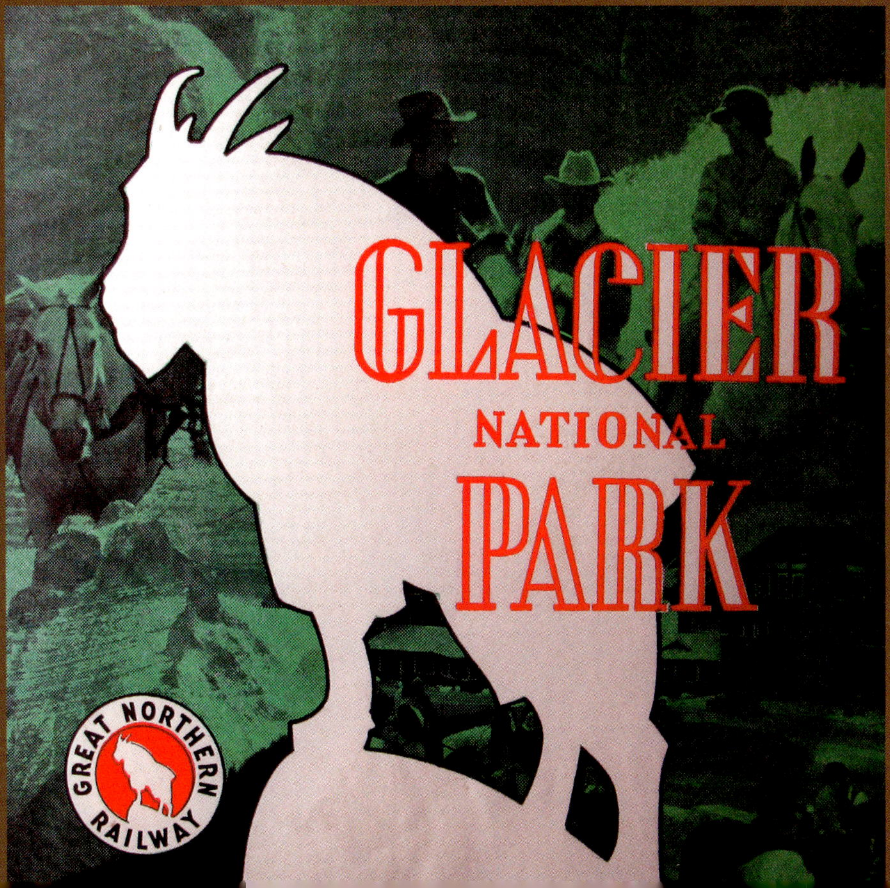

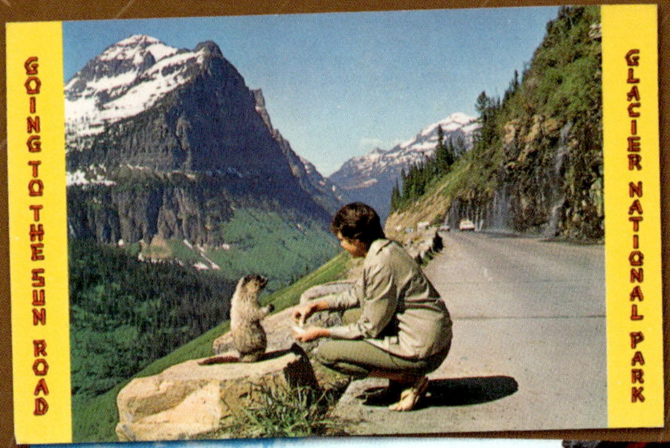

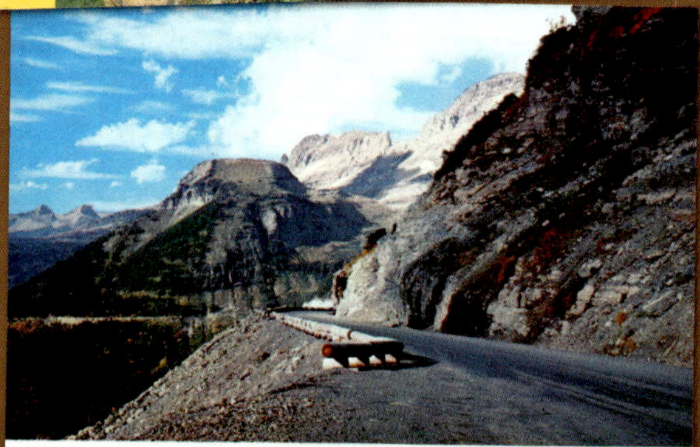

Going-To-The-Sun Highway affords the traveler America's most spectacular scenery.

The most popular trip in the park continues to be traveling along Going-to-the-Sun Road, which attracts approximately eighty percent of all visitors according to the park's research. The road stretches from Lake McDonald on the west to St. Mary's Lake on the east. Postcard of the road from an H. S. Crocker folder. Postcard of marmot by Plastichrome Bob Anderson Postcards.

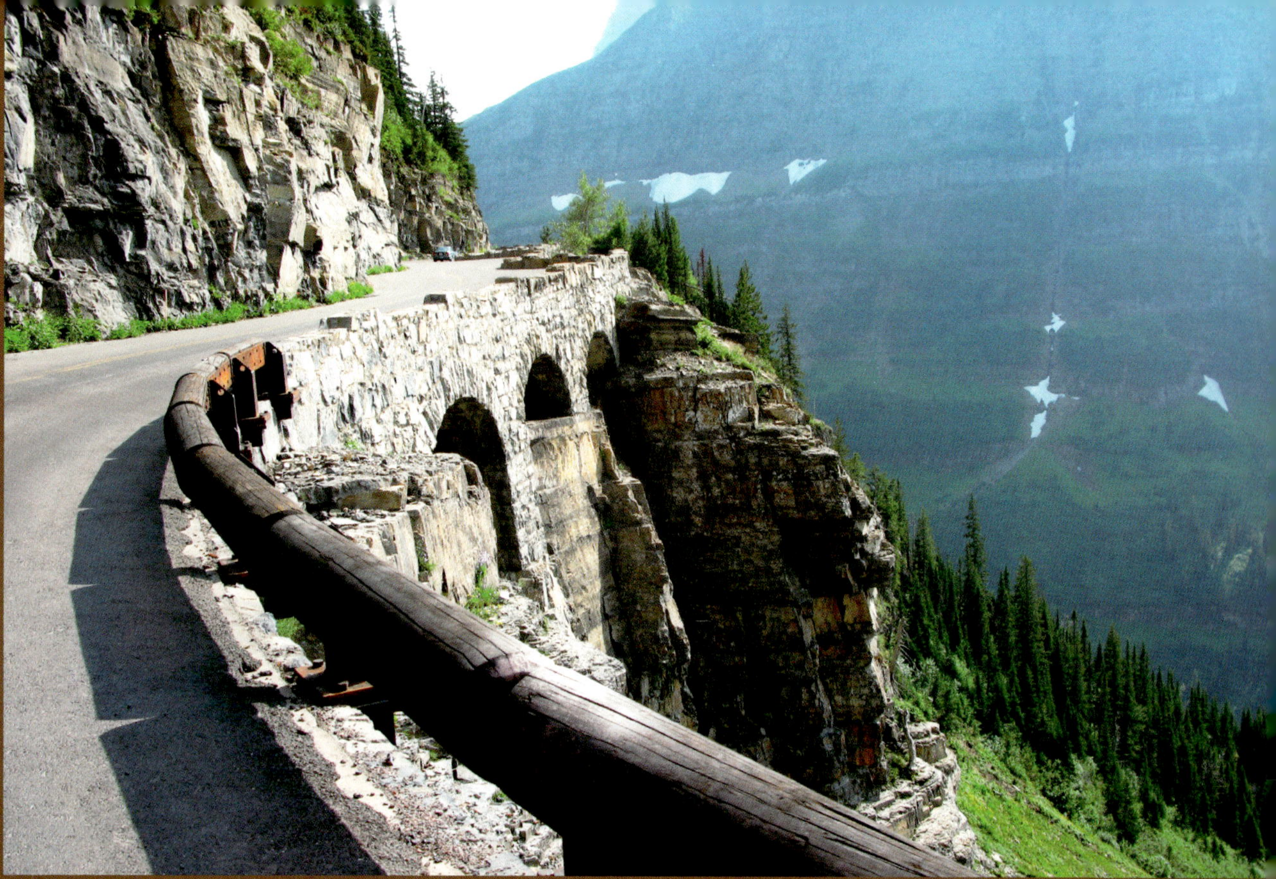

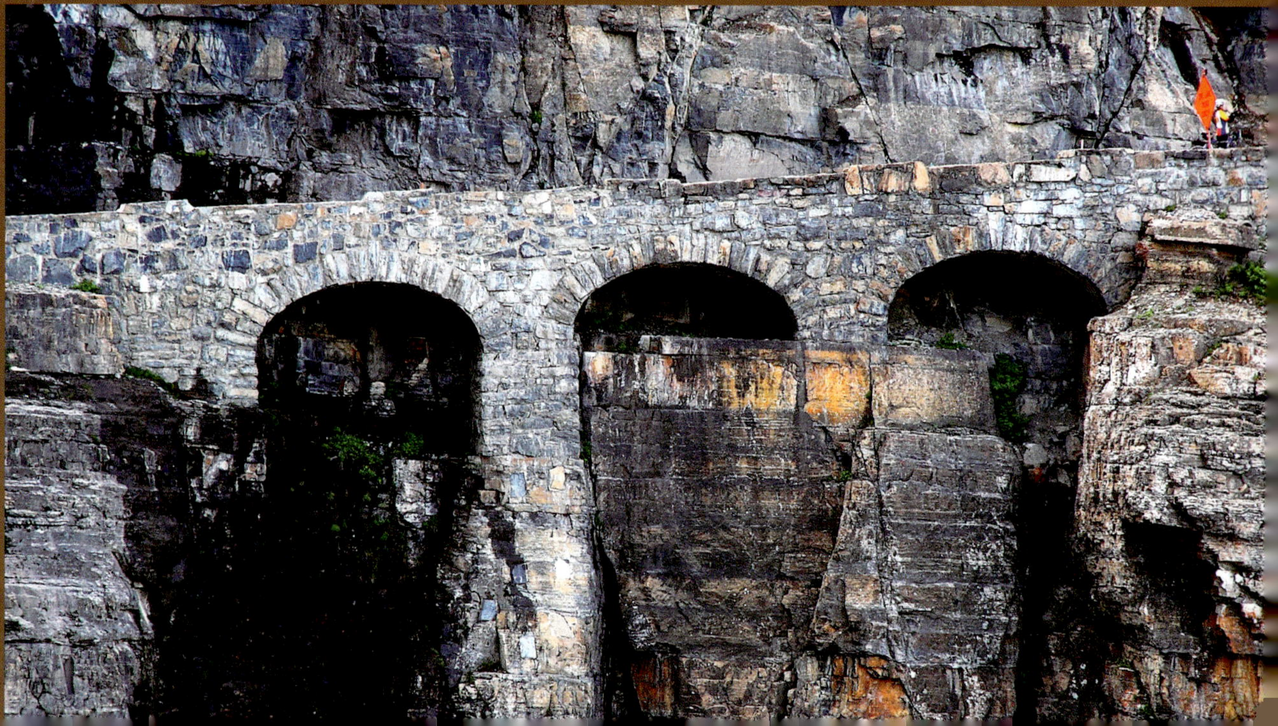

These photographs illustrate the extensive construction that was done to allow such a road to be built in the mountains, including the Triple Arches along the rock cliffs of Pollock Mt., which was considered to be an engineering innovation for its time. *Photo at right courtesy of I-Ting Chiang*.

Garden Wall, a jagged wall of rocks, can be seen for approximately ten miles. It is part of the Continental Divide where the waters on the west flow to the Pacific and the waters to the east flow to the Arctic or the Atlantic. Postcard by Security Lithograph Co.

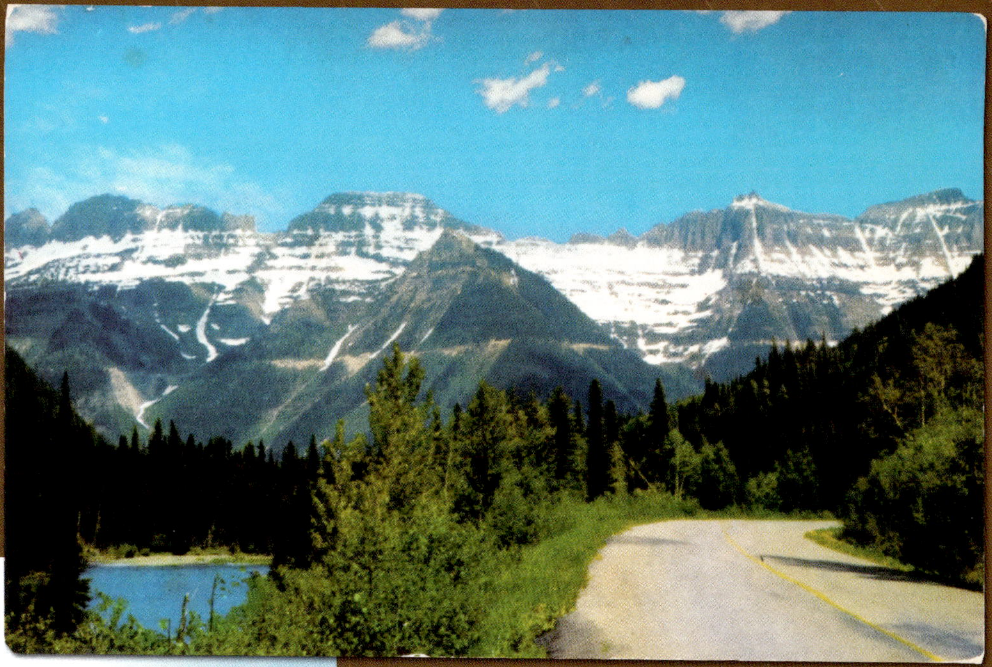

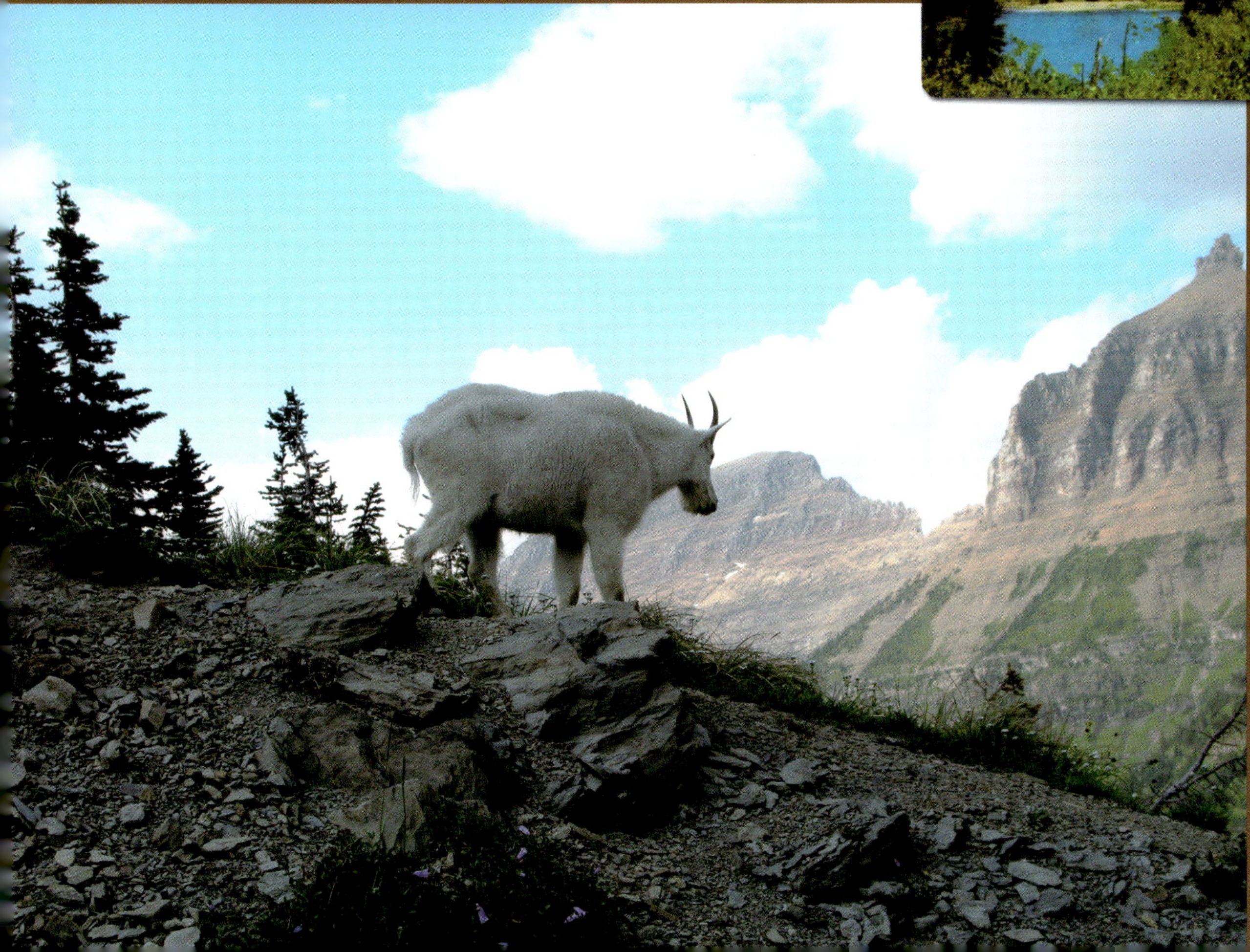

A mountain goat frames the Garden Wall in this recent photograph taken during a Red Bus Tour on Going-to-the-Sun Road.

Water features along the road are a photographer's delight. **RIGHT**: This photo postcard is of Weeping Wall, an awe-inspiring spectacle featuring eternal springs that feed the falls that gush from the mountainside. **BELOW**: Water, snow, and other elements create significant maintenance issues for the road year-round, including avalanches, mud slides, and rock slides. *Postcard by Northwest Curio & Post Card Co. Photograph courtesy of I-Ting Chiang.*

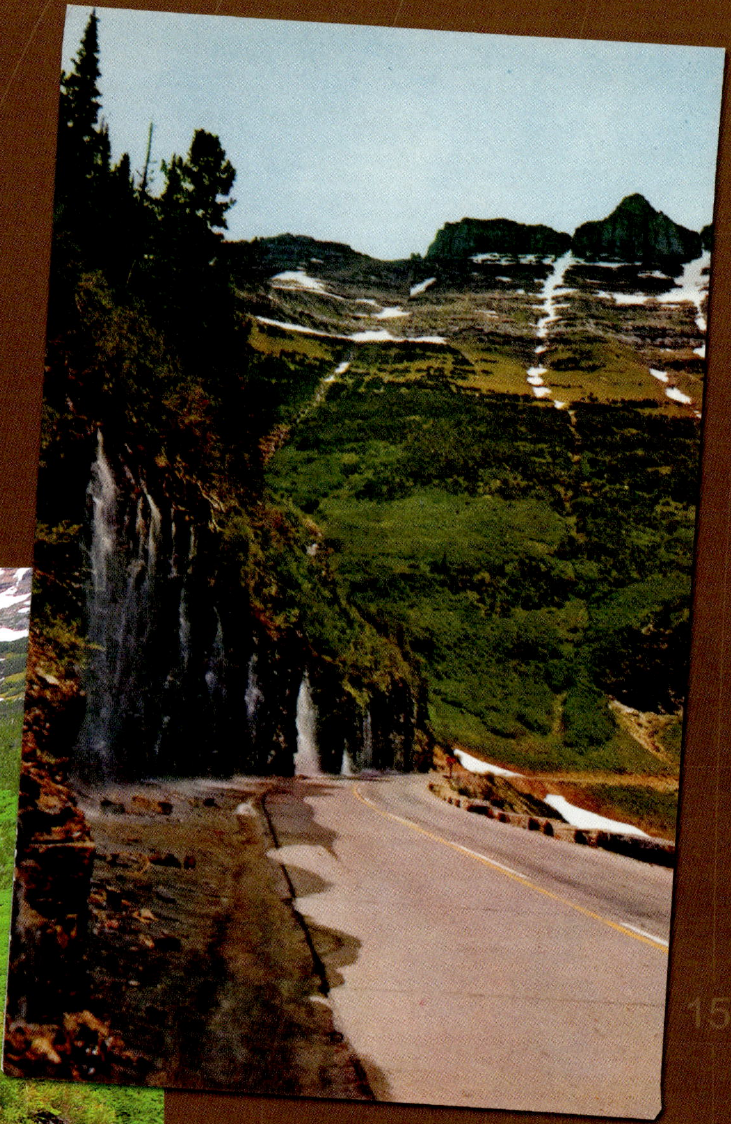

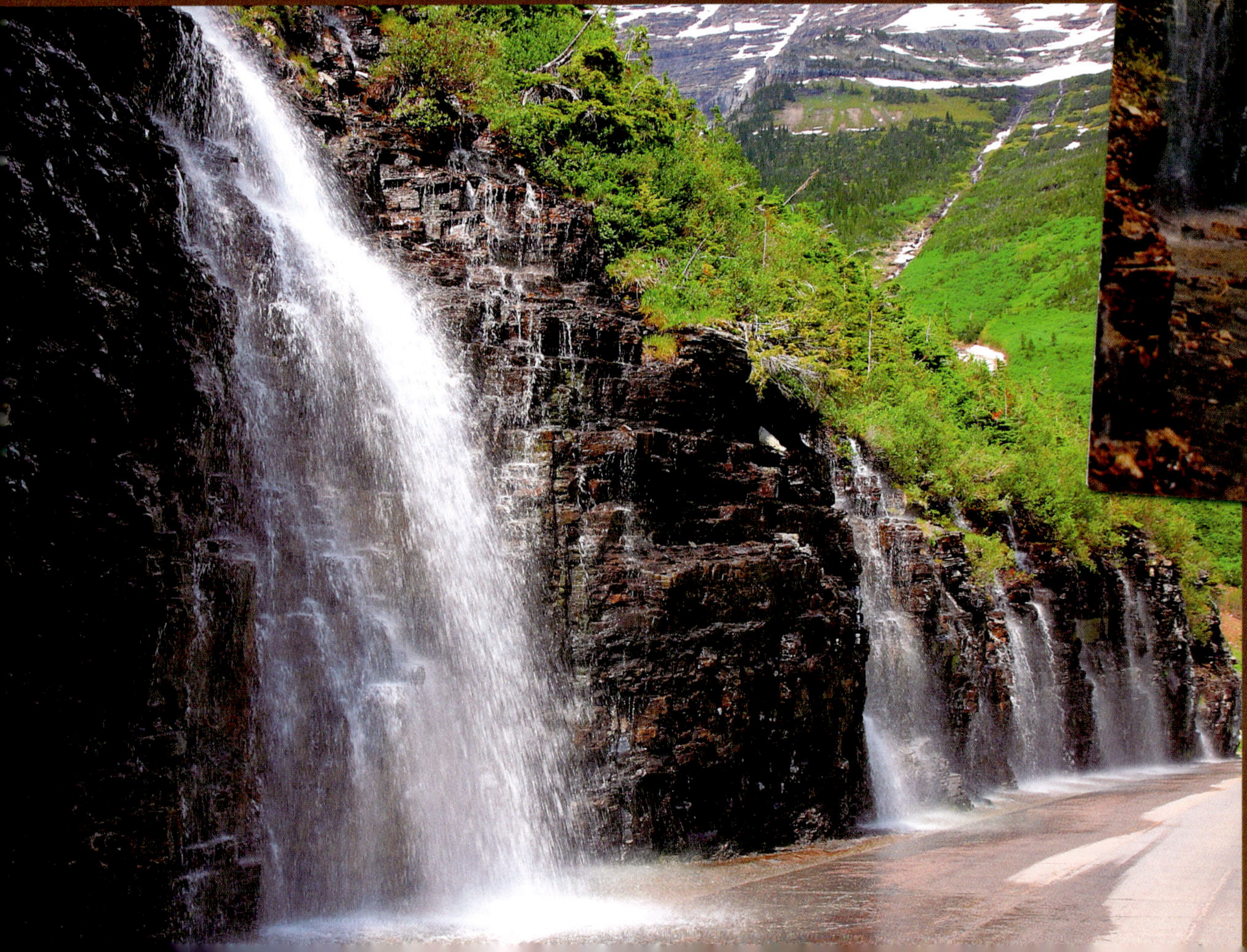

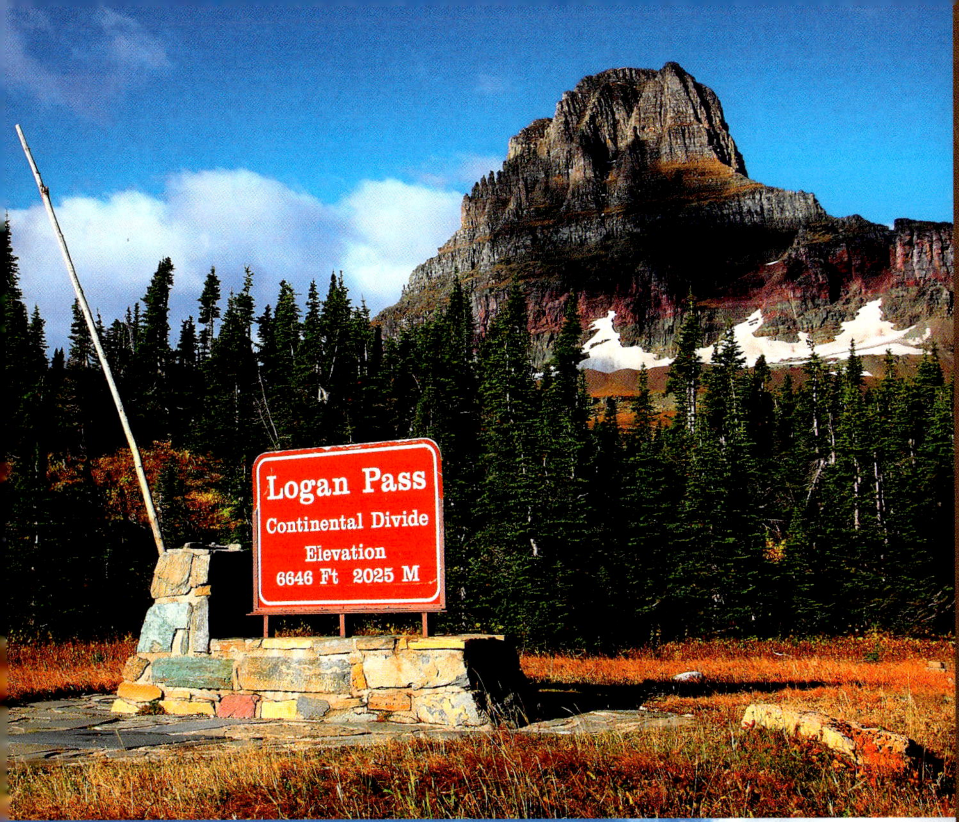

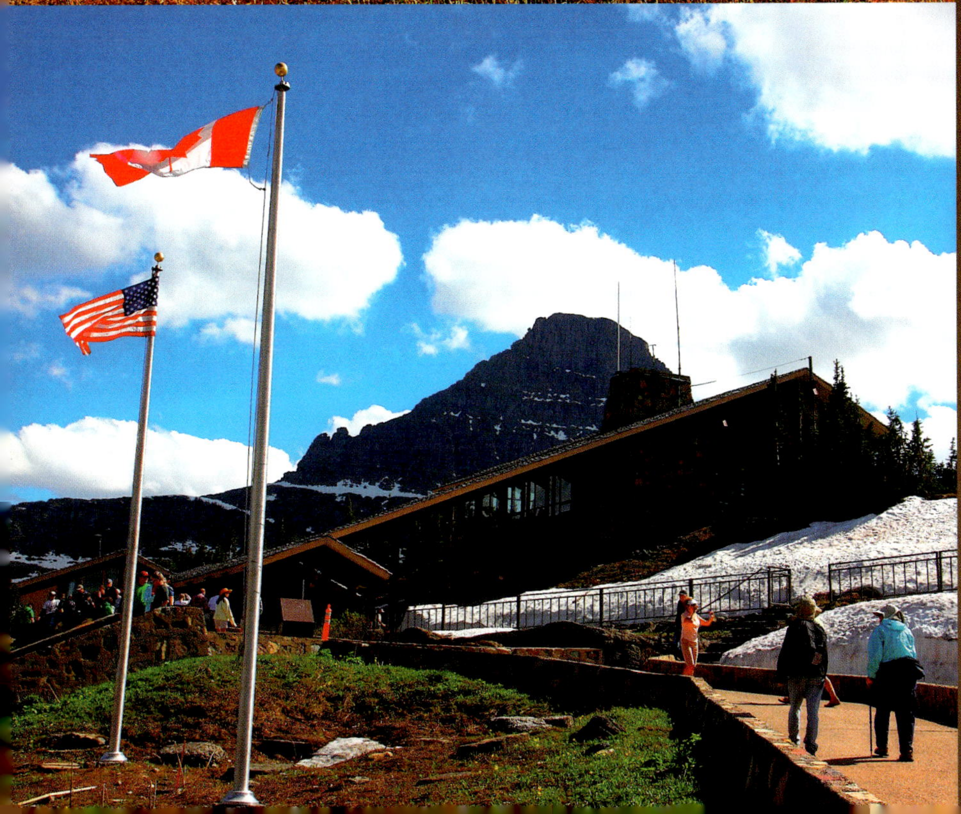

LEFT: Going-to-the-Sun Road crosses the Continental Divide at 6,646 feet at Logan Pass.
LOWER LEFT: The Logan Pass Visitor Center is located near the top of Logan Pass. It was built as part of the National Park's Mission 66 program and when it opened in 1966 it won an award for Historic Places. Visitors can take time to travel on a nearby nature trail to Hidden Lake or photograph the numerous mountain goats in the area. *Photos courtesy of I-Ting Chiang.*

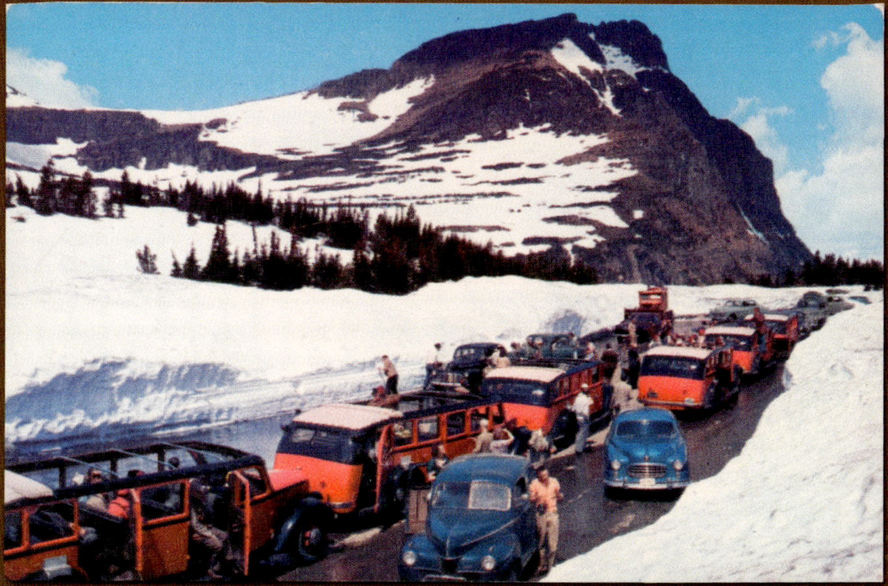

A view of the Logan Pass summit when it was covered with snow. A combination of tour buses and other vehicles make for quite a traffic jam. Postcard by H. S. Crocker, Inc.

Both these views were taken at the summit of Logan Pass with Clements Mountain in the distance. Greetings postcard by Northwest Curio & Post Card Co. Second card published by Bob Anderson Postcards.

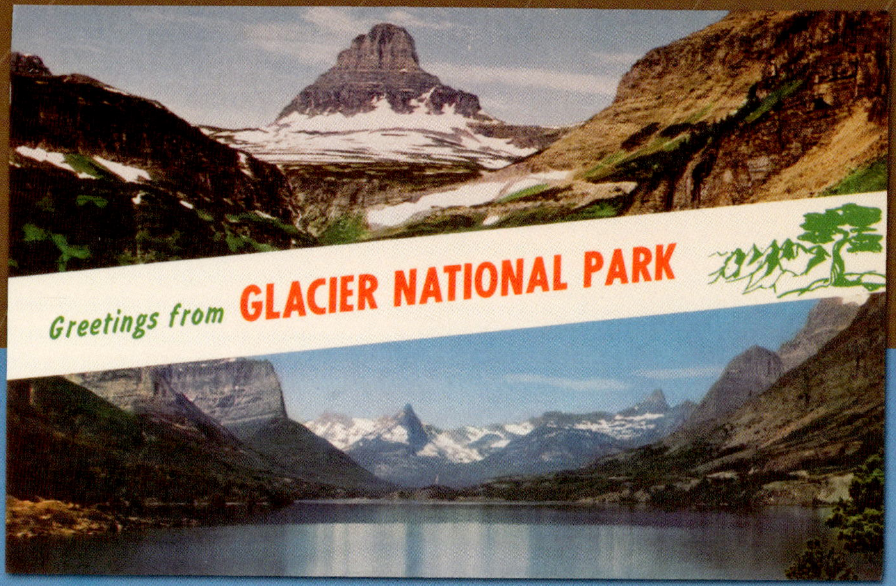

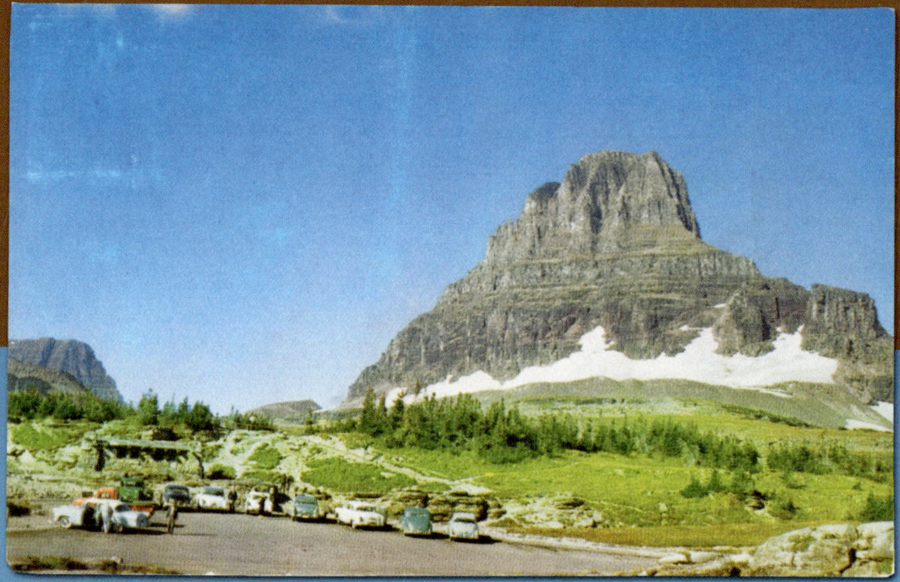

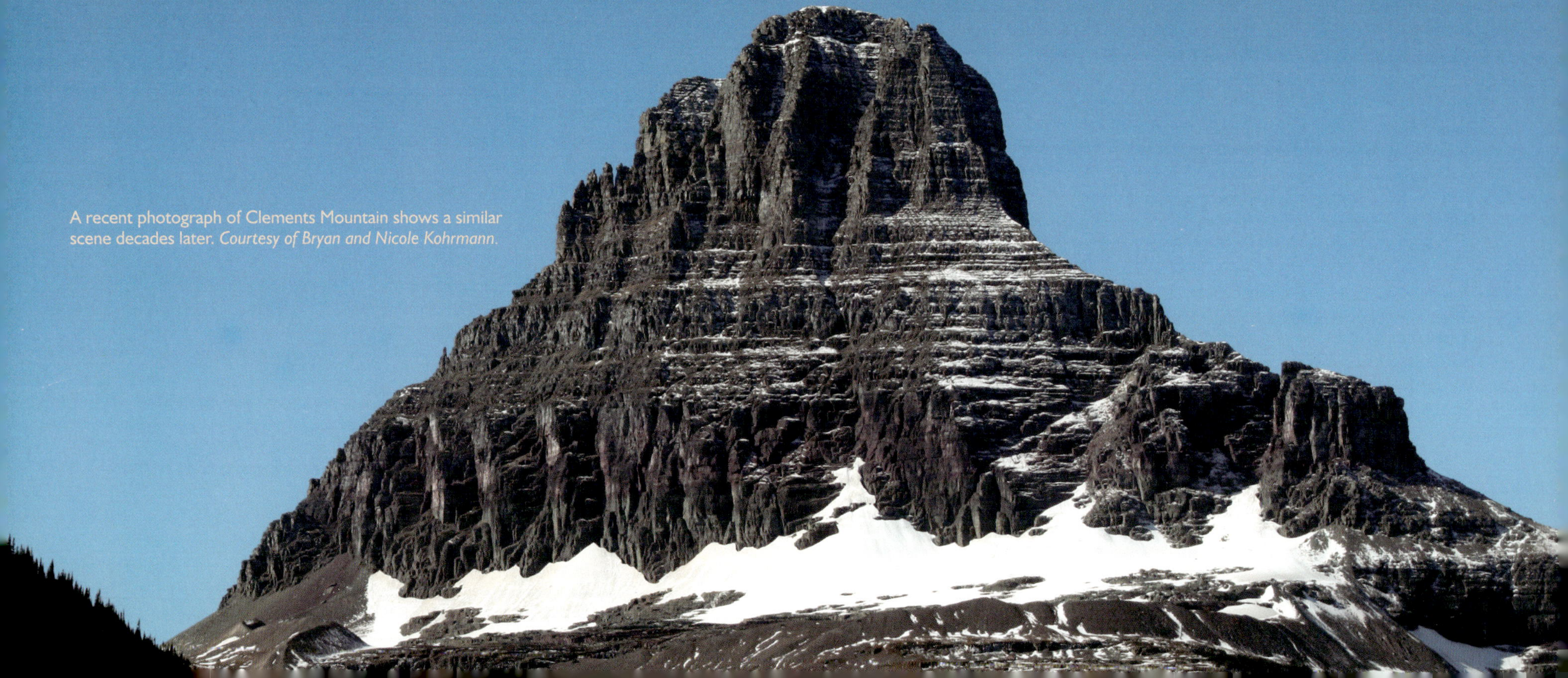

A recent photograph of Clements Mountain shows a similar scene decades later. *Courtesy of Bryan and Nicole Kohrmann.*

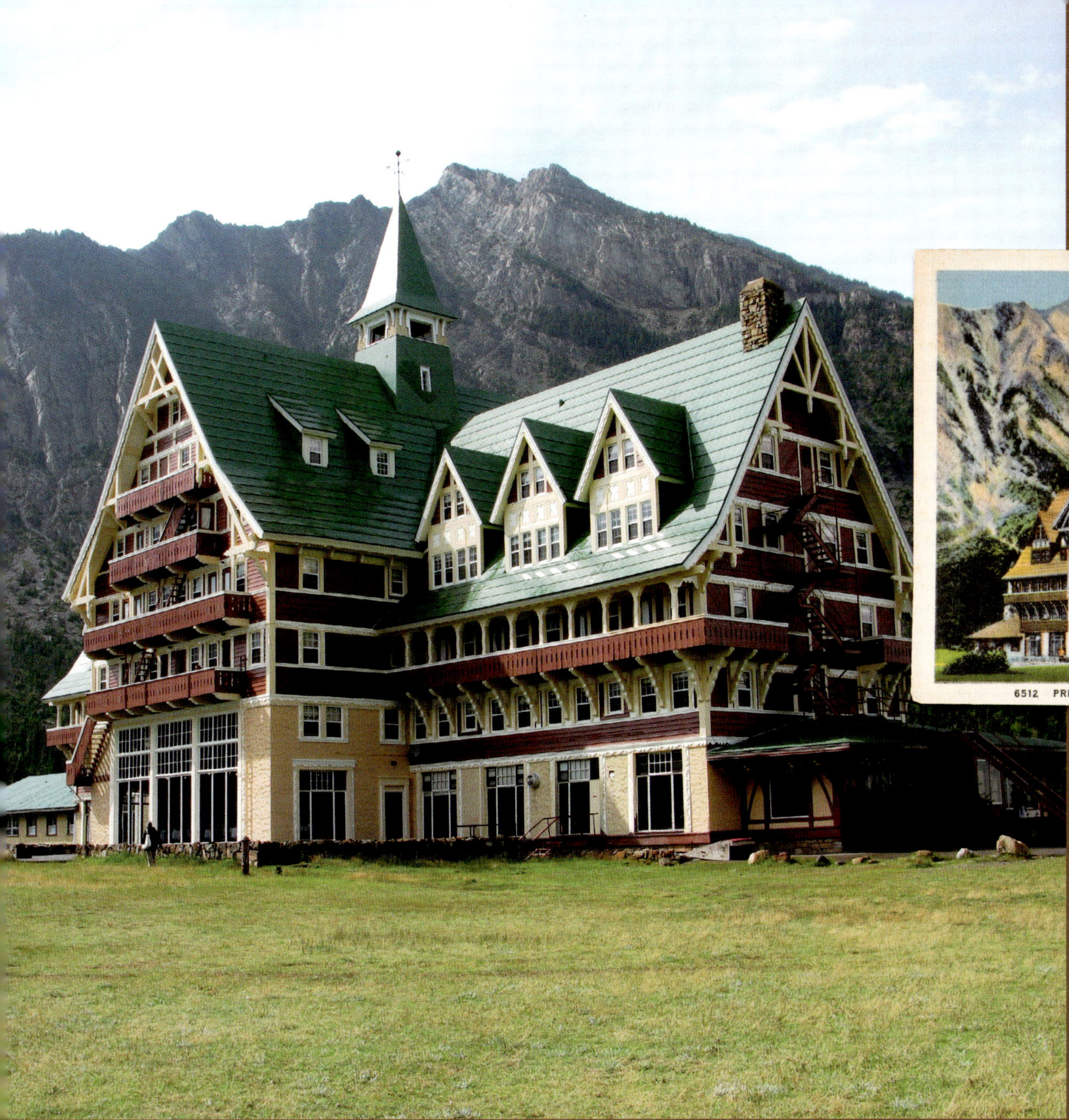

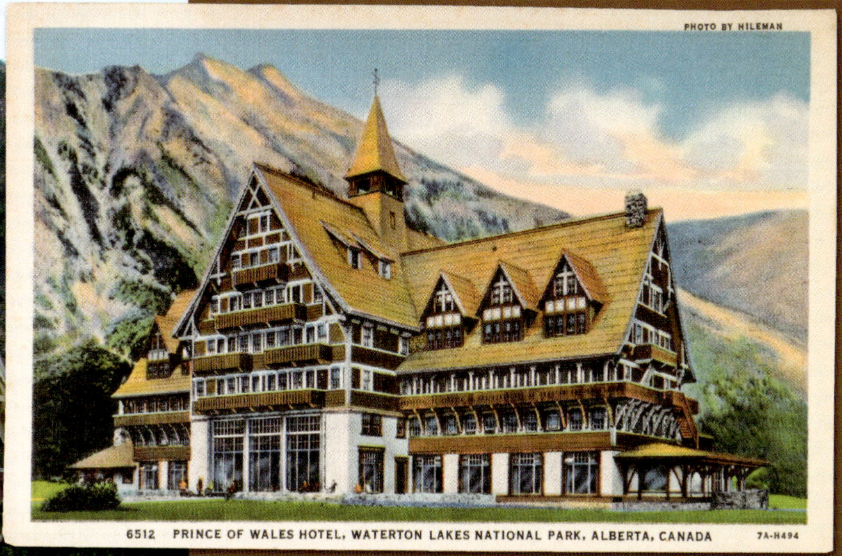

The Prince of Wales Hotel was built by Louis Hill and the Great Northern Railway after Hill received a land lease from the Canadian government. New roads were then completed to the site. Architects Thomas D. McMahon and Beaver Wade Day designed the chateau, which opened in 1927. It was the last of the lodges built by the railroad and the most exquisite. It includes seven stories with two five-story wings, a thirty-foot bell tower, and a single-story kitchen. The hotel was named for Prince Edward in anticipation of a royal tour of the countryside in 1927. Sadly, the prince never visited the hotel that bears his name. The property was named a National Historic Site in 1992. Linen postcard from a folder of views by C. T. Art-Colortone.

A longer outing could include a trip along the Chief Mountain International Highway to Waterton Lakes National Park in Canada. The highway is named after Chief Mountain, which stands 9,080 feet tall. One of the park's must-see places is the Prince of Wales Hotel. Perched high upon a bluff, the hotel offers magnificent views of Waterton Lakes and the township of Waterton, Alberta, Canada. The Waterton Lakes Park was designated as an International Peace Park along with Glacier National Park in 1932. This recent photograph shows few changes to the exterior other than stairways from the balconies.

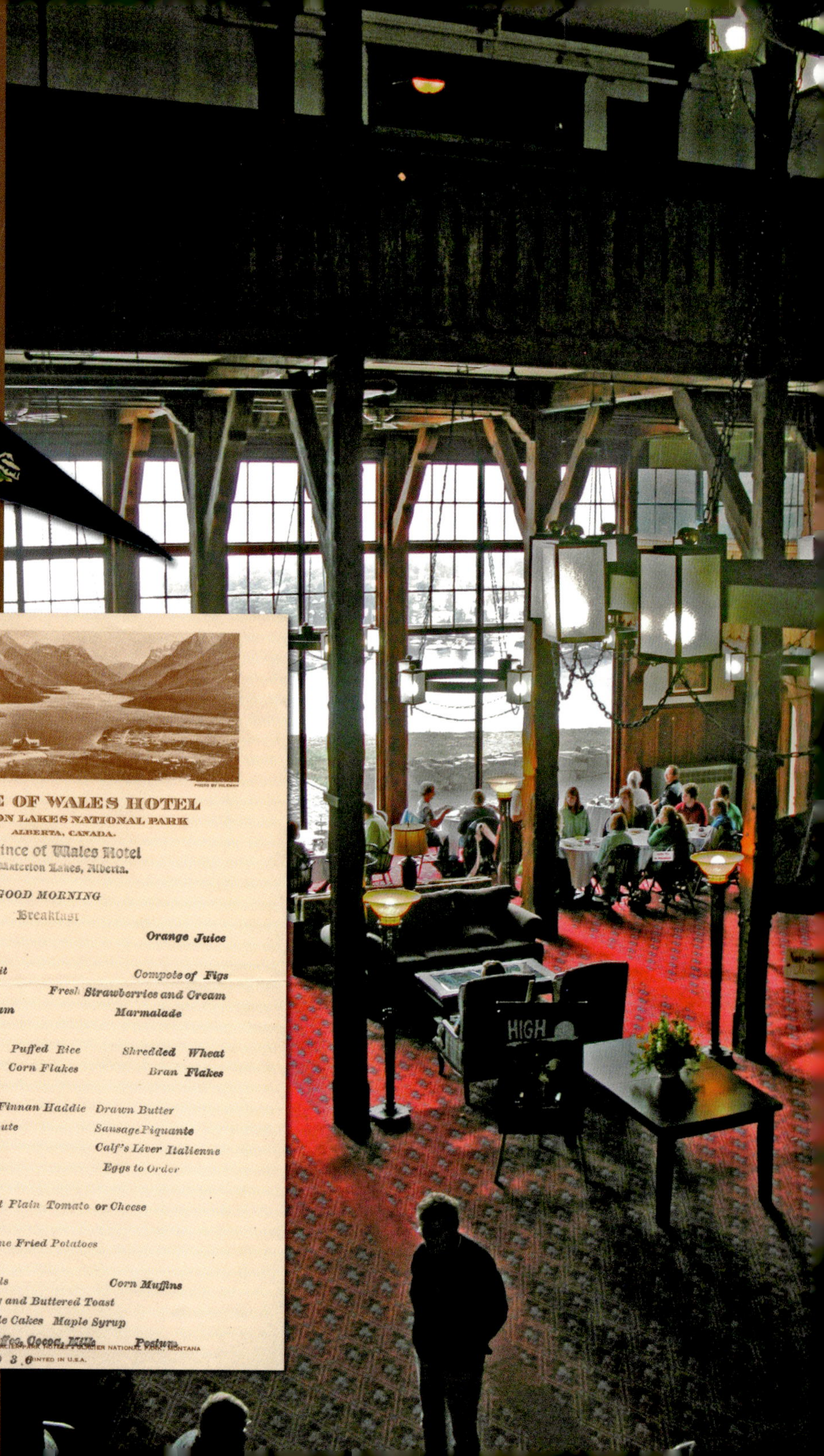

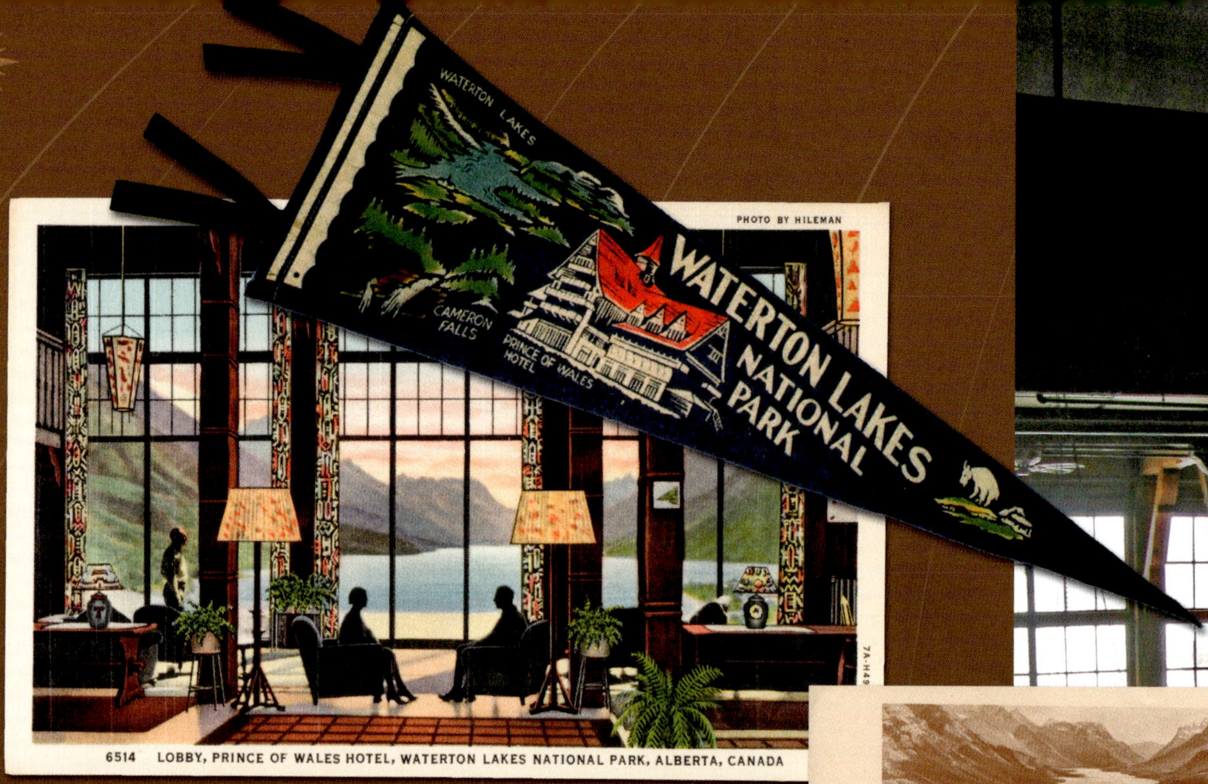

This linen postcard features the great hall or lobby of the hotel and its rustic-Tudor motif. A balcony on the second floor can be seen on two sides of the lobby. When the hotel opened, native pictographs decorated part of the lobby. The lobby's lights were moved to the Lake McDonald Hotel in the 1960s. Card by C. T. Art-Colortone.

135° 120° 105° 90°

PRINCE OF WALES HOTEL
WATERTON LAKES NATIONAL PARK
ALBERTA, CANADA.

Prince of Wales Hotel
Waterton Lakes, Alberta.

GOOD MORNING

Breakfast

Tomato Juice — Orange Juice

Chilled Grape Fruit — Compote of Figs
Stewed Prunes — Fresh Strawberries and Cream
Raspberry Jam — Marmalade

Rolled Oats — Puffed Rice — Shredded Wheat
Grape Nuts — Corn Flakes — Bran Flakes

Steamed Finnan Haddie Drawn Butter
Small Steak Minute — Sausage Piquante
Sugar Cured Ham — Calf's Liver Italienne
Breakfast Bacon — Eggs to Order

Omelet Plain Tomato or Cheese

Home Fried Potatoes

Assorted Rolls — Corn Muffins
Dry and Buttered Toast
Griddle Cakes Maple Syrup
Tea, Coffee, Cocoa, Milk — Postum

ASSOCIATED WITH THE GLACIER PARK HOTELS • GLACIER NATIONAL PARK, MONTANA
Tuesday 30 June, 19 3 6 PRINTED IN U.S.A.

The lobby's lights and other decor have changed through the years, but visitors are still drawn to the views from the eighteen-foot high windows. The hotel offers eighty-six guest rooms and is owned and operated by Glacier Park, Inc., which acquired the property from the railroad. Also shown is a vintage breakfast menu from the hotel.

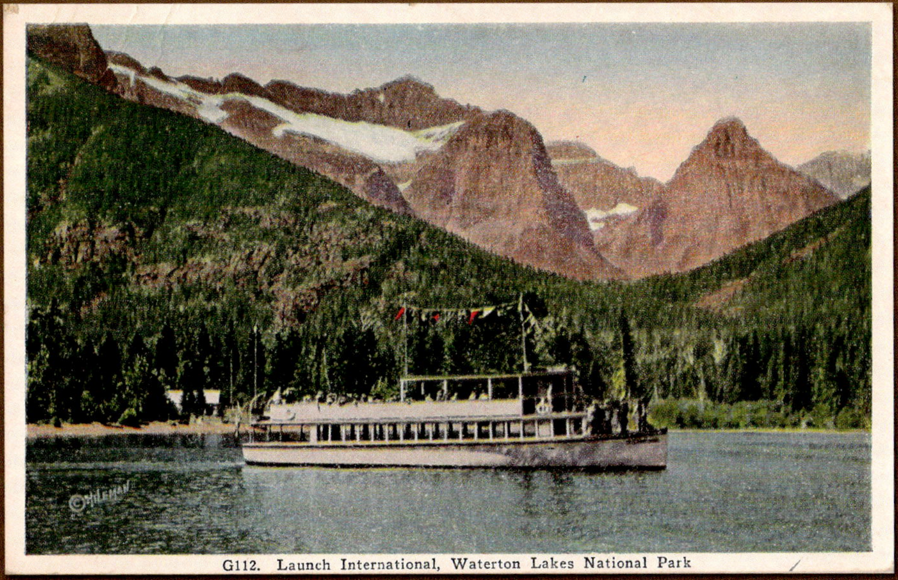

Boat tours by the *International* launch on Waterton Lakes were begun in 1928 and continue today. This postcard, mailed in 1938, shows the launch making such a trip in a Hileman photo. The card was published by the Glacier Hotel Co.

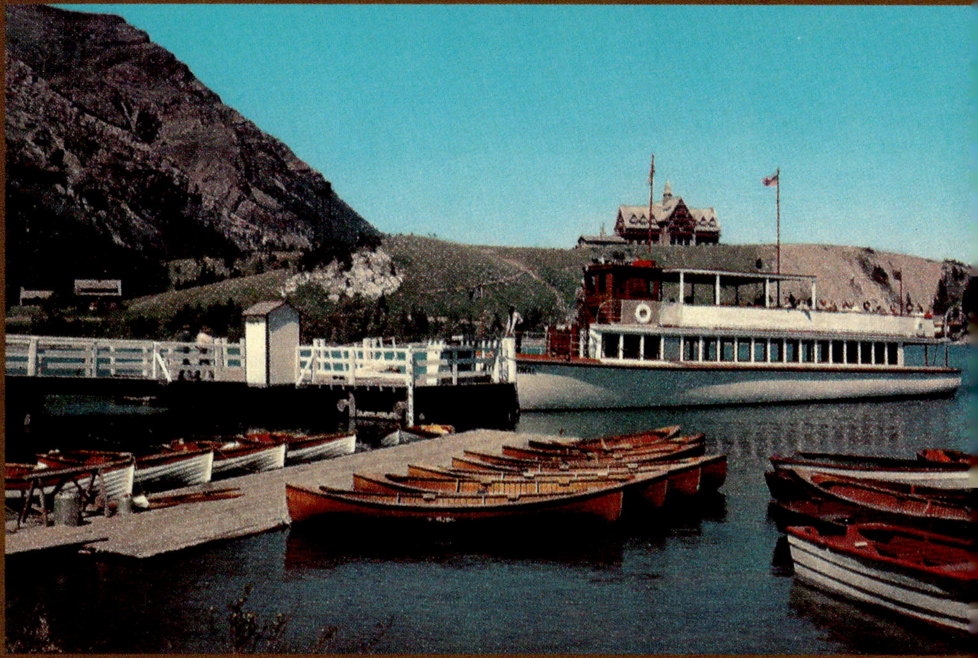

This later postcard, published by the Glacier Park Co., shows the *International* launch at the dock awaiting its next tourist excursion. The hotel can be seen in the background.

A similar scene in this recent photograph features a closer view of the hotel and more modern boating transportation.

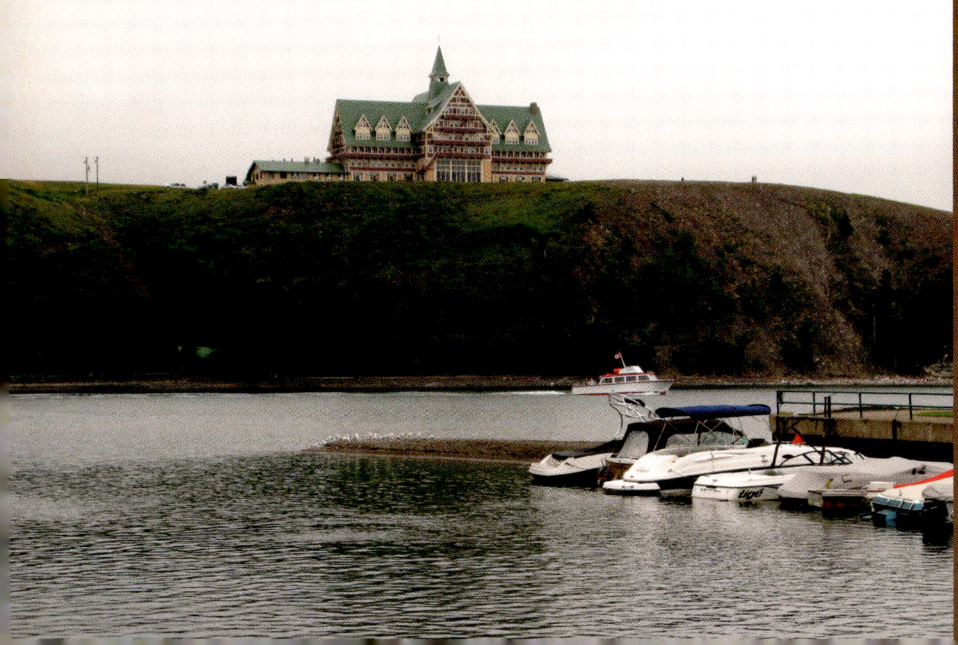

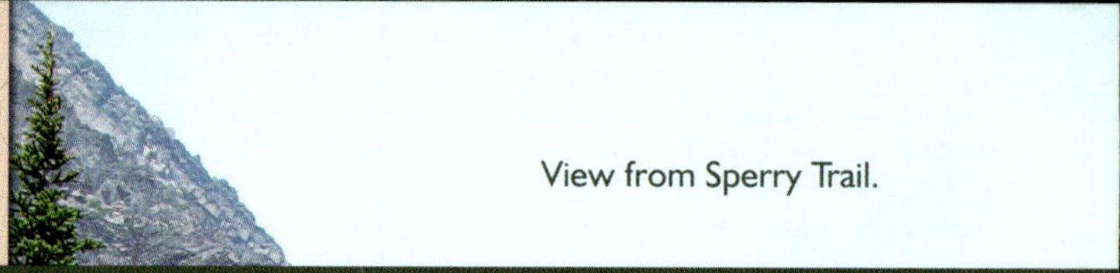

View from Sperry Trail.

CHANGES AND OUTLOOK

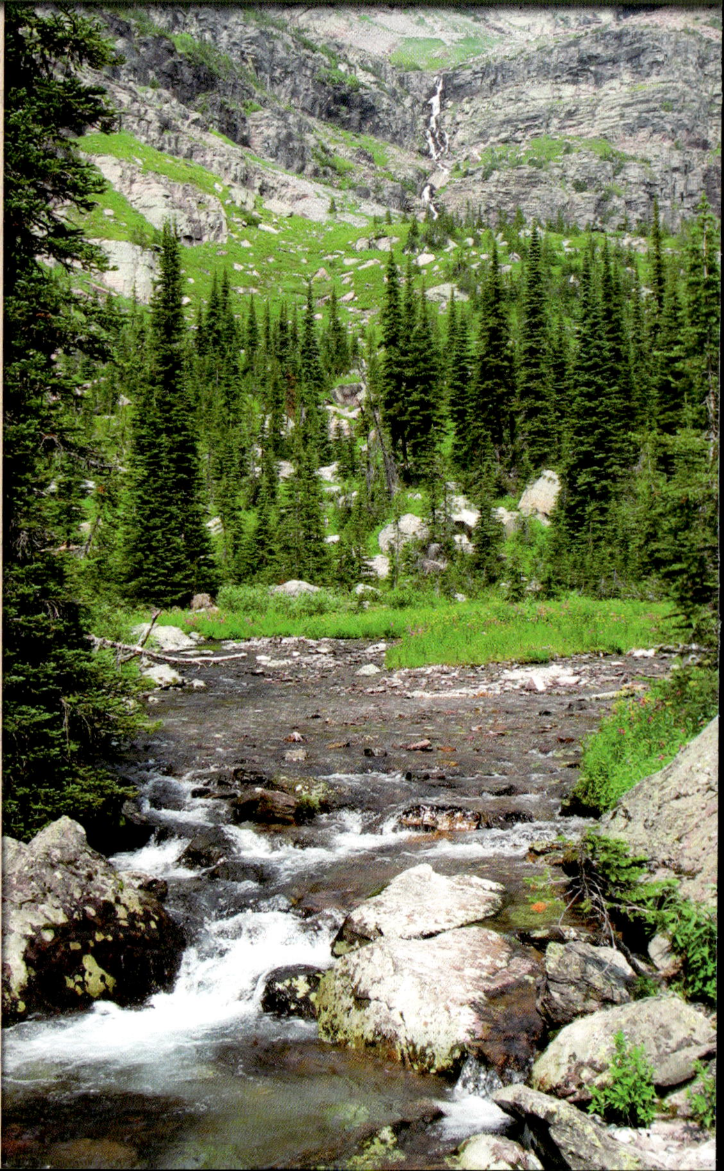

As the number of park visitors has increased from thousands to millions, management of the park and its facilities has evolved to reflect society's modernization. By the end of World War II, most of the chalets had been closed and the Great Northern Railway began selling its holdings to reflect a decrease in passenger train travel. Campgrounds and motels were added to accommodate visitors who now arrived in the family vehicle.

Mission 66, an initiative by the National Park Service to improve America's parks for its 50th anniversary celebration in 1966, provided Glacier with two award-winning visitor centers. Roads were also improved, campgrounds were added, and additional employee housing was constructed. In later years, the historic lodges have undergone multi-million dollar renovations, including the restoration of Lake McDonald Lodge in the 1980s and more recently Many Glacier Hotel. Extensive renovations planned for Going-to-the-Sun Road will ensure it remains a national treasure and engineering marvel.

Facilities aside, the park's greatest threats are environmental; there is grave concern for the future of the park's glaciers. The number has dwindled from 150 recorded in 1850, to only twenty-five in the most recent count. Researchers predict the remaining glaciers will disappear between 2020 and 2030 if existing climate conditions continue. As a result, significant global climate change research programs are underway at Glacier. The research includes an extensive inventory and monitoring of the park's ecosystems that are being used to help predict changes elsewhere in the United States and possible interventions.

Looking ahead, wilderness designations and protection from nearby mining and logging operations will add yet another chapter to the evolution of Glacier National Park for the enjoyment of future generations.

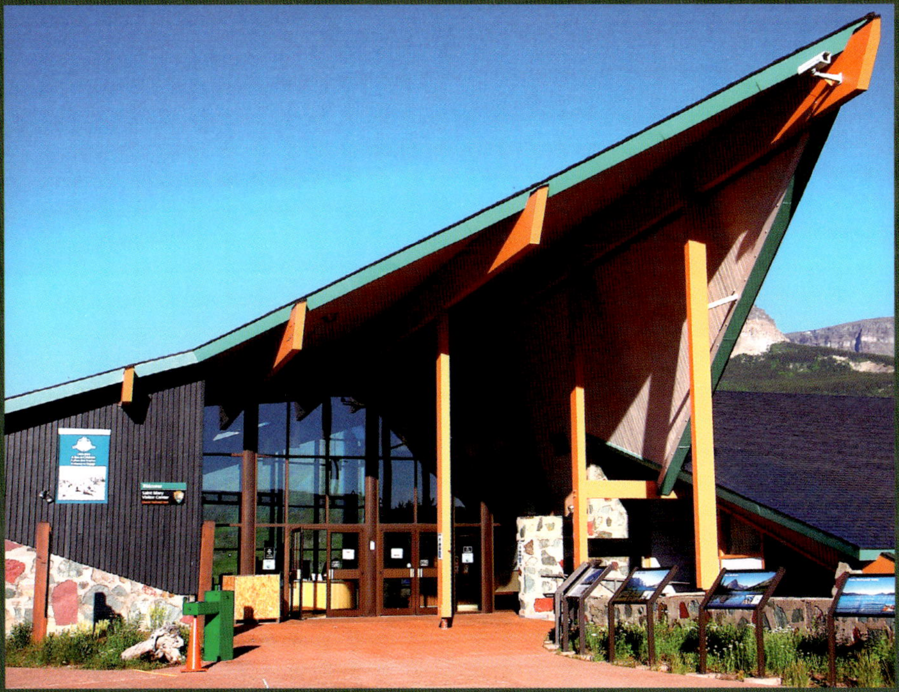

The St. Mary Visitor Center at the east entrance was built during the Mission 66 project and completed in 1967. It won an award for excellence, as did the Logan Pass Visitor Center. *Courtesy of I-Ting Chiang*.

BELOW: Lake McDonald Lodge underwent a large-scale renovation in 1988 and 1989 to remove some of the earlier updates that weren't in keeping with the original integrity of the architectural design. The renovation has created an authentic setting for visitors to enjoy.
LEFT: Many Glacier Hotel has also undergone recent exterior and ongoing interior renovations to allow this grand lodge to continue to serve Glacier visitors for many more years.

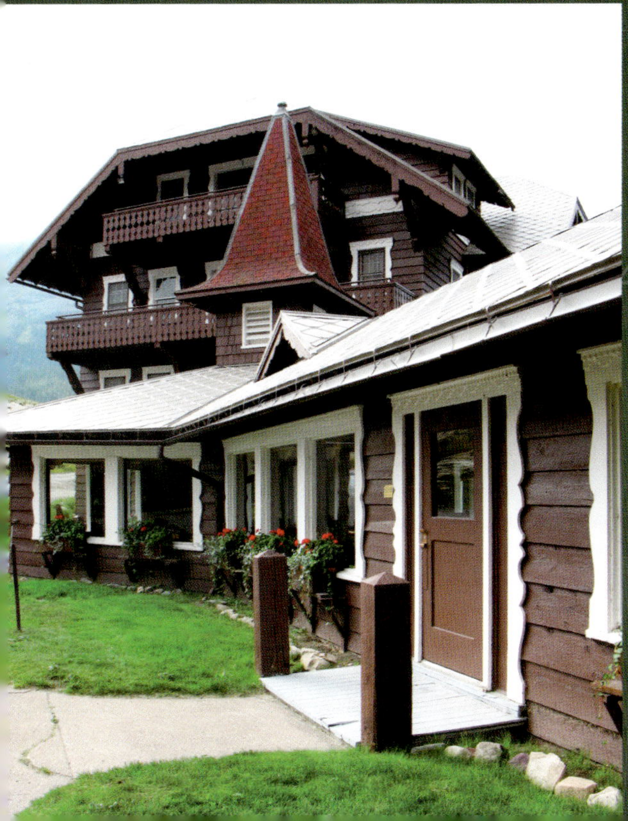

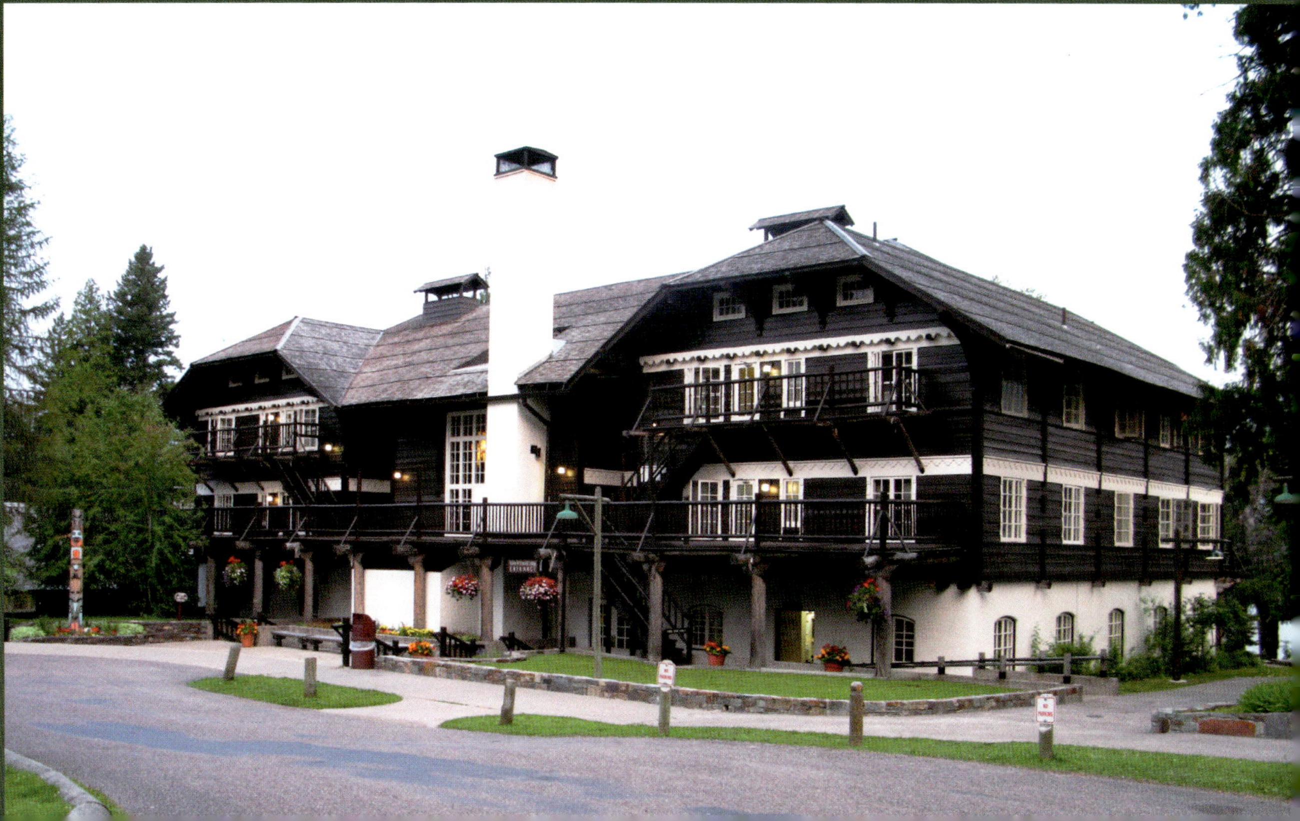

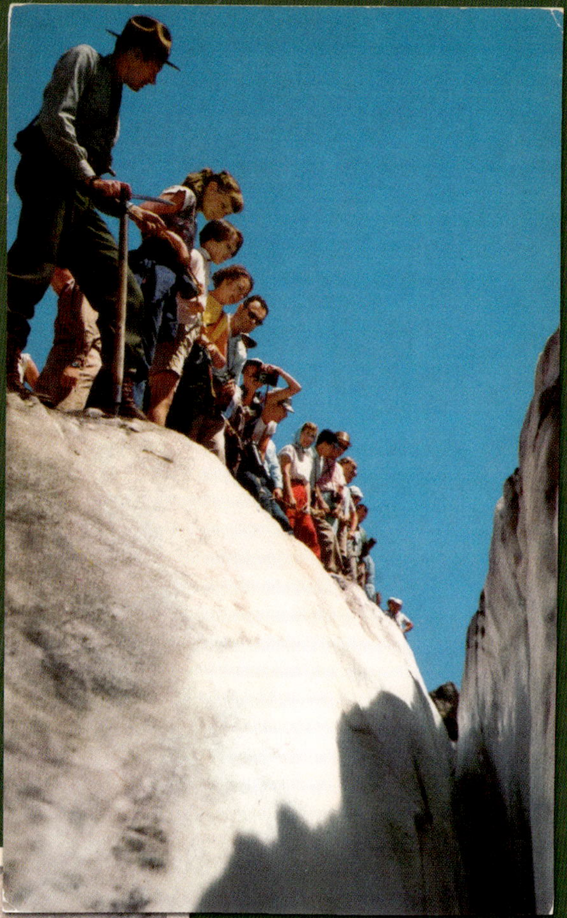

With the gradual disappearance of the glaciers, visitors are eager to explore what is left of them. The hike to the retreating Grinnell Glacier is six miles with an elevation gain of 1,600 feet and is one of the most scenic outings in the park. The trailhead is located at Swiftcurrent Lake. This vintage postcard by H. S. Crocker shows tourists on a ranger-led hike viewing an ice crevasse on the glacier.

While most of the park's natural wonders have been enjoyed for decades, one can only wonder what it was like to have visited the park a century ago when the glaciers were vast and plentiful. This Kiser viewcard from the Great Northern Railway's folder, postmarked 1920, shows Blackfeet Glacier, which was then the largest glacier in the park measuring five square miles in area.

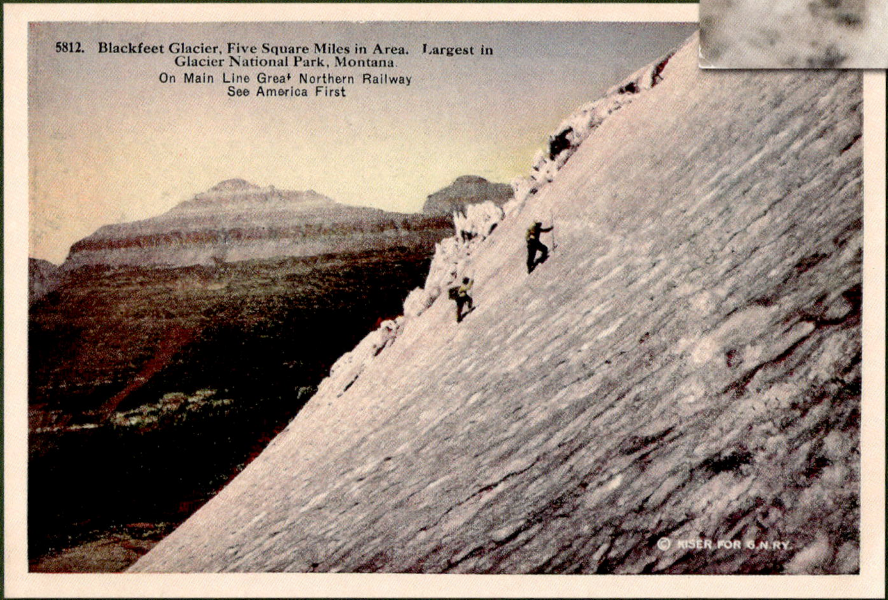

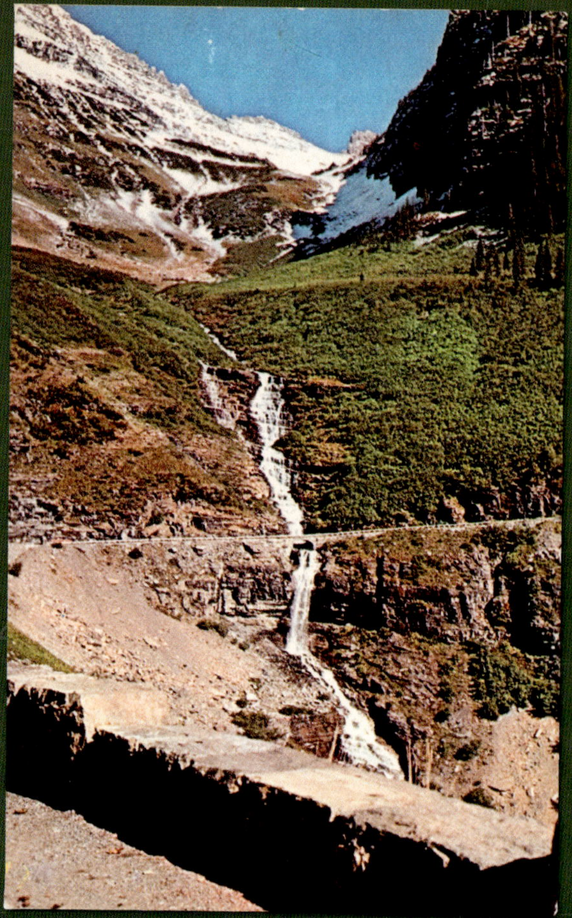

A multi-year restoration project now in progress on Going-to-the-Sun Road to repair damage caused by the harsh conditions will help preserve the road for future generations. While this scene may be a delightful sight, the rushing water poses significant maintenance challenges. Published by Plastichrome Bob Anderson Postcards.

ACKNOWLEDGMENTS

The untimely death of a close friend and neighbor in 2008 caused us to postpone a trip to Glacier National Park. When the trip was rescheduled a year later, we expanded our itinerary, took many more pictures than we had planned earlier, and thus, a book was born. Our thanks to Bryan and Nicole Kohrmann and the family of Terry Thompson for their contributions and continued friendship.

Many other people have helped make this book possible. We thank those who answered questions and helped with research including Tracey Baker, Minnesota Historical Society; Scott Burch, President and Owner, Glacier Park Boat Company; Ellen Feigin, Owner, Ellen Feigin Designs; Wendy Hill, Executive Director, Glacier Association; Jan Knox, Glacier National Park Accession Division; Christie Roberts, General Manager, Belton Chalet; Deirdre Shaw, Museum Curator, Glacier National Park; and Alicia Thompson, Director of Marketing and Business Relations, Glacier Park Lodge, Inc.

Thanks, also, to I-Ting Chiang of Fremont, California, for sharing his fondness of our national parks through his photography.

Lastly, thanks to my husband Mark for his patience and support, and son Prather, who assisted with the book's production. Additional recognition is extended to Schiffer Publishing Ltd. and its outstanding staff, especially editor Jennifer Marie Savage.

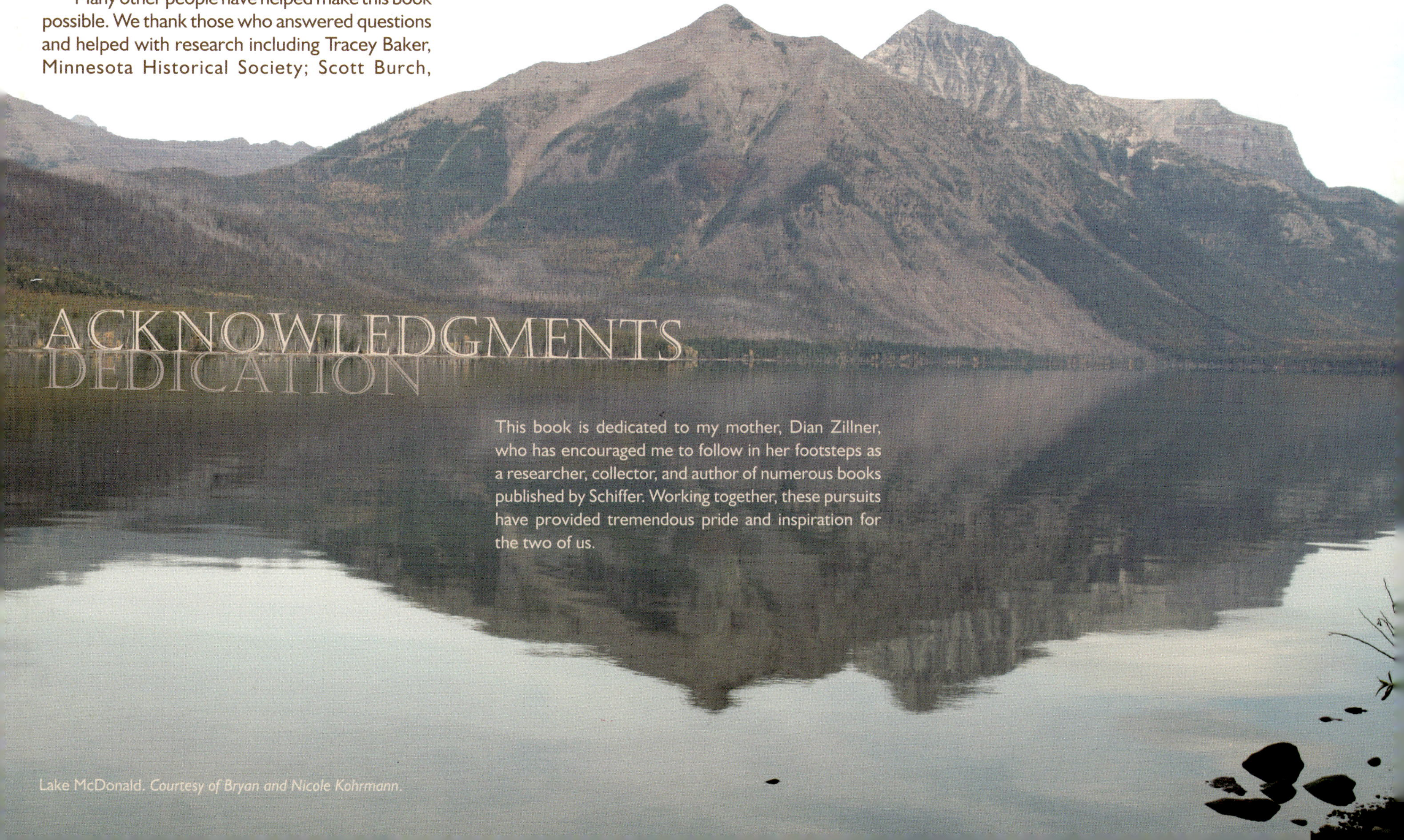

DEDICATION

This book is dedicated to my mother, Dian Zillner, who has encouraged me to follow in her footsteps as a researcher, collector, and author of numerous books published by Schiffer. Working together, these pursuits have provided tremendous pride and inspiration for the two of us.

Lake McDonald. *Courtesy of Bryan and Nicole Kohrmann.*

Bibliography

Books

Barnes, Christine, Photography by Pflughoft and Morris. *Great Lodges of the National Parks*. Companion Book to the PBS Television Series. Bend, Oregon: W. W. West, Inc., 2002.

Dujuff, Ray and Chris Morrison. *Glacier's Historic Hotels and Chalets: View With a Room*. Helena, Montana: Far Country Press, 2001.

Fodor's Complete Guide to the National Parks of the West. 1st Edition. New York: Fodor's Travel Publications, 2007.

Guthrie, C. W. *All Aboard for Glacier*. Helena, Montana: Far Country Press, 2004. *Going-to-the-Sun Road*. Helena, Montana: Far Country Press, 2006.

Moylan, Bridget. *Glacier's Grandest: A Pictorial History of the Hotels and Chalets of Glacier National Park*. Missoula, Montana: Pictorial Histories Publishing Co., Inc., 2007.

Scott, David L. and Kay W. *The Complete Guide to the National Park Lodges*. Fifth Ed. Gailford, Connecticut: Globe Pequot Press, 2006.

Pamphlets

Dyson, James. *Glaciers and Glaciation in Glacier National Park*. Glacier National History Association, 1952.

Glorious Glacier National Park. Glacier Park Co., 1959.

Great Northern Railroad: Glacier National Park and the New Logan Pass, circa 1930s.

Great Northern Railroad: Glacier National Park in Montana, Waterton Lakes National Park in Canada, 1956.

National Park Service. *Waterton/Glacier*. 1984, 2002, 2008.

Dept. of the Interior: Washington, D.C. *Glacier National Park*, circa 1917, circa 1930s. Additional pamphlets; 1946, 1951, 1953, 1958.

Websites

Glacier National Park: www.NPS.gov/glac

Glacier Park Boat Company: www.glacierparkboats.com

Glacier Park Inc.: www.glacierparkinc.com

Great Northern Railway Historical Society: www.gnrhs.org

Index

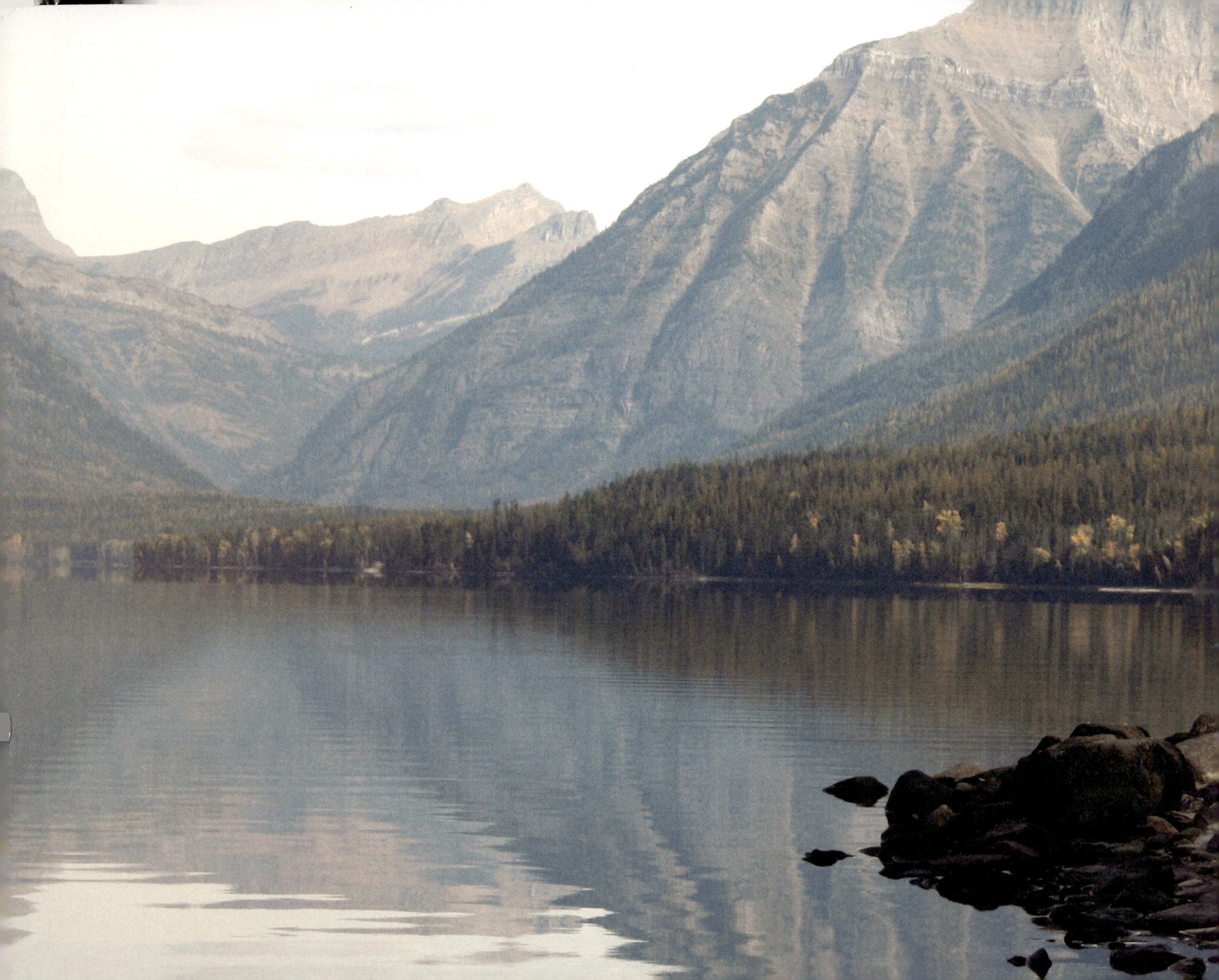